THE
DEAD
GIRL

THE
DEAD
GIRL

MELANIE
THERNSTROM

Kyle Cathie Limited

We have made every effort to trace the ownership of all copyrighted material and to secure permission from copyright holders when required. In the event of any question arising as to the use of any material, we will be pleased to make the necessary corrections in future printings. Grateful acknowledgement is made to the following for permission to reprint previously published material:

The Estate of Cecília Meireles: "Song" by Cecília Meireles. Reprinted by permission.
Farrar, Straus and Giroux: excerpts from "Questions of Travel" and "Poem" from *The Complete Poems, 1927–1979* by Elizabeth Bishop. Copyright © 1979, 1983 by Alice Helen Methfessel. Reprinted by permission of Farrar, Straus and Giroux, Inc.
The New Yorker: "Notes and Comment" column reprinted by special permission. Copyright © 1984 The New Yorker Magazine. All rights reserved.
The Radcliffe Quarterly: "Stanzas" by Melanie Thernstrom. Copyright © 1987. Reprinted by permission.

Newspaper headlines and excerpts used by permission of: *The Associated Press.* Copyright © 1988; *The Boston Globe.* Copyright © 1984; *The Boston Herald.* Copyright © 1984; *The Daily Californian.* Copyright © 1984, 1988; *The Oakland Tribune.* Copyright © 1986; *The San Francisco Chronicle.* Copyright © 1986; *The San Francisco Examiner.* Copyright © 1988.

Photographs and artwork used by permission of:
Museum of Fine Arts, Boston: *The Letter,* ca. 1891. Mary Cassatt, Gift of William Emerson and Charles Henry Hayden Fund. *Dekadrachm of Syracuse* (Demarateion), ca. 479 B.C., Theodora Wilbour Fund.
Cordon Art: "Three Worlds" by M.C. Escher. Copyright © 1989 by M.C. Escher Heirs/Cordon Art, Baarn Holland.
Ron Delany: "The Friends of Bibi Lee," photograph copyright © 1988 by Ron Delany. "Bradley Page at First Arraignment." Copyright © 1986 by Ron Delany.
Candida Donadio: "L is for Leo," from *Amphigorey* by Edward Gorey. Copyright © 1963, 1972 by Edward Gorey.
The National Portrait Gallery, London: "Oscar Wilde" photograph by Napoleon Sarony.
Fran Seigel: "Harlequin" by Kinuko Y. Craft. Copyright © 1981 by Kinuko Y. Craft.
David Yee: "The Page Family at the Second Trial." Copyright © 1988 by David Yee. "Bradley Page at Verdict." Copyright © 1988 by David Yee.
© Meg Luther, photographs on p.8, p.60 and p.429
The letters appearing in this book are not those of Roberta Lee. They have been created for this book.

While the events recounted here are accurate to the best of the author's recollection, some of the names of the people involved have been changed.

First published 1990 in Great Britain by
Kyle Cathie Limited
3 Vincent Square London SW1P 2LX.

ISBN 1 85626 039 9

Printed in the USA

In memory of Roberta Teresa Lee
1963–1984

He alone is dead who has been forgotten.

—Inscription on a Russian tombstone

Sometimes I try
to imagine

how things would have been
if you had lived. This is not

the right sort
of imagining. What means is

what is,
but imagined. Imagination builds

many-roomed houses with wood;
imagination does not wish

we were marble. Elegies
to reality

are hard to write.

—M.T.

ACKNOWLEDGMENTS

■ ■

One often finds lists of people thanked at the beginnings of books, to which authors sometimes add all the people in their life at the time, but I think in this book there is an especially close connection between the people in my life and the people in the book—the story and the story, as it were. In many respects this book is the making of many hands. So, among them:

Elaine Pfefferblit, my editor, who is patient and kind and passionate about writing and who indelibly improved the manuscript, and her able assistant Laura Cronin; Monroe Engel, without whom I never would have carried through; Michael Blumenthal, who has looked after my writing in many respects for many years; Lewis Hyde, in whose non-fiction class I began writing this book; Dr. Richard Shohet, who first taught me and Roberta how to write; Celeste Schenck, who knows all she has done; and Glen Hartley and Lynn Chu, my gifted agents, who did so much beyond the call of duty.

I also wish to thank the people whose judgment I have relied so heavily upon: Apollinaire Scherr, Tom Tox Reiss, Alyosha Donald, Elisheva Urbas, Robert Barr, Brian Hall, Lisa Ann Manshel, Michael Mahoney, Cynthia Baughman, and a huge thanks to David Edelstein for many late nights of work.

And among the many people who helped at various stages: Ari Z. Posner, Claudia Kolker, Lisa Moore, Annie Hope and Anne Peretz. Thanks, also, to Leon Friedman; and to Ed Sedarbaum, my copy editor. Thanks to Susan Klee and David Stoloff and Anna

Martinez and her family who gave me homes while I was researching the trial in California. Thanks to my own parents, who have in so many ways been a part of my hope to write. And thanks, finally, to the numbers of people through the years who have encouraged me in writing, who responded benevolently when I told them I wanted to be a writer, who did not ask me whether I had other plans.

CONTENTS

■ ■

PART 1: Memory: The Story   1

     CHAPTER 1   *Memory*   3
     CHAPTER 2   *The Story*   10

PART 2: The First Interpretation:
     The Household Deities   17

     CHAPTER 1   *Debts*   19
     CHAPTER 2   *Adam*   38

PART 3: The Second Interpretation:
     The Man with the Van   47

     CHAPTER 1   *Absolute Elsewhere*   49
     CHAPTER 2   *The Story of Suffering*   62
     CHAPTER 3   *Morning Unsung*   70
     CHAPTER 4   *The Grownups Organization*   75
     CHAPTER 5   *The Elusiveness of Meaning:*
                       Marcellus and Other Half Symbols   90
     CHAPTER 6   *A Suitable Ending*   99

PART 4: The Third Interpretation: Vertigo   117

     CHAPTER 1   *T'e Decision*   119
     CHAPTER 2   *Strangers*   124

PART 5: The Last Interpretation:
     The Little Match Girl   141

     CHAPTER 1   *Wounds*   143
     CHAPTER 2   *The Rock of Loss*   146
     CHAPTER 3   *Promise*   161
     CHAPTER 4   *A Broken Face*   178
     CHAPTER 5   *Every Soul Standeth Single*   183
     CHAPTER 6   *Matches*   192

PART 6: Uninterpreting: Characters   205

  CHAPTER 1 *Brad*   207
  CHAPTER 2 *Bibi*   249

PART 7: Rewriting: The Little Match Girl   265

  CHAPTER 1 *Bad Men and Scary Places*   267
  CHAPTER 2 *Doomed*   275
  CHAPTER 3 *Ugly*   279
  CHAPTER 4 *Through the Golden Windows*   297
  CHAPTER 5 *Matches and Matchlessness*   302
  CHAPTER 6 *Safety*   308
  CHAPTER 7 *The End of the Story*   311

PART 8: Misinterpreting:
    The True Story and Fictions of Memory   321

  CHAPTER 1 *Payments*   323
  CHAPTER 2 *Ways of Seeing: Fictions and Lies*   350
  CHAPTER 3 *The Warmth of Her Smile*   374
  CHAPTER 4 *We Don't Know*   382
  CHAPTER 5 *The Blue Screen*   386
  CHAPTER 6 *A Malignant and Abandoned Heart*   389

PART 9: A New Story: Memory   399

  CHAPTER 1 *The Story*   401
  CHAPTER 2 *Opening a Window and Lighting a Candle*   406
  CHAPTER 3 *Memory*   423

PART 1

Memory: The Story

■ ■

A man who dies at the age of thirty-five is at every point of his life a man who died at the age of thirty-five.

—Moritz Heimann

CHAPTER 1

Memory

You will never know Roberta. That could not happen now. You could be anywhere: walking on one of those lovely wide caféd streets in San Francisco decked with Asian girls in shorts and bright printed T-shirts, or in an underground coffee den in Cambridge where black-eyed girls listen to men telling stories of China or Algiers or any place other than the place they are in, and although she did go to school in Berkeley and her family was from Cambridge and she looked out at the world from dark, dark eyes and hair and colored cotton clothing, not one of those girls would be Roberta. Even if you hung out in the streets until the dusk fell and the stars came, even if you waited in the café where the guitar was the sweetest and the chocolate cake the blackest, even so she would not come. I know; I have waited—in the bath, over breakfast, at the movies, in evening. I am there, looking up at the sky, listening to the music, casually you might say, but not casually—for I am waiting, really waiting. I have gone to all the places I can remember. Can I have forgotten one? I must try to remember more clearly. Where can it be and why doesn't she come anymore to the places we could be together?

I am standing in Café Algiers and Roberta is late and I am afraid she is not going to come. She walks in, finally, and her hair is black and her eyes are dark and full of tears and she says she has something important to tell me. I am about to ask her what she means but before I get a chance to she is gone. Another memory: also dark eyed, Roberta there, but not quite there, or only there for a little while, but with urgency. What does she say? Not sure. But there is this other memory—this—where did it take place?—and she is crying and the last line she speaks sounds so final and I remember just how she repeats my name. "Melanie," she says, "I don't know, Melanie." "That isn't true, Melanie; the answer is no." And she is speaking with her particular emphasis, and the blackness is in her eyes and voice and—these memories all sound alike. They all sound so—*symbolic*.

At the time they were not symbolic. They are of a pattern now; then they were not patterned, as people are not patterns. Only characters are patterned, and people who are alive are not characters. They are almost characters, and the decisions they make each day about who they are and what they ought to do are constantly forming a character, but it is not formed, or not quite formed, because they are still deciding, and because the story has not been written yet. And as long as it is not written anything can happen, because the smallest changes change the story, and the story shapes its characters. Take a certain story, the Little Match Girl story for example, where the Little Match Girl froze to death on the snowy streets, lighting her matches one by one to keep herself warm until they were all used up. The last matches that illuminated the story—we have all thought so much about what these matches mean, and what kind of matches we ourselves might have—those matches need not have been metaphorical at all. If, for instance, someone had just happened to take a walk, and if that walk had happened to be on the very snowy street where the Little Match Girl froze to death, then instead of dying she might have sold him some matches and grown up and opened a match-making factory, and not turned out to be the girl in the tale at all. In fact there might not have been such a fairy tale because the smallest changes change the story and, as long as we are living, it can still be changed, because we don't know what the story is and we don't know what characters we are and with what endings.

What character might Roberta have been if she hadn't been the character that she was? If she were still making up her mind about the story she wanted to be writing? What color would her hair have been in ten years? Not the same color surely—not quite, not exactly. There. The story is looking different already. Only dark-haired girls die young and dramatically; middle-aged women have to have different tales. What kinds of things would she have said if she had been different, if she had had time to be different—or at least have had the possibility of difference, which is the difference between the living and dead?

The more I write about her, though, the less I remember those differences: between the girl in the story and Roberta. That blurry edge of possibility that the young wear, softening their distinctiveness, reminding you that they are unfinished still, is gone. The blurry irregularities are forgotten—the shape of her eyes, not perfectly almond, they must not have been perfectly almond, but only somewhat almond, and not truly dark, not only dark, but suggestive of darkness. The perfection and the darkness become continually clearer, a darkening clarity, while the blurriness fades, a significance too vague to be preserved.

But why do things have to be significant to be preserved? Bibi—I used to call her Bibi—Bebe, B.B.—now she is Roberta, Rosamunde, Mei-hua. Elaborate, formal, archetypal, literary, romantic, Chinese. She lived just down the street, she went to your school, remember, don't you remember? T-shirts and shorts, bread-baking, telephone conversations.

I have nine photographs. *Nine*—say it a few more times and even the number will seem significant. Ah, the significance of retrospect, invading, coloring, spoiling even the accidental. I was given the photographs; I could just as easily have been given ten. Or four. That is the kind of thing I like to forget. In two of the photos she is on cement steps: in one she sits, in the other she stands, her eyes look past you and then beneath you, hard and defiant, wearing three-fingered gloves and tight black jeans, defiant and vulnerable, her hair angled sharp and improbable. There is a small photo too, when her hair was still long, with white flower blossoms, dreamy and wistful, a little sad perhaps, although perhaps not. It is inscribed on the back: "I hope we are always together," she wrote in her lovely loopy handwriting, "Roberta,

Rosamunde, Bibi." It is the only photograph she herself ever gave me. There are two large ones of her face—one with fear and animal eyes, and the other a half smile. Similar, they must have been taken one after the other, but the shutter snapped at different moments, so they are different now. There is one large inscrutable one, where she wears a green sweatshirt, and two small ones, where she is stretched out on the floor leaning on patterned pillows, black ballet slippers on her feet, hands over her mouth, strands of hair catching, giggling. And there is one—just one— really smiling, sitting cross-legged on the carpet, hair blunt upon her shoulders, wearing an orange Whole Earth T-shirt, looking up into the orange light and smiling.

You're cheating again. You're *characterizing*. Listen to your rhetoric: dreamy and wistful, hard yet vulnerable, casual though serious, and smiling, finally smiling, the bath of orange light. How can you be talking about darkening clarity and almond eyes and the significance of retrospect, the endless revisions of the heart? This isn't Roberta; this is a Dead Girl. And any Dead Girl too, who died young and violently, who was beautiful but tragic, and whose memory people mourn in the language of mourning and speak of solemnly. The glossy finish of the photograph; the endless attempt to make sadness seductive. And it is seductive if you tell it well. People will cry for the girl who died if you tell it well enough, although all that is said in that kind of story is that the girl is dead. Your friend is what is forgotten among the glamour of symbolism, the pose of the photo, the closure of narrative.

Is there a way to write without glossing? Your writing, perhaps, is not specific enough. A few more telling personal details. Isn't that what they always tell you in beginning writing classes? *It's the telling personal details that make the characters come alive.* Red ink all over the margins. Remember, not symbolic details, not prescient details, but little things. *Be specific.*

In elementary school Roberta's hair is cut short and straight, with bangs. People think she is a boy; she does not like them for it. And there is some school production, where people dress up in costumes and Roberta does not want to dress up. She thinks it is stupid, and childish. And it is childish, but we are children, and my mother makes me a fairy plum princess costume but Roberta will have nothing to do with it. We talk about our childhoods years later, and Roberta says—that omnipresent note of slight despair—

"Oh, Melanie, I was just a small version of what I am now." In the class picture she is standing with her back to the camera. It is actually, or at least in retrospect, an incredible picture. Everyone else is looking into the lens and smiling, some squirming, some trying to stand tall, but Roberta is turned around. Her little shoulders are squared and she faces away. We are not friends.

No, this is not right, these little driftings toward symbolism. These are the few memories, selected for significance in light of who she was, who she later became. There must be thousands of other memories that are forgotten because they are not so telling, or don't tell what I want to tell. What are they?

I don't know. I don't—remember. Why do you keep asking? Roberta doesn't live down the street and she isn't wearing shorts, and no matter where I wait, and how long I wait, she won't be coming in. I've been waiting a long time; I might as well go home now. The wait in the imagination is only imagined.

But when you go home you leave the dead to the darkness and let your losses be lost. And there are so many dead; they are not differentiated one from the other as the living are. How do you make sure that Roberta will be different? How do you make sure she is—remembered?

Remember . . . we remember the things we love; to love is to remember, she is remembered, I remember. Not Roberta, but the memory of Roberta. Not waiting for Roberta to come in, but for the memory of her to be returned to you—the character of who she was. The story, not her life; the narrative, not the whole. The girl she thought she was, the girl you think she was, the girl described in her letters and pictured in her photographs; the girl she was making up, the girl in the story. Who was the girl in the story? What became of her; what was the story about? Were there tropes, themes, that kind of thing? There must have been themes. Lives always have themes—like stories, just like stories. Imagine, chisel, symbolize, shape it, like a statue. People look at statues; statues are not lost. We felt the Little Match Girl freeze to death in the belated dawn; we remember that story. We have thought about it. Her matches shed light still. Tell, tell her into a story, a story to remember.

But will a story suffice? Is the story important?

You know better than that; you're just pretending to have doubts. You always ask questions when you know you know.

What could be more important? The story is finished, and you are the one who can tell it. Roberta is dead, and you are the one who remembers.

It is August, and Roberta is leaving. I know she is going to leave in a few minutes, because someone is coming to pick her up, and then they arrive. The car pulls up and she turns to go. "Good-bye," she says, getting in.

Calling after her, anxious, the slight anxiety, "I'll see you soon—I'll see you at Christmastime."

She turns and looks at me through the glass, smiling, silent. The car pulls away. She did not reply, and the car pulled away. She did not think I would be able to hear her, perhaps; there was not time. There was not time. Your friend has to be leaving now; it is time for your friend to be leaving. Say good-bye to your friend now, Melanie—come now, come on, it's time to go now—say good-bye, Melanie, say good-bye.

CHAPTER 2
The Story

"... he tries to live his own life as if he were telling
a story."

—Jean-Paul Sartre
Nausea

Well Melanie,

I seem to be in sunny California. S.F. to be exact, but it's not exactly sunny. Is it really true Californians have more fun? This room
has mites. I'll be living in Berkeley starting Wednesday.
Here's my address:
B. B. Lee
Euclid Hall
177 Euclid Avenue
Berkeley, CA 94709
It's a co-op, all upperclassmen except for yours truly. A good situation to be in, since I can't stand all these fresh-off-the-boat types. Too
enthusiastic.
Procrastination . . . I'm in the co-op now. Signing up for classes
is an exercise in frustration. Not to mention a wade through the fires
of hell. I don't know what I'm doing here and hate feeling so lost. I

don't even have a bank account. But I'll adjust, I guess. If only I weren't
so slow-ow-ow-ow-ow. . . .
        Hey————think of me————

                                        Much love,
                                        Bibi

It is close to seven when the phone rings that Wednesday morning.
I don't hear it, but my roommate Kim comes up and knocks on my
door. She stands there in her flowered red and white flannel
nightgown, her eyes still bright with sleep but wide with sudden
worry too, and says, "Melanie, Veronica just called."

"Veronica," I murmur, sitting up, "you mean Roberta's sister
Veronica?"

"Yes, Veronica Lee."

"What did she want?"

"She said that Roberta is missing," Kim says, her voice getting
higher with a little rising note of anxiety. She looks very young,
her hair tousled on her shoulders and her eyes widening, and since
there cannot be two small and scared girls in the same conversation because someone has to be strong and practical or it will be
really scary, instead of panicking I get annoyed. How like Bibi! We
had been through this scenario so many times before. There she
was, always on the margin of everyone's consciousness, just out of
reach, threatening to fade. No one loved her enough, there was
nothing for her here, perhaps Madeira or Madagascar. No, even in
Madagascar she would not be happy, it would be better just to
vanish. And you would have to say, as you had said so many times
before, but no, I love you, I need you, I think your life is meaningful, you will be happy one day. You would know, too, that you
must not have been quite convincing because she had not been
convinced, and although you did not know how to do better you
were going to have to try again. Veronica had called—Bibi had
disappeared, whatever—here I was, going to have to be worried
again. And I would, but I would be annoyed as well.

"What exactly did Veronica say?" I ask Kim, but her answer is
so trembling and tear-threatening that I go down to the phone
impatiently and call Veronica. Veronica is about five years older
than Roberta; maybe twenty-six. She tells me the story.

Roberta—Bibi—who went to school at Berkeley, had gone

running on Sunday morning in Roberts Recreational Area in the Oakland hills with her boyfriend, Brad, and another girl, some blond girl who was someone's younger sister or something like that, called Robin. The Oakland hills are ten miles from the Berkeley campus so they had driven there. As they were running, Bibi had veered off on a different trail, and they assumed she would catch up with them, but she didn't. They waited for her at the end of the trail, and then jogged back to the car, but she wasn't there either. Brad drove along the highway that follows the trail to look for her, leaving Robin back at the parking lot. Sometime later he returned, saying he had not found her, and he and Robin drove home. At midnight Meg, Bibi's roommate, called him to ask where Bibi was, but Brad had been out for the day and did not know she had not come back. Meg called the police; the park was searched the next day. Nothing was found. Maybe Roberta would call me; I should let them know if she did. Veronica says she is sorry for calling so early and hopes I will be able to go back to sleep. At any rate, I should give her love to my parents. I say yes.

I hang up in the shock of confusion. At what level are we talking? How important is this information, and how does it alter normal things—like the incivility of calling at seven a.m. but remembering someone's parents when you do? Should I go back to sleep? Should I have breakfast? Should I call someone and tell them—what should I tell them? Kim was already sobbing in the corner. Should I cry? What would I be crying about—*what had just happened?* Is this my friend Bibi we are talking about? Are they sure? I had heard from her so recently—so amazingly recently—something new and important could hardly have happened between then and now. She would have told me about it because I got a letter just three days ago and a phone call last week and we were—we are—in really close touch just now, I point out to no one in particular.

What was I doing on Sunday? I was here in Cambridge doing nothing on Sunday, and I didn't think of Roberta that day. Therefore nothing important could have happened: after all, what does closeness mean if you're not aware of the important things that happen to the people you are close to? And we are close, aren't we? Should I go to my room to think about it and make sure? No, no, I do not want to think about it, I am not going to do that, I am going to go downstairs.

I knock on my roommate Don's door and ask him if I can come in. He says yeah, what is it, and I enter and sit on his bed. So, I just got this phone call, I say, this phone call—you know my friend Roberta? Anyway—no, not from her, about her, from her sister, her older sister Veronica. I tell him the story. I half expect he will give me some instant explanation. Only two days, she must be visiting a friend, maybe needed some time alone, don't indulge in the usual premature panic, whatever. Don is usually good at telling me my important emotions are not important—are often, in fact, silly. He has the perfect dry, sarcastic voice in which to do it.

"Sounds grim," he replies, shrugging. Grim? I think, Oh God, it does sound grim—distinctly grim, dear Lord, I think I will go into the living room to find Nicholas.

Nicholas—sensitive, comforting, small Nicholas—Nicholas will say something infinitely helpful. I recite what I have been told, and he puts his arms around me immediately and says in a low voice, "You have to realize, Mel, she might be dead." I nod dully, and I have no idea what he is talking about.

This is a story I tell often—over tea, in late-night confessional moments, at cocktail parties, pausing to wonder, between chapters, years later, what exactly I am saying. It was a long time ago: the things I felt then, I don't feel anymore. When I think of them now, they surprise me—they sound odd, childish, self-indulgent. But when I come to the finale, and I hear myself telling them that Roberta has died, that Roberta is dead, my voice sounds much as it did that morning: the same dull distance and vague stupidity, bewildering, the dragged-out sense of intermittence, broken by conversation, as we wait, always and halfheartedly, amidst half revelations and quarter meanings, for some definite kind of word: where she is, who she is, what—certain we have been listening all this time, certain we would understand it when it came.

■ ■

One day early in our senior year of high school, Roberta and I have gone into Harvard Square, and we are coming home on a bus. She wanted to stay longer, and I wanted to get back to do my homework. I have a French exam and a

Latin quiz and some reading for English and a biology lab to write up. Roberta must have these things to do too: we are in all the same classes. Also, I want to have dinner with my parents, although we eat later than the Lees, so she must already be late. She is annoyed at me getting on the bus.

A group we both know from our high school gets on, four girls and two guys from what Bibi calls the N.H.S. crowd (the National Honor Society—an organization to which neither of us was elected). They are wearing bright, thick-knit sweaters with matching scarves and mittens and blue jeans and making the requisite amount of noise. They are all active in other organizations as well. Roberta refers to them as Miniature Grownups, because she says that only Miniature Grownups would be excited about running dopey little organizational thingeys. Like *committees and thingeys,* she adds spitefully. But they are sitting down in the seats right ahead of me and I don't dislike them so I lean forward and say hi. They say hi back and we begin to chat animatedly. Conversation centers around a biology quiz: I gaily agree that it was very hard because I already know I have done well on it. I wonder if they know they have done well also, and if that is why they are bringing it up. Roberta does not mention how she thought she did. She does not like biology. I do not like biology either, of course, but my teacher thinks I do. It seems to me I have not been talking very long, not nearly long enough for Roberta to be mad or to feel left out, when all of a sudden she jumps up and gets off the bus. It happens so quickly it almost doesn't happen: I look at her seat again even though the bus is now driving by her, and it seems to me she could not possibly have disappeared this quickly. Another minute lags by: we are getting further and further away from the place at which she has gotten off. I run to the front of the bus and explain to the bus driver I need to get off too. He is old and cross. I shout at him, conscious that our classmates are staring at me and whispering among themselves. He lets me off, and I run back through the snowy street. We are somewhere in Arlington, miles from home. Finally I see Roberta walking slowly, her hand stuck in her pockets, her hair falling straight down the shoulders of her green ski jacket. "Roberta," I say, running toward her, "Roberta, what the hell do you think you're doing?"

"I wanted to get off," she says violently, turning to face me. "I can get off any time I want to," she insists, and starts walking again and will not say another word to me all the rest of the way home. The foreshadowing is so obvious I don't notice it, busy as I am wishing that she had gotten off a little closer to home, or that it was a better day for a long walk.

PART 2

The First Interpretation: The Household Deities

■ ■

We believe we are free. Everything we are told from our earliest age leads us to believe this is the case. It is not. We—the one animal almost without instincts, the cultural animal who invents himself—we are born into elaborate systems already owing allegiances to household deities which we will never in this life sufficiently appease. And this causes us much anguish and perplexity.

—Richard R. Niebuhr, in lecture

CHAPTER 1

Debts

Dear Mellie,

*GOT YOUR LETTER WEEKS AGO AND STILL HAVEN'T WRIT-
TEN BACK. I've got to get out of neutral.*

*Classes are oke. I'm not exactly thrilled by any of them. They're
just not interesting—or I'm not interested. Why can't I concentrate?
Why can't I get my shit together? The old question. If I knew what the
problems were, I wouldn't have them. And me? Worthless, no friends.*

*I JUST GOT A C+ ON MY FIRST PAPER. THAT IS A LOUSY
GRADE. NO WONDER WESLEYAN AND BROWN AND MIT
TURNED ME DOWN AND AWAY. I CALLED HOME AND IT WAS
TERRIBLE. NOTHING DOING//DOING NOTHING. NO ENERGY
NOTHING. WANT TO SLEEP. NO PEACE WHICH PASSETH UN-
DERSTANDING. RUNNING ON EMPTY, RUNNING*

RUNNING

Don't pay attention, it's just my mood these days. Berkeley isn't what I hoped it would be. Things will be oke, a little later. Thought you'd like the coins on the card. I'm not such a basketcase.

> *Love,*
> *Rosamunde*

I am sitting at the Lees' kitchen table, with Mrs. Lee and Veronica. They have given me an orange and Chinese tea in a big Chinese teacup with a flowered lid on it. There are peels scattered all over the table; no one else is eating anything. The Oakland hills are fifteen miles from campus, Mrs. Lee is saying. How did Bradley expect her to get home?

He left her there, she says, he left her there alone.

But we don't know, I say. We don't know what their arrangement was.

But he drove Robin home. How come it was Bibi who was by herself? How come he and Robin went home together?

We know nothing about Robin; we know nothing about Brad; we know nothing about their relationship. We don't know what the story is.

He left Roberta in order to go to the Exploratorium for the day. Did you know that was his pressing engagement—that he had to hurry back to campus in order to get to the Exploratorium with a group of his friends?

The Exploratorium? What is an Exploratorium?

Some touchy-feely California science museum. *And not only that, but Roberta was supposed to go with them.* When they asked him where she was, he apologized for her. He didn't tell them he had left her up in the hills. *He didn't tell them he had left her there.*

But we don't know what he said to his friends. Maybe he was embarrassed, maybe he expected her to meet him there, maybe he was angry that she didn't.

How did he expect that she would get home? Oakland is twenty miles from campus; they had driven there.

I thought it was ten. Or seven. Maybe he thought she would run; maybe he thought she had gotten a ride; maybe he didn't think about it.

Who would she get a ride from? A stranger? Would she have hitchhiked? Would Roberta have tried to hitchhike home?

No, she wouldn't hitchhike; she would know that was unsafe.

Meg said she used to hitchhike around Berkeley.

Hitchhiking around campus is different; she wouldn't hitchhike in Oakland.

She hitchhiked to Mexico.

Wasn't she with some people then? Some guys? Maybe she—maybe—did she have money with her? What was she wearing?

Black and white striped jogging shorts and a dark long-sleeved cotton shirt. And sneakers and bobby socks, and her purse is at home next to her dresser.

Maybe she had her money card with her and withdrew some money from her bank account.

The money card is in her purse, and the bank is in Berkeley.

Maybe she was carrying some money with her, like a ten stuck in her shoe.

Do you think she would have done that?

She might.

I always told her not to go anyplace without money. She probably wouldn't have gone anyplace without money.

She might have decided to take the money to visit a friend she hadn't seen in a long time and headed toward L.A. or Santa Fe or—anywhere really. You know how she liked to surprise people—to drop in on them—because she was sick of school or wanting an adventure. You never know with Bibi, you just never know.

And she'll probably call us when she gets there.

But the police have called all her friends. Her address book was in her room, with her date book and her diary and her purse and the clothes she changed out of to put on her running clothes. Her friends say they have no idea where she is. Her friends are worried; her friends want us to call them when we find her.

Maybe she didn't visit a friend. Maybe she took a bus from Oakland. She wouldn't need much money for that. Even if she just had a dollar she could take a bus and anyway she could probably talk the bus driver into it if she wanted to. Is there a bus that goes by Roberts Park?

There might be a bus that goes by Roberts Park! Maybe we should call transit information. There must be a bus that goes somewhere near there, to Berkeley. I'm almost sure of it—she wouldn't hitchhike if there was a bus that went right to campus, would she?

Why would she hitchhike if there was a bus? Maybe we should find out; we should call the bus company. Do you have a phone book; what should we look up? See, there are lots of possibilities; we haven't thought very long and we've already thought of a good one: think what we'll think of if we think a little longer.

"But Melanie," Veronica says suddenly, her black eyes dark, "if she had taken a bus, if she had hitchhiked, if she had walked, *if she had had sex with a taxi driver and, in return, he had driven her to her doorstep*—if whatever she had done had turned out okay," she says, pausing, trembling over the word *okay*, so that I know how she is going to finish the sentence: "she would be home by now. She would be home by now."

■ ■

"I had a fight with my mother last night," Roberta is saying one afternoon in high school.

"What happened?" I ask, smiling a little. So many of our conversations start this way.

"She accused me of being unhappy, and I said yes. So she looked it up in her Dr. Spock book—you now, the one Good Parents memorize—and between the chapter on taking your child to the art museum (Cultural Education), spending the summer on Cape Cod (Discovery of Nature), and encouraging them to read (Key to Success), she couldn't find a section on Unhappiness. So she decided that if it wasn't a legitimate category, then it must be the result of a deficiency in some other category, which implied she had been deficient. And since she has been through the list so many times, and everything has been checked off—carefully, painfully, look how hard she worked to make sure everything got checked off—she decided to get mad at me instead."

"Yes," I say, "yes."

"And of course she has worked hard," Roberta adds thoughtfully, "and truly done everything to be A Good Mother. So I guess it is legitimate that she feels she deserves something to show for it—to tell the neighbors and friends and hang on the refrigerator next to my report card. She can't hang it up as long as I'm unhappy, can she? That's the last item on the résumé, the unwritten failure that spoils all the rest.

"And since the usual bullying, bribing, and coercion is

not going to work—not about happiness, it isn't—I guess
there's nothing she can do.

"Which leaves them about at the end of their powers,
doesn't it? Maybe I will go to school in California next year.

"It must be funny for her, having had such a hard
childhood in China and finally coming to America and Dad
being so successful and a computer science professor at
MIT and also starting his own company and this nice house
in Lexington and all these things so I can grow up happy
and privileged without having to struggle as they did, and
after all this—after all this, with absolutely nothing to struggle about or against or for, why look: *I'm just miserable.*"

She looks at me darkly, her eyes tearful. "But you
know, Melanie," she adds, more softly, "it's kind of funny
for me too."

■ ■

"Melanie, Melanie," Roberta says, telephoning, her voice
low and choked, "I got rejected by MIT."

"Oh, stop it, Roberta. Don't give me this rejected business. You've spent your whole life trying not to get into
MIT. You did poorly in every one of the sciences and math,
and you started crying in the middle of your alumnus
interview.

"So, great—be happy about it—you didn't get into
MIT."

"But my father being a professor there and my older
brother and two older sisters all going and graduating with
extreme and excessive honors, and all of us being able to
go there for free, I am wasting my parents' hard-earned
money—"

"And are wicked and ungrateful?" I say, thinking how I
was going to school at Harvard, ten miles from home, where
my parents teach, and that I wasn't even allowed to apply
to Berkeley. Why would you go to school far away if you
could go close to home? say my parents. My mother went
to school far from home, and she was so unhappy she had
to transfer back. They just don't want the same thing to
happen to me.

"You want to go," I tell Roberta, "and what you want

to do—what is going to make you happy—is the most important thing."

"That is not true," says Roberta. "Whoever told you
that? No one ever told me that. That's not the only thing
that's important at all."

■ ■

"The Parental Committee has reached a verdict."

"Yes?" I ask, smiling.

"The decision is in favor of me going to Berkeley."

"That's wonderful, Roberta."

"It's like they've given up on me."

I am afraid she is going to cry, and I say quickly, "No, it
is not like that. They are just letting you go. Like you've
always wanted them to. That's not the same thing as giving
up, now, is it?"

"I don't know," she says dubiously.

■ ■

"Have you heard from Roberta recently?" Mrs. Lee asks me.

"Yes, I have," I say proudly. "As a matter of fact I have heard
from her very recently indeed. She called just two weeks before—
before—I mean just a couple of weeks ago, and then on Thursday—
last Thursday, I mean—I got this letter from her. This really long
nice letter—the first letter I had had in a while and it was great."

"Oh," says Mrs. Lee. "Do you think I could look at it?"

"Well," I say, considering, "if you'll give it back."

■ ■

Roberta comes home from Berkeley for summer vacation
after our sophomore year of college. We go into the Square
one day so I can introduce her to Bob; I have been waiting
for her to come home so they can meet. Bob is a senior at
Harvard; I hope they are going to like each other. My
mother wants me to do something else—to get my passport
photo taken at the photo shop, I think.

"This is my friend Rosamunde—Bibi," I say, trying to
remember how I have referred to her with him before. I had

been in the Rosamunde habit for the past couple of months, I thought. "And Roberta," I add quickly, just in case.

"Oh," he says, surprised, laughing, "I thought those were all different friends."

"By any chance," he asks in the sudden way he has, looking right at her, "do you have an identity problem?"

I would have taken his tone as ironic if I were Roberta, and laughed, but it is hard to tell with Bob. His tones are ironic, they are always ironic, but you can take them however you like. The suddenness gives it the effect of seriousness, but his face is deadpan, as if he is parodying seriousness. And yet the things he says really are serious. He puts in the irony, I think, just to be kind, so you don't have to take them seriously if you don't want to. Roberta always elects to take everything seriously, though, and so she cries passionately: "Yes. I do. And my parents call me Mei-hua," she says, pronouncing a Chinese name I have never heard, "or Number Four. Chinese parents number their children. I'm not kidding. Only sometimes they make a mistake and call me Number Five—I don't know who they think the extra is—maybe the cat. It's funny how they never *upgrade* my number, though."

I relax: they are going to like each other after all.

My mother is cross when I get home, as expected. "It was important," I say.

"So is your passport photo—if you want to go on our vacation, that is," she says. My mother is a busy and efficient person: she is a political scientist, and she is writing a book on the effects of the 1965 Voting Rights Act, and she Gets Things Accomplished. We puzzle one another.

"What exactly was it you did for the afternoon?" she asks again.

"Something important," I repeat passionately, wishing I could think of something important and specific to make up.

"Yes?" She waits. I can't think of anything compelling, so she stays cross. It's easy to make things up, but hard to be specific about it. But I was right, actually; no need for fictions. Bob now knows Roberta. He is not one of the people who did not know Roberta. It is so simple, after all. If we hadn't gone for coffee that day, he would be.

■ ■

I call Bob that night, to tell him the news. I have not called him for a while since he moved to San Francisco to start medical school; I had been saving calling him, and it is queer to realize that this is the occasion on which I shall use it. I do not tell the news well. The more I think about it, the less surprised and the more depressed I get, so by the time I speak it has none of the saving passion of the shock and protest of sudden bad news. As I am explaining, he suddenly interrupts and says: "She's your best friend and you're already giving up on her after three days! You're talking like—she's dead.

"Be hopeful," he tells me, and suddenly feeling I have disappointed him—and Roberta as well—I resolve to do better. I resolve to be hopeful.

■ ■

It is the summer after her sophomore year, and Bibi is trying to decide what to do. She wants to go away: she spends most of her time thinking about going away—lots of places, different places, all of them far. She had thought about taking the year off from school, as I was going to take the year off: she didn't like school, she was unhappy in school, perhaps she could spend the year in Paris. She would go to Paris and I would go to Benares and we would both be happy and faraway, she said. We talked about this a lot: what it would be like to be happy and faraway. Her parents disagreed. Lots of people take a year off from college, and they get back on track, she argued—it doesn't necessarily mean you are dropping out forever, she said—it doesn't necessarily mean anything like that. Her parents were not convinced. So she stayed at Berkeley, and I took the year off and didn't go to Benares—lived, in fact, in Somerville a few miles from Harvard. She thought of going away for the summer, at least. She had some money: her parents insisted she get a job working nights at a computer company after high school. She didn't just dislike the job, as people often dislike jobs, because they are routine or monotonous; she hated it. She used to call me from there and say it frightened her how much she hated it. She likes

the idea of taking all that money and using it to go someplace far away—Tibet, Paraguay, Tierra del Fuego. Not that
it would make up for the job, she reminds me, and the way
that she felt all those hours working at it—Jesus, nothing
could make up for that—but at least it might add some
consoling irony to think she subsequently squandered all
her earnings on faraway places in summertime.

"Oh," I tell her. "Go squander it all on summertime.
Don't give it a second thought."

■ ■

"So, when are you leaving, Bibi? Did you buy your plane
ticket?"

"No. I talked to Veronica."

"So?"

"Veronica said I had to come home. She said it was
irresponsible; it was running away. She said I had better
come home and attend to my responsibilities."

"Oh," I say, "yes." And then: "Wait—what responsibilities? Responsibilities to do what?"

"You know," she says, "to do things. To work on my
things."

"I know," I say, quiet, knowing. Practice the piano,
write, save money, be productive, take a course, be unhappy. Responsibilities.

Oh Bibi, I almost cry, if you can't go away next year,
couldn't you at least take the summer off? I don't say
anything, though, because I already know the answer: if
you took any time off, a year or even a summer, a whole
long strange summer a million miles away from yourself
and your troubles and your responsibility to be your troubled self, you might never pick them up again. And perhaps Veronica was right: who would want responsibilities
when they could be in Tibet? I used to think about this a
lot: whether that summer, the last summer, would have
been the last summer had she not used it as she did. It
was curious: she spent most of her life planning to go
away, but she never did until she stopped trying and simply disappeared—just as I never went anywhere, until I
followed in her wake looking for her. She came home that

summer, as I came home—we had plenty of ideas, both of us—but in the end we decided always to come home. I wonder what would have happened had even one of her plans to go away—to lead a different life at least for a little while—worked: had she not grown weary of plans and planning and waiting for things that didn't happen. I wonder, too, what would have happened had I gone to Benares— had I really gone, gone and not left an address—gone so far that the mail was lost or so late that by the time I heard it was all out of date. I'm so sorry, but I didn't hear in time—I'm so sorry, but by the time I heard it was too late to be sorry. Had I done, in fact, anything besides what I did, and had she gone anyplace other than where she was, and had we been anything other than what we were— trapped and unhappy—I wonder what would have happened: had I not been here to mourn, that is, had she not been there to die.

■ ■

The Lees call me the next day. Mr. Lee is already in California, searching. The police are searching, students are searching, volunteers with dogs are searching, no one has found Roberta. Veronica would like to go out to California too, but she is worried about leaving her mother alone.

"I'll stay with her," I say without thinking, and then realizing of course I should, I say: "I mean of course I'll stay with her."

"Really?" says Veronica. "Oh, thank you. Thank you."

Mrs. Lee calls me the next day. "I'm going to California," she says triumphantly in her thick Chinese accent.

"You are?"

"Yes," she says. "I am going to California with the rest of my family. Can you take care of the house while we are gone? We want someone to be here to answer the phone—so that— We want somebody to be home . . . if Roberta calls."

"Oh. Yes. Yes. Umm—when will you come back?" I ask quickly.

"When I find my daughter," she says.

■ ■

Brad shows up at her house in Lexington one day that summer on a motorcycle. He doesn't call or write or let Roberta know beforehand; he just shows up on his Honda, leather jacketed, blond hair gleaming. Brad is twenty-two, about to be a senior, and he also lives in Lothlorien, their vegetarian co-op. She had known him about a year, and they had been dating on and off since Christmas, I think, of the previous year, but there had been other people as well, for both of them. Her letters were filled with stray names— Ben, Courtney the Bearboy, and then Brad, Bradley Page. Still, in their own fashions—his distant and hers ambivalent about commitment, of any sort, ever—they had been together a surprisingly long time.

Brad assumes he can stay the night. The Lees consider: they have never talked about men, they have never spoken of sex, they have never told her she can date, but they let her go to school in California. He is the world; he is California. He has come to take their daughter; he thinks he is free to sleep in her bedroom any night he likes. Send him to a hotel, says Mr. Lee. Roberta tells me this: My father, she says, said Brad should go to a hotel. I wonder, now, where he slept that night. It seems to me that he stayed with Roberta; I don't remember for certain, but I think he did. Perhaps the Lees had wondered if they were being unreasonable.

■ ■

At the end of July, Roberta begins to think she is pregnant. She and Brad had not used birth control; her pelvis is oddly tilted, and she can't use a diaphragm. We lock ourselves in my bedroom and read *Our Bodies, Ourselves*. It says that people do get pregnant; that if you are over one week late getting your period you may be pregnant, and that you should get a test. We call my old pediatrician, who is a very nice man. He keeps slipping, though, while he is talking, and saying "you," and I correct him with "my friend," and he keeps talking. He says I should tell my parents; I say my friend's parents would never speak to her again. He says that girls who tell their parents have a much easier time with abortions, and that parents can be much more understanding than one might imagine. I say I have not found that to be true, I have found just the opposite to be true, and he says your parents, and I say hers, and he says you and I say she, and then we both start to talk at once and I hang up. Roberta and I look through the phone book and call hotlines; they tell us the same thing. My mother keeps knocking at the door. She wants to know if we want to come down for dinner; she wants to know when we are going to be off the phone; she wants us to know that we can't tie up the phone too long because people might want to be calling her; she wants to know what we are doing in there—*girls, what are you doing in there?*

■ ■

"Do you think I should call Brad to tell him?"

"Yes, *of course* I think you should call Brad," I say, feeling a general female indignation.

"You think he'll want me to call him?"

"Of course he'll want you to call him. After all, it will be his baby, won't it?"

"Yes," she says, "it will be his baby."

■ ■

"I called Brad."

"Oh! Great! What did he say?"

"He said he was training hard to try out for the Olympic crew team, and also practicing for the triathlon and doing some cross-country running, and he was in good shape and he would probably do well, and he was glad to hear from me—"

"But what did he say about the pregnancy?"

"He told me how something similar had happened to him while he was in France and he was psychologically raped by the mother of the family he was living with, and—"

"But what'd he say about the pregnancy?" I ask, too impatient to ask what psychological rape was or how it applied.

"He said if I ever needed anything I should call.

"But, you know, Melanie," she adds, pausing, "the thing is, I *was* calling. I was calling."

■ ■

That night we call Adam. Adam was my boyfriend, and he did not know Roberta very well because he lived in New York, but with Adam that would not matter. She can stay with him, he says instantly, he will give her the money and make the arrangements. No, she needn't worry about it; he is glad to do it—more than glad, he says, he wants to.

"Thank you, thank you so much," she says hesitantly. "I mean, I'm sorry—I hate to be an imposition—I'm always such a burden on everybody—and on myself—"

"It's no problem, no problem at all," he proclaims in his large, easy, definite voice.

"Really?" she asks again.

"Really," he says.

■ ■

It is time, I decide, to talk to Adam. I have left two messages for him on his answering machine, but although I know that he must not have gotten them because he always calls me back immediately, I pretend that he has and wait diligently for him to call. If his roommate DeWitt doesn't remember to give him the messages for another couple of days, I might not need to tell him about it at all because she might be found by then. Adam is a practical person: he is a journalist, he takes events seriously. He will take this event very seriously. He will not understand that it might not be as definite as it sounds just because I am still thinking about it, because Roberta is a complex person, and everything she does has many possible meanings. It needn't necessarily be taken at face value, her having disappeared, because if I hadn't been home when Veronica called me, or if she hadn't told Kim what it was about and Kim hadn't woken me up, *then I wouldn't know and things would be exactly the same.* I don't need to talk to her or see her very often—I could go a long time without seeing her, at least a year, maybe two, because most of the time she is at school there and I am at school here.

So: *why can't I trade five minutes of after-time for before-time?*

I know that the forward motion of time is one of life's most definite rules—no exceptions permitted, yes, of course that includes you. Why shouldn't it include you? Time progresses forward at exactly the same measure; it only seems sometimes to go faster. And it only seems sometimes to stand still, like a still lake, as if you could look down to the very bottom and see the shape of the trapped leaves, and the colors, and you imagine the past is accessible to you, but—you are wrong. It's a trick of the light. See how difficult it is to think without metaphor. It's metaphor that makes time appear like still lakes. Time isn't anything or like anything. It moves forward, neither fast nor slow, just forward. And once it has moved a beat ahead, as it has always just moved a beat ahead, it doesn't go back, even for a small minute. *Never.* We already said there were no negotiations: this is a rule, and you can't cheat. Why do you always imagine you can cheat on everything, and bend the rules so they come out your way? Time doesn't care what little manipulations you can do in your mind. This isn't a poem; it's *reality.* It's amazing you've gotten to be this old without understanding about reality.

However, since I have gotten this old I try to see if I can argue my way out of changing for just a little longer. *Suppose,* I propose, in my most winning and persuasive way: suppose I altered it *just a little bit.* Suppose, for example, I called the old number and no one was home or the line was busy or I hung up quick before they had a chance to answer. Then it would be just as if Roberta were out or missed the phone or were talking on the other line—like before. Just like before, that is, if I didn't know. But of course I do—I do know.

I call Adam.

"Oh God, sweetheart," he says in a low, pained voice, "that is the saddest thing I ever heard. You stay right there. I'll come up right away."

"No, I'm okay. I mean—it'll probably—be different soon. I mean she probably—I don't know— Don't come up yet. I guess something will probably happen soon. Wouldn't you think?"

"I'll call you tonight," he says.

■ ■

She has a test, and the test is positive, and they ask her when she has the abortion whether she would like to be

sleeping or awake. I ask what she told them, and she says asleep I guess, and holds her palms out flat in front of her. Her hands are small and slightly misshapen, as in one of those drawings children do where they trace around a hand on a piece of paper, except the paper was slightly crooked, or was pulled out before the drawing was done.

"This will definitely," she says, looking past me, her eyes black with fear like an animal's, crossing her hands in front of her body protectively, "be the end of adolescence."

I reach toward her face and brush a tear off her lashes.

■ ■

"The woman at the clinic called me."

"She did?"

"Yeah. She fucking left a message saying tell Roberta that Natalie at the clinic is trying to reach her. What clinic? my father wanted to know. She fucking left a message with my father. Don't they know *anything* about families?"

"What did she say?"

"She says that I should come in again and get another test because she thinks that test wasn't valid after all, because it looked like the ring was a little *jagged* or something, and somebody might have *knocked* the test tube. Fucking assholes."

"They did? The test might not be true? But I thought that never happened! I thought that if they say it's negative, they might be wrong, but if it comes back positive, it's positive. *Our Bodies, Ourselves* said that never happens. Well, no kidding. Aren't you lucky! Somebody must be looking out for you, baby."

"No," she says, suddenly looking right at me. "No, I don't think that they are."

■ ■

Reporters begin to call me. I cannot imagine how they got my number. I am taking the year off from school and living in an attic in an ancient, ugly house in Somerville and I keep her letters and pictures buried deep in the diary that is hidden under my bed. My pictures of her look nothing like the pictures in the paper—which are prim and Chinese and schoolgirlish, taken from her passport perhaps or from some ancient class photo—and the accompanying little descriptions in the articles sound nothing like her descriptions of herself in her letters. But suddenly there are men on the phone asking for me, wanting to know what Roberta was like—what she did, how she looked, how she felt about her family, whether she was happy.

"*Happy!*" I finally spit out at some man on the telephone. "Happy!" I am so angry I can barely speak. No, she most certainly was not happy. She had dropped out of school two weeks before, she had called a week ago and when I asked her whether she was all right she said no, and she had said good-bye in her last letter. It wasn't signed, it didn't say see you soon or write back or take care or even Love, Roberta: it said bye—"*bye bye.*" And all along—for years and years—she had been saying she was frightened, she was depressed, something was going to happen, and happen soon, *and nobody listened to her.* Everybody said we were bright young promising high school girls and dark thoughts were attributable to adolescence. Lots of people are unhappy when they are young, they all said, but they outgrow it. Well, she wasn't wrong, and she wasn't making it up, and she's not going to outgrow it now because something finally has happened, and now, *now* you're calling. Now you're interested, now you're concerned, now you want me to tell you what it was all about. *Hah.* A bit late, buddy.

"She wasn't happy?" the man says, surprised. "But she did so many things. I have here—the last person I talked to said she knew three languages and ran and was in training for a triathlon and played the viola and tutored Asian students and wrote poetry and worked at the women's center and took dance classes and was modeling in a hair show and—"

"Four," I interrupt sullenly. "It was four languages. Latin, Chinese, French, German." I puzzle about this for a while, trying to think whether she actually knew German or had just been thinking about learning it. What about Greek? "She wanted to learn Russian too," I add. "She loved to be able to talk to people— like if you knew Russian, you could talk to two hundred million more people in the world. It was one of her favorite ideas." And then, remembering, with a passionate, almost desperate sense that whatever I say will not be enough, will not convince him of how important it is, I cry: "*She was incredibly unhappy.* She was almost . . . suicidal."

"She was?" the man says. "No one has said that before."

I suddenly realize I have made a mistake. "Oh," I say. "Maybe—I guess I shouldn't have said anything. I don't know what her family wants people to say. I'm sorry—I take it back. Could you—could you erase that from the record?"

"All right," he says after a moment, and then adds, "But you're lucky. It happens that I'm a good guy and I won't print anything you don't want. But not everyone would be so scrupulous. It's interesting, and it's a new angle, and it would make a very, very hot story."

■ ■

Adam calls me that night. "Listen, hon," he says, "you don't have to talk to anyone you don't want to."

"Oh," I say, surprised. "No, no, I won't." I haven't told him about the reporter because I am ashamed.

"You aren't experienced with this kind of thing, and you don't know how they can twist around what you say, so make sure they don't make you say anything you don't want to. And if they give you any trouble, you have them call me."

"Yes," I say. "I'll do that. I will definitely do that."

■ ■

"Roberta," I say, "Roberta, I'm so glad you called. I've missed you! How are you? How's school and stuff? How's Brad? Did you talk—I mean about everything that happened last summer? Are you still going out?"

"I am dropping out of school," she says coldly, her voice flat, "and I am going to owe my parents forty-four hundred dollars, which they will collect. I don't have anything to pay them with and I have no idea what I'm going to do next because there is nothing I want to do next, but I'm going to do it anyway because I don't want to be in school. I don't want to and I can't—I can't do it anymore. And I was never going out with Bradley. We're just sleeping together."

"That's not true!" I exclaim, almost hurt. And then: "Wait—I'm sorry—are you okay? You are okay, aren't you?"

"No," says Roberta.

It is October 21, and I don't know how, but somehow—I managed to let her hang up without asking her exactly what she meant. I don't know; maybe I figured I would ask her next time we talked; maybe I figured it was a temporary depression; maybe I figured she didn't really mean it. I don't know; I don't know why I'm even bothering to make up reasons; whatever I figured, I was wrong. Very wrong, obviously.

■ ■

The article comes out the next day. It dutifully reports that she was doing this and this and this and was well liked and has lots of friends, and that Naomi and I, her best friends, are sad and shocked and totally surprised. I reread the first paragraph, "Roberta—affectionately called Bibi—is described as a dynamic young woman . . ."

Ah, I think, after all this time. After all this time and worry—the worry that our parents worried, the worry that we ourselves worried, the worry that we would not, after all, turn out all right—is over. The report has been made. Here it is, in black and white: she was a paragon of accomplishment, everybody's favorite person, a tragic loss, truly. The verdict is in. And I—who lived my entire life as if I were writing it on an application that was never accepted but eternally under consideration—had to keep on writing. Her life was stamped and sealed; she could put down her pen at last. I was almost jealous.

■ ■

I am standing in a gleaming white room of an expensive California health spa. Bright complicated exercise equipment is spaced all around, and it too gleams, metallically. Roberta is lying in the room, dead, stretched out cold and dark. She opens her eyes for a moment, and I catch my breath. I know that if only I can get someone else to see then she will have to stay alive. If someone else sees what I see in my dream then it will not be a dream, it will be documented reality, and in documented reality alive people and dead people are different. It is as if they are in different rooms, they are that different. I am pretty certain this is true. Roberta would have to be in one room or the

other, so if they see her alive, alive she would be. I turn toward the door, and Roberta tells me not to bother: she will be dead before I get back. She says it just like that: flat and cold, don't bother, I'll be dead before you get back. I freeze, and then I see a vending machine in one corner. I know that if only I can get a cherry pie out of it and feed it to her she won't be able to die again because she will have eaten. But in the same way that I know this, I already know that I don't have enough money to buy one, and as I am pulling out handfuls of pennies and lint and gritty lipsticks, looking for some kind of forgotten quarter, even though there are no forgotten quarters—I've been through my purse before and there aren't any—Roberta dies again. Because there is nothing else to do I go into the next room, where they are showing a pornographic movie, and the audience is waist deep in a shallow Jacuzzi watching in the dark. I don't want to watch, but I can't go back to the other room, and after a while it becomes clear that it is a snuff film: the music gets thicker, it has that feeling about it, you can tell from how you feel and from how your feeling matches the music that they are going to rape and murder someone when the ending finally comes. And because it is a dream we are not just watching the film, we are the film, so that someone has to be me. Who else could it be? They are already closing in when I awaken.

I just wish I had had a quarter, I say to myself, awakening.

But that's ridiculous, I protest, seeing the improvement in daylight. I do have a quarter, I have lots of quarters. My purse is full of quarters. They must not have been the right kind; they must not have been symbolic quarters.

Symbolic? Symbolic of what? I just wish, I say, revising my wish, I just wish I knew precisely what was being paid for, and what kind of coin was required.

CHAPTER 2
Adam

Well Mel—

  I think it would be very nice to begin this letter saying my classes
are going great guns, I'm busy as a bee, this is really turning out to
be the most productive period of my life, I'm swimming eight miles a
day, and Mr. Right is asleep in my loft. HA!
  (Ha.)
  In fact, as usual I cannot seem to generate a large amount of interest in all those little details like classes and papers that I'm supposed
to be busily generating interest in. NOT ORGANIZED. Where is the
balance?
  I look around and wonder if everybody's in on some secret no one is
telling me. I try. I do try. I actually start work. I fall asleep. Sleep as
a way to check out of reality is the worst. I just wish I could be a little
more inspired.
  In truth, things are not well with me. My classes are really taxing
and unexceptional and the burden is too heavy (for one such as me). If
anyone told me they were leading their life this way I would tell them
they were sick. I met my roommate and she is a zero.
  Melanie at moments like these I begin to think there is nothing for
me but my hopeless stream of words. I know it isn't true but you forget
when you talk too much and not enough happens. I have hundreds of

Chinese characters to memorize and I can hardly string together an
English sentence.

    Too many linguistics classes! Not enough Dante!

    I guess I won't be going to law or computer or medicine school—or,
in fact, any more school at all. So young to have closed so many doors.
Did I tell you how bad my grades are? There is a special room in the
inferno for people who get grades as bad as mine.

Love,
Your Friend Roberta

P.S. I reread your letters and they made me feel better. Send me some
more to read and reread.

Adam arrives the next day out of nowhere. I am staring at the
photographs one more time in the midst of the late-afternoon gray,
which is exactly the same as the late-afternoon gray of the day
before, and realizing that everything was still there—just as it
always was. The photographs are exactly the same: the same
number, the same expressions, the same pages, *the same.* Everything I knew about her, I still know; everything I felt, I still feel.

    (The same? The same as what? What did I know; what do I
feel?)

    And all of a sudden there is Adam, green eyed and earnest, big
and nice, out of nowhere, as he always appears to come out of
nowhere, and although he is, factually speaking, not a new thing
in my life, I never get accustomed to him. I am surprised with the
same surprise I felt when he remembered my name when I was
fifteen, and when I saw him a year and a summer later and he still
remembered, and I am amazed and guilty. He is also from Lexington, but he is four years older, and so he graduated from high
school the year I entered it. I met him once, when I was a
sophomore in high school and he was a sophomore at Harvard,
and then I bumped into him a year later the summer I turned
seventeen and *he remembered my name.* And it turned out that he
and his family went to the same church I had just begun to go to.
That was the summer I had read the Gospels for the first time and
decided I wanted to be religious, except I had no notion of how to
begin. There was no religion anywhere in our household: my
mother was Jewish, and my father was nothing. I remember telling
my mother once, puzzled, that she wasn't really Jewish either, and

she said of course she was, and I said she didn't believe in God, did she, but I was pretty certain that she didn't, and she said that had nothing to do with it. And then she named lots of other of their very Jewish friends, the so-and-sos, for example, she said, were certainly Jewish—they were active Zionists—they wrote about Jewish history and Jewish politics and went to fundraisers and were devastated when their children dated non-Jews, there was no one more Jewish than the so-and-sos, and they didn't believe in God. I asked her if she had ever asked them specifically, and she put her hands on her hips and said, "Funny girl," and I thought to myself: I would like to be a Christian. I didn't know any Christians who believed in Christianity though—because, says my father, when intellectual people grow up they become atheists, because religion, he likes to add, is the opiate of the masses, unless you are Jewish, and then it's culture. It was queer, there was no reason I could think for it, and I know it didn't used to be so because Donne and Herbert and all the best poets and people used to be Ministers and Men of God, but there seemed to be some peculiar condition of the twentieth century whereby it had now been arranged that all the intelligent and admirable people were Jewish or atheists or both, which meant that everyone was really nothing, but some people didn't eat milk and meat at the same time. Absurd, of course, in six different ways, but that was as it seemed to me then. So I started going to church, and my parents kept referring to it as a *phase*, a religious phase (as in: the so-and-sos' daughter went through that cheerleading phase when she was in high school, and they were nearly in despair, and then she outgrew it and went to medical school and married someone Jewish). The whole idea was just on the point of dissolving, like some stray New Year's resolution (no one, says my mother, makes more New Year's resolutions than Melanie or forgets them quicker), when I met Adam and his family. I had never met a family before who were religious: who had faith.

And then I finished high school, and graduated the same day Adam graduated from Harvard, so that I had to miss most of his graduation, although his mother showed me the pictures, and Adam said it was a good thing too because he was getting tired of explaining to his friends why he was going out with a high school girl. He moved to New York that year, though, to write for *The New Yorker*, and I was certain he would forget about me then, but he didn't. Of all the lucky things that could happen to me, it seemed he was the luckiest, and it still does, but not for him. "I'm not sure," I say. "I don't think you should come up—it's not a good time. I—I don't know."

"I'll be there on the five o'clock train," he says. And suddenly, magically, just as the things he says always materialize and are true, he is here, holding me.

■ ■

The night he arrives we go for a drive and pull over onto a dark side street. This is the perfect moment to cry, I think, while I am all nicely held—I ought to cry more at times like this, instead of when I am alone in the attic and it truly is desolate—but I don't. It seems to me that if I take even fifteen minutes out from thinking about Roberta the situation could change. She might disintegrate in tears, and what would I be crying about, exactly, anyway? I don't know. I don't know what has happened; I need to think about it and whether tears would suffice. So I only tell Adam I am hungry and we pull out of the moment, its darkness unanswered, and drive away in search of hamburgers.

■ ■

He tells me, in the restaurant, that he is going to California and he wants to take me with him. He is like that: someone disappears—a friend or a friend of a friend or someone he read about in the papers—it doesn't make a difference: when someone gets lost he goes to look for them. With me, however, I have to think about it.

"It's so dramatic," I say, worried. "People will think I'm too dramatic. They'll want to know what I'm doing there, how I can be any help. I can't, obviously I can't, but there I'll be, always needing to be in on things, trying to cash in on emotions while other people have serious things to do, like putting up posters. And won't it be typical, won't it be Melanie, won't everyone—*hate me?*" I ask, suddenly passionate. But because Adam is never hateful he never has to worry about considerations of this sort. Emotion and action are not misallied; his gestures are complete and adequate, and the relationship between what he feels and what he does is so natural he does not even stop to consider how it could be otherwise. So before I have even begun to explain, he puts his fingers over my

mouth and cheeks, as if blotting tears, and says: "No, angel, not at
all. Get some clothes together."

■ ■

I call my friend Judy that night to tell her I am going to California.
"Why?" she asks.

"So I can help in the search!" I say, trying to give an Adam
answer.

"What help can you be?" she asks, not unkindly. Judy is an
engineer. She markets medical technology.

"Well," I say, "well." I flounder and finally come up with: "I
want to see her room, and look at her books and—water her
plants. Her plants might be dying!"

Judy wishes me a safe trip.

■ ■

I pack woolen skirts and blouses and scarves and stockings and
underwear and shoes and boots and jewelry—a pearl necklace
and a black cotton jumpsuit and a flannel nightgown and a silk
one too and a slip with a ruffle and a gray woolen bathrobe with
red braid which is also very nice. I take out the iron I have not
used since I bought it three years ago and all of a sudden I am
pressing I am mending I am hemming I am excited. I am not going
to fall apart, I am not going to leave ugly and unpacked, I am not
going to put on a black sweater and never take it off again. Adam
has come, we are going to California, we are going to California!

■ ■

I wear my pink smock dress to the airport the next morning. It
is pale pink, and it goes over a crimson and white striped leotard
and it has big pink pockets. Adam tells me I look like an illustration in a very happy children's story. I must remember that, I think
to myself, and write it down in my diary, and hope that if my life is
a story that line will be read as a definitive comment. Girls in
children's stories do not have their best friends murdered, I remind
whoever might be writing the story—not in *modern* children's
stories, I add, thinking of certain fairy tales—because in happy
modern children's stories it would be a terrible violation of genre,

and genre, as everyone who knows anything about stories knows—
genre, I pronounce suddenly, why *genre is everything*. I just hope it
is clear from the outset that I am in the same genre as Adam. I
reach for his hand and hold it tightly.

■ ■

But suddenly, suddenly I am sick. I am nauseous, drowning, I
have never been so sick before. I lie down on the lobby seats in the
airport and Adam pats my hair awkwardly and looks worried and
tells me I am a good girl. And then they announce that it is
boarding time, and I get up, reluctantly, hostile, and wobble
toward the plane, and Adam orders me to smile. I stop and wonder
for a moment if, after all, we are in quite the same genre. He
senses my silence and tells me that he was just worried they won't
let me on the plane—you look so ill sweetheart, he says, tugging at
my hair, but I know that is not why he said it. He believes that one
should be brave in the face of crisis, cheerful even, and I guess I
believe this too, but it sometimes seems to me that it is not being
true to one's feelings—it is *keeping up a pretense*, and a difficult
pretense at that. Not only does one then have the misery of being
miserable, one also has the misery of having to pretend not to be
miserable, which is, in a sense, twice as much misery. For Adam
the two miseries cancel each other out, but for me, I think, they
accrue. I could be wrong, but they feel accrued. But since my and
Roberta's ideas about such things have not brought much happiness
so far, have led only to this moment here, and since of all the things
I have ever wanted I think that most in this life I would want Adam
to think well of me, I try to smile, and in the immense effort that
smile requires, the plane pulls into the gate and we are in California.

■ ■

**Roberta and I are sitting on my bed eating yogurt after
school trying to figure out what we could possibly do when
we are Grownup. Roberta eats plain yogurt and sliced ba-
nana with a spoon. We've had this discussion before: we
have it, in fact, almost every time we get together. It always
lasts from the middle of the afternoon until dinnertime,
when the light darkens and we've come up with college
and there is nothing more to come up with.**

Bibi,
Autumn 1984
Berkeley

"Oh well," I say, finishing the discussion by echoing my mother, "never mind, then, you're still young!"

"Yeah," says Roberta contemptuously. "Young and hopeful." And then: "Young and hopeful—isn't that just the worst phrase! Doesn't that just make you so—angry? Who the fuck is it who fucking invents phrases like that?"

"Young and hopeful," I echo again, and then, wondering, almost curious, "there is nothing particularly hopeful about being young, is there?"

"No," says Roberta, stirring her yogurt thoughtfully, "nothing particularly."

PART 3

The Second Interpretation: The Man with the Van

■ ■

Oh, must we dream our dreams
and have them, too? . . .
Is it lack of imagination that makes us come
to imagined places, not just stay at home?

—Elizabeth Bishop
"Questions of Travel"

CHAPTER 1

Absolute Elsewhere

*I'm—oh God I don't know. I don't know what it is. I just have
this certain small feeling—this feeling like—well—like* I'M IN A BOX
WITH NO HOLES. *Now that's a cliché, Roberta, besides which it's demeaning to speak of oneself as if one were a laboratory rat.* BUT THE
WALLS ARE CLOSING IN. *Shit. I'm—I can't think of the right word for
a change—"going out"? (bad); "dating"? (worse, sounds like the 50's).
Anyway, I'm (grit my teeth) "going" (going where?) with a guy who
lives in the co-op. We do a good job of misunderstanding one another.
I think it's my fault. But he comes across as an open book and then you
find out all the pages are blank. He frightens me—what if I like him
more than he likes me? God that's so jejune. . . .*

"So tell me everything!"

"What do you want to know?"

"What's he like? What does he look like, what does he
dress like, what do you do together, what do you like
about him? C'mon."

"I don't know—I don't know what he's like."

"What do you mean—you're going out with him, Roberta."

"I don't, I don't. He's not like that, he's—I don't know.
He's like a lake. You assume it has great depths, pure
undisturbed undiscoverable depths. You assume depths must
be there because the surface is so flat—pretty and flat and

utterly unrevealing. Boring almost, you might say. If you didn't know about the depths, that is, if you didn't believe they were there. And there are depths, aren't there? I mean there have to be depths because people are deep.

"Everybody is deep, aren't they?" she demands suddenly, philosophically, interrupting herself.

"I guess," I say, unimpressed. "But really I don't see what good depths do you if you don't have access to them. Brad could be the most fascinating person in the world, but if you don't know what he's really like, and he doesn't share himself with you, who cares what's 'really' down there—if there is anything really down there, if 'really' really means anything in such a case."

"Ah, well," she says, smiling, it seems to me, over the telephone, her deep mysterious smile, "I like mystery. And you can't have mystery without depths, can you? Or depths without mystery? Think of a poem. How interesting would a poem be if there were no hidden levels of meaning?"

"I guess," I say again, puzzled, because this is true, or at least it is true of poems, and I like poems, and poemy people and thinking of things in terms of poems, but I wonder suddenly—disloyally almost—if this is always necessarily the very best way to think.

■ ■

The night air opens up fragrant and beautiful and there are palm trees in the concrete jungle gym of the airport. So we are, after all, someplace different, I realize, and turn to Adam, suddenly smiling. Things happen, one goes places, arrivals occur. I stand by the suitcases, thinking about this, happy, while Adam makes some phone calls, and Brad pulls up in what I remember as a neat little red sports car, but people have subsequently assured me was an old pale blue station wagon. He gets out of his car jauntily, and I peer up into his face and see that he is handsome. He has straight dark blond hair that falls over his eyes, and high sculpted cheekbones, and he is tall and wide at the shoulders and narrow at the hips and long and easy of stride. His eyes were brown—or maybe blue. He seemed like the kind of person who would have had blue eyes; I am certain of that. I look again, waiting for the emotional reading, the deeper vision, and see—the same thing. I am annoyed

and intrigued. This is our first meeting; a significant moment, it
seems to me. Here standing before me is the unknown character
whose face is supposed to make all things clear, and all I can see is
that he is handsome. What about depth? What about revelation?
What about the lake?

Disappointed, I take a step back and remember that Roberta,
too, must have felt the same disappointment—looking at Brad,
thinking about Brad, telling me he was like a lake just to make
something up—to lend a little metaphorical meaning or invent a
way of interpreting someone who would not interpret himself
because we both liked and needed and believed in interpretation so
much. It's not that I don't remember exactly how I met him; I do
remember. I even remember wishing at the time I would have
more to remember. And standing as she must have stood, puzzled
and piqued and infinitely interested, I remember reaching for her
gesture, and, feeling happier than I had in a long time—imagining
suddenly I was doing the right thing, the Roberta thing—I remember kissing Bradley hello.

■ ■

Dear Melanie,

*O.K.—Where the hell is he? We did have plans; now is the lout
here? No. Is he even remotely here? NOOO.*

*Did he forget or is he just trying to torture me? Crumbs. And now
it is midnight or a little past and too late to do anything else.*

When will the girl learn?

Especially, when will she learn not to give a shit.

*Oh rot. Fear of rejection, abandonment, unworthiness. Precisely the
diagnosis I myself would have made. Poor child, I wonder if she will
get well.*

> *A Lonely Letter From,*
> *B.B.*

I am alone in the back seat of the strange disorienting darkness of
the car. Adam begins to speak to Brad about something; Adam is
good at male talk. I can recognize the shape of it without ever
being able to quite follow the content, although male talk is funny
that way, in having so much content. Politics, events, things, hap-
penings, the game, the game, who's who in the game, Magic

Johnson, although they just call him Magic, more things—male talk has so many Things in it, it is hard to see what they are talking about. I listen for a moment, and then lean into the back seat, safe in my exclusion, and close my eyes. It is so anonymous, the movement of this dark space along an empty highway, this nowhere-in-particular space, less located than sleep because less personal and dream-crowded, that I feel almost safe. It is so rare to feel safe. You have to catch it between times—after you've left home, before you have arrived at the next place, that temporary safety of being lost in the smooth darkness of the passing highway.

■ ■

Roberta puts her face down on the desk, her black hair spread over her back like a shroud. "Roberta," I say, "Roberta!"

There is no reply.

"Roberta, are you okay? Was—umm—class okay?

"Do you want anything? Can I do anything for you? Do you want to go someplace? Do you want to go home?"

"Away," she says, "I would like to go away."

"What do you mean away? Like vacation away? Paris, Greece, Rome, Zermatt, London away?"

"No. Not that kind of away—no place in particular. I want to go elsewhere—Absolute Elsewhere."

"Absolute Elsewhere," I say, "hmm." And then: "I like that—Absolute Elsewhere. I have to remember that, and write it down. A.E. Elsewhere, Absolutely."

■ ■

Roberta is receiving some kind of advice from an Advisor, and I am waiting for her so we can walk home together. There is an empty chair in front of her, but she isn't sitting in it, she is standing straight and awkward, and the Advisory Person is harassing her about some pre-pre-college forms.

"You know," she says, her red-lipsticked mouth moving quickly, "if you hadn't dropped track you could get an excellent recommendation from the track coach. She thought very highly of you—and you could have waited to drop it until after applications were in. Well, never mind. You'll just have to play up the China card. And the violin. Kerry Williams—"

"It's a viola," Roberta interrupts, hostile, with the beginnings of tears. "I play the viola." She was able to do both things at once: to speak fierce and frightening, and cry soft and dark. The Advisor only noticed the first, and went on speaking, annoyed. I saw Roberta was looking down at the desk, and on sudden thought I traced "A.E." on the desktop with my fingertips.

She understands, and looks up at me pleased—pleased at the idea, pleased that I remembered, pleased the Advisor would not know what she was pleased about. Mainly the last, I think—a favorite pleasure, the pleasure of secret pleasures.

■ ■

Absolute Elsewhere, I think, A.E. Is there something menacing about the concept's seductiveness? Where is Roberta now? Where is Roberta now? I sit up quickly and the men give me their attention. Tell me what happened, I demand, and Brad begins his version.

"We were supposed to meet at eight a.m. Robin and I went down to the courtyard, to wait for her. She went up to my room and, not finding us there, assumed we had left without her and wrote Robin a note ('I guess you guys left . . .'). When she bumped into me downstairs she said accusingly, 'Well, you *might* have waited.' And we tried to tell her, look, we did wait, we are waiting—what we're doing is waiting—but it was too late. She wouldn't listen."

I knew exactly how it would have happened. She would conclude she was neglected, unloved, and abandoned at the slightest pretext—*you did something without me?*—and by the time evidence to the contrary came, the feeling had settled in and it was too late.

"The ride to Roberts Park took about twenty minutes. Roberta did not say a word the entire time. We were both uncomfortable."

There was no one who could be as convincingly unhappy as Roberta. When other people are unhappy for no reason they look silly, and you ask them why and if they don't come up with an explanation you laugh at them. But when Roberta was unhappy, she was so very unhappy that it did not even occur to you to look for a reason. It was curious, how quickly you got used to it. It just seemed to be part of her, like having black eyes and hair and being Chinese. There may have been family problems, of course, as there usually are. I don't know what they were, but the important thing is I don't think Roberta knew either. I remember asking her once about her parents' childhoods, and she said she didn't know—they hardly spoke of them. "But don't you ask—don't you want to know?" I persisted, and she shrugged. "You don't understand," she said, frustrated, "it's not like that in our family. You can't just ask things you want to know and find out. You don't understand; they're *Chinese*."

"My parents are fighting," I remember her saying another day, with one of her memorable looks.

"Oh well," I said. "My parents fight too, sometimes."

"But I feel frightened. I feel like the family is falling apart."

"Well, what are they fighting about?" I asked. I was so little help to Roberta.

"I don't know," she said, "they fight in Chinese. They talk to me in English, and to each other in Chinese. They ask me if I've finished my homework, and I say no in English, and they say we see to each other in Chinese. Chinese is such a tangled way to speak—syllables all stuck together, dead ends and twisted syntax. It's such a perplexing language," she says.

"Chinese," she finishes bitterly, "is deliberately labyrinthical."

"But Roberta, how can you not understand a language you've grown up hearing all your life? I mean Chinese isn't perplexing for the Chinese, is it?"

"That about sums it up, doesn't it?" she said sarcastically, and I suddenly caught what she meant. And that, in fact, did sum it up: there was this constant sourceless unhappiness, which surfaced at the merest of incidents, and which there was no way to trace. I imagined Brad feeling the same impotence, wondering what little thing he had done to start it, begging Roberta to tell him what it was. And Roberta shaking her head silently, not just refusing to talk but really silent—silent because she had nothing to say. I had thought about it for years, I had talked about and around it with Roberta the whole time we were together, and yet we never came up with any particular explanation. It was like sawdust, the un-happiness: it infiltrated everything, everything was a problem, everything made her cry—school, homework, boyfriends, the future, the lack of future, the uncertainty of future, fear of the future, fear in general—but it was so hard to say exactly what the problem was in the first place. Was she orphaned? Friendless? Untalented, unintelligent, unpretty, unathletic, abused? Did her parents, in truth, not adore her, and were they unwilling, really, to do anything in the world for her?

All right then, what exactly was the problem?

"What exactly is the problem?" I remember demanding of her one day. "I mean the *underlying* problem."

"You sound just like an Advisory Person," she retorted, and began to cry.

"I'm sorry," I said, feeling sorry. "I just kind of . . . *wondered.*"

"Well, I wonder too," she said, looking right at me, her eyes wide open. I felt sorry for Brad, driving that Sunday morning to the park and wondering, as he glanced uneasily at the girl beside him—Roberta, silent and unhappy by his side.

■ ■

"We began to run at a slow pace," Brad continues, "but Roberta fell behind, and then veered off onto another trail. We waited at the end of the trail, and then ran back to the parking lot. She wasn't there either. Robin stayed there while I drove my car along the road, looking for her. I didn't follow her earlier because I didn't know if she wanted to be followed."

I thought I knew, as others might not, that this was accurate. It was hard to tell with Roberta: I had followed her out of parties, left classes, called her back when she hung up on me, went over to her house when she wouldn't answer, and I was never sure if any of these things were the right things to do. Maybe she left because she wanted to be followed; maybe she wanted to be alone. Maybe it was a cry for help; maybe not. Maybe only she could solve her problems. She had, after all, had a lot of help: endless psychiatrists and friends and teachers and guidance counselors. Maybe she needed more concern, or less—or something, perhaps, entirely different.

"When she wasn't there, I gave up and went home," Brad continues.

"How long did you look?" I ask, knowing that was the question everybody would ask.

"Twenty minutes," he replies coolly. The accusation—the collective accusation—rises easily to mind. *Twenty minutes is not very long.* And it isn't, either, if you really thought you should wait.

"I wanted to get back to campus because I had like ten friends waiting to use my car to go to the Exploratorium. And then I got kind of caught up . . ."

I understood so well what he was saying. Not only was it unclear whether or not she really wanted to be found, but it was tiringly unclear. I could feel his urge to put his foot on the gas and pretend that Roberta might magically reappear at campus—to pretend, that is, that it would still be possible to meet his friends at the Exploratorium and call it a good day.

"A woman called into the hotline," Brad says, "who claims that she saw a girl who matches Roberta's description being forced into a van. And the dogs show that her scent stops at a point in the road where she must have gotten into a car."

I catch my breath. I try to reach for Adam's hand, but it is too far away. I lean forward to see Brad's face, but he is looking ahead. I try to look at him again, but I still can't see him. And I think to myself: You haven't seen his face once during the trip. The version you are coining is your own. How Brad feels, you have no idea.

"We're trying to shield this from Robin because this is kind of—her first real-life experience," Brad says, "but seven women have disappeared in California in the past year who were all murdered in similar ways. Apparently there is a group of men who hide out in the mountains and keep them alive for varying amounts of time, torturing them sexually and psychologically."

I wrap my arms around my body, trying to curl into a ball. It is so hard to think about the facts. Men are torturing her sexually and psychologically. *Men are torturing her psychologically and sexually.*

The sexual aspect seemed almost silly. It had that absurd pornographic-movie unreality—too really scary to be scary. But her mind. Dear God, what were they doing to Roberta's mind? They were fucking with her mind. Christ, it had been so fucked with already. Think of the kind of people who would be putting their fingerprints on Roberta's mind, the kinds of things she would be thinking now. Think of her black countenance growing blacker: thinking life had proven her right after all. I would never convince her otherwise now. I would never get their traces to come off clean. They would be smeared all over the inside of her mind. That horrible sticky stuff: the stickiness of adulthood. Jesus—I would rather she were safe in the ground.

Dear Melanie

> *Forgive me for unloading all my miseries on you.*
> *I wish I could get free.*
> *I wish*
> *I want*
> *I hope*
> *to doeth better!*

Roberta

"So teach us to number our days that we may get a heart of wisdom."
—*Psalms 90:12*

Also: "A merry heart doeth good like a medicine."

She must be wondering as she pushes her way through matted branches just where it is she is going. Behind her is the road where Brad in his blue car and Robin by his side are waiting. He would take her back to campus if she turned around. She is not really that angry with him, she admits to herself suddenly, she simply does not wish to turn around. It is a simple thing, really, this sudden distaste for her room and all that it holds. She thinks of her notebook, lying exposed, her diary available for anyone to read. Shouldn't she be getting back before someone reads her diary? Doesn't she have to write about this morning's trip? Pinpoint the memorable moments? No, she thinks, it's more than distaste she feels—it's nausea. Somewhere in front of her must be the highway, busy with cars going places. Perhaps one would take her where she wants to go. Where does she want to go? Mexico? She had always liked the idea of Mexico, painted small and bright, flowers on pottery, things old and triangular. Children selling tacos for pennies, spicy with heat. She did like the idea, she reminds herself, until she went there over spring break with Ben. Now when she thinks about Mexico, all she thinks about is Ben, getting on the bus with Ben, and coming home without him. No, that is not true, she remembers some other

things, like the watermelon ices. But when she thinks of
the ices, she thinks of Ben too, what happened between
them, and what didn't happen.

All right, then, she would have to go someplace else.
Like Guatemala. She had heard there was a jungle where it
rained every single day. Rain splashing through the thick
canopy of jungle leaves so that it was only mist by the time
it fell through to the snake-black earth. And the snakes
were also green, of course, large and green and spotted so
that they were hard to tell from the leaves, until they bit.
Then you would know what a wonderful weight they had,
how smooth and cold and coiling, almost like singing. Or
like rain. And the fact too, that for the first time in your
life you were in a place where it was never ever dry. Dry,
she thinks, as she has spent most of her life, with a hor-
ble unending dryness like cheap chalk on your hands, but
on the inside too.

But what would she do in Guatemala? Would she bring
that notebook on her desk in order to write? What would
she write? She would write about her feelings, her thoughts,
being alone. She would write about herself; as always. Oh
God, is there anything else to write about? What do people
do who do things besides write? Writing was no good; that
was precisely why she was going away. It was not herself
that would be good; it was the jungle. Could she just write
about the jungle? Could she be in the jungle without it
being herself who was being there? No, even syntactically,
the idea doesn't make sense: she and herself are the same
thing. And knowing that, it was already spoiled. That omnipresent layer of consciousness, gray as chalk and not at
all like rain, which seeped into everything wherever she
went and made it all just like her, would sift over the
entire jungle like spoiled flour. She would be lonely, she
would be unhappy, she would be self-absorbed. She would
feel homeless and write too many letters home, describing
alienation and homesickness. She would meet someone,
they would have a relationship, and it would be exactly
like all the other relationships—problematic. He would
be Ben or Courtney or Brad or someone like them, and
she would be herself. No, no, it had to be something
else, far, so far it was not even a place. Elsewhere, she

wanted to go Elsewhere, Absolute Elsewhere. Yes, she says aloud, pleased, remembering, an absolute kind of elsewhere, as she stops, confused, hesitant, imprisoned suddenly in quivering branches, wondering which direction it lies in, perhaps, as I wonder too, looking up, which way she went, and how to follow.

Bibi,
Autumn 1984
Berkeley

By LEIGH ANNE JONES

It seems like everyone I talk to knows Bibi, or knows someone who knows Bibi. And they're all worried.

I knew Bibi way back when, but time split us apart. I always had things to do, and so did she, until it got to the point where when we talked, we weren't sure what to say. We were both busy, intensely involved in the pressures of day-to-day life, and there didn't seem to be much point in trying to fill each other in as time went by. Two weeks ago, I really felt like calling her. But I didn't.

We used to sit in the back of our western civilization section and laugh at all the pseudo-intellectuals kissing up to the TA, asking questions which gave away the fact that they already knew the answers and were just trying to make themselves look good. The way I figured it, I could laugh because it was funny, but Bibi could laugh because she was a *real* intellectual.

We would argue over who had more cause to be awed and intimidated by the other. I still maintain that I have more reason to respect her ≠ she is brilliant in my eyes. But I don't know her now. I wish I did.

If you haven't yet had the chance to be completely unnerved by the story, here it is:

Roberta "Bibi" Lee was jogging down a trail in Redwood Regional Park with her boyfriend, Brad Page, and another friend, Robin Shaw. Something was said, and Bibi just shot off down the path.

They ran after her, called her name. Checked back at the car, the pool area. Nothing.

That was Sunday morning. Nobody has seen her since.

A Chronicle story quoted Berkeley P.D. Detective Michael Holland: "We have serious concern about this because it is not her pattern of doing things. In fact, her friends say for her to disappear for several days is totally out of character."

So what happened? It's easy to imagine the worst. But Bibi is wary, athletic, savvy. She is a complex person with dark moods. She has a calm, serious face which hides the pressure, the expectations never spoken, always felt. Mutual friends tell me she'd been having problems: school, life, the usual. And when I knew her Bibi tended to internalize her problems. Her roommate, Meg Luther, said Bibi was in a bad mood that day. It wasn't uncommon for her to leave for a couple hours if she wanted to be alone.

A few weeks ago, Bibi called a friend about the work she had missed in a class. The friend said she seemed distracted. She said Bibi asked her how she had been, and she had launched into a long, detailed monologue. Then she asked Bibi the same question. There was a long pause, but she knew Bibi had heard the question. Finally, Bibi laughed a harsh laugh and said something about school. The friend told Bibi to consider withdrawing from classes and taking a break. Bibi listened for a while and then, abruptly, said she had to go and hung up.

The Chronicle story also reported that a woman fitting Bibi's description was seen with a man in a bank in Montclair; another report mentions a church.

We've all thought about what it would be like to just take off. Leave the pressure. Just to see what would happen.

CHAPTER 2

The Story of Suffering

. . . Oh, Melanie, I have been so unhappy of late, for no good reason, and guilty. I lie, I lie, I lie. I have been suffering from my own delusions and illusions, and need to be slapped in the face and told to shut up. But then, I always do put myself down and present my inner world in fluorescent lights. I've been crying a lot, again. I'm so blind, so self-centered; you should take me to task for being so shell-bound. But there I go again, making demands. Still, why aren't you here?

If I had to do it over again,

I wouldn't. (John Berryman, Dream Songs)

> *Neither would I.*
> *B.B.*

Come back, I say to the Man with the Van, and then, afraid I've intimidated him, I say in a smaller voice: please come back. You see, I explain patiently but instinctively, you don't understand what you're doing—what you're taking—I mean whom you're taking. That young woman, that bare-shouldered, bare-legged waif girl, standing by the side of the road with her thumb stuck out, barely having had time to do anything and never having had time to be happy—

that girl is an inconceivably weighty and significant person. You cannot conceive of the things she is bringing with her, the attachments she is bound by, the place she has in other people's imagination. I don't think you thought about that: I mean I'm sure you did think, but I don't think you thought enough or in the right way because you couldn't know the things I am about to tell you. Let me explain.

I understand, I add reassuringly, I can imagine exactly how it happened. You were driving along, thinking how little life has given you, and how little even of that you have been able to keep, and never a woman, when all of a sudden there was this girl, just standing by the side of the road. And so you pulled over, hesitantly at first, and you couldn't believe it—she just got in. Just like that—like she was free. So you figured you could take her and not give her back, and no one would notice. It was as if she were life's gift to you—a real girl, a pretty girl—to make up for all it had not given you in the past.

And I'm sorry life hasn't given you much—I really am— I say again, but you were wrong about that, about her being free. She only looked bare-shouldered and empty-handed, but really, I explain passionately, really it isn't so. She isn't free; she is attached. Your action will mean things you can't imagine—queer things, funny things, serious things, horrible things. You thought no one would notice because the road was so empty that day, and no one saw when you stopped your van, but it has been seen now. It has been seen and reseen; it will be imagined and reimagined for-ever. For you it was something you did just once, but for us it will be paradigmatic. We will think of our whole lives differently: we will think of ourselves differently. You don't know this, but it's true. If you had thought of all this, you would have kept driving.

I feel I am not being concrete enough. Maybe the Man with the Van has a very concrete mind. I try to explain a little more specifically. For some reason, it is difficult for me to be specific about anything that matters to me.

First of all, I begin, thinking hard, there is the meaning to Brad. Think of what this is going to do to Brad, having left her there in the woods and all. And of course he should feel guilty for that, but not as guilty as he's going to feel if you don't bring her back. And too there is the meaning to her friends, to Meg and Naomi and Scott and me. Me— obviously you haven't thought about me. You don't know how a long time from now I will meet a man and because I won't know him he will be a stranger, and because you are a stranger I will imagine he could be you and be frightened. You don't know what it will be like for me to have a life in which I am always frightened, and can't be talked out of the fear because I have a story to confirm it, and the story will be you and what you did. And her family. I think you have forgotten about the family. You can't have thought about them—I can't imagine all the things it will mean to them, and I know them. There is very much you will have to answer for to the family. There are the household deities, I say, and then, remembering he doesn't know about the deities, I change it to ancestors, lots and lots of ancestors, and the long inherited story of suffering. You can't envision what your role will be—what a frightening story it is—you might not want to be in such a frightening story. I would not want you to have us always think of you as the frightening person in a frightening story.

I look up, frightened.

No reaction from the Man with the Van. Funny, I am so right, I think to myself; I wonder how it could be he is not convinced. How . . . surprising. Surprising, I think again with surprising innocence, like a child's surprise: the Man with the Van can't hear what you have to say and wouldn't be interested in your opinions if he could. But it's a childish surprise too, and surprising that I haven't outgrown this kind of thinking—these conversations with imaginary figures bearing real names, where the real and the imagined so clearly have nothing to do with one another and never will. Surprising that so many of my thoughts are so futile, and surprising—most surprising—that I know this and keep thinking them anyway.

KIDNAPPING

BIBI LEE WAS LAST SEEN BEING FORCED TOWARD A VAN
BY THE SUSPECT AROUND NOON ON SUNDAY NOV. 4 NEAR
THE MONTERY ENTRANCE TO HIGHWAY 13, SOUTH OF PARK
BLVD. IN THE MONTCLAIR SECTION OF OAKLAND.

ROBERTA THERESA LEE
Nickname "BiBi"
Asian female 21 years of age
Resident of Berkeley
Student of University of California
5 feet 6 inches, 115 pounds
Black shoulder length hair
Brown eyes, medium complexion

Black and white 1" vertical stripe
nylon jogging shorts, maroon or blue
long sleeve cotton T-shirt, gray jogging
shoes with light blue stripe.

HAVE YOU SEEN THIS MAN

SUSPECT: White male approximately 40 to 45 years old,
bloated facial appearance, beer belly,
6 feet to 6 feet 3 inches, 220 to 250 pounds
unkempt curly brown collar length hair,
full curly beard and mustache,
wearing a tan sleeveless T-shirt
and tan pants.

VEHICLE: 1978 to 1983 van,
Dodge, Ford or Chevy,
MEDIUM GOLDEN BROW
metallic color, sligh
raised in back, rear
double doors with
"smoked" windows.
driver's side has o
one window, no tri
did not appear to be
modified.

We pull up outside the apartment of someone called Ron, whom
Roberta and Veronica had known from China. Roberta and Veronica had spent a year at a boarding school in China, except that
halfway through the year Roberta had a bad fight with Veronica
and moved in with her boyfriend, an English actor named Chris,
and when Veronica informed their parents that Roberta was sleeping
with some strange guy, she was sent home, shamed. Roberta was mad
about it for years afterward. She was fourteen years old at the time.

We go into Ron's, where we are staying the night, Adam

dragging my purse and book bag and suitcase and second suitcase
for the damp clothing I hadn't had time to put in the dryer, and I
carrying his backpack with a change of underwear. Veronica is
sitting at the table, her face down on its wooden top and her
smooth black hair spread about her, falling away from the delicate
bones of her neck and shoulders. She could be Roberta, posed that
way. I take a step backward and stare at her. Ron is standing
behind her, awkwardly stroking her hair while she speaks in a low,
prophetic, and lyrical voice, somewhere between a murmur and a
moan. Her voice is wonderfully haunting, in the particular fashion
Roberta's was. I realize, suddenly, that this is as it is meant to be: it
is not just that they suffer, as many or even most people do suffer,
but that it is done in such a way as to make suffering beautiful,
significant, seductive, as a sad story is seductive because it has to
be, because stories are written to elicit response. You wouldn't read
them if they weren't. I listen with awe; she is so compelling. I look
at Adam to see if he is struck with the sight, but he is busy with the
suitcase. It's funny—Adam is so sensitive to suffering. He set up a
shelter in his church in New York City, he writes about poverty all
the time, and he never passes a homeless man on the street
without reaching in his pockets, and as he does you can see his
face tightening with anger at the world and with compassion for its
victims, yet he is not arrested by the sight of Veronica. But it's a
different kind of suffering, of course, this kind of suffering, from
the cold of a night when you're sleeping on the streets and no one,
no place, is thinking about you.

"*A thirteen-year-old,*" Veronica whispers. "A thirteen-year-old
Vietnamese girl from Philadelphia was abducted today. So young—
they take them so young . . ."

"Don't torture yourself," Ron says soothingly.

"The psychic told me he had to take someone with him into
the forest to find Bibi."

(*To go into the forest. To go into the forest where Bibi was lost.*)

"When he was leading me through the forest," she continues,
"I closed my eyes and could feel Bibi very near. She was hurt—
wounded—suffering. She was calling for help, and no one could hear
her. I felt Bibi's pain in my very own body. My legs became stiff
and leaden, and my feet ached, as if the arches had been carved too
deeply. There was a wound on the side of my head, and my eye was
bleeding. And I was calling, calling, and no one would come . . .

"I can't go through with it again—I can't—I can't," Veronica cries, much too quietly. Bibi too would surprise you with quietness just when you expected noise, the noisy theatrics of red-lipsticked American women whose makeup smears as they begin to cry.

"You won't do it again," Ron says. "I won't let you torture yourself."

Veronica makes a gesture with her hands, as if brushing his words away.

"It has to be someone very close to Bibi," she says intently, "someone who can sense her—who can feel the wounds in their very own body . . ."

"I will!" I cry suddenly.

"No!" Adam says instantly.

I look at him, surprised out of the spell of her words, but his face is resolute. I wonder why he doesn't want me to help. Adam believes in help more than anyone in the world. He will put up a hundred thousand posters in the next three days and probably reorganize the search center; why wouldn't he want me to give the one kind of help I can?

"No," he says again, as if I were a child who, overhearing her parents' financial troubles, bursts in to tell them she will support the family from then on.

"When will the trouble end?" Veronica cries. "The Lee cycle— it goes on and on—China—the sickness—the suffering—these things, all the things that have happened to our family—my mother, my father, my brother and sister, me, and now—now my little sister is *lost!* It can't go on any longer; when is something going to make it end? *When is something going to happen?*"

But, I almost say to her, but something *has* happened.

I look at Adam instead, confused, but he thinks I am asking about the psychic again, and silently voices no, again, but nicely. No, I say to myself. I, too, am good at this kind of drama. I could so easily step in, imagine the pain which is Roberta's, spend the rest of my life leading psychics to the place where it happened, and explaining to strangers what it is about, the nature of this suffering, the elusive nature. No, I say again, no. Roberta has gotten into the van. We're done with psychics now: we're finished with imagined suffering. They didn't help; they never helped before; they had a lot of years to help—they and the psychiatrists and all the other people with whom unhappiness was talked and thought about. If they were going to lead us to the place where the hurt happened, they would already have done so. You can't think your way out of

suffering you got yourself into by thinking too much about suffering. This is not part of the family story—it is a new suffering,
real as pictures of missing children. Roberta has stepped out of the
drama: she wanted it to end. Whatever she suffers now is different.
Something has happened, I think to myself, something has happened.

■ ■

**Roberta is drawing up lists of things she might want to be
when she grows up, if she grows up. She likes to add that
little qualification just so you know not to take it for granted.
It's curious: the list is so long and there are so many possibilities because we are such promising young girls—endless
possibilities, almost, you might imagine, but you would be
wrong. When you try to think of them specifically you see
then that all of them were only possible possibilities, but
none of them were actual possibilities. Actually, all possibilities disintegrate.**

"Maybe I will be a doll maker," she says wearily.

"Maybe," I say. I love dolls. "Maybe I will too."

**"How do people become doll makers? Are there doll
makers?" she asks.**

**"I don't know," I say, "I'm not sure how dolls get
made. Are there doll-making schools? Is there such a thing?"**

**"I could be a—a lawyer," she says defiantly. I don't say
anything. We both know whatever she is, she will never be
an attorney.**

**"What will become of me?" she cries. "You go through
the whole list, and you figure out one by one how none of
the things work. What happens when you get to the end?
What happens when all the possibilities run out?"**

**I get up and stand behind her chair and put my hands
on her shoulders. I half expect her to move away, to shake
them off. She doesn't, though; she sits there with her feet
beneath her in ballet shoes, small and curled, her eyes full
of tears. I start to say something to comfort her, and hesitate, wondering what the right phrase is, but for some
reason nothing, not even "things will be okay," comes to
mind. I remember this so clearly: standing there unable to
think of anything, although it is so obvious now—the phrase,
the missing phrase. Worry, stop worrying, you shouldn't**

worry so about plans and planning. It's pointless, really pointless—you alone and you especially need never worry. You're different from others, and lucky that way—you'll die young.

CHAPTER 3

Morning Unsung

The familiar combination of bloated and jumpy, with feelings of profound annoyance. How can I explain . . . hmmm, imagine being shut out of a carnival that everyone else was streaming into and out of. Bad (trite) metaphor, but that's how it's been with me—bad-metaphor-ish.

How she lives: Skipped folklore, went to modern dance. My days spent in ways that would drive my parents crazy. I fell asleep twice this morning in class and then dragged myself home just in time to miss another class and a section and fall asleep on the living room floor. Now I'm wondering if I can make it through lecture this afternoon. Can she? No, she can't. I'm still so weak I can barely carry my crumpled clothes from the chair to the closet, let alone do any real work. Lord knows I have more than my share of Real Work. Schubert coaxed the evening on. Tonight it was starless and damp. It takes so long to get from nowhere to nowhere.

B.B.

I am dreaming and in my dream I am running through the forest and it is Sunday morning, except that I am watching the dream too, as if it is a movie, or a book I am reading, and thinking about as I read. I am running on a Sunday morning, I decide afterward, excessively analytically as usual, because Sunday is when one goes to church, and church represents finding oneself, whereas running represents losing oneself in something big and beautiful, such as, for example, a forest. A lover is with me: he has brought me to the forest. I could not have gotten there without him, but as soon as we arrive it is necessary to lose him, for he is a hindrance to getting lost—really lost, beyond recovery. He doesn't want to be lost; he comes after me, trying to take me back, but I begin to run. I ran, she ran, she began to run so he wouldn't be able to find her. I have figured it out, I think to myself; I have figured it out.

Just at that moment, however, Adam begins to stir, and tosses off the covers. I recognize the familiar gesture: he always awakens like this, instantly happy, as if there were nothing he was dreaming about. He wakes up happy, I think jealously: he awakens without regret.

In *Island of the Blue Dolphins* the girl in the story, whose name is Karena, is left on an island alone. She wasn't always alone; at the beginning of the story she was with her whole tribe, but the tribe decided to leave the island and sail away on a big ship. Karena's little brother leaves his favorite spear behind, however, and goes back for it, and Karena goes back for her brother. Her brother is eaten by wild dogs a few days later and Karena is left alone on the island. In 1853, eighteen years later, some otter hunters from California chance to find her, and they take her back to the Santa Barbara Mission, but apparently the ship with her whole tribe on it had sunk. It is a true story. No one was ever found who spoke her language, and she never learned English. She died in a convent in northern California and is known as the Lost Woman of San Nicolas. No one knows what she did or thought all those years alone on the island because no one was ever able to talk to her; the author, Scott O'Dell, had to make it up. She died alone; she died without telling. I wake up lonely. I don't know how we got here last night; I can't remember whose apartment we are in.

"What's the matter?" Adam asks, pulling on his socks.

"Do I have to get up?" I ask, sniffling a little.

"No, hon, you stay and sleep."

I lie there watching while he dons a clean shirt. He is so lovely and male and efficient. He pulls on his blue jeans, all stiff and crinkly from having just been washed. My heart always breaks at the thought of him doing his own laundry in some late-night Laundromat, a long walk from his apartment, putting quarters in with his big clumsy fingers and studying the soapbox carefully because there is no one to tell him how much soap is the right amount of soap. He laces his hiking boots quickly. He wears hiking boots or sneakers all year round, even though he lives in New York City and works at a fancy job, he always goes out in the world clad thus, as if the city were just like the forest, or as if it doesn't matter because he is free wherever he goes. And he is right: it doesn't matter for him because he is as he is wherever he is. We are different this way. I want to ask him why this is, and how I can be like him—*I want to be exactly like you, why should I be any different from you?*—the old voice, the plaintive voice, but already he is bending down and kissing me good-bye and saying see you later and banging the door behind him. It bangs loudly.

I think about going back to sleep. The room is empty with sunlight. It worries me, its being so still: as if there might be nothing to wake up to, and I will know this, somehow, in my sleep and not bother trying.

I stand up and throw my nightgown off. The gesture requires all my energy, though, and I'm not sure what to do next. I put my hands on my stomach. It feels round. I try to remember that it is mine, this rounded shape, and therefore it must have something to do with what I feel and think and believe. It must; *it's your body.* It is so hard to think what that might be. Puzzled, I move away and wander around the room touching things: the rough linen of the red-stained curtains in whose texture you can feel the redness, cold as a crushed cranberry, and the twisted shape of the frosted pink vase on the dining room table. I pull a few petals off the flowers in order to be surprised by the ease of their give in my fingers. I like to touch things. I will wait a long time in a museum for the guard to leave so I can touch the sculpture; Adam caught me once and deeply disapproved. He is so careful never to say anything self-righteous—because, I suppose, he is right so much of the time—but I knew what he was thinking: *suppose Everyone touched the statues, Melanie. . . .* But for some reason, although Everyone arguments are absolutely decisive with him, they never seem to factor into my thinking at all. Or rather they do, but only after I have had what I wanted.

What do I want? What is it—what is it? It is so hard to know. I turn toward the window. Perhaps I can think about the sunlight coming through the pane, how wide the glass is, and warm the light on my skin. Other people talk about that a lot, sunlight on their skin. A little girl walks below, in black shiny shoes, trailing a red jump rope and an older boy. I like the fact that I am standing naked before an open window, and anyone could look up and see me, but no one will know I am there. It is more private than being behind closed doors. I know perfectly well that if I had any shame I would be at the search center long before Adam *(What are you doing? For God's sake whose friend was she anyway?)* but I cannot hurry, I will not hurry, the morning is exempt. It's funny how I spend my life looking for exempt moments and am permitted so few. Fewer even than Adam, who never looks for them, and never lingers in the morning. "What are you thinking?" I will demand anxiously of him sometimes. "Nothing," he will reply, and then, surprised at my suspiciousness, "really, Melanie, nothing at all." And finally: "I would tell you if I were thinking anything, sweetheart," and I will realize with infinite jealousy and longing that he is telling the truth: he really isn't thinking anything. He has been given the moment off. I wonder, for the thousandth time, why I am never given any moments off—time to rest, in which you don't have to wonder how the moment is meaningful. You might be able to figure it out if you thought hard enough, of course, and certainly you can always make something up, but it won't be the same as if you hadn't thought—if you had just felt it. Like if you just felt the sunlight instead of thinking: *ah hah*, sunlight on skin—meaning: *a sunlight-on-girl-in-morning-meaningful-poetry moment.* It might happen to truly be such a moment, of course, but the thought gets mixed up with the sunlight and spoils it, like a woman wearing too much makeup and hoping too hard you will think she is beautiful. Adam is beautiful; he doesn't have to hope. He's not handsome; he's beautiful and he wakes up early and happy and is the first one at the center putting up posters, while I wake up old and tired and cross and worried. He doesn't even realize what a gift this is because it is not a gift for him: all moments are moments off because he does not think of things this way, just as all time is meaningful time because he never asks about meaning.

I go into the kitchen to look for food. Should I skip it? Do I have time? No, I am not going to skip it no matter what time it is; I have been through these negotiations thousands of times and since I never do skip it, I'm not going to skip it now. Especially not now. For even if it were only a small thing like giving up breakfast, any slight twinge of hunger might remind me of deprivation—of starvation and emptiness—and it might occur to me that it is not really food that I am lacking, just as it is not only this morning I don't have it. I know it's going to occur to me one of these mornings. I'm going to wake up and realize: *I have nothing.* I know it already. *Nothing nothing.* It is true.

But since I know it—this premonition of some inner poverty I want so much not to have—I know too that I must keep doing things, little things, anything, to make sure this morning does not become that morning. So I go into the kitchen and search through the cupboards and find some tea in an old tea tin. I put water in the kettle and boil it and pour it into a teapot and wait for it to brew and become nice and brewed so I can add milk. It does not mean much, of course, but it might mean something, these little gestures of allusion, like allusions to books you once read a long time ago. I concentrate as hard as I can on thinking about how many people in fairy tales stumble upon a warm well-lighted house after they have been out in the cold nearly forever and are almost frozen, when they are just then invited in by someone kindly and given tea brewed with milk.

CHAPTER 4

The Grownups Organization

Dear Mellie,

The thing about depression is (someone said this, I read it some-where): if there was a pill which you were absolutely certain would cure it and it was sitting five feet away from you, you'd be too depressed to go and get it.

How do I feel today? Let me count the ways. (Oh no, shut that girl up!) I'm basically feeling kind of tense and anxious, but there is this mean streak of irritability and a mile-wide mood of to-hell-with-it. A little wilted too, like lettuce.

The saga of lost love (LOVE) continues. We went into San Francisco yesterday for some good clean platonic fun and I kept smiling, yep, here we are just friends isn't this great? Then I had a long chat with Babycakes (Bradley) under the starlight of the streetlight after he got out of work last night, and it was almost pleasant.

So what? So why am I so starry-eyed about the bloke? Ask me if I've never met a nice guy from Lafayette before? I mean really Roberta.

Actually, I've been meeting a lot of interesting people here of late. No one whom, unfortunately, I'll keep in touch with. But people are like that, you know—changeable. One, two, three, and then I was gone.

I got three letters today. One from you, one from my mother and one from the bank. You are so dear to have written to me; you know I save your letters and have them always—I shall give them back when we are old.

A psychic did a meditation reading of me and said that there was a tear in my heart. How do you like that? A tear. Those were his precise words too. I didn't even bother asking how it might be mended.

I dried a flower for you today. I picked it and put it in a book of Chinese prosody. Remind me to send the petals to you in a year, when they'll be dry.

LATER:

It is morning now. The time has arrived for morning to arrive. Why it's taking so long, I couldn't tell you, but it's no closer now than when I left. I've so many homeworks I don't try to keep count. They get handed to me in bundles by strangers in different lumps and colors and wrappings—bows and trimmings and papers with black and white spots on them. Frightening, how huge they are, especially the ones in the classes I'm not taking.

The letter, again.

I'm just not going to be able to finish. I have an exam on stuff I never read in languages I don't speak. A paper due 11 days ago and I haven't even begun it. I'm supposed to be in a hairshow, and I don't want people to look at me.

I—I—I

Oh it's impossible.

> *Rosamunde*
> *B.B.*
> *Mei-hua*

The walk across campus does not take long. The campus is sunny and grassy and looks like a movie made in California. Everyone is pretty; most people are even blond. The kiosks are littered with advertisements for plays and a movie called *Death As Usual* and a lecture on the latest breakthrough in the mathematics of knots ("Knots—the most perplexing problem Mother Nature ever threw at Physics") and another lecture on birth control in Yucatán. The end of the word *Yucatán* blots out Bibi's face, although I can see it is there. Handouts for a rally protesting Capitalism and Prejudice litter the green of the lawn, and someone is selling popcorn. I worry, momentarily, that there might be posters of Roberta on the ground too. I don't see any, but I walk carefully, just in case. The whole scene looks so much like a playground that I stop and buy some popcorn, even though I'm not hungry. If it is a playground, though, I'm not sure what was being played, but whatever it was I am glad it is over, I think to myself, and walk quicker, and open the door to the hotline center, breathless.

On each of the walls are enormous maps of surrounding areas, dotted in red where they have already been postered. There is a long table in the center with three phones that are constantly ringing, and a dozen or so students are answering them, taking notes on yellow pads. On the middle window are two large pieces of cardboard with a number written on each in thick black Magic Marker. Beneath them it says DAY, written in smaller letters. I stare at this for several minutes before I realize the number is the number of days Roberta has been missing. A large number of days at this point, I notice. A short large woman with a thin line of a mouth is ordering Brad, dressed in bright pink shirt and a long dangling earring, to do something. Brad seems to be obeying in slow motion. The phones are ringing constantly; the students look very young. In fierce Chinese, Mrs. Lee is scolding Veronica, who is holding what appears, amazingly, to be a small brown teddy bear. The center, which people refer to as Treehaven, has been set up in a student called Ken Lao's

The Friends of Bibi Lee

apartment; a friend, perhaps, I have never heard of. I wonder where Ken Lao is going to live now. The entire thing seems so improbable: I puzzle for a while about where it all could have materialized from. Treehaven—The Friends of Bibi Lee. It looks so different from her bedroom, I think to myself stupidly. The Operation, the Rescue Operation—some of the papers, I remember, actually referred to it as a Rescue Operation, and I wait with relief so sudden and extreme that it is almost happiness for someone to tell me what to do. The Grownups have come; they won't ask me what I have been thinking. Thinking has nothing to do with it. It is a Rescue Operation.

One mustn't gloat over meaningless victories; after all, where does this leave me?
For one thing, further behind in my work than ever . . . I hate work, but (curious) I hate not working too. So why not work?

I soon see, however, that I was wrong about this—about being rescued. The pile of envelopes before me is so large. I feel somewhat sad: I pick up an envelope and try to close it. I do another, and another, and it occurs to me that if I address another five or ten or hundred envelopes, I will be much more bored than sad, and that will really be sad. I skim through the names. Mr. Joe Desolto runs a gas station in Texas. *"Dear Mr. Desolto,"* reads the letter that I am folding and stuffing in the envelope: *"We are trying to help Mr. and Mrs. Lee recover their daughter, Roberta (Bibi). Bibi was last seen . . ."*

I try to remember if Roberta ever mentioned a Mr. Joe Desolto. (What kind of name is Desolto anyway? An unlikely name, an improbable name; a fictional name, no doubt, possessed by someone nonexistent.) No, of course she didn't mention Mr. Desolto; he lives in Texas and she hated Texas and Texans. She had never actually been there, of course: it was the idea of Texas she hated. It occurs to me she might have been wrong about that, though, but anyway there was no point in sending letters to Texas. I sift through the envelopes again: none of the other names are familiar either. No point, no point, no point. It occurs to me momentarily that Roberta might be in Texas anyway, or anyplace else for that matter, because the place might have nothing to do with her or her former life—it might be someplace *random*—but this thought is worse than the previous thoughts so I discard it as quickly as I can by going into the kitchen to look for food. The pile of envelopes topples and scatters all over the floor as I get up.

■ ■

Treehaven is being run by the woman with the thin-lined mouth. Her name is Lena Grady. Everyone defers to her; Veronica consults her on every move, the students look worried when she is not pleased with them, and even Brad seems to respect her. She is short and plump and stands too close to you when she talks and speaks always in a whisper. It is difficult to tell how old she is, her face behind round owl glasses could be in the thirties or forties, although she has a grownup son so perhaps she is in her forties or fifties. Her voice is husky and compelling, both babyish and seductive. I can't figure out where she comes from, and what she has to do with us. I want to ask who exactly she is and why she is here, but I can't think of any way to ask that isn't rude. Like: who are you and how did you spend your time the day before yesterday? Why do tragedies collect strangers, and what do you want with us? She is there when I come in the morning and there when I leave at the end of the day, and I never see her go out.

On one occasion, when I am particularly pressing about her situation, she admits that she had been a nurse in her former life.

"Do you mean you were a nurse and you just quit because you read about Roberta in the papers one day?" I want to ask, but instead I only say, "A nurse?" somewhat questioningly, and annoyed, she adds hastily, "*I* am the person in California who knows how to run a recovery operation, you know." I don't like the way she says "recovery"—it sounds like what you would do to a dead body ("The body was recovered," the paper said, "from the area just north . . . The girl had been missing for several months . . ."). I nod, though, because I want her to keep talking. Then she tells me that there is a well-documented rule about how the chances of finding a missing person decline exponentially with the number of days passed: halving at certain intervals, always down. I don't listen carefully enough to figure out how many days have passed, and where we are located now on that graph.

"The police don't really *care*, you know," she says. There is something about the way she says "you know" that manages to imply the opposite: we didn't know—she knows. The police don't care—you were wrong when you thought that the police care.

"They don't?" I echo, dutifully appalled, wondering what else
we don't know—like what we don't know about her, for example.
"No," she says, "they don't. We are the ones who can find Bibi."

I don't like the way she calls her Bibi. Nobody but very close
friends used to call her Bibi, and now everybody nicknames her,
even the newspapers use her pet name—the media's intimacy with
the famous or the dead—but I smile at her anyway. She was right,
though: I always forget this, but it turned out to be true. She
did just what she said she would do. If it weren't for Lena Grady
we'd still be writing to churches in Miami and gun shops in Oregon.

■ ■

**Adam and I are driving to Roberta's house to pick her up.
It is a cold snowy day, and Adam is driving carefully, so as
not to skid. He keeps one arm around me as he drives, his
hands both still on the steering wheel. Adam always does
the driving when we are together; he is a good driver, a
safe driver.**

**"No," her mother tells us, opening their yellow door,
"Roberta is not here. She left. She said she was going to
walk to the library."**

"That's funny," I say, "she knew we were coming over."

**"Oh, well," Adam says easily, "we'll catch up with her
then." And then, seeing my doubtful face, "Look, there's
only one way to go."**

**And although there was only one way to go, she was
not on that one way. We drove back and forth along the
road from the library to the house over and over, but no
Roberta. I asked her about it later, and she shrugged and
said she was there, where else could she have been? But
she wasn't there, we looked, I'm certain of it. Even Adam
remembers, and Adam never remembers this kind of thing.
You remember for a particular reason—not because it was
so odd, but because it was so typical: in so many of my
memories of Roberta, Roberta is not there.**

■ ■

I realize, after a few days, that nobody talks about Roberta. It
bothers me, and I start to several times, but I find, after all, that I

can't think of anything to say. There is the how-did-you-know-Bibi-and-how-well-did-you-know-her question, but since I knew her better and longer, and once I ask they are compelled to ask me back, my intentions look poor. Someone will occasionally say, "She was a nice girl—wasn't she?" "Yeah, a really special person," I will reply, and then we will look at each other suspiciously, wondering, each, what the other one knows.

It seems impossible that no one knows more. Here was this whole organization, suddenly sprung up, with telephones and people and reporters and maps, *all because Roberta went running one day*. Not a likely story. There had to be more to it than that—and someone must know what it was. And Lena, we all decided, would be the one the person who knew would tell. The students talked to her and the Lees talked to her, even though the Lees never talked to the students. Especially they avoided her boyfriend.

Mrs. Lee said to me once, "But Brad *lost* Roberta," and I tried to protest that it was, of course, factually true, but it wasn't true like that—it wasn't italicized true. But she turned away angrily.

I think that the reason the Lees didn't trust the students is that so few of them were Chinese. It was so Roberta-like, that she had so few Chinese friends. With anyone else this would simply be because they felt more comfortable with Americans, but with Roberta I knew it was just the opposite: she didn't want to be comfortable. If she were comfortable, she wouldn't be alienated, and if she weren't alienated, she would be—she would be, I think, and stop, trying to imagine Roberta not alienated—why, she would be someone entirely different.

The strangest thing—the thing I would look up from the preparation of posters and be surprised by with the same surprise as half an hour before—was the public nature of the event. Along with the Berkeley and the Oakland police, the FBI had come into the case. It was said to be the largest search operation since the kidnapping of Patty Hearst. Senator Kennedy's office would call the Berkeley police periodically to check on progress and make phone calls to the right people. I wasn't sure where the Kennedy connection came from—perhaps Naomi's mother, who had worked in politics. The posters were translated into Korean, Japanese, Chinese, Spanish, Vietnamese, and Thai: one of the papers said three million were eventually circulated, another said fifty thousand. And there were phone calls all day, every day: people saying they had seen someone who looked like Roberta maybe, people calling to ask what Roberta looked like, people calling to find out what other people had called to say. The Man-with-the-Van idea caught on incredibly quickly: everyone had seen him everywhere—in the other lane just before the light turned green; at the dry cleaner's last Tuesday; at the auto dealer's, the man selling vans looked a little threatening and he might be the Man with the Van.

I didn't understand how it could have become so public. Children grow up retarded because they don't have enough to eat. You see pictures of them; their heads are too big. More were slaughtered in genocides since World War II than died in the Holocaust and you had thought the Holocaust was the worst thing you had ever heard of. There are places people die of diseases that were cured a century ago, because the medicine costs a penny a day. In Soviet labor camps they fed prisoners porridge made of grass because people can't digest grass and they wanted to see the effects of long-term starvation. In the camps they said they learned it from the Chinese. After a cold night in New York City, they find bodies in the morning. In the tropics, there is elephantiasis. Adam told me some of these things. Yet there she was, one young woman who didn't have time to do anything but make a few friends, and everyone was interested. Everyone was concerned, and everyone had told their mother and she was concerned too. It was so peculiar. Each night people would gather around the television to watch the latest report on the news. It had almost the feel of watching the game, and there would be glee and cheering when they showed pictures of us on TV.

One night after Veronica had been interviewed by a particularly famous woman reporter who had made a big fuss over her being a member of the inner circle, she looked at me seriously and said: "You know, I'd give up all this for Bibi."

Shocked, I replied instantly: "Yes, of course." We looked at each other again, and I repeated: "Of course you would," and she echoed after me, "Of course," and we looked at each other again. Of course all this time is being spent granting interviews and preparing statements and directing operations and writing, but really it must all be for Bibi, somehow. Well. Hmm. Somehow. What else could it be? But of course.

■ ■

I pick up the pile of envelopes again and look around the room—everyone is working so hard. Shining through the gray of the cheap reproduction on leaflet after leaflet is Roberta's face. Even through the newsprint gray it is stunningly beautiful. Veronica notices me staring at it too long, and comes and snatches it away.

"Maybe you should try another area," she says sarcastically, as if she were annoyed merely because I am being slow.

■ ■

We are sitting at the Lees' kitchen table. Olivia, the eldest sister, is home for the weekend.

"How do you like being a doctor?" I ask casually, but really curious, really wanting to know.

"She hates it," Roberta answers for her, viciously. "And she owes the army the rest of her life." Olivia has paid for medical school by joining R.O.T.C.—for every year she was in school, she owes them a year in the army.

"It's not as bad as I thought it would be," Olivia says cautiously.

"Oh. It isn't what you wanted to do?" I ask, surprised.

"No, of course not." And then: "I wanted to be a pianist. But it wasn't practical. I used to try to practice when I got home from the hospital or lab or classes, but I'd always be too tired. At one point during medical school I thought I'd drop out and I auditioned for Juilliard. I got in, but it was no use, you know, it wasn't practical. The only real effect was that I missed the week we were studying the heart. Now when my patients have heart problems I won't be able to help them.

"It's funny, you know, how things turn out—it's the one organ that always kind of appealed to me."

"But why wasn't it practical?" I ask, appalled. Of course we all lived by phrases—and that particular one governs my life too—but every once in a while you hear them spoken by someone else and it occurs to you to protest.

"Because it wasn't practical," she repeats.

"But why?"

"Because—it was just an idea. You know how when you're young you get an idea about what you want to do, and then you get older and you have a career instead. And it's not that bad—it's rewarding, in its own way.

"You'll see what I mean," she adds, smiling at us.

"No I won't," says Roberta.

"But you have to," she insists. "It's not so bad," she says again. "I decided to become a psychiatrist, so I'll be able to keep my own hours that way and maybe even have children. You make the best of it. I mean, you have to—that's what growing up means."

"Well," says Roberta, pouting, willful, almost coy, but speaking darkly, too: "Maybe I won't grow up."

"But you have to," Olivia says for the third time, and I don't see why she is so insistent.

Roberta gets up and smiles and shakes her hair all over her face. We both look at her surprised: she is so pretty, so stunningly amazingly definitively pretty, that it is momentarily convincing: She in herself will be all and enough. She will not have cars and houses and careers and marriages and arrangements and rearrangements; she will not have to consent to the same concessions that others consent to—she will remain forever alienated and critical and beautiful and twenty-one. She will be herself and only herself forever. She is that beautiful, it is that convincing how beautiful she is.

But of course "just being yourself" is the same sort of phrase as "it isn't practical." There are so many of these phrases; it is curious how rarely one asks what they mean.

■ ■

"Why don't you go out for a while? Go to a movie, go out to dinner, take a walk. You're working so hard," I say to Veronica nervously.

"I can't," she says, "I have to be here in case anything happens—in case Roberta is found and there are *decisions that need to be made.*"

"But what kind of decisions couldn't wait a few hours?"

"There might be decisions that need to be made right away," she says menacingly. "Things might happen that I will need to be here for."

What kind of things, I want to ask, are we talking about? What is going to happen that can't wait till you get back?

I don't ask, of course, but it worries me, as it would worry Roberta, how hard Veronica is working. Debts are so difficult to repay.

■ ■

I ask Veronica once about her job, and what is happening with it. She does some kind of technical writing for a computer company in Cambridge called Mark of the Unicorn—a lovely name, I think, for a computer company. Veronica shrugs. She says she told them she didn't know when she would be coming back, and if they wanted to find someone else they could.

"Oh no," I say.

"What could I do?" she asks, with an angry defeated gesture. She and Roberta had the same cheekbones, the same straight smooth hair, same slant of shoulder and pallor of skin. They would have looked alike, but Veronica was thinner and more angular and five years older and had gone to MIT and then worked for a computer company. Bibi had not gone to MIT, she had gone to Berkeley: she had gone to Berkeley and dropped out of school, and then dropped, even, out of dropping out, just like that, disappeared, and Veronica had been left, as always somehow, to do all the work: to send mailings to Mr. Joe Desolto. It was as it always was. What else could she do?

■ ■

I am addressing envelopes again, and waiting for the day to be over. It is not nearly over though, it is not even twelve-thirty. Veronica comes over to look at my progress. At least there is a pile for her to look at, I think thankfully.

"All the envelopes have been addressed on the wrong side," she says very quietly. "Return addresses go on the upper left-hand corner because stamps go on the right."

"Well," says Lena, scurrying over in the way that someone large scurries. I look at her, hoping she will explain it to Veronica.

"Have you ever lived abroad, Melanie?" she asks.

"Well," I tell her, "I once lived in England."

Did nothing today. STOP. Wonder if tomorrow will be more. STOP.
Productive. Stop, Stop.
The girl in the card looks so engaged.

"There you go," she says. "In England they put stamps in the other corner."

"It was in ninth grade," Veronica says dryly. This is true. I look around the room. Everybody else is busy with something.

"All right," says Veronica, with the same dryness. "Why don't you go take a little walk and get us some copies of these photographs of Roberta. Think you can handle that?"

I nod miserably. "And take playboy over there in the corner with you," she adds, more sarcastically. Brad looks up and gives us his big golden smile. We bang the door behind us. On the way we stop for frozen yogurt. I get mango. Babycakes, I think, recalling Bibi's letter.

Adam, I see looking around, is busy directing things in another corner, scanning maps of places yet to be covered. He likes to be busy: he is not happy with the task—not dumb oblivious smiling—but undefeated nevertheless, and strong with conviction. His eyes are wide lashed and shining, his movements easy and definite, you think often how tall and easy he is. I am idle and calculating; he has green eyes. If Mr. Joe Desolto turns out to have seen Roberta, I calculate, then this afternoon's work will have been meaningful. If not, it will have been a waste. Adam would like to find Roberta, too, of course, but because of Roberta, not because of his afternoon. He does not keep track of his afternoons that way, to see whether in retrospect they turned out to be wasted. The afternoon is not a waste now, it is green-eyed with hope, and it will not be a waste later because he will not remember it. He has no need to remember because he can afford to lose as many as he likes. He doesn't even keep a diary.

I look down at the pile of envelopes again. I fold up a piece of paper and put it in. I fold up another piece of paper. I put it in the envelope, and then lick it and run my fingers along the flap. I lick the first envelope in the same way, and then the second. The third doesn't quite stick. I try to lick it again. My lips are so dry it seems to me they are going to crack. I run the edge of the envelope along them as hard as I can, and they bleed slightly from the paper cut. The wetness of the blood makes me feel a little better in a funny way. *I'm still so weak I can barely carry my crumpled clothes from the closet to the chair, let alone do any real work. Schubert coaxed the evening on. Tonight it was starless and damp. It takes so long to get from nowhere to nowhere.* Whenever the task before you bears for the afternoon the burden of the meaning and music of the whole of your life, there will always be, I realize in sudden defeat, a scarcity of music. Whatever man the plea is sent to will not be the right man, and no amount of envelopes enough envelopes.

It is embarrassing, of course, to be so unhelpful. No matter for how long one manages to find an excuse to leave the center, one still has to come back and be embarrassed. Nobody likes me for it: Veronica especially is angry with me, Lena thinks I'm nice but not too bright, and Adam is too nice himself to notice. It is worth it, though, I decide, because whatever I do I don't want to make the Organization any more organized than it already is. I have become increasingly worried that if it gets too busy nobody will notice if Roberta walks in, or if they do notice, they won't have time to do more than look up briefly. The Organization was already getting to be a Fact. Big plans were being made and they got bigger every day. Veronica was talking about purchasing a machine that would dial random numbers and repeat a recorded message giving people a brief version of what happened and urging them to call the hotline center with information. Apparently some precise high percentage, such as 87 percent of the people called, will listen for a modicum of time, like three minutes and a quarter. Some firm was considering donating highway billboards so an enormous picture of her could be blown up and put on the freeway. For the news, they had already filmed a reenactment. It showed a dark-haired girl running along a highway and being forced into a van by a moon-faced man, in order to try to trigger viewers' memories. This last plan bothered me most: it was as if they were no longer waiting for Roberta, but had decided to synthesize a substitute. The more we did, the more plans that were made and the more money spent, the less and less likely it seemed to me that she would come back. I kept worrying what Roberta would say if she walked in and saw that they had hired somebody else to play her. She would understand that the Organization had an existence of its own and could not now be unassembled—not without paying, that is, for all that had already been done.

She would know how in debt she was after this many days of being missing. (*Look how thin Veronica is getting. Look how concerned the Kennedys are. Look how devastated your mother is. Devastated. You'll have to pay it back, you know. Interest accrues. We've kept all the receipts and it's more than a pound of flesh you owe—as it always was. You'll have to pay in flesh if you can't come up with it any other way, and there are no other ways. Ordinary work won't do; you have worked hard all your life, and it has never been sufficient before. It won't be enough now either: think of the cost of the postage we've used, writing all those letters; think how much you owe us in postage alone.*)

She hears them—the voices—because she has already heard them. She knows what they are saying; it is always the same. She won't answer; the household deities are insatiable. You cannot pay your family back for all they have done for you because it has all already been done. They love you too much; they have done too much, consanguinity is in every vein. Blood is that thick, blood is too thick to be repaid except in kind. She was never able to appease them before: why imagine she could appease them now? She is not going to try, she is not coming back. She is never coming back; she will never come this way again.

CHAPTER 5

The Elusiveness of Meaning: Marcellus and Other Half Symbols

Dear Melody,

Hope things are oke with you. Glad to talk to you; there was so much to say and my roommate Caitlyn isn't really capable of contributing. She's a dear (you're such a dear) but also a computer jock (calculus, physics) and our conversations haven't been particularly profound. Oh well, we don't have to be best friends. I wish she weren't so aware of her possessions (as in, "this is mine, that is yours"). Maybe it gets on my nerves because I'm like that too.

By the way, the results are in: A in Chinese, A– in French and a skin-of-the-teeth B in Western Civilization. NOW I've got to keep it up. Sic 'em. Take no prisoners.

Be well to you!

Love,
Rosamunde

Veronica finds out that we stayed with Meg and slept in Roberta's bedroom last night. This does not please her. It is so very apparent, her face darkening with displeasure, that it almost makes me feel warmly toward her. When she first got to California she had wanted to stay in Roberta's room, but Meg had let Brad stay there instead. I know Veronica will not tell me that, however, and I wonder what she will say by way of justification. Veronica is compelled to use only logical justifications. This is because she was not the youngest.

"You know, Meg called me up the other night and asked if I would be on her talk show. She hosts one of the student radio stations—for some *women's organization* or something—and she wants to do some program on *kidnapping*, and use Roberta as an example. I guess she thinks it would add authenticity or publicity or *atmosphere* or something, when we're trying to find Bibi!"

"Oh," I say. To claim that one is using Roberta is the ugliest of accusations: at the center we constantly scrutinize each other in order to assuage the anxiety of scrutinizing ourselves. I am especially anxious around the Lees—sure they are going to uncover some motive of my own any minute and discover that, rhetoric aside, I do not really love Roberta and am using her for some as-yet-to-be-understood talk show of my own—and I wish I had pronounced "Oh" with more emphasis. And yet: what talk show? What motive could I have—or could Meg have? There is nothing to suggest that Meg cared more about the talk show than about Roberta, or that they were mutually exclusive.

"Moreover," says Veronica, in a tone of deep personal injury and grievance, "she stole things from Bibi." She sounds as if the things had been stolen from her.

"What exactly did she steal?" I ask.

"A little gold heart on a chain from her bedroom, *a heart Bibi wore next to her own heart.*"

Look, I want to tell her, you can't have everything of Roberta's, you know, other people might want some things too. Meg might want some things and I might want some things and Roberta might have wanted us to have some things. But I like the fact that she noticed the funny little symbolism of the necklace: that Roberta wore an image of a heart over her own heart. I remembered how she called her stuffed mice Mouse, or her large gray elephant L'Elephant. Roberta liked stuffed animals and mouse houses; I had dolls. I wish I had stolen something, I think jealously, and console myself by plotting to steal it back from Meg someday—if Meg had actually managed to get anything of Bibi's, that is. And I think to myself, depressed: Veronica probably made it up.

It was odd that way, though: how suspicious we all were of each other, right from the beginning—tangled, always, in this question of motive.

■ ■

Brad begins to wear bits of Bibi's clothing: a red flannel shirt, a furry alpaca sweater with pictures of camels in geometric designs. At first it strikes me as the perfect symbol of love: to wear another's clothing, to dress in their dress, and I wish I had something of hers to wear. But as soon as it strikes me as a symbol, I remember what Dr. Shohet told us about symbols in our high school English class: how they represent both themselves and the opposite of themselves. To dress in love, but not really to love: to have the appearance of love but not the reality. I catch Veronica looking at Brad askance, and I hear her whisper something to Lena. He is so fair of face he must be foul of heart, and Lena, not fair of face, must therefore, we assume, be trustworthy. She had no prettiness to hide behind; therefore she could not be hiding anything. She'd have nothing to hide it with. It is a funny way to think about people, as if they were like poetry, and could be interpreted thus, but we did think like this, and several times I heard Lena referring to The Beautiful People, or even more pointedly: The Beautiful Person. *The person we all think is beautiful, though really we know better.*

And yet "really" what? What was it we knew? There was nothing we knew. It was funny, no one liking Brad—or rather everyone liking him, very much, and all of us waiting to be shown what a mistake it was.

■ ■

The brown teddy bear that is being carried around Treehaven is Roberta's bear, Marcellus. He is stylish and French and I am dying to hold him. Veronica and Brad carry him the most. I am surprised Veronica carries him, and does not see him as subversive. He seems to me the one symbol of Roberta in the entire organization: the symbol of anti-Grownupness. And yet he makes me sad too, for he is already a little ragged, and ragged too from the fact that he is only a small brown bear, and it is a lot of symbolism to be carried by a small brown bear.

■ ■

I am sitting on the floor of the center drawing flowers on envelopes. Not big flowers—small flowers, twisted, with intricate vines and tiny unblossomed buds. The kind that would be in a garland a girl would wear on her head if she were an illustration in a fairy tale about a girl with a garland to whom something magical happened. (*What happened? Tell me what happened?* I can't tell you: you have to wait and find out.) You can tell it is a story with magic in it, though, because of the illustrations. There are garlands of rosebuds all over the cover, telling you what the girl inside is going to look like, and what kind of girl she will be. I haven't drawn her yet, but I am just about to. I could be writing addresses on the envelopes instead, of course, but I am almost in a good mood. When I look up next it is evening, and time to go. I begin to gather my things. Veronica hands me my pink sweater and a bottle of contact lens solution. The brand, I notice, is unfamiliar.

"Would you like this?" she asks.

"Oh," I say, looking at it, wondering.

And then: *"It was Bibi's."*

"Oh!" I say again, unsure, and look at it for a while, and finally, for lack of other conclusion, put it in my purse to take back to Boston. It was two-thirds full. I did take it back to Boston, and I remember it sitting on my bathroom shelf next to some nail polish that happened to be a shade of green I would never wear so someone must have given me that too. I don't know where it is now, though, so I must have lost track of it at some point. It was always this way, somehow. I felt bad throwing it out; I felt bad keeping it; I feel bad not knowing where it is. Half symbols; false, indifferent, unhappy uncertain symbols, symbols—lost, misplaced and unplaceable.

■ ■

Adam and Brad drive to the Oakland hills, searching. The hills are vast and desolate, chalky and craggy. After they have been wandering around for about three hours, Brad carrying the bear, in the middle of nowhere they bump into the psychic. It's strange,

Adam says, I mean not that he found Roberta, because he didn't, but that he found us. The hills were so vast, and we were so lost in them, and he just happened to find us.

■ ■

One day I am looking wistfully at Marcellus when Veronica says, "Would you like to hold him, Melanie?"

"Oh yes," I say, infinitely grateful and surprised. I must have replied too quickly, though, and with too much desire, because she immediately draws back and says, "Actually, maybe I'd better keep him."

I don't say anything, and she adds pointedly: "After all, he was Roberta's."

"Yes," I say. "He was."

■ ■

A woman from Greens, a fancy vegetarian restaurant, calls to confirm a reservation for two for Roberta Lee and friend. Brad answers the phone. The hotline is still using Roberta's old phone number. Shocked, Brad remembers Roberta planned to take him for what he tells Veronica would have been an engagement dinner, of sorts. I had never heard anything of the kind: what sort of engagement? I wonder. He thinks about going anyway, he says, and taking Marcellus to sit opposite him, but he doesn't.

Veronica tells me the story. Brad had told her. It is a sad little story, I guess, and I guess that is why it is told.

■ ■

As I am waiting in line one day at a sandwich shop, having left Treehaven with the idea of lunch, it occurs to me that I am missing my chance. I have come to California to figure out what happened. The evidence is still intact, her plants are still healthy, her books undisturbed. All the clues must still be there because she disappeared so recently—if only I could read them correctly. I start from the line, but I don't know where to go. I don't want to go to the center because I have already been there.

The woman ahead is asking what they put in their tuna fish. The man does not understand—tuna fish, wha'd you think, lady?—

and I understand that what she wants to know is whether there is mayonnaise in the tuna because mayonnaise is fattening and she wants to be thin because to be thin is to be beautiful and American women want to be beautiful. And obviously she does not want to demean herself by discussing this in a public place and opening up the opportunity for him to speculate on what her chances of being beautiful are, even if she were thin, which she is not, and about which I am already speculating dubiously because I am an American woman too. And meanwhile I have forgotten that my friend may be dying or hurt, and the chance to find her will be gone, and it is my fault as I thought it was my fault, as I knew it would turn out to be. The woman continues to ask veiled questions about the tuna fish and the minute is passing, the minute is passing, I begin to cry because the line is too long and there is nothing I can do. By the time I get my sandwich, however, the tears have passed too and I have decided that it is too late and there is nothing I can do, as there was nothing I could do, and I blow my nose and begin to eat, and hate myself, completely.

■ ■

Bob has driven in from San Francisco for the day. He steps out of his car into the sunlight, slim and smiling and looking like someone from California, and I'm incredibly glad to see him—him and his car and wherever he is going to take me, away from here.

It has been, I think, about a year since he moved here to start medical school. It strikes me, suddenly, as an odd coincidence that he happened to move to where Roberta was. A good coincidence, considering the situation. Not a good situation, though, I think, a bad situation, and I don't know if you can have a really good coincidence in a bad situation. I stand there, considering this, staring at him and thinking with satisfaction that he looks just as I thought he would look.

He is tall and strikingly slender, with the thin androgynous angularity of a model, so that sweaters drape nicely on him and clothes hang well, as upon a mannequin. He has long arms and legs and feet, and long white piano-playing hands. His hair is close-cropped, straight and brown, and he has light-lashed, perfectly brown eyes. There is something curiously disarming about this: most eyes have a touch of gray or green or black in them but his are only brown. He has a long neck and a high forehead and his nose is aquiline and the bones on his wrists and hips and shoulder blades are noticeable. One thinks of him this way: in terms of bone structure. His lips are almost white, or rather they are perpetually chapped and the chapping eats away at the faint color beneath. He puts waxes or Chap Sticks on them often, with a characteristic gesture, but they remain always chapped. For some reason this has always appealed to me. He often licks them or runs his fingers over them when he is thinking.

He has an extremely pale complexion—that white whiteness that is usually found only in the British, with a light sprinkling of freckles over his nose and forehead. The underside of his wrists and the skin around his eyes are so white as to be almost transparent, with that odd delicate gleam through which you can see to some fainter layer of faint blue flesh. There is something surprisingly vulnerable about this, as if you had just startled him from sleep, and you imagine suddenly that all the gloss and hard-edged irony must have come later, and he must, in fact, have been a very serious, solemn child—sickly even, with that meditative otherworldly emaciated transparency one associates with dying children. He must have been constantly told to eat more as a child; one can imagine his mother trying to bribe him to eat cheese. They are looks one likes if one likes him, and likes too that this is true: you wouldn't see any warmth in him unless you believed it was there.

He is usually so animate in his gestures, though, that it is difficult to get a precise impression of what he looks like at all. His voice is smooth and quick and casts a spell over everything so that you cannot see him properly because you are always listening; it has so many myriad interlocking tones, each too quick to be identified, so that one has an impression of pervasive movement. He tilts his head, slightly, while he is talking. He doesn't like to be studied: even as I am staring at him I can see that he is impatient, and about to say something or move away to divert attention.

"Well," he says efficiently. "Hi, Melanie." He has brought me a bouquet of pastel-colored snapdragons; I can see him holding them full in both of his hands, the deep velvet blossoms just the right size for me to put my fingers into—pinks and blues and purples.

"Hi," I say happily, although I know he doesn't like it when I'm too happy to see him. He is glad to see me too, of course: he has brought me flowers to signify the very thing, perhaps, that I am feeling—*you, I've missed you.* You would think, then, that we feel the same, but we don't—not often, not at the same moments because we don't like the same kind of moments. I remember we were once waiting for the phone and watching this Spanish woman, Anna, whom Bob lived with, talk to her lover. She barked something guttural at him in Spanish, tossed her mane of hair, and slammed down the phone. "I like that," Bob said, watching.

"I don't," I replied. "I like long good-byes, where you arrange when you're going to talk next and then you say you miss them and then maybe you say something else just to keep on the phone a little while longer, because you hate to let them go, and you both know why you said it, and you cradle the phone a little closer and laugh."

"I'd rather just feel it," Bob said. "It's minimalist," he added, teasing, and I remember staring through the veil of levity and thinking I would remember this, as one always remembers such stark illustrations and the occasions in which they occur: *we are different.* It sometimes seems to me his whole manner is calculated to render expressions of emotion unnecessary—antiquated and uncomfortable, the way eighteenth-century garb would feel on a Calvin Klein man. He has always particularly disliked greetings and farewells, and raw awkward heart-in-the-throat occasions. Even on television he makes fun of them: *Touching,* he says, when the heroine begins to cry, oh beautiful and touching. If she has to ask him if he loves her, Bob says, the answer doesn't count. I wouldn't be here if I weren't happy to see you, he tells me; if you don't tell me that you're happy, I think to myself, I don't feel that it's true.

"So," he says, trying to move the moment forward. "What do you want to do? Do you want to go someplace?"

"Mmm-hmm," I say, still not moving.

"Where? Do you need anything?" He is practical this way; he often asks me if there are things that I need.

"Umm," I say, thinking. "Shopping maybe. For tea." And then: "Yes," I say, liking the idea more, "let's go shopping for tea."

I do want some tea, and think it might help. Also I like the idea of being taken away from Treehaven. Mainly it is that, of course.

"All right," he says, "let's go then."

The supermarket is strange and enormous and artichoke gleaming, just as I remember it from when I was little and we lived in

California and I used to beg my mother to take me shopping so I could pick out things.

"What kind of tea do you want?" Bob asks, as we are standing in front of the wonderful array.

"Almond Sunset," I say, pleased. He takes it off the shelf and I trail behind him to the cash register.

"You know, almond tea was Roberta's favorite kind," I add, to establish that this is not just any shopping trip, and it is not just that I can't do without my favorite tea for a couple of days.

"You mean it's your favorite," he says, laughing softly.

I am about to protest darkly, and I am not exactly lying because it did happen to be a kind of tea she liked, when he turns to look at me. Flipping the package up in the air and catching it deftly, suddenly serious, he says: "You know you don't have to try so hard to make everything *meaningful*. This isn't some novel where tea has to be tied in with Roberta so this can be a significant half hour. If you just want some tea—just because you want it, no symbolism involved—you can still have it.

"I mean I'd still get it for you," he adds, putting it down on the counter and turning to look at me, "no questions asked."

And I, who imagine that everything I do has to be meaningful—that I make my very living, as it were, through meaningful interpretations—am astonished.

"So," he adds confidentially, "if you really did pick it out because it's her favorite kind, there's still time to go back and get something you really like." But because I hear his voice to be friendlier now, I admit that actually it was what I wanted—of course it was what I wanted all along.

CHAPTER 6
A Suitable Ending

Dear Melanie,

My life's a shambles. On the romance front, nutso. Courtney is being a jerk and I'm not coping well with Brad's lingering Francie fancy. Maybe it's time to cut my losses and creep off. But I don't think I have the strength. And if that weren't enough, I'm fat. (And I'm not being anorexic; if you could see a picture of me you'd see I'm FAT.)

I got my hair cut today. It wouldn't behave itself so SLASH. Off with it! At least some things can be managed.

I just don't know.

I don't know how to be or whom to trust with what I am. Why is there no difference between who I am on the outside and what's on the inside? Why can't I keep up a public front like everyone else—like certain people I seem to become "involved" with?

I'm taking Linguistics, Modern Novel, Anthropology, Syntax, a folklore class and I'm in but may soon be out of a Feminist Lit. class. If I drop it I'll have to get into another course pronto. Drat. I'm sure I've forgotten at least one other class. Plus I'm doling out soup to the homeless, working with an East Asian feminist magazine and ushering. Nothing like time on one's hands, eh?

I feel far away from everything and everyone. I don't want to doubt people. But what choice is there when you don't know?

So far away,
Roberta

EDITORIAL

Suitable ending   by Brad Page

Thin worn shells once coloured with life
Now rags and loose ends in a last formless dance
Empty from the closet into paper-bag brown.

Plastic jewels draped in elegance.
Layers to the seasons
Buttoned up tight to chill glances
Always revealed to warm glares a beauty disrobed.

Sextant poised, shivering for warmth, she continually in-
                                        spected society's gusts.

Sway back,
Challenging the winds head on she sailed, never luffing,
Never in irons.
She cut forward gently parting the waves of complacency
Who in awe, embarrassment lapped against her gunwales.

On a warm Winter's day terror howled in the soul
As the appetite of the mind's eye took a second look but
                                        didn't see
Witnessed by one, viewed by millions,
The rest fed on the 6 o'clock news with coffee and dessert
And a well described man with
A positively identified friend
Drove slowly away in an instant.

The last scarf lay in order in a half empty box – taped shut
No postage, no cost;
Returned to sender.

To bibi: who dressed me in love, 11-18-84

*This poem, written by missing person Roberta "Bibi"
Lee's boyfriend, is not an epitaph. Torn from the heart of a
lover, it is a glimpse of a soul too powerful to ever be
extinguished.*

*Bibi's dissappearance has brought tears to the eyes of
many; some who are among this editorialist's dearest
friends. They are tears of sadness and frustration, but they
have not washed away the hope.*

*Bibi vanished two weeks ago. Since then her many friends
have formed a search network that has blanketed the Bay
Area with posters. If you're going home for the holidays,
please help. Stop by Sproul Plaza and pick up some posters
from the "Friends of Bibi." Plaster them on every gas station and rest stop on your way home.*

We can find Bibi.   **– ed.**

I am walking out of the center one day, when Brad comes up the stairs carrying a pile of newspapers. I stop: he is not just coming up the stairs, he is skipping. "My *poem* has been published!" he announces gaily. Skimming a paper off the top with a nice flourish, he tosses it at me. It's the student paper, the *Daily Cal.*

I look up quickly to try to catch the expression on his face, to see what it says about the poem, but he is gone. I read the poem again. Shells, sextant, gunwales, dessert, no postage: what *is* he talking about? I start to slip it in my purse ashamed: I am someone who is supposed to know about poetry. And then I see that the editor had explicated it on the bottom after all: *"This poem . . . is not an epitaph. Torn from the heart of a lover, it is a glimpse of a soul too powerful to ever be extinguished.*

"Bibi's disappearance has brought tears to the eyes of many, some who are among this editorialist's dearest friends. They are tears of sadness and frustration, but they have not washed away the hope." And finally: *"We can find Bibi."*

I wish I had thought of writing a poem.

■ ■

Veronica comes over to me, as I am back at the envelopes, and wordlessly hands me a copy of the *San Francisco Chronicle.* I look down and see that it is a piece by Adam.

INSIDE THE SEARCH FOR BIBI

Roberta (Bibi) Lee, 21, disappeared at 9 a.m. Sunday, November 3, when she split off from her friends while jogging in Redwood Regional Park in Oakland. She is described as Asian, 5-feet-6, weighing 115 pounds with shoulder-length hair and brown eyes.

Roberta (Bibi) Lee, a girl I went to high school with in Massachusetts some years ago, was walking in the Montclair area two weeks ago when a bearded, beer-bellied man forced her into his brown van. Despite the posting of hundreds of thousands of fliers, and several hundred tips a day phoned into the police and to a special hotline, she has not been seen since.

Still, each day dozens of her friends from Berkeley and from back East fan out through Northern California, searching. A search, it seems to me (this is the first I've ever been involved in and I hope the last), is a peculiar process. Full of hope twisted on edge and despair turned somehow into energy.

The search headquarters, a fourth-floor apartment in a building not far from the UC Berkeley campus, is wallpapered with maps of the area, with blocks outlined in red if the street has been leafletted, if posters have been put up and gas stations and restaurants alerted. Yellow means the area is not yet covered—there is still a lot of yellow.

The young people sitting around the room, waiting for a ride so they can turn some neighborhood from yellow to red, are not solemn, not weepy. The human mechanism can't stand the strain of unabated grief and still function, so these people have learned, over the two weeks, to joke about the weather, or the classes they're missing, or whatever, and thus keep thoughts of that brown van at bay.

But the thoughts creep back in anyway, and only hard work will exorcise them. The work, in some sad but necessary fashion, is divorced from its ultimate goal. People do not go out the door to "find Bibi": they go out the door to put leaflets in the window of every bar and every diner and every Quik Mart in the mountains along, say, Route 9—in Boulder Creek and Ben Lomand and Felton.

That way, at day's end, one has accomplished *something,* even if it is something that may turn out to be meaningless. The man in the van may never drive down Route 9; he may be in Mexico or in Chicago or hidden so far back in the forest he won't be seen till spring.

Hope needs regular pushes to keep it strong. So, in this search, there are minor victories along the way. Not victories of substance— only finding Bibi will amount to that—but victories of process. The news that the Swingline company is donating 200 stapleguns and a million staples restores the spirit. Each kind shopkeeper who says, sure, go ahead and put your poster in my window, makes it that much easier to go on.

People who have worked on a political campaign will find some of what I'm describing familiar. But a political campaign points ahead to a single day, and it gathers speed and momentum as that day draws near.

In a search, the rhythm is reversed—the enthusiasm is greatest at its start and slowly, painfully, it dwindles. There is a horror in that withering away, especially for those so close to Roberta that they can never really resume their normal lives.

There is no set date for a search to end—it will end when Roberta is found, and who knows when that will be.

But those last are despairing thoughts, and no room can be made for despair—once it gets its foot in the door it expands, till it occupies every chamber of your heart.

Despair, I think, *"No room can be made for despair":* Adam makes no room for despair. *"Once it gets its foot in the door it expands, till it occupies every chamber of your heart."* Adam doesn't have to make room for despair because his heart is like the heart he is writing about: it is that big—it has that many chambers to feel things, like sadness and hope. I wouldn't despair either if I had any simple good feelings like Adam. I pick up the paper and nuzzle it against my cheek, and then look around ashamed. It's not as if Adam and Adam's writing and Adam's way of thinking and feeling are going to rub off on me whatever I do to that piece of paper. I always try to take metaphors too literally—a bad sign, I think.

Veronica tells me later that she doesn't like the piece. I ask her why, surprised, never having heard of anyone who does not like Adam and everything he writes. He stands outlined in my mind as clearly as those medieval depictions of saints before perspective was discovered—the ones shown among beasts and men in the bright confusion of the ancient cities, flat and blue and red and gold. They are not contemplative saints, the medieval ones: they are all tangled up with the world. You can always tell the saint from all the other men, though, because he is outlined in such clear gold lines, so that although he is tangled, he is not lost in the confusion. He is too busy directing sheep and cattle and men to be lost. Veronica tells me that she doesn't like Adam's piece for the same reason that she doesn't like the newspaper articles about Roberta. They aren't how she sees it, she says, that's all. She has Roberta's clipped epigrammatic manner of speaking. They aren't, of course, how I see it either, and Adam's version no more than any other. His is the interpretation of faith. There is hope and despair: the belief that we are going to find her is hope, and the thought that we aren't is despair. Hope is Roberta and despair is the Man with the Van, and we choose hope over despair because it is better. Adam isn't naive; he knows that despair would be more sensible, but he chooses hope anyway—like that, a choice. He doesn't say so in the piece but I know he does. And he doesn't mention, of course, either, the fact that despair is Roberta too—that Roberta might have despaired of a lot of things before the Man ever drove by; that if she were forced into the Van she might have wanted to be forced in; that she might have gotten in precisely because she despaired, and that the despair might be that we don't know exactly what she was despairing of, and she didn't know either. He doesn't say that because he would never say that. He would never even think that because once this thought occurs to you it ruins everything. Once you have the secret miserable irrational suspicion that at any level Roberta *wanted* to be missing, all of a sudden you can't put up posters and write beautiful pieces. I carried Adam's piece in my purse for almost a year, and then pasted it ragged and yellow into my diary. I look at it sometimes still, even though it has been a long time now since she was even missing.

■ ■

Brad comes into the center each day, dressed elaborately. A pink T-shirt, a purple scarf, a single feather earring. He looks pretty, but I wonder why he wants us to think about how he looks. I recall the dedication to his poem: *"To Bibi: who dressed me in love."* To dress; to dress. To reveal, to cover, to cover up? Self-revelation or self-disguise; depth or surface? Or does Brad not believe in these differences? For Adam, of course, does not think in these terms; for him everything is both: integrated, without discrepancies. He is what he seems and he seems what he is: good, true, beautiful—the old words, the platonic triangular three. But Adam is different from other people this way, and when other people seem to be like him, you are usually missing their complexities. What was it Brad said about the clothes? *"Thin worn shells once coloured with life / Now rags and loose ends in a last formless dance / Empty from the closet into paper-bag brown."* So he too knew Bibi was gone—there was no meaning to collecting artifacts, contact lens solutions. *"The last scarf lay in order in a half-empty box—taped shut. / No postage, no cost; / Returned to sender."*

Why? What did he think had happened? *"On a warm Winter's day terror howled in the soul / . . . Witnessed by one, viewed by millions, / The rest fed on the 6 o'clock news with coffee and dessert."* Who was I then, or Brad? Clearly not the millions, the people having dessert, who don't know anything. Those were the people watching the reenactment on television. We must be the one, the one who witnessed it. What had I come to California for if not to witness? Brad must be here for the same reason, for he was being no help with the posters either. *". . . terror howled in the soul / As the appetite of the mind's eye / took a second look but didn't see."* To see without seeing—yes, exactly—that was exactly what it was like.

What was it we knew but didn't know? The title of the poem

is "Suitable ending." Ah, yes, the suitable ending, of course, that's what we saw: an ending that ended our story suitably.

But why did it make so much sense? What story had to end this way? What was the story *about?*

The Man with the Van? No, he is some stranger, some random jerk. How could he hold the secret meaning or be the one who witnesses? He is one of the dessert-and-coffee people. The meaning must be more personal; there must be a more personal meaning. I so want to ask Brad what he knows.

■ ■

"How," I ask Lena tentatively one day, but determined to find out, "did you get involved with this?"

She puts her hand on my arm and leads me out to the balcony off one of the bedrooms. Bob, who is with me, follows a bit warily. "Mels," she says. "We can talk out here, Mels," she tells me. Bob's nose wrinkles: she is not on Mels terms with me.

"I *am*, you know," she says, "*the* person in California who knows how to run a rescue operation."

"Really!" I say encouragingly, with what I hope is the proper amount of round-eyedness. I was prepared though: I had heard this line before. Bob moves a definite step backward. He does not consent to even temporary alliances, because the precondition of "join my club and I will tell you all our secrets" is that you leave your skepticism at the door, and Bob never goes anywhere without it. This is because he is from L.A. Also, in my mind, because he is Jewish. It is not an attitude Adam would ever have, for example: he would consider it uncharitable.

Apparently satisfied with my response, she continues: "My son's girlfriend, Tracy, was taken just last April. She was sitting in a park, a public park only three blocks from their house, reading a book, when she was taken."

"Really!" I say again, pleased that after all there is going to be a story to back up her claims. I hope it will be a good one.

"Yes, she was sitting there innocently reading on Easter Sunday afternoon in the sight of hundreds of people."

"Oh!" I fill the pause. I feel the beginnings of horror-story pleasure, the poor grownup version of ghost stories.

A little ashamed, as when you turn the page of the *National*

Enquirer because you want to know how the body is laid out and what color her hair was, I ask: "Was she . . . pretty?"

"She was—umm—somewhat plain," Lena replies awkwardly. I am instantly sorry to have interrupted, and ask contritely: "How was she taken?"

"They must have been wearing police uniforms or shown her some kind of ID. She would have respected authority because of the way she was brought up."

"Ohhh," I say, beginning to get worried. Policemen are absolutely trustworthy to me too—*Hill Street Blues,* red flannel shirts, chopping wood on weekends—Regular Guys, like Adam, only more so.

"But," she adds menacingly, to keep, perhaps, my thoughts on track, "they kept her alive for three days, and we didn't find her until the fifth day because someone in the police office *lost* the crucial clue. It was misplaced—they put it on the wrong desk. It turned up after she was dead."

As soon as she says it I realize I must have been waiting all along for her to explain why it was she and not the police who had to run the rescue operation.

"They lost it!" I exclaim, more worried. I lose things too.

But Lena wants more than worry.

"Melanie, *the things they did to her body!* No, I won't even tell you the things they did to her body."

She won't tell me. Why won't she tell me?

"There was nothing she could do—nothing—to save herself?"

"Nothing," Lena says darkly.

"And they—they—"

"She was murdered."

Tracy, I think passionately, blinking back tears, whoever you are, I hope you can't hear this conversation. Tracy, I hope you understand, it isn't really you we are talking about. It's only the narrative that is being exploited.

"And such a sweet and innocent girl," Lena adds, capitalizing on her success. "Naive, young, vulnerable, helpless, you know the type—*the type these things happen to*—the type Bibi must have been—the type you are—"

I catch my breath.

"The type you are," she repeats with finality. "Just like you."

Bob snorts, and says, "Let's go," and the story is finished.

"How can you let people say those things about you?" he whispers, yanking me along by the arm. "How can you even let them think them? Why doesn't it bother you? It bothers me, damn it. You aren't naive, you aren't helpless, and you aren't a *type*. Especially you aren't a type. How can you let people type you?"

I look at him, surprised, and see that he is genuinely angry.

"But it doesn't matter what Lena thinks, does it?" I ask tentatively. "I mean, if I know it's not really me? Or Roberta?"

"Oh, I don't believe you," he says. "There's a reason you let people say those things about you, and the reason is you don't totally dismiss them. You don't see anyone describing me as the perfect victim for a *National Enquirer* crime, do you? And you know why that particular characterization makes me so angry? Because it's not just stupid and wrong—it's dangerous. That girl— that flimsy female paper-doll *girl*—may be just a fiction of Lena's, a pathetic pornographic fantasy that has nothing to do with Tracy herself. But that type, as Lena so eloquently put it, gets raped and murdered.

"God," he says quietly, "I hate people who try to turn you into that.

"So I really think," he finishes, heavier with irony, releasing my arm, "you ought to make more of a point of distinguishing yourself from her."

■ ■

I am getting dressed in a square sunlit room. Adam, who has been up for a while, is sitting on a chair reading the newspaper. He looks up and watches me sit on the edge of the bed brushing my hair. The sound of the brush strokes is the only sound in the room. I stand up and walk over to my suitcase and take out a pair of jeans. I reach down and begin to pull them over my legs.

"You look nice in those pants," Adam says quietly.

"No I do not. I do not look nice in these pants or any other pants because I have ugly thighs. I hate them; I wish I could cut them off." The violence in my voice surprises me.

"Don't talk like that!" Adam says deeply. He hesitates for a moment, trying perhaps to decide what to say. He has tried the

but-I-like-your-body-and-since-I'm-your-boyfriend-isn't-that-what-
counts argument so many times in the past four years, and although I do think that it is what counts, for some reason it has, in
fact, not counted.

"Just think what a good nice lap you will have for children to
sit in. You remember that: if you didn't have thighs, you wouldn't
have a lap for our children to sit in."

I look up at him in surprise, suddenly realizing, yes: this
counts. An alternative mythology. Of course, it might not be this
way for me by myself, but then I am not by myself. There is Adam,
and he is there in that happy beautiful place where we are going to
have happy beautiful children and I and my loathsome hateful
useless body and loathsome hateful useless self are going to be
different because they will be useful to somebody else. My thighs—
instead of being objects to be scrutinized—will become a lap.
Children will settle on them. I am sure of it because Adam is
sure: more than sure, he is already there, waiting in the happy
place. I ought to hurry and make up my mind and get there
before he gets tired of waiting and gives up. I wish I knew
how exactly to get there. I remember starting to cross the street
with my friend Jerry once, and him yanking me back roughly,
saying, "Jesus, Melanie, why don't you ever look where you're
going? I'm starting to cross the street and you're on the outside
so I'm assuming, *just assuming*, that you've looked, *because people
generally do*, and then I remember: Oh no, I'm with Melanie,
and Melanie never looks where she's going. You know you're
going to kill yourself someday, don't you? Yes, my dear, I guess
you do know that."

I was about to say, "That's not true," but instead I stood still,
taking, as I often do, other people's casual remarks as prophecy. I
don't know whether he sensed my fear and changed his mind, but
he looked at me for a moment and then said: "Actually, I take it
back. If you had a child with you, you would stop and look both
ways and take the child's hand so your little one wouldn't run
ahead, wouldn't you? When you have a child you'll change. It's
selfishness that allows you to be so preoccupied. Adolescent selfishness. You'll outgrow it."

"I will?" I asked earnestly, and then, realizing it was hardly
for him to answer, shrugged, embarrassed, and we crossed the
street. We crossed safely, though, and remembering now, I feel
better and throw on my woolly white sweater and Adam and I

walk out and toward Treehaven, and as we walk we begin to argue our favorite argument. He likes names like Tom and Daisy and I like names like Tadzio and Demelza, and I think his names are ordinary and boring and he thinks to find ordinariness boring is a matter of misplaced imagination. And since I know that in some pervasive sense misplaced imagination is the theme of my life, but can never quite figure out what it is misplaced onto, or I would be able to change, I smile at him, yes, I like them too, yes, your names are better names.

■ ■

I finally contrive it so that Brad and I are walking out of the center at the same time. I ask him where he is going, and then tell him I am going in that direction too. I am leaving in two days.

"So, umm," I begin, floundering, surprisingly. Usually I am good at taking advantage of such moments. "So, ahh, I guess it must be really hard to be in school at the same time—I mean to have to be taking classes now and stuff."

"It's not so bad," Brad says, smiling at me. I wonder if he is smiling because he sees through my question, or whether there is another reason.

"Actually," he drawls, "I'm only taking three courses, and one of them is in linguistics, and one is in jazz dance, and the other is in creative writing and I showed my teacher my poem, and she said it was very sensitive, and they are all, actually, going just fine."

■ ■

Looking around at Treehaven at the plans and posters and calls and donations I feel almost smug. *We were right, you see; we were right we were right we were right.* We weren't making it up and it wasn't imagination. There really was something wrong and not all the money and resources and ambition and energy in the world rescued us. We had known that for years; everybody else was finally going to know it too. The system saves no one. I flatten myself against the wall, watching the incredible commotion of the center. It strikes me as so pointless, I am afraid I am going to cry.

Adam sees me and comes over. He follows my gaze, realizing I am watching everyone at work, and I imagine that he is about to voice my thoughts. "One thing this center sure makes clear," he says, "is that if there is one bad person, there are about two hundred good people in this world." I almost think for a minute that the one bad person is me, or maybe Roberta, but then I realize he means the Man with the Van. "It really makes one confident about the world, doesn't it?" he adds thoughtfully. I stare at him, but his eyes are clear of irony. I feel the particular mixture of alienation and affection toward him that I always feel when he completely misreads my thoughts and misinterprets the situation. I wonder if we will think more alike as time goes by, or whether we should even bother talking. But for some unfathomable reason of long-standing arrangement this indecision translates in my mind to a feeling only of love, so although I had been about to say, "That's *not* what I was thinking—not at all was that what I was thinking," instead I think to myself once again that I love him utterly; I could not love him more than I do.

■ ■

Meg and I are walking out of the center. I am on my way to get lunch; she is on her way to class. She tells me that when Roberta was first missing, two psychologists came to speak at Lothlorien.

"And the psychologists had the nerve to say we should understand that Roberta was not going to come back—or if by any remote chance she did she would not be the same person at all! Like we hadn't even finished putting up our posters and they were already trying to tell us to give up on Bibi! I mean isn't that sick; doesn't that just go to show how worthless professionals are!"

I glance over at her. Her eyes are big and brown and full of earnestness and conviction—that particularly wonderful young-girl brown-eyed earnest conviction. I wonder if I have ever worn that expression.

■ ■

Adam and I are walking to an Italian restaurant in Berkeley. Dusk is falling; the day is closing, lovely and gray. There are just the two of us, walking side by side in the blue-thick blackening dusk already a moment changed from the gray in which we began. The lights from the houses and streets and shops are so small and far away that it seems that he is very near me. I wish I liked beginnings as much as I like closings. We are having one of those conversations that happen endlessly between lovers and never between friends, in which we are both saying one thing, and thinking another, and thinking about what the other is thinking and wondering if the other is doing the same. At least I am wondering what he is really thinking, and whether he knows what I am thinking, or if he even thinks this way. He is talking about someone he knows, his roommate DeWitt, I think, and thinking probably of Roberta, and I am pretending to be thinking of Roberta, but thinking definitely of myself. What he is trying to say, I think, although he does not say it directly because he imagines it might not be a Christian thing to think, is that it is hard for him to be friends with someone who is unhappy because you have to try to make them happy or you aren't a friend, and yet you can't make someone happy who is not happy. You think you can, but you can't. Unhappy people are unhappy. I think that, yes, this is true, and I mean to say casually: "I guess you feel that way about me too," but instead I catch my breath and ask, suddenly brave, "So you feel that way about me too?"

And Adam replies easily, "You aren't fucked up; you just think you are."

I look at him, surprised, shocked, and am about to reply: But thinking is *everything*—it's no use saying it's just my thoughts that are the problem, when obviously they are indeed the problem— when it occurs to me that if thinking were really everything, then I could just as easily think that he was right. I'm not fucked up; I just thought I was. I am fine. Really, I think I'm fine. Just like that. *Just because I think so.* End of adolescence. Roberta might come back. Roberta might not have been missing in the first place. Nothing was wrong; *you just thought there was.* I tug at Adam's hand to make him stop walking so I can figure out if this is true.

It's funny about truth and true moments. I decided a long time ago that there are certain moments that are *true moments* and others that seem to be, but aren't. Like Revelation and Obvious Contrivance. It's easy to understand if you think about the situation as if it were in a novel. If, early in the story, someone tells the doomed girl that she is not doomed, when she knows and the author knows and everyone who is reading the novel knows perfectly well: *she's going to die when the story ends,* then that's not a true moment. It's neither prophetic nor revealing; it is, in fact, a lie. And this is apparent to all good readers.

If she's trying to picture her life, however, and she suddenly realizes she can't imagine herself older than twenty-five, then that's true—an authentic little insight. When Anna Karenina heard of the watchman who fell in front of the train at the beginning of the book and looked at the train tracks and felt a shiver of premonition, *that was true.* That told you what was going to happen later. You might think the reason I don't know whether this moment with Adam is true is because we haven't got to the end of the story yet: read a little longer and then you will know. Did she marry him, did he marry her, did their story end well or not? In *Anna Karenina* you know that that initial scene is a foreshadowing from the moment you read it, if you read well. You don't have to wait six hundred pages to watch her actually jump in front of the train before you say: this is a tragedy. You know not because you know the story but because you know the genre. When the hero in a Harlequin romance tells the heroine not to worry, everything will be fine, that's true. Everything really will be fine: *it's a Harlequin.* We can be certain because in books events are meaningfully ordered, and people are suited to their fates: if the heroine looks beautiful and tragic, then it's a tragedy. If, on the other hand, her name is Eden Ariel and she has long blond hair and is incapable of a deep thought, it must be that deep thought is not required. She looks great in her white dress; she is surely destined for handsome love and nice houses because that is happiness for a Harlequin heroine. When Anna Karenina looked tragic and beautiful at the first ball, all in black, whereas Kitty, on the other hand, was cozy and domestic in pale pink tulle, those were true too: Anna dies; Kitty has fine babies.

Adam is trying to tell me what my qualities are, and what kind of character I will be—you were wrong, he wants to tell me, when you thought you were the troubled kind—and I would like to believe him except that I don't know how to know if he is telling the truth. We'd like our story to be a happy one, of course—the kind of book where you come to the end and say, isn't that nice—but revelation is so difficult to distinguish from wishful thinking and there's no way to know what genre you are in. If you get a good report card from school, for example, it might bear all the trappings of an important personal evaluation, but if you try to make that into a revelation, you've made a mistake. And if you phone someone like Adam and ask whether you're really a Good Person and, when he says yes, ask if he's *positive*, as I do several times a week, that's not just wishful thinking—it's cheating. Adam has told me so easily though that there's nothing wrong—you're not fucked up, he said, you just think you are—and he seems so innocent of implications and unmanipulated by me, and is, in fact, already beginning to talk of something else, that I wonder if it might be genuine. I tug at his hand again, but he doesn't understand that it means I want him to stop walking, so he only squeezes my hand back and continues on, and before I have decided, the scene has already closed on a candlelight dinner where we are bent in earnest conversation over forgotten things and pasta.

■ ■

I corner Brad, finally, one day in the kitchen of the center. He flashes me a white-toothed smile; I wish I had planned what I was going to say to him.

Finally I come up with a question about Lothlorien. He tells me that it is indeed vegetarian, which I already knew, and that they make their own bread and have no sugar. "No sugar!" I exclaim, trying to taste life without sweetness.

"Yes," he says, "but every once in a while I go buy two dozen donuts and go on a binge." His tone is even, not at all confessional. It strikes me as odd; I cannot imagine Brad, blond easy Brad, his fingers deep in raspberry filling, gobbling white sugared crumbs. It is not, for example, the kind of thing Adam would ever do, or at least not in the same way—not with the same jelly-smeared horror. Adam can eat dozens of donuts, but happily, with animal contentment. He has many nice mooselike qualities.

I asked Brad, then, if he would send me copies of the photographs of Bibi when they were developed, and he promised he would and that was all. This was the sum total of my exchanges with Bradley Page. So you see I came to large conclusions based on small remarks because I had nothing else to base them on, and because I like to conclude. It seems to me now that these remarks were meaningful—Marcellus, the poem, wearing her clothing, the jazz dance class, no sugar, jelly donuts. They may very well not be; they probably are not, but they are what I knew. I didn't know much, of course, but I don't think Roberta did either. She told me that once, after they had been seeing each other several months, she asked him how he felt about her, and he replied that she looked sexy in black. "But how do you *feel?*" she asked again— with that strange urgency that would not allow her to let any remark be a casual remark or any moment incidental. And he smiled his large smile, and said: "I like you."

"*But what does that mean?*" she went on, unable to help asking. "I like *strawberry jam,* too."

And so I was going to have to leave California without his having opened his heart to me, even though I was so interested. I am sorry to say how interested I was. I hope I am not making him sound too interesting, writing about him. Adam, reading something I had written about Brad, had an odd little grimace on his face; Adam once said—although in a completely different context and several years later—that he didn't want to be just a nice guy, although he is a nice guy; he wanted to be *mysterious.* And Bibi, dismissing Courtney, the boyfriend she had abandoned for Brad, told me she wasn't interested any more because he wasn't mysterious. He'd been mysterious before, but then she got to know him.

I want her to know she is wrong about this, as I was wrong in California. Brad is as mysterious as a face-down card. You don't know what it signifies. You don't know: that's all there is. You can pretend and imagine and interpret and think him dark and interesting, but the truth is: you know nothing about him. Turn the card over and you'd know. There's no lake to fathom; it was merely inadequate information. There was more information about him in time, of course, but not necessarily more meaningful information. No one knows why Brad did the things that he did; even he may not know. Even to himself he may be a face-down card. Adam, on the other hand, who will tell you anything about himself you want to know, to whom you can turn at any time of night and he will be sleeping; Adam, who does not keep a diary, and has no skeletons in his closet or interpretations of his childhood, and never says anything shifting ambiguous elusive paradoxical troubling; *Adam, who you might almost say has no personal history at all:* Adam is mysterious. He has the mystery of clarity. I wish I could tell Roberta how much more interesting it is.

And later, walking back, I try to picture something different, I try to imagine the joyful reunion. Bibi walks in (walks in? Where does she walk in from?) and she is so surprised to see me and Adam, she says, Melanie, what are you and Adam doing here? And I say—no, Adam says—Oh, we just wondered what you were up to—and he puts his arm around her jovially in his understated blue-jeaned way, not wanting the magnitude of his concern to be oppressive—so we thought we'd come check it out, B. In spite of his breeziness she would suddenly understand, and would exclaim, surprised, as she was always surprised that she had friends: You came all the way out here for me? Conversation stops. Do I ask her where she has been? No, maybe Adam would ask her. Uncertain, I glance up and see her face for the first time. Her eyes are black. I can't see what happened. What is she thinking? Why can't I see? They must contain a secret, the way a lake contains the secret of a drowned body. Frightened, I don't want to hear. She is going to tell me an unbearable story if I don't stop thinking about it now. I start to hum the Talking Heads song "Heaven" as loudly as I can, *"Heaven—heaven is a place—a place where nothing—nothing—ever—happens,"* and I tell myself that this will never happen, nothing more is ever going to happen because there is nothing more that can happen now. Even this many years later, as I am writing in my nice blue room with my nice flannel nightgown and my nicest friend Claudia sleeping small and blanketed just down the hall in my blue study, even now it frightens me, and I have to say once again she is dead. She is dead, and she was dead long before I ever got to California. Nothing I thought or worried or imagined matters. Roberta isn't thinking, and wasn't even then. She wasn't thinking, she was dead: dead and safe and underground where no man's hands could ever touch her again, safe in my mind, where only I could think of her in the right ways, whenever I wanted and only with love. The absoluteness of absolute elsewhere is that it is elsewhere from imagination too. It doesn't matter what you think. She was dead.

PART 4

The Third Interpretation: Vertigo

■ ■

Anyone whose goal is "something higher" must expect some day to suffer vertigo. What is vertigo? Fear of falling? Then why do we feel it even when the observation tower comes equipped with a sturdy handrail? No, vertigo is something other than the fear of falling. It is the voice of the emptiness below us which tempts and lures us, it is the desire to fall, against which, terrified, we defend ourselves.

—Milan Kundera
The Unbearable Lightness of Being

CHAPTER 1
The Decision

Dear Melani,

A distressing card, I know. Disturbing, on many levels and dimensions. Why is the fish floating upside down? Is it always that gray or is it dead?

I saw a New Yorker cartoon the other day with one admiral saying to the other admiral that more and more he saw things as gray— battleship gray, he added, but still gray. Made me wonder what kind of gray is my gray. Like—like what?

Nothing's better. Everything's worse. No one told me California had a rainy season. Nobody seems to like me and I draw further in. Getting fatter. Did I mention that before? Disgusting.

I can picture my mother holding her head over me, shaking her head. At a loss what to do, ever since I can remember. Why shouldn't she be? I'm at a loss, too.

Oh Melanie, I don't know. . . .

Still don't know where I am, what I'm doing. Wish it would come. Like a telegraph. Come home. Immediately. Come.

I guess I

I . . .

Roberta

It occurs to me, riding in the taxi from the airport to home (not even cold or hungry, but thinking I must be I am slumped so small and sick, watching the meter tick past the teens), that if this were a book it would be a sad situation, but an exciting sad situation, like a mystery-story sad situation, and I might be the heroine in the mystery story. Like Nancy Drew, for example. Mmm, not quite like Nancy Drew, but not quite as unlike Nancy Drew as it feels—not quite as completely unexciting and ungratifying. The taxi pulls up to the house, and I try to sit up a little, as she might sit up, and when I step out I try to step out tall and beautiful. I'm not doing a very good job, though, it seems to me: if the mystery story were made into a movie, they might not hire me to play the part. It worries me, that they might not hire me.

I get out and walk up the three wooden steps to our house. As I walk I say to myself: I am coming home; this is my home. What I like about thinking this, you see, is that you would never guess it. It is just one poor dark shambly house in a whole row of poor dark shambly houses in a Portuguese neighborhood not convenient to the Square, and there is nothing about it that would tell you it is any different from the other houses, except it is different: it is my house. A year ago I might have walked by it, and I never would have been able to see what would happen tonight, tall and nause-ated, stepping out of the taxicab. As I step out of the taxi I repeat our favorite phrase with its favorite prophetic pronouncement: *Things Are Not Quite What They Seem To Be.* The house I grew up in thinks it is what it seems to be. It thinks that all the things in it are very Thernstrom and labeled clearly like suitcases at the airport so they won't be taken home by the wrong people. I worry, sometimes, that my parents think I am one of the things in their house: a thing of theirs, a thing on their list of things to be appraised. I want to tell them I'm not, but I never do because I get too worried that they've already figured this out, and that they must be disappointed about it, or feel cheated—I have been so expensive in so many different ways. An expensive thing, to be sure, if not a pretty, intelligent thing. A thing that didn't pay off, that, all tallied, you could hardly call a bargain. I remember talking about it with Roberta once and in a rare moment of filial sympathy saying, "Well, I guess it's a bummer for them too, steeped in the catalog theory of life, and having it be us who arrived. I mean we could feel sorry for them, too, if we wanted."

"You can feel sorry for them," she said sarcastically. "I'm kind of busy feeling sorry for *us*—having been ordered in the first place. *Other* people's children were born, not *ordered.*"

"Me too," I said, conciliatory. "I just thought we could con-sider taking a break for a while."

"You can't take a break from your *feelings,*" she said, com-pletely seriously. It was unusual the way she could be like that, completely serious, all of the time.

Nervously I knock on the door.

Max opens the door and yells, and Don comes partway down the staircase, and Nicholas takes my suitcase. "So, how was Cali-fornia?" they ask curiously, faces all turned toward me. I blank on my lines. There are only three of them, but it seems that there are too many faces looking at me. Everything I can think of is embarrassing somehow. Anyway, was there anything to tell?

"It was okay," I manage, this familiar vagueness coming over me. It is thicker than usual though; it is difficult to speak.

"Did you learn anything new?" Nicholas asks helpfully, while Max asks about Adam and Don tells me my parents called, six times. Did I learn anything new, I wonder, did I learn anything new?

"Well, what did you do the whole time you were there?" Don prompts.

"Was it interesting?" This comes, I think, from Nicholas again.

"Did you get to see San Francisco?"

"Yes," I say, and then stop. Are San Francisco and Berkeley the same thing? Where did we buy the tea?

"How was the weather?"

"The weather," I say, "the weather in California is all right."

"Roberta didn't get found?" someone asks. I wonder momentarily if he is joking, but by the time I stop wondering, and think of something conclusive to say about California, they have already begun to drift away. I wander into the kitchen to look for something to eat. I'm not sure if I'm hungry. I don't think so, but I'm not sure.

Kim is cooking something pancakey in the kitchen, which smells like burnt milk. It is such a homey kind of disaster, the burning of milk—the thick cream bubbling, the burnt black crust. She looks up quickly, a cross little line under her short blond bangs. I smile at her, and she widens her lips in return and then says, a little hysterically, "Oh, the blintzes! You're looking at the blintzes!" Kim knows what a nice sparkly laugh she has, and giggles often. "I was trying to make this recipe, this recipe I cut out here from this magazine, and it said to put cottage cheese in it, and I thought it meant on the outside, but really they meant on the inside, so when I . . ."

Kim and Roberta had been best friends in junior high school, and then Kim decided she wanted to be something else, she wanted to be *popular,* and she started curling her hair and wearing it fluffy and barretted, and Roberta became, well, "more Roberta," as she would sometimes sign letters. Then Kim went to college and Roberta would call her on vacations and she would always be busy—going to a party or just about to go to a party or just about to go shopping for a dress to wear to the party—and Roberta would hang up abruptly in a black mood.

"Why do you keep bothering to call?" I would ask, not understanding Kim's appeal. "Of course there are problems," Roberta said thoughtfully once, "but old friends are like old coats. You know where the lumps and bumps are," she said, not explaining the rest of the analogy. Two years and a thousand parties later Kim decided she had no Real Friends and maybe it was time to give Bibi a call. And she was just about to, any month now, when what we know happened, happened. But standing there in the kitchen, wanting to stay for one more minute to watch the skim from the milk bubble over the iron skillet and spill down the stove, I wonder what to say. She doesn't want to hear about my feelings; she doesn't want to hear my consolations for her feelings, or lack of feeling. This leaves me, I realize, nothing to say to Kim.

I have nothing to say to any of them, I think. And quite coldly I think to myself—I remember exactly the way I thought it, standing there with Kim still explaining about the blintzes—that for the first time in my life I am going to be depressed. My life, I recall, made a brief protest for itself. (But what about your *plans?* Your diet? Your job, calendar, dates, resolution to exercise and practice your French and keep up your correspondence and be neat— organized—peppy—psyched? What about your poetry? Nancy Drew doesn't drop her life, no matter what's going on. She looks good all the way through; that's why she's the heroine.)

Nancy Drew, I reminded myself, has *nothing whatsoever to do with it.* Nancy Drew doesn't *care* about the missing people in the mystery. That's what makes those stories what they are. It changes everything, once you care. And then I apologized briefly, and explained that I understand the importance of all those things. I really have tried to keep up on them, all my life, and not just drop them for emotional reasons. I would if I could, I explained, go on in just the fashion I have been doing all this time, but then, suddenly worried I would not be allowed to drop anything, even for a moment, I screech: BUT IT CAN'T BE DONE ANYMORE. It just can't be done. I mean, I can't do it anymore, and besides, I'm not going to. It was funny, I had wanted and needed and hoped and longed and thought about it for so long—always, actually—but there had never been a good enough reason to disregard all the other good reasons on the eternal list of things to be done. Now, finally, it was going to happen. I was almost pleased.

CHAPTER 2
Strangers

Between Halloween and Thanksgiving, Bibi began to
reflect some concern with what she was going to do with
her life. She dropped out ... Their relationship was still
very much up in the air on November 4th. There had been
incidents of jealousy, each saw other people; nothing was
settled.

At five o'clock, the previous spring of sophomore year, on
the day on which housing cards are due, I find I have not
turned anything in. I stare at the clock until five-fifteen
and then call Bob up, miserable.

"Look, Melanie," he says, "you've been wanting to take
time off from school all year. So good, you're going to do it.
I'm excited."

"But—but I'm *frightened.*"

"Frightened of what, exactly?" he asks impatiently.

"Something terrible happening?"

"Like?"

"I don't know. Like, you know the way you feel—like
there's something scary going on but you don't know exactly what—or rather there would be something scary going
on if you weren't a privileged-in-school person, which makes
it sort of improbable that something scary is really going
on. But once I'm not in school ..."

"What?"

"Then I could—"

"Yes?"

"Fall into the indifferent abyss."

"There's no indifferent abyss," he says definitively. "That's not real life, that's literature. Real life is getting up in the morning and having breakfast and driving to work like everybody else. Maybe you just don't know enough about real life. You've been imagining it too long, hon."

"Do you think that's the only problem?" I ask hopefully, because I love it when people distinguish life from literature for me.

"Well, I didn't say that's your *only* problem," he laughs. "But, yes, I do think that's a problem."

I nod into the phone again.

Dear Melanie,

This semester will probably finish me off for good. I'm assistant cook one night a week and have to clean up after lunch once a week, plus all my courses, volunteer work, dance class and the Marx-Freud-Nietzsche triple threat.

A crummy week. I liked these two men, but one turned out to be rotten and I could tell the other was also bad news—some mid-life Italian who kept trying to put his hands up my skirt. I met a boy last week, but who knows. I was out in the rain this morning so long the dye in my blue boots turned my feet blue. There was a poem I read about an abortion a long time ago; in the last line the man says: ''come out of the rain baby/your socks are turning blue.''

Love,
Roberta

The five of us are sitting at the kitchen table in the lamplight, darkness already fallen outside, eating macaroni and cheese. Max has made it because it is his night to cook, and it is not very good. He must have tried hard: there are recipe books scattered all over the kitchen, and at one point he had come upstairs and asked me sweetly whether bubbling water was the same as boiling water. I had cooked last night with the cookbook I baked from when I was a little girl. My mother, who is a wonderful cook and makes exactly the kind of food that the family likes to eat, would let me make pies for my father. He was always so happy to come home from work and find I had made a pie for dinner; I would think all afternoon about how happy he was going to be. When it was my turn to cook last night I made a shepherd's pie. The recipe had a wonderful little pen-and-ink illustration below it of a shepherd's cottage with shepherd's pie in it being eaten by a shepherd. Nobody seemed to like it much, though, or to take into account the illustration. Nicholas makes hot salads and bok choy and sprouts in the wok and Don makes *boeuf bourguignon* and French things painstakingly directed by Julia Child, and he is inevitably in a lousy mood about them long before they are ready. Kim has the predictable flair for whipping up nifty concoctions—pineapple Jell-O and Bisquick bake and the like—perhaps cut out from *Good Housekeeping*, perhaps intuited naturally. It's funny that no one cooks what anybody else likes to eat. It's curious, too, we are all so unhappy. If I described us briefly you wouldn't think it would be so.

I am the only one not in school at Harvard this year. Max and Nicholas are seniors: Nicholas is half-Japanese and a social studies major. He is talented at music, and already has an album out and a number of other accomplishments, and is concerned about the welfare of the world. Max is a Jewish English major from Connecticut who is applying to teach at private schools next year and makes self-deprecating jokes, and his older brother DeWitt is Adam's roommate and also a good friend of mine. Once a month he comes out of his room in a good mood and is incredibly funny, and the rest of the time he broods. Don is from an Irish-Catholic family in a small town in New Hampshire and graduated last year in art history and is now taking organic chemistry because even though it is quite clear to everyone else that he has no interest in medicine, it is not clear to his parents. He has lovely curly red hair, and he lights his cigarettes at the kitchen stove because he never has matches, and he knows a lot of women. He likes heavy-metal music; there are pictures of Jimi Hendrix scattered all over his room. Earnestness, one discovers eventually, is not within his emotional range. He once found a rare Rolling Stones album in my bedroom that Adam had given me, and looked at me, for the only time, with clear, impressed open-eyed attentiveness as he asked: "Wherever did you get that, Melanie? That's a good album!"

Kim is a junior studying history and thinking maybe of architecture, and she draws and dances and sails and plays tennis and squash and likes to travel and has an amazing sweater collection.

She is pretty and petite—not beautiful, which would be too serious anyway. She is neither stupid nor unappealingly vain, yet
there is something about her that utterly precludes intimacy. I was
once with my friend Jerry when we bumped into her. We talked
for three or four minutes, and I agreed to pick her up somewhere
later. As soon as she walked away Jerry said, "You shouldn't be
friends with that girl." I stared at him because Kim always makes
such a good first impression, and he said, "She doesn't like you."
When I tried to ask what he meant and how he knew—it had been
a lively conversation, a friendly conversation: she asked me to do
her a favor and I agreed—he shrugged. "It was obvious. I mean
just that, and I know because I'm your friend—because I like
you." And when I told my friend Mary Rose that Kim and I were
roommates she said, "Oh, *Kimberly Taylor has no soul.*"

And this remark—this unfair unjustified cruel cheap remark,
which is definitively untrue: of course she has a soul—nevertheless occurs to me every time I see Kim, sitting across the dinner
table from me just now in her blue and white Fair Isle cardigan
with the snowdrop flower pattern and freshwater pearls, chatting
earnestly with Don about how new-wave music is not really that
new anymore. "Guess I missed it," I say when they attempt to
include me in the conversation. "Is Elvis Costello new wave?"

There is an awkward pause: people say little things to break it
up. Everyone does have a soul, of course. I take another forkful of
macaroni. All right, I say to myself, we are trying. You'll have a
real family, maybe another day. Goodness—eat your dinner.

■ ■

"You know it could have happened to anyone," Nicholas says out
of the blue at lunch one day. I know what he is referring to, but
I pick up the paper and study the state of the deficit. He asks
knowingly if I would like to see Miss Manners, but I tell him no, I
am reading this. It could not have happened to anyone, I recall: it
happened because she grew up, as I grew up. I stare at the financial
column. My eyes hurt. I get a Kleenex from the bathroom. But on
the way I can't remember what it had to do with growing up, and I
sit down again.

Well, *to begin with*, if she had been a child she wouldn't have
gone to the forest with him. Children live within the circle of tightly
held hands that is their family; it is grownups who have been cast

outside that circle and have to make the best of strangers. And if the stranger prefers the company of a blonde or has a pressing engagement at the Exploratorium there is nothing one can do. One has to find another stranger to take one home, and hope that he is, indeed, inclined to go.

Children are taken by strangers sometimes too. Look at all the pictures of children on the subway.

Well, of course, *sometimes,* but only when they *slip out of that ring and everybody is very sorry and very very surprised*—only when they *accidentally* slip. It does not happen because they handed themselves over. Besides, when strangers take them they do not do the same things to them; and if they do the child does not understand. They are frightened; they are hungry and thirsty and feel pain and wonder why they are not given juice or allowed to pee, but they do not understand as Roberta understands. It is not informed suffering, darkness confirmed. They have nothing by which to interpret it. It is merely the darkness of another good-night, which they have no way of knowing is a final good-night because they have no way of knowing what finality is made of. It is sad and nothing besides sad; it is not personal. It is just sad.

But just because she wasn't a child, I remind myself, doesn't mean it had to be Roberta. There are millions of young women; he only happened to pick her. He didn't know who she was—he picked her because she was pretty, probably, and golden-shouldered. And although she was pretty, so are a million other people. Becky Evers, for example, is very pretty. If Becky Evers had gone to Berkeley, and had been standing by the side of the road on the way back from some eternal club meeting, wearing a short skirt and a high ponytail and the smile you could cut out of your high school yearbook, he would have picked her up too.

But if he had picked up Becky it would not have meant the same things. Becky would have been planning to be somebody's well-dressed wife; instead she would be dead. It would be a random thing—an *accident,* an incident. No reflection on Becky. A sad incident, of course, for everybody concerned, but incidents do not make a way of thinking, and incidental darkness is not our darkness.

But the man did not know Roberta: the man did not know what she was thinking, the man does not know what you know: *the man was a stranger.*

If indeed he was a stranger, as they say he is a stranger, he is not that strange: he is not strange enough.

■ ■

"You know it wouldn't be so bad," I say to Bob on the phone later that night, "if it had been an accident. A car accident, for example, would not be nearly as bad."

"A car accident," he repeats incredulously. "I've been thinking for a while that you vastly underestimate the amount it would hurt if she were killed another way. I wish you'd think more about the fact that what's scary is not the neat dark way this all kind of fits together, but the fact that you might never get to have lunch with her again." He pauses in case I want to say something, and when I don't he goes on in his characteristic frustrated almost-annoyed tone. I know I am allowed to interrupt and ask if he cares, and if that's why he's being so mean, or if there is *another* reason—a meaner reason—and although he will probably not answer, he will change his tone. But because I know I can—I know that that was what his pause meant—I let him go on.

"You sound as if you think it's the *significance* or the *symbolism* of the events which is so disturbing. *Ugh,*" he says. "That part is so unimportant. You talk as if the whole thing is only as meaningful as the interesting interpretations you can turn it into, when the issue is so obviously lunch. People are so much more serious than interpretation. You'll miss her company. You would miss it if she were killed in an accident just as much as if she were murdered. Who cares how? What if your friend Bibi won't meet you at Café Algiers anytime soon, or ever? Concentrate on that fact for a while 'cause it's a shitty one, but not shitty in the way that you're feeling now. What I'm saying is, concentrate on Bibi a little more."

"But," I ask, hesitating, "but do you think that's how Roberta would see it? Don't you think she would think about it exactly the way I do?"

"I don't know," he says. "Maybe she would." And then, his conviction returning—the confidence, perhaps, that he has a nicer turn of phrase than I have, and therefore owns always the last word: "But then again, maybe she'd be wrong."

■ ■

An accident, I say to myself in the darkness of my room later that night. *A car accident.* Like the girl who died prom night at our high school—just like that. Sad, but not more than sad. What was her name? Ginnie? Annabel?

Not a metaphor: a mistake. *A mistake.* An unmetaphorical mistake.

The darkness is not impressed. I sit down at my desk. Writing is impressive. Hunched over, the splinters of the stained wood showing through the paper, my elbows hurting, I print out as heavily as I can with my black ink pen:

A car accident. Like—

Like when you're driving
along a dark highway late at night
because it is late and the highway
is dark and you know you are going too fast because
you are going too fast and you close your eyes, and wait, sudden,
to hear
the splintering of glass
the rush of blood
in approach of quiet

Only, I think looking up, only not quite like that. And I add the last line, discarding the pen:

Only more personal.

■ ■

I go to visit my friend Michael in Central Square. Intimidated by the maze of one-way streets and spotting an easy parking place, I decide to park and walk the five blocks to his house. I don't leave until almost one a.m., and as he stands at the door bidding me good night I feel an uncommon fear. Since I am not in school now, I think to myself, things can happen. And even though I know it's a foolish distinction, I ask him to walk me to my car. As soon as we reach it, he says see ya and turns away. I almost call after him, Wait, I'll give you a ride, but suddenly shy, I watch him walk away. On the way home two men hold a butcher knife to his throat and strip him of his gold watch and a hundred dollars. The next day he shows me the slice where the knife pressed slightly too hard. The men were crouched behind a car at the end of his street; they must have watched us walk by.

■ ■

Today, Pete and Scott (and Brad was going to come but he decided not to) took me to an odd little town called Bolinas in Marin which hides its signs (really—they don't want anyone to be able to find them). We went to the beach; I met two men who were nude. One stared at Scott, and his friend came over to me. I was amazed at his poise, seeing that he had no clothing on. These totally laid-back and laid out Californians—blond looks and blank eyes—are full of shit, you know?

I find myself at a party one night. It is dark and because I am not smoking, I am dancing. I am dancing with a bunch of people, but then the song ends and another starts and I am dancing with one person. The music softens to slow dancing—*It's those restless hearts,* someone sings, *which never mend*—and he puts his arms around me, and we slow-dance too. And then it is late and the night is over so he walks me home because I am a woman and cannot walk home alone. We stand at the steps of my door and he wants to know if he can see me again. *He is trying to pick me up:* the phrase floats into my mind like a piece of stray music from the party. To pick up, to be picked up. He picked her up after a party, I think, listening and missing Adam vaguely. But she invited him in. She did invite him in, though. Don't forget who invited whom into their apartment. I close the door and lean against it heavily. I found out later his name was Chris, and he was one of Don's old roommates and Bob's little sister's freshman outdoor program leader, and his father had died recently of cancer, and he was doubtless very very nice. I don't know, though; I never returned his phone calls.

■ ■

Dear Melanie,

More love troubles. What else? I was mooning after one fellow, who was, after all, an asshole. Then there was an older guy, even worse, from Australia, who foisted himself on me and my bed and now I've got

*to give him the heave-ho before I get completely ground down. Don't
trust 31-year-olds who like 20-year-olds. That's like me going after a
seven-year-old. Shit, maybe it would finally work out, ar ar ar.*

*Hallo! A message from Marcellus, my bear. Such a pretty bear.
And his accent is nice too.*

*Don't worry about me and Courtney the Fictional (the boy with
the drop-dead blue eyes). I threw the idea out along with some papers
on my desk. How trivial I am.*

*Love,
B.B.*

"Did you call Danny back?" Nicholas asks at the kitchen table one
afternoon. I shake my head.

"Well, that must be why he called three times this afternoon
while I was trying to study."

"Yeah," I say, looking at the pear I am holding and turning it
so it catches the light. Pear-light, I think: round.

"I told him you already had his number, but he left it anyway."

"Which is why I made sure to give you the message yesterday
so you'd have time to get back to him before he calls back today,"
Nicholas continues.

"Yeah," I say, wondering where Adam is.

"Yeah," says Nicholas. "Shall I pass that friendly little message
along? I mean if you don't want to talk to anyone anymore then
fine I won't take any more messages—it won't break my heart,
believe me; her whereabouts are unknown, I'll tell all callers—but
if you want me to keep writing their names down then I think you
should call people back. Everyone who calls you, you should call
back—but especially Danny. Danny is a *nice* guy. And Oliver. It's
rude not to call people back.

"Within the time frame they called you," he adds.

"Mmhmm," I say.

"You shouldn't be afraid of sex," he says.

I look down at my plate, hating him. "Fuck off, Nicholas," I
say, "I just don't want to talk to them."

■ ■

Dear Melanie,

   In RESPONSE to your letter:

A. *Gregory, the nervous, self-absorbed actor—I don't know I guess he wasn't so cool after all. Right?*
B. *Forget B. Why B?*
C. *Guilt with or about or around Ross. Don't feel guilty.*
D. *Drugs. Don't do drugs.*
E. *I thought about your dilemma over your hair: I don't think you should cut it ALL off. But shorten it; maybe eight or nine inches. You do depend on it, your friend Abby is right. But if you get your hair cut very short, you would be just like everyone else. So don't do that. The extreme length of your hair is the crutch.*
Am I becoming a dullard? Then I shall be off.

                      Blessings,
                      Rosamunde

I am driving painstakingly along some twisted streets in Central Square. It is late afternoon, gray is falling. In sudden strange elation I put my foot on the gas, and the car sails forward beneath me. I see the other car coming, but I can't do anything and the moment is such a large moment I relax into it and think how curious that now, after all this time, when I was not thinking about it at all, it is happening. The wonderful thing is that I cannot change my mind, there are no negotiations or deliberations, it is happening, finally happening, and there is no anguish. The anguish, I suddenly realize, must have come from having thought about it so long beforehand—from the late long nights of trying to divine the opaque and undivinable. If I had known this then, I think, I would never have bothered. I remember how my grandmother told me that in the middle of her operation, when they thought she would die, she realized suddenly: So all those papers on my desk don't matter anymore. And I remember how when she told me, I thought, No, I will never feel that, my papers *do* matter, they will never in this life not matter. I have to finish them, I have to sort them, I have to worry about what will happen to them, into whose hands they will fall and for what purposes they might be read and misread. I have to get them right, so no one will think I am someone else, and I have to make them interesting, so they won't get bored halfway through and quit and be left with incom-

plete information forever. Yet even this problem of misreading—
the one thing I never thought I would feel differently about—I do
feel differently about because it is such a long moment, the space
between knowing it will happen and having it happen, that there
is so much time to think and to change. Let go. Things will change
in a moment anyway, you might as well let go of the old orderings
before they smash apart. I wonder, vaguely, if I have ever had a
moment long enough to change in before now. And then the cars
collide.

But after the sound of glass breaking, after the screech and the
door crumpling in and the coming-to-rest sound, after all this, I am
still there. I am slumped in my seat, the seatbelt tight around me,
just as it was before, and the man in the other car is getting out
stiffly and walking toward me, and a policeman is walking with
him. The radio is still on, and the sweet seductive voice of Madonna
coos, calling, and I am listening. It is annoying; I am annoyed at
myself, almost, but it is no use: the strand of tune is playing itself
out, small and complex, meshed and woven, suggestive of something, maybe of love; if you follow you will understand, maybe or
almost, follow I am following, her voice is so interesting: what I
mean is I am so very interested.

■ ■

The latest on the emotional rollercoaster: There was a T.A. I had
last year, one of the best I ever had, very intelligent and good-looking.
I had the feeling he was attracted to me, too, there was definitely some
tension there. After all this build-up, two weeks ago we went out and
he turned out to be a chump, rather cruel and very manipulative. So
now I have to avoid him, which I do by not going to campus and miss-
ing all my classes. Why is this true of so many people? You scratch the
surface and all the polish comes off—underneath is junk.

Don comes into the kitchen as I am sitting at the table. How's it
going? he says, and tells me his organic chemistry test was a
bummer. Pity, I say. Pity, too, I could say, that my best friend may
have been murdered or raped or strangled or cut into little pieces
and hidden in a box somewhere, which we haven't found yet—not
even the box. And then Don would say something back, but
sooner or later he would have to say, well, better make this
sandwich now, or get back to my organic, or nice talking to you

Melanie, though not that nice, given, you know, the subject. I get up and ask if he would like me to make him a sandwich. He nods okay.

■ ■

Nicholas is on his way home from South Boston. He is stopped by a gang of Chicano men, who pull up in a car and strip him of his backpack. It contained his wallet and some material from his thesis on Haitian refugees and two Widener Library books for which he has to pay a hundred-dollar penalty apiece. He tries to explain to the library that it wasn't his fault, and he shouldn't have to pay a penalty as well as the price of the books, because there was nothing he could do about it—they were *stolen*—but explanations changed nothing, of course. They aren't charging him because they thought it was his fault, but because the books are gone. They are the same: losses, thefts, carelessness, misplacements or misunderstandings, the cost is the same.

■ ■

I think everyone agrees (don't they) that there are correct ways for dealing with rejection, but I can't seem to find or follow any of them. Certainly, you're not supposed to lose your pride and your dignity and call them up yet again with a plaintive "Hi how are ya" when they ("they, they" I mean "he," the Bearboy with the bear just like Marcellus— you remember my telling you about him?) when he hasn't been calling me back, or calling me first, or calling me at all. How much are you supposed to humiliate yourself? I mean, Jesus. But if I don't call him does that somehow get me any further? Who's keeping points in this game, and why do I care? Heads you win, tails I lose. I have to face the possibility that he simply doesn't like me. That hurts.

I am driving to my job as a security guard in Burlington. Although it is my fifth night on the job I am lost and I stop at a gas station to ask directions. It turns out to be self-service, however, so there is no attendant to ask. Standing by the pump, squinting his eyes as if trying to read the price, is a man filling a small truck. He is wearing a red-checked flannel shirt that hangs loosely over his faded blue jeans, and since Adam and Daddy dress like that I decide he is a Regular Guy. A Regular Guy is a nice guy—he works hard at some

job to save for a ring for his high school girlfriend, Sandy. He and
Sandy are good to each other. It's not a complicated thing: they
watch television in the evenings and they don't play mind games
or have talks that last forever. Television is important. In our
household it was long ago determined that television is a waste of
time (the term my parents use is *mindless*—as in "*mindless stupidity*"). And since no one ever has time to waste—not even on
holidays, not even if one were very sick, since there are always
Russian novels—we didn't watch much television. We do have a
token set, but it is in my parents' bedroom, so if you want to watch
anything, you also have to listen to them making fun of whatever
you're watching and asking whether you don't have anything
better to do. And of course it has to be off by nine-thirty, which
consistently eliminates *David Letterman*, which is the only show I
really like anyway. They're not actually going to sleep at nine-
thirty, but they're settling in, maybe doing a little reading—they
don't have to have specific reasons, *they don't want you in there*,
turning up the volume. In the Regular Guy's family there is a
special room called the television room. It is downstairs and it has
plum-colored wall-to-wall carpeting and they all sit there together
every evening and nobody thinks about whether it is a waste of time
because they have time. They can watch anything they want whenever they want because *no one is that busy*. I wonder what it would
be like to have plenty of time and not to be busy all of your life.

The man comes closer, however, and I realize that I have
misplaced him. There is something wrong with his blue eyes: the
whites glint too much, and roll upward slightly. But I have already
started to smile warmly, in preparation for the other family, and it
seems too late to take it back because I do not want to hurt his
feelings and I do not want to be wrong. So I roll down the window
and ask him if he knows how to get to the job. He does, he tells
me, and wants to know where exactly I am going. I tell him the
name of the company and he asks what I am going to do there in
the middle of the night. I explain that I am the security guard.

"You work alone?" He sticks his hands in his pockets and
spreads his legs a little. I willfully ignore the fact that the question
is not that casual.

"Oh yes," I tell him blithely. "But it doesn't bother me. I
mean actually I chose the midnight shift specially so I wouldn't
have to have other people around—no noise and bother and dis-
traction and such. It's good; it's quiet. I like it."

I hardly dare look up. "And it's not really lonely—I like working alone." I try to smile, thinking perhaps if I look more like Sandy he will recall his role and begin to be nice to me. Like he might help me find the place.

"I hope I'll be able to follow your directions. I'm horrible at finding things," I say. When I first got my driver's license my friend Steven said he didn't really see the point since knowing how to steer is only half of it—knowing where to steer *to* is the rest. He wanted to go along when I took my driving test so he could sit in the back seat and laugh at me, but I wouldn't invite him.

I look up, hopeful, but his eyes are still glinty.

"I'll tell you what," the man says. "I'll get in the car with you and help you find it, and my buddy over there will follow behind in the truck. That way you'll be sure to get there safely."

"Thanks, but—" The dialogue is over. I press the button that rolls up the window, as his hand reaches for the car door. Mercifully it is an up-to-date car, so the doors lock with just one button. I jab my finger at it and put my foot on the gas. As I drive away his truck comes roaring up and passes me and zooms down the road. I turn around and go home, and call the security company from our brown-flowered tablecloth on our table in our nice red and white kitchen. The man who answers is not concerned.

■ ■

The winter night is iced over; I am driving back to my parents' home. It is taking so long it is painful and absurd; I steer the car over the ice carefully, braking all the time, but it occurs to me, sudden and clear as the cold I am breathing, *I will never get home.* It is too far away; this is not the right way, you will never get there, you will never get home. And I stop braking, just for this moment, less than a moment perhaps, and the car slides over the ice and into the web of brambles and berries waiting, bright and dark, at the side of the road.

■ ■

I wake up several times that night—cold, dreaming shallowly, conscious in each dream that it is only a dream, and tasting greedily the thinness of the illusion. Toward dawn I get up and go over to the phonograph. I riffle through the pile of records, searching, and finally find an old tape of Crosby, Stills, Nash and Young. It is the third song on the second side. The familiar high wailing sound fills the room with horrible haunted lyrics, the voice so slow every word is distinct. *And in my mind I still need a place to go . . . The chains are locked across the door.* I listen, huddled in my nightgown on the mauve rug in the thick light of the slanted attic room, three flights above where the others sleep. The rest of the tape is filled with pleasant songs about love and summer breezes and pentagrams and Guinnevere in her garden. And then there is "Helpless." Who wrote it? Why do they repeat the word *helpless* so many times, and why does it arise from their memory of the lost place— that chained door like the childhood of a relative who died before you had a chance to ask them what it was like? I wonder what the singer was thinking of as he sang. The name of the album is *Déjà Vu.* I listen to it again, trying to count the number of times the voice sings that one word—*helpless*—but there are too many.

■ ■

I met a girl who met a man who met someone who knows THE BEARBOY. (I know you haven't forgotten.) She says he's sweet and sincere and she was really surprised when she found out he goes with this space cadet of a Valley Girl. I say: Say what? So that's the answer. It's nothing mysterious, no Big Question about the nature of my soul, my infinite unlikability, no—he's a nice guy who digs blondes who hold on to his arm and listen to what he says. That's it. That does it. That's the reason. I'm just not glittery and golden enough. How flattering. And I still feel this pathetic longing for the chump. Melanie, please tell me (write right away): when will I learn?
    Troubles, troubles, troubles said the oyster to the clam . . .
    Miracles are not/ Worth waiting for.

■ ■

It is late afternoon and I am tired and it is already clear that I am not going to be able to go to sleep that night, certainly not early, maybe not before morning. Someone wrote me a prescription for sleeping pills once, which I never filled; I think about walking to the drugstore to buy some, but I already know what the man at the counter will think. A young woman, you wouldn't think something would be wrong, but something is wrong. Look at her face—

the flesh under her eyes, thin and blue, the softness of her voice. I wonder what is wrong. You won't find out what is wrong, though, until many scenes later, but since you have already seen this sort of movie and read this sort of book you know what the last scene looks like, and since she has read it too—since she knows it, in fact, so well that she is writing it—you wonder why she doesn't just go ahead and buy more than one bottle.

PART 5

The Last Interpretation: The Little Match Girl

■■

It was terribly cold. . . . Soon it would be quite dark; for it was the last day of the year. . . . Along the streets, in the same cold and dark, went a poor little girl in bare feet . . . simply blue with cold. The snowflakes settled on her long flaxen hair, . . . lights were shining in every window, and out into the street came the lovely smell of roast goose. . . . She only got colder and colder. She didn't dare go home, for she hadn't sold a single match nor earned a single penny. . . . Ah, but a little match—that would be a comfort. If only she dared pull one out of the bunch, just one. . . .

—Hans Christian Andersen
"The Little Match-Seller"

CHAPTER 1

Wounds

Nicholas is sitting up straight on the couch when I come down to breakfast one morning. His face is very stiff.

"Caroline Isenberg has been murdered," he says.

"Caroline?" I say. "You mean Caroline with the red hair?" The whole existence of the girl that I used to have breakfast with freshman year, and who would take me to different houses so I could meet upperclassmen—whom I was never really friends with, but I was almost friends with, suddenly depends upon her red hair.

"Caroline Isenberg," he repeats, and hands me a newspaper. The photograph, in black and white, her hair in tones of gray, shows that it is indeed Caroline. I think how I hate it when people from my high school ask: "Bibi Lee—the runner?"

"What happened?"

"She was murdered." His voice is very flat.

"By . . . whom?"

"Some man," he says, throwing down the paper.

"Who?" I ask again.

"I don't know."

"But did she know him?"

"NO," he shouts, "it was a stranger. Would she be likely to know someone who would murder her?" His voice breaks.

"I'm sorry," I say, and offer him my hand. He takes it, trembling. I come around and put my arms around him. This seems to be the right thing to do. I remember the last time I saw Caroline. It was in the summer and Nicholas and I were having coffee at an outside table in the Square, and she waved to us and then came over. She was wearing a black sundress with a tight ribbed bodice and little red flowers, and she looked plump and white-skinned. She had fair very creamy skin. It was a good August for sundresses. She told us she was moving to New York to go to acting school in the fall. She looked at Nicholas most of the time when she talked, since we might have been friends, but had not turned out to be friends. Nicholas said acting school, and she laughed and said stardom, fame and fortune, and curtsied, quickly. She and someone called Susan were going to live together, and Susan's mother had found them jobs waitressing.

"Where?" Nicholas asked.

"Buddy's," she said, in a deep male tone, in imitation of the way a man called Buddy might pronounce his name, and laughed again. As she laughed she pushed back her straight red hair, coiling it behind her ears. But since her hair was shoulder length it fell immediately forward again. For some reason I remember wishing it were thicker so that it would stay back.

I ask Nicholas if he wants to tell me what happened. I know what has happened, of course, from looking at the newspaper article, but I don't know what to ask. Horror is so specific. I babysat once for a little girl who could not go to sleep because she had seen a horror movie on television. I had read the whole time because I don't like horror movies. Finally I sat her down on my lap and asked her what was so frightening. "The *movie!*" she sobbed. "But what about the movie?" I asked, realizing that she could not be crying about the whole thing, because there must have been too many different scary moments in it to be scared by them all at once. "Are you sure you won't be scared?" she asked, looking up from her tears. I said yes, and she whispered in my ear that—it was when—and stopped and asked me again if I was sure it was all right to tell, and I said I was very sure, and she told me the man had stuck a knife between the woman's legs. "That is horrible!" I said, but somehow it didn't matter anymore what I said. She slid off my lap, yawning, and toddled back to bed.

"Caroline was in Lowell House when I first moved in," Nicholas begins in a low tone. "I didn't know many people, and it was kind of—you know, lonely, Mel. And she was nice to me. So we kind of went out for a while. . . . I mean we never . . . but . . ."

I nod to tell him I understand and he goes on.

"And then we stopped seeing each other.

"Some man was waiting in the elevator of her building when she came home at night. And he took her up to the roof to rape her, and she struggled to get away and he stabbed her. All the while she was screaming. Somebody finally called the police, but the man got away. While he was stabbing her she was screaming to the police: 'It's me, Caroline, I'm over here,' while they were looking on the wrong rooftop. 'He's stabbing me! I'm being killed!' She lived for six hours in the hospital, and they thought she was going to make it, but they couldn't control the bleeding. She bled to death in the morning.

"He stabbed her eight times—eight. He stuck a knife in her flesh eight times because she wouldn't let him rape her. . . . My—my memories of Caroline are so physical."

I know what he is trying to tell me: he had not slept with her and they had stopped seeing each other, and this stranger, who had also wanted to sleep with her, had stabbed her. There is nothing for me to say, so I try to pat his hair. Four weeks ago Roberta disappeared. He reaches out and rests his fingers momentarily on my stomach, lightly, tentatively, the way you would with a pregnant woman, as if afraid it will hurt me. It doesn't hurt, of course, but I almost recoil from surprise. I realize in time, though, how important it is not to withdraw. He looks at me in wonder and gratitude: the wonder, I suppose, of intactness: the wonder that I am still so intact.

CHAPTER 2
The Rock of Loss

Dear Melanie,

I've finally put this stupid and trivial relationship behind me. The only question is why it took so long. To make short of a long story (can you say that? after you study linguistics you're not sure anything you say is correct)—anyway, to make it brief, we were supposed to go out for dinner and he was going to call me about the day and then he never called. So I told him etc. etc. It's all over and well behind me. I say, no more of these types. Avaunt!

But one mustn't gloat over meaningless victories; after all, where does this leave me?

For one thing, further behind in my work than ever. ''Catch-up'' (which is my new name for ''work'') is hopeless. I hate work, but (curious) I hate not working too. So why not work?

Y naught?

And another: the Bradley story. ''Chain, chain, chain—chain of fools.'' He likes me, he likes me not, who knows what he thinks and what I think of that, blah blah the old pattern, more emotional roller-coasters invented by Yours Truly for her own dubious amusement. Met his Mother and Father, very white, very upper-this and that, divorced, calm and aspiring to upperer and calmer levels of high-California bland-ness. Rather unsimilar to me and my tribe.

Ick, I smell like onions. Vidalia onions, my roommate Felicia just received a whole box of Vidalia onions from the Deep South. She claims they can be eaten like apples, but (I know this for a fact) it's not true. So now our whole room smells oniony. Felicia is spoiled rotten.

I went to this really faaabulous used clothing shop in Berkeley and bought some old silvery things—something old and something new, something borrowed and something blue. What occasion is that auspicious for? Marriage, she says, wrinkling her nose. Ick!

Got a nice letter from your mother today to the effect that I should not keep going out with slobs. So it's official. No more slobs.

I went on two ten-mile runs this week and then this afternoon I went to a birthday party for the Buddha. He was very old. There were balloons and flowers and cake with icing. Happy Birthday, dear Buddha.

And he probably didn't even know I cared.

And now it is time for dinner! More hand-to-mouth action. Some uncontrolled face-stuffing should calm me down.

I liked writing this letter. I hope you liked reading it; at least the paper is rather lovely, thick and tea-colored and stripey too. I'd love to get one back soon. Take care of yourself and I'll try to do the same. Expect presents. How does the Desiderata end? Do not distress yourself with imaginings (who me?). Many fears are born of fatigue and loneliness. Be careful. Strive to be happy.

> *Love among the ruins,*
> *Bibi*

"Well, I guess I'd better go," Nicholas says some hours later, looking at his watch, then staring at me miserably as if waiting for something. He picks up his backpack, but doesn't gather the books that go in it from the floor.

"Where are you going?" I ask helpfully, after a minute.

"To try to find some appropriate way of mourning for Caroline," he says dubiously. He puts the pack on his shoulder, shrugging a little, the movement almost jaunty, and it seems to me I have never seen anything so brave before. Nicholas, small Nicholas, who is only five feet three and whose child's body you can still see, though developed now, muscular, and who took on burdens when he was small—big burdens, the burden of his whole life—getting into Harvard and taking out loans and working his way through, word-processing and security-guarding, and getting good grades and writing music and making a record and volunteering at a food shelter and heading the Haitian refugee committee and

directing a show and writing a thesis, but who is still a child—small
and orphaned and unloved—with no more resources than he ever
had to change that, or he would have already. He has changed
everything, but he has not changed his orphanedness. Fifteen-
odd years removed from his childhood, he stands here in the living
room with the old childhood desolation, looking at his watch and
thinking with grownup thoughts that it is time to walk away
because he has always walked away because it is better to do
something than to cry. And although he does not know what it is
you're supposed to do about mourning he still picks up his empty
backpack.

I get up from the empty couch. I clear up Nicholas's breakfast
dishes—there is only a cup and a saucer and a fork. I put them in
the dishwasher, and then take them out and wash them by hand.
The sponge is large and yellow; I pour too much soap in it, and it
foams nice and too full. The hot water splashes out clean; I dry the
dishes quickly, with a faded blue dishtowel that is also very clean. I
adjust the blue shawl on the living room armchair; it is always
slipping down.

The phone rings and it is my mother. How are you? she says.
How are you? Did you hear about Caroline Isenberg? So-and-so
who works with her father called—he called and talked for a
whole hour, he was so upset and he didn't even know her. Did
you know her? You didn't know her, did you?

"Yes," I say, stumbling, "I mean—not really."

"Did you? I didn't know that you knew her at all! You
weren't in the same circles at school! She was an actress, I thought.
Was she in the Signet? How are you feeling about it? It's a terrible
thing. *Terrible*. How are you feeling?"

The particular confusion I often feel when I talk to my mother
begins to set in. There is a pause, and in the pause I somehow
forget what I am supposed to say. She has told me it is a terrible
thing. It is a terrible thing. Am I permitted to just agree, I wonder;
does agreement constitute something to say?

"How are you feeling about it?" she asks again, trying to be
helpful, but still waiting.

"I'm concerned about you," she says. There is another little
silence. She sounds concerned. What am I supposed to say? She
is—I think—she is concerned because of my feelings, because of
how she thinks I might be feeling.

I would be feeling, of course, that this is a terrible thing.

Because it is terrible. *Terrible.* I start to tell her I am feeling terrible and then stop. It's a queer thing with my mother, but for some reason it's as if we can't both have emotions at the same time. Some mothers never talk to their daughters; she wants to be able to talk: to share our feelings. This is a nice thing; her intentions are fine. As soon as she asks me anything personal, however, I always panic, and it suddenly seems as if I might have no feelings. I've heard of such people. I've even heard my mother talk about them. *Empty-handed, empty-hearted. Her heart was made of sawdust. He had no emotions.* He didn't really care; he didn't care about anything besides himself. *You talk to them awhile and you find out there's nothing there.* Nothing there; there's just nothing there.

"I have to go, Mummy," I say, and hang up before she has a chance to ask me where I have to go, and how it could be more important than what I am feeling—if I am feeling anything, that is, if I have any feelings.

I move the shawl from the armchair to the couch. You can see it better there, and besides it may not slip down so often. The shawl is a certain shade of blue—flat, not navy, but not pastel—a French blue; the couch is dark brown. I am not sure about that— French blue and dark brown. I had a dress once of brown and blue; some people can wear those kinds of colors. I gave it away. There is my room, of course, which could be vacuumed. I think for a while about whether to vacuum or to dust. Kim will probably come home eventually, and we could make dinner together. I could write some letters, make some phone calls, go to a dance class. I could work on my poetry, read, be sad. I could be sad.

(*You don't seem to be sad.*)

I am sad.

(What are you doing about being sad? You haven't cried much. Why haven't you cried? What are you going to do all afternoon?)

At four I call Bob. "Bob, I'm so upset," I say, getting upset. "I mean I'm not so upset—I mean my mother called, and she wanted to know how I was feeling—how I was really feeling—and it was like *I didn't have anything to say.* My best friend is missing, a girl I know has been stabbed and bled to death—and I don't have anything to say? Do you think there is something—somewhat— *wrong with me?*"

"Do I think there's something somewhat wrong with you?" he repeats. And then, laughing: "Oh, I forgot, you just talked to your mother. That usually does it, doesn't it?"

"No, no, we weren't having a fight. She was being nice; she was being concerned. She wanted to know how I was feeling because she was being concerned."

"How you were really and truly feeling?" he asks. He has a way of making words like "really and truly" sound suspicious and childish. "Like there's some secret proper appropriate way to be feeling which if you're not articulate and eloquent about pretty fast, you are disqualified from forever?

"Have I got the picture, or what?"

"Yes," I say, "I am failing."

"At what?" he asks, as if taking patient-history notes, withholding comment.

"Feeling," I say, frustrated, beginning to cry. *"It's like I'm failing. At feeling.* And it's the worst thing because it's not like I'm someone who does things instead, like you and Adam. I don't do anything, and I don't even have any feelings."

"Okay, okay, stop crying," he says, in such a way that I can tell he isn't note-taking anymore. "Look, you have to stop crying because otherwise I won't be able to understand what you're saying."

I stop crying a little because I can tell he is going to answer now—he is going to give it his attention.

"Better," he says airily, in a way that might be funny if I weren't too glum to notice. "A little better, anyway. I see we're onto your favorite subject—Moral Failure 101. Too bad—there are a lot of other more interesting things we could talk about. For example, I just bought that book by your poetry teacher. I just walked into a bookstore and said, 'Do you have *Days We Would Rather Know?'* I thought of you—"

"You did!" I say. "And you had never bought a book of poetry before!"

"But I guess it isn't on the agenda today." He likes to allude to all the more interesting conversations we could be having if I didn't have such a tedious one-track mind. It's a funny technique; he's good at it, and I too would rather talk about poetry, yet it never makes me abandon the original concerns.

"Look," he says, "I have to be at the hospital in fifteen minutes, so let me see if I've got this straight. Why don't you run it by me again. No, never mind, I have it straight, of course. Know why?

"Want to guess?" he offers again, breezily, and then, as if he has just thought of it, snapping his fingers in sudden recollection: *"Because I've heard it before—that's why."* He always throws out a lot of quick interjections because he has a restless mind, and because he likes to keep up the illusion of improvisation—as if the things he says are more glib and sarcastic than they actually are.

It seems to me he is right, though, and we have, somehow, talked about it before, but I can't remember what we said.

"Okay, one," he says. "Do you think I care? Do you think I really give a shit? Do I waste two percent of my time thinking about your moral failures? Do you think *anyone* does?

"Okay, maybe your mother," he concedes, amused, "but does she count? Do we even like her? Isn't it funny I didn't happen to be thinking to myself when you called, yup, that Melanie, she seems awfully *happy* these days? Doesn't she know there's a tragedy going on here? Doesn't this just prove what a *cruel insensitive and fundamentally shallow person* she is, forgetting her friends before they're even cold—doesn't it prove, in fact, just exactly what we've always known about her? Wait till I tell her parents! You know what they say: *Once a wicked child, always a wicked child!* Too bad I didn't consult *them* before I got to know her!"

I put my hand over the mouthpiece.

"Do you detect any familiar themes?" he asks. "Yes, we definitely have had this conversation before. And stop crying—if you're crying you won't be able to take notes. I mean it—I don't want to have to run through it too many more times again. Aren't you a little bored with it? Okay, Point Number One. Important. Pay attention."

I nod, feeling both the pleasantness and unpleasantness of being commanded.

"Somehow," he says, "you have obtained the pathetic misguided willfully ridiculous notion that every incident life presents is some kind of weird test to see if you have the right kind of emotions because that in turn will determine whether you are the right kind of person. You are calling me because you don't think you're doing well on the test, and you want to know if I think you can do better. Before I answer, let's take a few minutes out and look at the whole arrangement. Now, I realize it's kind of a big thing to ask someone to give up their dominant life metaphor, even if it is stupid and misguided, but let's talk about it."

"Yes," I say, aware of the temptation of the offer: you do the talking. Relinquish the burden of narration. I think with gratefulness: not many people could do this for me.

"First of all, there's an interesting little logical problem—who's doing the testing? I'm not going to because as I just explained I'm not interested—I have *better* things to do. I'm going to med school in order to learn to cure people, not to ask them whether they *deserve* to have their diseases or what their diseases mean to them. Your mother can't do it because we've already established that she disqualifies herself by not liking you enough, Adam disqualifies himself by liking you too much. Besides, it's against his principles to think ill of the people he loves."

Yes, I think, depressed: there is no one to tell you. Eventually everyone disqualifies themselves. That's why you have to keep asking.

"Roberta couldn't because she was too busy taking the test with you. And that about covers the main characters in your life, doesn't it?

"So, that leaves you, Mel, to be the judge. You are the one who has to be forever anxiously scanning your heart and trying to decide whether it measures up. You are the one who has to think every five minutes of every idle afternoon: hmm, might there be a meaning here? Am I being good, am I being bad, what am I supposed to be doing with this potentially significant five minutes? *'In a minute there is time for decisions and revisions which a minute will reverse.'* And even if I know what I am supposed to be doing now—say I am supposed to be being sad for Roberta this afternoon— how do I know I am really doing it and not just pretending?"

"I don't know," I say. "How?"

"However—and this might be Point Number Two, I'm not sure, but write it down anyway—one of the peculiarities of the test seems to be that you can't alter the outcome. Your judgment is purely the discerning sort: trying to figure out what you're like without having any power to influence it. I mean, why can't you just get psyched to be good and then make it happen? You don't feel that you can, do you? It's such an odd, antiquated idea—that people are impotent with regard to their own souls. Like that Puritan belief—"

"The Calvinist doctrine of the elect," I say.

"Right," he says. "Like whether you're saved or damned, foul or fair, chalk or cheese, has all been written down since before you were born, and not one line could be rewritten because it was done by God. But since no one knew who was elected and who was canned, you still had to be painfully good and worry and wonder all your life just in order not to exclude yourself from the possibility of being saved—just *in case* you were—unlikely though it always is.

"You're kind of being had both ways, aren't you?"

"Yes," I say, "you are." You are trapped because you can't know, because how would you know if you were good or bad? And it isn't just up to you either: really good people like Adam don't just try their way into it. They try to be good, but only because they are good. Anyone can try, but not everyone can be Adam. When I was little I used to want to be a saint when I grew up and my parents would laugh about it: even when I was seven, it was a family joke. We thought, my mother would say, you were planning to be a pirate.

"But since there's no way of knowing for sure," Bob says, "you've developed all sorts of bizarre indirect methods for trying to figure out the gloomy heart of the matter of your authentic identity, which you try to fit into the most inappropriate situations. Like this afternoon," he says. "Kind of a worrisome way to lead your life, eh? No wonder you can't sleep nights."

It *is* a worrisome way to lead a life, I think, admiring his style. He's adept at tossing off such analogies: tying together Calvinism and sleeplessness. And adept, too, at dropping them before you have a chance to inspect too closely. Worrisome: as if it were merely some unpaid bill or unanswered invitation.

"But even though it's an agonizing process, you don't really want it to end because, what if I tell you you're bad? What are you going to do then? Even though the overt purpose of this phone call is to enlist my help in this process, you must already know there isn't anything I can say. If I say yeah, you're right, you aren't feeling the right things and haven't been all along and don't even bother trying because if it doesn't come naturally then it isn't deep, sincere, real emotion—are you going to hang up and slit your wrists? And if I say no, honest, I think you're sad in precisely the perfect and optimally appropriate way, are you going to believe me? Do you feel any better when Adam says: *'Why, no. I think you're just perfect, Pet, Precious, Brightness and Beauty'?"*

"He never calls me those things."

"But does it *ever* work? For more than five minutes? You don't believe him, as you wouldn't believe me if I did answer your question—which is why I'm not going to. I'm your friend, I don't want you to slit your wrists, et cetera. And even if I could convince you that I'm sincere, not just coddling, I might be wrong. After all, as you're trying to tell me yourself, I don't know the real you because you have me under your powers, as you have Adam and everybody else bewitched—except your mother, who is, of course, immune to enchantment. It's something you put in the water; she told us about it. Since there's no answer I can give and there's no answer anyone else can give and everyone has been disqualified," he says, pausing dramatically so that I know just what he is going to say, "and there's certainly no answer you can give—then *what is the point of the question?*"

"I don't know," I say. "You always tell me my questions are useless when you don't want to answer them. Besides, I don't like your tone."

And yet, with a child's mixture of resentment and relief, I don't really mind: a scolding, I am being scolded. He is after all the only person who has ever been able to successfully criticize me. And his voice, his magical magical voice, weaves its familiar spell, smooth and golden, through all its sarcasm an offer outstanding: *you could change, you could be happier. I just know you could be happier.* And: *Yes, yes, I know it too, I do so want to be happier.*

"Which bring us nicely to Point Number Three," he says. "I trust you're making a note of it."

"I always note down everything you say and read it before I go to sleep. Do you write down everything I say?"

"Before I tell you what it is I'll tell you how I know that it's right," he says, conciliatory, as if holding out a confidence. I prick up my ears: I like confidences. "Whenever you're asking a question for which there is no possible satisfactory answer, it ought to read as a clue that the question sucks. No-win mental constructs are a waste of time, and you have a penchant for wasting time this way. Whether you're good or bad, truly feel or feel somewhat, isn't up for debate. Your mother's opinion or mine or the man at the grocery store's or even your own doesn't matter. Ask questions about trivial things; deep ones, like goodness, smart people take for granted. It's as stupid as the old how-do-you-know-you-exist nonsense. Well, you don't, but if you assume it you can get on with things, and if you don't, you can waste a lot of time having long long-distance conversations.

"Here," he says, "I will give you a list of appropriate topics of conversation. You can ask me what I think of a poem you wrote, and I'll be happy to give you my uninformed opinion and you can feel secure in the knowledge that you know more about poetry than I do so you're free to throw away what I say. You could ask me what I think of your last haircut, and whether you should have permed it, and I will tell you your hair ought to be straight. Why did you cut your hair?" he asks, and I almost smile because I knew he would bring everything to cosmetics—he always does. I'm trying to make the conversation deeper and deeper and he's trying to make it more and more superficial. I want to know if I'm a good person and he wants to discuss my hair. Yet it's a deep thing too, his commitment to cocktail party discourse: ask yourself the things that matter. With others, talk pleasantries.

"You can ask me," he drawls, "whether I'm tired of talking about your insecurities—"

"Wait," I say, "are you tired of talking about my insecurities?"

"No," he laughs. "I enjoy berating you. It makes me feel in control. Men like that. But we ought to wrap it up," he says easily, "so shall we settle it now? This question, which you've been trying to slip into every conversation for years and years, is not legitimate. It is destructive and futile and *mistaken*. It's damaging to be asking yourself or anyone else what they think of your soul—it's not up for evaluation—particularly not *negative* evaluation. Yuck—" he says definitively, "that's the worst kind. Give yourself a break. Life isn't a test. Your mother won one fight a long time ago—"

"Oh," I say, listening hard. "What fight was that?"

"The fight that there even is a 'real you' that ought to be generating 'real tears.' The fight that it's worthwhile talking about what you 'really feel' and whether it's 'really right' or could 'really be better.' *That* fight.

"Say you're fine next time she talks to you. Ask her how she is. Ask her whether she's bought any new clothes lately. *Change the subject.*"

"But what if she thinks I'm . . . superficial?"

"I am a patient person," he says. "But we are back at square one, aren't we? Look, Melanie, either decide you aren't and it's an outdated romantic concept anyway, or be unhappy and fret about it forever.

"And bore me as well," he adds. "And waste my time."

"I knew you were getting to that, about your time," I say, friendly, happy. "And your being bored. Why haven't I cried?"

"You got me," he laughs. "I give up—why? Could be this afternoon isn't the right afternoon. Maybe it's too scary right now to be entirely sad. Are you too alone; do your roommates need your attention; does the dishwasher need unloading? *Are you putting too much pressure on yourself?* Maybe a lot of things. You have feelings; there is nothing wrong with your heart; you do love other people, people do love you, you do love Roberta. You do love Roberta. Is that what we've been getting at all this time?"

"You promise?" I try to laugh a little as I say it, because I see how absurd it is, to have to be asking people not whether they love you, but whether you love them. It's funny; I always thought not being loved was the worst idea in the world, but it's not. It's nothing like the suspicion that you yourself are the Tin Man.

"I promise," he says. "Boy—that might have been our concluding point. How *exciting!* Have you got it now? From now on, instead of thinking that just because you aren't feeling anything this particular second your heart might be hollow—you'll assume it's just not the right second to feel it. And relax until the right second comes. Someday, sometime, you'll be someplace—like sitting on a rock or something—and you'll be feeling strong because your life is going well or because you're so far away from your life in that place, and then you'll remember and it will be a safe place to cry, and it will be good. I'm not trying to change you into an unreflective person, God forbid, it's just that your thoughtfulness is so misdirected and distorted—"

"The things I feel are not stupid," I say.

"Of course not. They're just so totally out of proportion and exaggerated so much of the time, it hurts to listen. You don't have to throw all your thoughts and doubts away—just save them for a rock. And meantime, try to take it easy a little, huh?

"At least till I get back from the hospital?

"I've got to go.

"Bye, Melanie."

■ ■

Kim comes in with the groceries and sings, "I was able to use my Co-op Card *even though I didn't do any work last month.* I bought this cashew-butter stuff, it's like peanut butter only it's made of cashews, and it was five-sixty, only I didn't buy jam to go with it, I hope the guys like it. Do you think the guys will like it? Also I bought lamb chunks so we can make a lamb stew for dinner tonight, before they all come home, if you're not doing anything—are you doing anything?"

I heat up some oil in a heavy metal pan and begin to sauté the meat as Kim slices cucumbers onto a china plate. As we work, we begin to talk about her favorite subject, her lost romance, Leslie. I ask questions at appropriate intervals; she sighs nicely. I listen with all the interest with which I would listen to a good television program. Every young woman should have a lost romance—preferably between the ages of sixteen and twenty. I try to decide if I have had any, while Kim sets the table. At six-thirty, when the lamb stew is almost done and I am trying to decide whether to add lemon juice and wine or wine and cream, Nicholas walks in. He looks small and drenched; it had started to rain on his way home.

"Oh, poor Nicholas," Kim coos, "you look small and drenched. Would you like me to get you some dinner?" She curtsies as she speaks, as if pretending to be a housewife.

He does not smile, but he does sit down. I offer him a towel, and then some tea. He stares down at the cup and wraps his hand around it.

"So, ahh, so what did you do today, Nicholas?"

"I went to the arboretum. It was raining. There were lots of people there, but then it started to rain so they left and I didn't know whether I should leave too—I didn't know—" His voice starts to break, and he swallows and then says, "So I took the subway home."

He clenches his hands tighter around the cup, as if trying to break it. After a couple of minutes I say: "Well, that's okay, Nicholas. I'm glad you came home. That was a good thing to do."

His face crumples and a tear squeezes out. It stands silver for a moment on his brown cheek. "But see," he says, "I just don't know—how to feel better."

How to feel better. And then I remember that I spent the whole afternoon talking to Bob about how to feel worse, and that they're really the same thing, just the converse—these endless attempts to second-guess your emotions with moral or psychological formulas until there isn't anything left. So I exclaim, passionately: "But you don't have to feel better! Whoever said you have to feel better? Why, you can be sad just as long as you want to—years even. Didn't someone once say something to the effect that all neurosis is a result of incomplete mourning? You haven't even spent a whole day being sad and you're already disturbed you don't have a strategy for getting back to being well adjusted."

"I tried," said Nicholas. "I went to the arboretum. It rained."

"You'll be fine in a handful of days," I say. "I wouldn't worry about it. The worst thing about someone's dying is not being so sad and missing them so much; it's knowing what a short time those feelings will last. It's knowing there's going to come a day when you feel fine, just fine, no really—busy, a little overextended this semester maybe, but not sad—no, not sad at all. And whenever that day comes it'll be too soon: it will be a betrayal and an abandonment, not just of your friend but of yourself, and your emotions and your faith in their significance and reality—and that day will come. You imagine you have to get better because people do get better because it is too hard not to because you read in some high school psychology textbook that there is an immutable law of human nature which says that in the long run people always do the easiest thing because that's evolution. Or else they die of heartbreak. So you figure as long as you're going to get over it eventually, you might as well get over it now and not lose any time—right? And knowing that ahead of time, it's like you have already betrayed and abandoned, and you wonder what the point of starting to feel anything is—if indeed you do feel anything . . .

"But it's not true," I say again quickly, backing off, afraid I have explained too clearly the inevitability of the trivialization of loss and the disintegration of emotion. "Sadness is real—important— it might be important forever. It might be there is no day far and happy enough that you won't be able to cry real tears in it. It might be that we will never ever have to say: oh my childhood best friend, oh my college sweetheart, oh the loves and losses of youth, how long ago they seem. What did she look like again? Photos— does anyone have any photos anymore? Funny, how I used to feel so much and now I feel nothing. Amazing, isn't it, how everything fades?

"And look," I add, in sudden excitement, remembering the rock, "it might even be that not only will your losses still be with you in that place, but you'll be able to picture them more clearly, with the clarity of distance. Time doesn't heal all wounds. We wouldn't want it to."

"Yeah," he says caustically, "I can just imagine my father calling me and asking what I'm doing these days and my saying, oh, I'm being sad for Caroline. Bummer I can't put it on my

résumé and it doesn't pay the rent, and I know it happened almost
three years ago, but really, Dad, it's a full-time occupation.
Consuming—interesting—rewarding—honest. You should try it
sometime. Do you have anything to be sad about, Dad?

"Not," he adds, "that my father ever calls me anyway." His
voice changes. I withdraw a little; it almost hurts to hear it. I
complain ceaselessly about my family, but of course they call all
the time. He has never mentioned his before.

"But—but—but . . ." He gets up, and puts his hands on top of
the cup and leans down hard. It does not break. He begins to cry.
"I don't have anything to be sad about. *We never had an affair.*" He
sits down again and puts his head on the table and covers it with
his arms. Kim gets up and starts to come over and then sits down
abruptly.

"I never went out with Leslie either!" she cries. "All the letters
that I wrote him this fall—he sent them back to me. He said that I
was just writing because I was lonely, and my letters had nothing
to do with him. But he didn't understand. How could they—I
didn't know him that well because *there wasn't anything between us.*
Leslie never liked me! People say I should try and get over him—
that it's hard but I need to let go. But they don't understand how
hard it is to get over something that didn't happen—to let go of
something you never had."

"I know," I say. "I feel that way too, sometimes—about
Roberta—about everything. It's like mourning for the disintegration of the happy family you never had, and the end of the
adolescence that in truth was kind of troubled, and the time when
you were little and blond and tree-house happy except that it's
someone else's childhood you're thinking of.

"But, of course," I say, remembering what Bob said again,
"even if what you have is emptiness and loss, those count. They
are a something—a form of sadness, as meaningful as any other.
Sadness for what you didn't have is just as sad as for what you
did—sadder even. In fact it's so sad it's hard to realize it yourself
and feel it, and feel good about your feelings. You have to be in a
very strong place—a rock-safe place—to be able to do that and
have it not be unbearable. Maybe the arboretum isn't the place,
and maybe Kim isn't going to let go of Leslie until she's married.
But that's okay, you can wait for it—for the place where you can
realize all your old losses and not mind them anymore. A place
like—like when you're sitting on a rock or something," I add,

wishing I could remember exactly what Bob had said. It's always like that with Bob. I know so exactly what he means while he is speaking, and I've been waiting so many years for someone to explain it to me—but as soon as he hangs up I don't quite have it. Perhaps I don't take good enough notes after all.

Nicholas looks up blankly. "There is no place," he says almost sarcastically, picking up his teacup and holding it to his lips, dry-eyed: the draught of emptiness, the drink of defeat, "that will ever be that safe."

CHAPTER 3
Promise

A. [Brad] Her two roommates and Bibi, I remember, and I think there might have been someone else. At one point during dinner, Bibi said she wanted to go for a walk, and I said, sure . . .

But she didn't get up, and right after the dinner she got up and walked out the door. And I thought she wanted to go for a walk, so I got up and followed after her. She went down through the courtyard. . . . And she abruptly turned and went out the other entrance of the courtyard, got to the street, turned around abruptly again and just went down the street. . . .

Q. Did you see her again that evening?
A. No.
Q. Did you ask her why she had left you abruptly?
A. Yes.
Q. And what did she say?
A. She didn't have a reason.
Q. Now, at the time this occurred, were you angry with Bibi?
A. I was upset not knowing what happened and expected some explanation. Never received one, but she said that she was sorry it happened, but she couldn't promise it wouldn't happen again.

**Q. Did you discuss what she meant by she couldn't prom-
ise it would never happen again?**
A. No.

And then one night it is time to go to work again. I pack two
peanut butter and blackberry jam sandwiches and a big sweater of
my father's, and Max lends me his Walkman with his tapes of
Purple Rain and *Stop Making Sense*. I take a map and study it
carefully before I go, and get Nicholas to draw me a simplified
version, and then at midnight I drive to my job as a security guard
in Burlington.

The other security guard says he is glad I am here, he wanted
to be getting home, and I watch him walk toward the door, and
listen to the sound of the car starting and then pulling away, and
then there is no more sound and I am alone. I walk over to my
desk, take out my sandwiches, and realize I am fine, really fine,
and happy to be here.

I think about opening one of my books; it seems to me it has
been months since I have last had time to read, and I wonder
momentarily what I have been doing instead. But the thought
makes me sad, so I brush it away and hastily pick up the book. It is
not exactly what I want, though, like when you're hungry and
don't know exactly what you want to eat but nothing on the
menu. And then I remember what I want, but before I remember
that I can't have it—or rather, before I get the feeling of not being
able to have it; the empty feeling; the feeling, in fact, I have been
trying to avoid feeling all of this time—I realize I have her letters
stuck at the end of my diary. I have reread most of them, of course,
but not all of them; I have not reread her last letter. It was written,
I think, about a week before she disappeared.

*"Life has only one real attraction—the attraction of a gamble. But sup-
posing that it is a matter of indifference to us whether we win or lose?"*
                                              —Baudelaire

                    BAUDELAIRE HAD AN UNHAPPY LIFE.

Oh Melanie . . .
    *I do do things, I feel like I have to do something, so I go out
and then just spend the day wandering around looking in shop windows watching the punked-out kids and teenagers with ghetto blasters,*

just hanging out, and then this compulsion to move on. I ended up in
a record shop called "Shadows" with a headache and some heavy metal
tapes of bands which depress me. I'd like to do some shopping but in-
stead I seem to be lightening my load, giving things away. I gave some
clothing to MEG and my radio to SCOTT.

WHY?

"... the little that we get for free
the little of our earthly trust ..."

I am dropping out of school. I haven't told the Parents. I know I
will owe them $4,400 ugly mean dollars in lost tuition. (As if that was
the only thing that is being lost.) I feel as though it's what I want, though,
and I do think that ought to count for something. I cannot stand being
in school anymore. I am sick with worry about things which don't mat-
ter. I am not going to write these papers. "Life and the memory of
it, cramped, on a piece of dim Bristol board ..." *How does the rest*
go? What's for free?

"Not much.
About the size of our abidance
along with theirs: the munching cows
the iris, crisp and shivering, the water
still standing from spring freshets,
the yet-to-be-dismantled elms, the geese."

The yet-to-be-dismantled elms. The geese. I like that. Elizabeth
Bishop was right on.

And us? Who can say? We're always trying to look back ahead of
time and it's impossible and doesn't work.

I love you, Melanie, do be careful ...

I'm going to stop now.

I picture us, years from now—not even years, but someplace else,
meeting, as in a teahouse, crisscrossed by shade and light. We're old—
but not bony and immobile, coaxed by strangers, but together: keeping
house and gardens of herbs and rabbits, books of poetry, cups of tea.
You're reading aloud and I'm doing something else. Somewhat like
witches, but somewhat like us. I'll be thinking of you. You think too.

bye
bye

I pick up the letter and hold it to my heart, and the gesture does
not even seem inadequate. I imagine that place, the teacups (lid-
ded, with etchings of flowers, not sentimental English roses but

Chinese peonies, floppy and scarlet and enormous) and the rabbit in the garden (a nice brown rabbit, not a white Easter bunny) and the books (all poetry, no prose whatsoever, Chinese poetry that she is going to translate for me while I make the tea and pour it into the peony-covered teacups with the large flat lids). But before it occurs to me that I am not there, that it is a passage in a letter in which she says she is giving away her things (why is she giving away her things? Wait—*why is she fucking giving away her things?*), and the letter says good-bye, and the end sounds like more than a casual good-bye, and isn't signed (every other letter is signed. Why isn't this one signed—*why is this the only letter she ever wrote me in which there is no signature, which ends simply ''bye bye''?*), the telephone rings. I am so glad to hear it ringing that I answer all breathless, and it is Bob just as I had hoped it would be Bob, and I say hi Bob, happy. I used to not like his voice, it is so polished and L.A., but after a while it came to remind me of white running water falling on small round pebbles, which shows how adaptive metaphor is: the things you love come to remind you of the things that you love if you love them long enough. After we have talked about *The Man Who Mistook His Wife for a Hat* and Kimberly and whether he should go into radiology or neurology or psychiatry or ob/gyn—I think psychiatry or ob/gyn and he thinks neurology or radiology—he says we ought to be hanging up because his last phone bill exceeded his rent, and his rent is not cheap. I say, "Okay," reluctantly, stalling, "umm, thanks, so, for calling."

"Will you be home tomorrow?"

"I'll be at work again tomorrow night."

"No, I mean during the day." I am puzzled. He never calls me during the day—he has classes from seven to seven, it is too expensive, and I like talking to him late at night anyway. His voice is flat as he asks, but drama is not in his repertoire of tones because he thinks it is the same as melodrama, and I monopolized that role long ago.

"Why?" I say suspiciously.

"Look, Melanie," he says, after less than half a pause, "I'm going to tell you something. I was going to tell you tomorrow, but I can't let you hang up without telling you." His voice is still noncommittal, but I know that he is breaking his own rules in using a phrase like "I'm going to tell you something," and I clutch the phone.

"On the news tonight they said they found a body. They

haven't confirmed the identity yet—they're still doing tests," and then, lowering his voice, as if about to confide something intimate, so that I almost begin to feel the pleasure of a confidence before I realize what he is going to say: "But I'm pretty sure it's her.

"Melanie . . . Mel . . . are you there?

"Melanie? Talk to me."

I struggle to formulate something, but the news is so simple—what I have been waiting for, here and in California, all this time—is so simple after all that I hold my breath and can't think of anything to say. This was the news. Because I don't want to hurt Bob, I resist an urge to hang up the phone and be done with it.

"You mean," I say slowly, "you mean. What you're saying is, she's dead."

"Ahh," he says softly, "you knew that. Nothing new has happened."

Silence.

"Mel?"

No, I think; at one moment she was a girl writing about books and teacups and shivering iris, struggles and hopes and the struggle to hope, and at the next she was a body, unidentified, uncovered by men with dogs, and somewhere in there there was a change—a big change—and I missed it. Before it was too early, and now it's too late because now we know. The entire time she was lying dead under a bush—the first night, the second night, when it rained, all the subsequent nights. A month, a month and a half now; weeks before you got to California she was dead, all that time she was dead, as she is dead now. I try to cry but I don't have the breath.

"Melanie," Bob says sharply.

"Melanie!" I remember him and tighten my fingers around the phone to catch hold of his voice. And then I realize that I am the one who has to say something, and it seems to me that before I have thought of what it would be I say easily, quickly, "I wish I could die." It surprises me, I've never said it before, but then I realize that yes, that would be exactly right. It will end the conversation, and all the conversations like it that led to this conversation.

"Why?" he asks, with what sounds almost like hurt.

"So we'd be together."

"You wouldn't be dead together," he says, his voice changing, almost as if he is joking, the tone somewhere between sarcasm and sadness, wistfulness and intimacy, but elusive, not settling into any mode. I know—I have replayed it in each of these modes, and it was not quite any of them, although each held some kind of love: "You'd be dead separately."

"But then I wouldn't have to know she was dead," I say, as darkly as I can, afraid perhaps he will tease me out of it.

"That's true," he says flatly. There is a silence, and I close my eyes and wait for things to get vaguer. I've almost forgotten he is there again, when all of a sudden he interrupts crossly and says: "What about me?"

"What about you?" I reply sullenly, a little annoyed, but glad too.

"I guess you're planning to leave me alone?" he demands. "You—ahh—overlooked that angle?"

I have not, actually, thought of this. I feel a twinge of shame and am about to be convinced, when the doubt returns. "Wait," I say. "Are we definitely going to be friends always?"

" 'Course."

"No," I say desperately, needing to know with an absolute certainty, as certain as being dead would be certain, and afraid he won't be able to give it to me. *"I mean definitely."* It is difficult to convey just how definite it would have to be.

"Definitely," he says, his voice too smooth for reassurance.

"Wait—do you promise?"

"I promise."

I hesitate, but his voice is completely solemn. It seems to me I have never heard him be completely solemn before—his tone is always so infiltrated with irony—that I am awed with thankfulness. I am afraid to say anything that will spoil the gift of that solemnity, but I realize I can't quite picture it and I have to ask: "But—I mean—it's not like that when you're grownup. What about being Grownup? We'll marry different people and move to different cities, and then see each other once a year, maybe, if our husbands and wives like each other, which they probably won't. And then all we would do is maybe have dinner in some expensive restaurant, and talk about how our careers are progressing, and how no, we haven't been doing much else, it's so hard to find time to read, you know, and I'll say yes, I know, but do come back to our establishment for coffee so that we can discuss these things at more length, and that's just when your wife will say we'd love to but we can't—it's late, the babysitter, obligations, whatever, you know—and I'll say I know again, and that'll be it for another year. And we'll never talk about Roberta because she'll have been a high school friend—*high school.* No one stays in touch with high school friends. No one reads Rilke—do you know anyone who reads Rilke? Have you ever noticed how when you ask about poetry, people always say: well, in college I used to like . . . And it's true, they don't read, they can't read because they have to pay Taxes. It takes almost all year to figure out your taxes when you make grownup amounts of money, and the rest of the time you spend fixing things. Fuses, for example, and water boilers, and storm windows that have to be taken off in the summer and put on again in the winter and horrible hateful abhorrent mean frustrating things that erode your entire life with petty domestic cares. And too you have to listen to your kids tell you you don't understand, you don't know who they are, and you have to get mad back, and tell your kids that they don't understand either, the burdens and responsibilities of being Grownup, like sending them to college so they can have meaningful times and talks like this. And it sounds pretty feeble, and it is pretty feeble, but you don't have any choice, because Grownupness is *feeble.* I'm not excited about it, I've never been excited about it, and I'm not going to do it—not now—not now."

"You aren't scaring me," he laughs. "It's like a story you're telling. And not that good a story either," he says good-naturedly, but with what I think is a note almost of pleading. "It's *silly,* Mellie. Do you really think my life or your life will be anything like that? There are, I suppose, people who live that way, but then they did when they were our age too. Adolescence, makeup, boys, music, parties and shit. College—the same, but you pay more for the drugs. Any age is superficial if you are superficial. The Establishment isn't going to run your life then, because it doesn't now. As for the idea that our spouses aren't going to let us be friends, that's also totally stupid. They won't be jealous—they can't. We were fishing buddies."

"Fishing buddies?"

"Mmhmm," he says thoughtfully. "Don't you remember the time you rescued me from the sharks, in the middle of the storm, off the coast of Guatemala? Funny, I remember it perfectly. You're so good with boats too. Fishing buddies don't go out to stuffy restaurants or have superficial conversations. Look, the point is, we'll tell them anything we want, and we'll lead our lives any way we want, because we're the ones who will be grownup, and grownupness will work around us, not vice versa. Deep Grownups have deep friendships, just as deep children do. Deeper, probably, because meaning . . . accumulates. Don't you feel deeper than when you were eleven?"

"Yesss . . . but—"

"Okay then. What makes you think it's going to stop? It's not going to stop, I promise."

"Oh." And then: "Wait—don't forget about old and ugly. Don't forget I'm going to be old and ugly then."

"If your chief joy in life was having good skin, I would worry because you're right: your skin isn't going to be as good at fifty as at twenty. Not much argument there. But if that were true, then you'd have absolutely no excuse for being unhappy now, and not enjoying your good complexion while it lasts. But if it's depth you want, that's time's return for ruining your complexion.

"You know, as I was saying all this in general, I was actually thinking that you, in particular, more than anyone else I know are going to like being old. You know how you are with kids— relaxed, and happy and free to be so because you're not burdened by having to prove you're smart or accomplished or pretty, because kids don't care about that kind of shit. I mean—am I wrong?—but it seems like that's the time you feel most unevaluated, and being unevaluated seems to be your favorite mode of being. Well, all relationships will be like that then. The whole business of what will happen when you're old and ugly is especially absurd because I know you think you can't do without it, but you don't realize what a big fucking drag it is to have to worry whether you're pretty all the time. You have to worry if you're failing that people won't like you anymore, and if you're succeeding, they'll like you for the wrong reasons. Think how much fun it will be when the issue evaporates. Think how much fun it will be to be yourself, and to know you're liked for it. I mean you are anyway, but since you don't know it, you can't enjoy it. Well, when you're old it's going to be like that *all the time*. You won't just have problems; you'll have worked them out. You won't have to worry anymore about whether you deserve to be contributed to; you'll be the contributor. You'll have my role in every conversation. It's a great role; I know you're going to be great at it. I can't wait to hear you. Aren't you excited? You don't need to die or do anything dramatic to escape old problems—you're going to *outgrow* them. You're going to get *older*. You always act like the problem is so unique, but the answer is really so simple it's beautiful. People mature. I guess you'd shortcut some problems if you killed yourself, but you'd never outgrow them. Besides, it's cheating, and anyway, I don't see why you'd want to—it's going to be great. I can't wait for you to be old—for us to be old."

"Oh," I say, quiet, feeling a moment's relief from envying Roberta, who would always be beautiful and twenty-one now.

And then: "But Bob?"

"Yeah?"

"What if you die too?" The suspiciousness is upon me, as if I am being tricked somehow—after all his fine words he'll be the one who dies and I'll be left to wither. It sounds like a familiar scenario somehow.

"I'm not going to die young."

"Are you sure? How do you know?"

"I'm positive," he says. "I promise."

"Oh."

"So you promise too."

Go ahead, I tell myself, lie, and although usually I'm not scrupulous this way—whatever you say now you can always change your mind later, particularly when it's your life you're promising away—I'm superstitious suddenly, as if it will be overheard and I'll have to stick by it even if it's not the right thing for me. The idea of being bound to life by a promise too deep to break—no cheating—is too frightening. It's like promising never to fall asleep. What if I need to, what if I'm tired? What if I'm unhappy—what if I want to be with her, or not be without her? What if I miss Roberta? I might be sad; I might get tired of being sad, or I just might not feel like it anymore. But Bob is still waiting and I am sorry to disappoint him, so I say finally: "I promise if I ever think about it I'll think about you too."

"You can't do better than that?"

"No."

There is a pause, and then he says, "All right." I feel a sudden gratefulness, both for not making me promise that and for giving me something good to promise, and in my gratefulness I suddenly remember something and ask: "But why didn't you tell me when you first called?"

"I didn't want you to be alone in a building late at night with it," he says quietly.

"Oh," I say, overwhelmed at his consideration. "It's okay. You were with me." And as I say it, I realize for the first time that it is okay—it will be okay for him to hang up because I will be okay.

"Wait," I add anxiously, "I love you."

"I know," he replies easily. Almost, I must have thought he would dispute it—ask what I meant, or if I were sure and how I knew I was sure—but he has not contradicted me, and in the freedom of that ease I hang up. I must, I think, never have had so much feeling before, or I would always have been happy. I walk outside and look at the sky and it is thick and starry, and the thickness lasts all the way until morning, and a little farther.

■ ■

Q. Now, what happened after that? What was the operation after that?

A. [Veronica] Well, I think I said to Lena at that point, "Oh my God, it's Bibi." And she said to me: "We don't know that." And I said "okay." And we continued to work on mailings to gun shops in Oregon and on a tip we had received and just kept working.

Q. Was there any discussion of where the body had been found?

A. No.

Q. Why not?

A. I think we all had our fears but we all had our hopes that it wasn't her. And to discuss anything would have been mere speculation and would have made it worse.

It's just not the kind of thing that you wanted to say at the time. It wasn't like a party or anything. We were sitting scared. We didn't want to know. You know. We weren't anxious to know. We didn't want to call up the police and say: what's wrong? Why? You were scared of the answer that was going to come out.

Q. When the call finally came?

A. I can't remember her exact words, but I think Lena said the I.D. has been confirmed.

Q. Do you recall saying anything else?

A. No. There was nothing else to say.

At seven o'clock I want to go home. The receptionist does not come until eight, but because I am still happy I know that I can do what I want, so I put my sandwiches back in my bag and lock the door and leave. The air is frosty and bright as I walk toward my car; I turn on the radio and drive through the still streets. The song playing is "Starlight" as the news comes on. "In Redwood Regional Park in Oakland, California, today, the body of a young woman . . . ," says the swift voice of the announcer. I reach for the dial and switch it as fast as I can, but the new station is playing "Fire and Rain"—*I've seen fire and I've seen rain*—and the edges around the feeling of fullness begin to dissolve into the lyrics—*but I always thought*—so I switch it off and, still thinking of the end of the song—*but I always thought I'd see you one more time, babe*—I drive the rest of the way in silence.

The living room is filled with the lovely quiet rustle and smell of our Christmas tree. I could turn on the tree's white lights, I think, and sit in the white dark of the early morning, but sometime between getting out of the car and fumbling for my keys in the frozen dawn, a little more of the happiness has ebbed, so I go upstairs and open Nicholas's door.

"Oh, Mel," he says, opening his eyes. "What is it?"

I stand in the doorframe, suddenly shy and unsure.

"Is something wrong?" he asks, and then: "Why are you standing in my doorway?"

"They found Roberta's body," I tell him.

"Oh my God—when?"

"Last night."

"Why didn't you call us?"

"Ohh—I don't know—it was okay—then."

"My *God.*" He jumps out of bed and begins to yank on his jeans. "I'll just be putting some pants on," he says reassuringly, like a doctor explaining to a patient all of his movements so as not to be threatening. "And finding my shirt, and why don't you just lie down here, Melanie?" He pats his bed, kindly, as if I might not see what he means.

"Oh," I say, confused. "I don't know."

But he says, "Come on," with a soothing definiteness, and when I think about explaining, I realize that I'm even less full and happy than when I came in, and I am, in fact, tired and cold and hungry. So I crawl under the down comforter. "You can cry if you want," Nicholas says, and it occurs to me that although this is not as safe as Adam's bed, which is the safest place I know, it is pretty safe, and safer than my attic, so it would be a good place to cry. Nicholas rubs my back in a circle, as if I were a sick child, and I try to cry a little, but my eyes are dry. Dully, from downstairs, the phone sounds. We listen to it for a moment, and then Nicholas says apologetically, "Do you think I should answer that?" I say I guess, and realize that the night, the beautiful night with its long interlude, is over. It is morning now; others will tell it differently. I listen to the sound of Nicholas's feet pattering down the stairs, as if he were wearing pajama feet, and think how public the news will become when he reaches the bottom. Slowly, preoccupied with the threat of intrusion, I get out of bed and go down the stairs myself.

"It's Kimmy's mom," Nicholas says, holding his hand over the receiver. "I guess we'd better go get her."

"I guess," I say again, and Nicholas goes upstairs and leads her down, in her blue Lanz nightgown with the yoke of big flowers, and hands her the phone. She listens for a moment, and I look away so as not to see the news on her face. She hangs up immediately and screams accusingly: "ROBERTA'S DEAD WHY DIDN'T YOU TELL ME?" and then begins to pace up and down the room, sobbing violently. I stand against the wall in a corner, so as not to get in her way, and try to think of something to do to stop the noise. It seems to me that it is the worst noise in the world.

"Maybe we should call the hotline center," I say suddenly. "Maybe they have some new news, or maybe this isn't the right news, or maybe—I don't know." My voice trails off, out of possibilities, but hopeful somehow that someone will say something else.

Kim looks up from her weeping momentarily.

"Yes, let's call the hotline center," I say, encouraged.

"It'll be five in the morning there," she says, the quaver still in her voice but the tears subsided.

"Well," I say, and begin to dial. In the middle of dialing I get confused and have to start again, repeatedly. And then it rings and Lena Grady picks up the phone.

"Friends of Bibi Lee," she says briskly, the familiar greeting startling.

"Friends of Bibi Lee," she repeats, a little annoyed now.

"Umm—Lena?" I ask stupidly.

"Yes? Speaking?"

"Umm—it's umm—Melanie calling," I come out with finally, and then relax, as if that explains everything.

"Yes, Melanie?" She is definitely annoyed now. I look at Nicholas for help; he gestures encouragingly.

"I was—umm—wondering—Nicholas—mm—or Kim—was it—
Roberta?"

"Yes, the ID has been confirmed. The investigation has now
been switched to homicide," she tells me informatively.

"Oh," I say. There is a silence and I'm not sure what to do
next. And then, wondering: "What's homicide?"

"IT'S MURDER!" Kim screeches in the background, and begins to walk up and down again.

"Oh," I say again.

I want to hang up, but I can't quite think of how. I think that
maybe I should apologize for having called so early, so I start to say
that I hope I didn't wake them up, but as I am in the middle of
saying it I realize that of course I have, it is five in the morning
there, Kim told me that before I called, and I stop, dismayed.

"It's okay, Mel," she tells me sweetly. "If you were here I
would slap your face."

For some reason this idea cheers me sufficiently to say good-bye.

Kim immediately resumes sobbing when I hang up. I realize that I
have heard nothing new from the hotline, and I try to remember
how Bob explained it, but I can't, so I decide to call some other
people. I try to call Adam, but he is not home, so I tell his
answering machine: "Hi, it's Melanie. They found Roberta's body
this morning." Kim looks at me, appalled, I guess at how easy it is
for me to say it—how un-tear-choked my voice is—and suddenly I
am appalled too and hang up quickly. I try Dr. Shohet next. Dr.
Shohet was our favorite teacher in high school, and one of the only
adults I remember Roberta approving of.

"You see," I start to explain to him earnestly, a little gladness
coming back in the confidence that he will understand: "You see,
in her last letter—in her last letter she said we would be together.
Wait, let me get it—listen: *'I picture us, years from now—not even
years, but someplace else, meeting, as in a teahouse, crisscrossed by
shade and light. We're old . . . but together, keeping gardens of herbs
and rabbits, books of poetry, cups of tea . . . Somewhat like witches, but
somewhat like us. I'll be thinking of you. You think too. bye bye.'* And
see, that time, that time is the future, where we will be happy and
life good. That's what is going to make this all worthwhile, all
these years. . . . And now, now it turned out to be all a lie. Now
that time is never going to happen. No garden days—no simplicity

and goodness—no poetry—no *time*. There's no time left for us to be together. Roberta doesn't have any more time."

There is a silence, and I can hear he is considering. A sense of gratefulness mutes my own words as I realize that he truly is thinking about what he is going to say—he is giving it his best consideration and will, therefore, come up with something: a better way of thinking, a happier understanding.

"Maybe that time can still happen," he says finally. "I don't know—maybe it can."

"But how? She promised we were going to be together, and now we're not. She had nothing to promise with, as it turned out. She was just unhappy, and the promise that you always have with you—that things will be different some other day—is broken. There isn't anything other than what there was, and what there was wasn't good . . . enough. If she had known how things were going to turn out she would have killed herself a long time ago."

"No," he says, "that's not true. You don't know that. You don't know there is nothing more. You don't know what the promise is, you don't know what the promise means, you don't know whether and how it is being kept. You can't say. You can't judge."

"But she didn't get to grow up. She didn't get to be happy—she didn't even get to be *happy*."

"There's no promise of that," he says heavily. "We were never promised that."

"She didn't get to have children."

"We aren't even promised that, kiddo."

"What *is* promised? How could it be anything good now? How could that time still happen?"

"I don't know. I'm sorry, kid—that's the best I can do." I hear a note of self-reproach in his voice, as if he thinks he has not been all that I would have wanted him to be, and I so want him to know that he has, and that I am completely consoled, that I say passionately, "Oh no, I believe you." And realize as I say it, having said it, because I said it, it is a promise too.

■ ■

It is time, I decide, to call my parents. My dad picks up right away. "Oh, Mels!" he says warmly. "You're calling early—what's up?"

His voice is so homey that I begin to cry a little as I say, "They found Roberta's body this morning, Daddy."

"Ahh—that's terrible, sweetie," he says, his voice husky.

"Daddy—you don't understand—*it's awful!*" and I start to cry harder, although I'm waiting at the same time for him to stop me and say something to prove he more than understands—he knows better.

Even as I am waiting, though, I am sorry to put him to such a test. What if he fails? And what really is he supposed to say anyway? What does he know about this sort of thing? He is a quantitative historian, and his specialty is nineteenth-century America. He is particularly interested in demographics, immigration and social mobility, and he likes to read old census reports to discover income patterns in towns that have been dust a hundred years. Once when we were camping my mother mistook a bear for him. We were asleep in our tent when a brown bear lumbered in and my mother told it to shut up Stephan, you'll wake the children. He smokes a pipe and plays a hard game of squash and never ever thinks in terms of infinite consolation.

"Well, hon," he begins, and I can tell he is worried too. Then all of a sudden he says, with love and conviction: "If you come home I'll make you pancakes."

I am so moved I can hardly speak.

"Any time," he repeats happily, "any time you want to come home you can."

"Really?" The question comes out in a whisper, and I am startled at how serious my voice is, for of course I can always come home, they've never said I couldn't come home, my mother only said it once and it was a long time ago.

"Promise," he says happily, the word complete.

■ ■

The phone rings a few minutes later, and it is my mother. She is crying, and asks through sobs, "Did they really find Roberta?"

"Yes," I say, flat and cold, somehow withdrawing, "I think." She keeps crying, and it seems to me she is calling specifically to make me hear that she is crying, and for some reason the sound is much worse than Kim's. Like nails on a blackboard, like the blackboard is a heart and the heart is mine. "Yes," I say again, "yes," as quickly as I can, and feeling mean but unable to listen to her sob for one more second, I hang up. Just as I hang up, though, the phone rings again, and this time it is Adam.

■ ■

"I got your message," he says, low and defeated. I have never heard him be defeated before, and I know that it is breaking his own rules, not to be brave and cheerful. I know too that he will restore them momentarily, and that he could have called me after he restored them, and I am breathless with the honor that he chose not to. I listen, afraid I'll sniffle or do something that will make him be brave again.

"A guy who works at my office was shot this morning," he says. "A young black kid, one of the copyboys. Someone pulled a gun on him in the housing project where he lived and shot him in the head. A good guy—he was taking night courses, and doing good here—trying to get out of the ghetto—and he was just . . . blown away.

"It's a bad world," he says rawly. I can hear he is feeling it as he says it.

"This is evil," he says softly, and I realize I have never heard him use the word before.

"Sometimes it seems that I'm going to spend my life watching people die." His voice is gravelly. I can hear the sharpness with which he speaks against this idea: "Although I know that's not true. I know that I'm also going to bring life into the world—or rather, you're going to bring life, and I'm going to watch."

"Yes," I say, "yes." I want to tell him that I have thought of this last night and I know that it is true, but I can't remember exactly why, only the feeling, the feeling of promise, and so I say yes, again, yes.

■ ■

But later, I realize that I am more tired and cold, and I have to go to sleep. I think about putting it off a little longer, but I can't think of anything else to do so I go up to my room alone, and get under the covers, and don't get warm. I try again to remember last night's conversation, and the enveloping feeling, but it is completely gone. I try instead to imagine Adam's hands covering my face. Sometimes when I am lying awake in the night Adam will

sense in his sleep that I am not asleep too, and without waking up
he will reach over and rest his hand on my face, with the same
unconscious gesture with which he covers my eyes in the scary
parts at the movies. And his hand is so big and definite that I will
have the peculiar sensation of not being able to see my own
nightmares anymore, so that nothing bad can happen to me. And
in the perfect safety of that promise, I will sleep. Because I have
never spoiled the feeling with analysis in the morning, it works like
a blessing, and sometimes even just remembering it works. I close
my eyes and try to feel that weight across my cheeks. Yes, it is
there, I think, and start to fall asleep. But then I realize that the
hand is not quite big enough anymore. There is a crack between
the fingers, and I can barely look through it, but I can look through
a little, and I think I see something, and the something spoils the
feeling. And because it is spoiling, because it is already spoiled, in
order to spoil it completely I sit up and let myself think it, and it is
a word, and a question, and the word is *homicide* and the question
is: Who did it? Exactly at that moment it seemed to me that I could
hear the phone ringing downstairs—it seems unlikely now that it
rang at exactly that moment, but I remember it as being exactly
then, and I remember too knowing for certain it was for me, and
getting up and going downstairs. And it was Adam again, and he
said: "It was Brad, Melanie, it was Brad. Why didn't we guess? It
was Brad, of course, it was Brad all along.

"Shows what a good judge of character I am," he added, and
then with more grievance: *"And I helped him edit his poem."*

CHAPTER 4
A Broken Face

Here's a poem from this great book of poetry (do you have it?)
called Poets of the World. *Someone gave me his own copy. And*
now I shall copy a poem out for you.

> *Song*
>
> *I placed my dream in a boat*
> *and the boat into the sea;*
> *Then I ripped my sea with my hands*
> *so that my dream would sink.*
>
> *My hands are still wet*
> *with the blue of splashed waves,*
> *and the color that runs from my fingers*
> *colors the deserted sands.*
>
> *The wind arrives from far away,*
> *night bends itself with the cold;*
> *under the water in a boat*
> *my dream is dying away.*
>
> *I'll cry as much as necessary*
> *to make the sea grow*

so that my boat will sink to the bottom
and my dream disappear.

Then everything will be perfect:
the beach smooth, the waters orderly,
my eyes dry like stones
and my two hands—broken.

—Cecília Meireles
Brazil, 1901–1964

It seems to me that the house is suddenly flooded with newspapers. Whenever I come into the kitchen, it is covered with papers we never used to buy: the *Boston Herald*, the *Tribune*, the *Washington Post*. I wonder who is buying them now. I skim through, and although I keep saying that there is nothing I don't know, there is nothing they can tell me now, I read them anyway, and remember them. When I am in the car, the news is always on, and even if it is only a sentence, I remember exactly the phrase that they used. I never realized it before, but the same news is on five or six times a day, for an hour or half an hour or three and a half minutes, but they repeat the same news in case you missed it earlier. I am pretending to mix something in the kitchen a day or two after the first news reports, and Don is watching television in the other room, and suddenly I can hear a voice saying calmly and clearly: "The badly decayed body of Roberta Lee has been identified today, using dental records. Investigators were unable to determine at first whether the body was that of a man or a woman . . ."

Stunned, momentarily I think I must have heard him wrong. How could they not tell Roberta is a woman? I riffle through the pile of discarded newspapers, looking for yesterday's article, and actually read it for the first time. "Found in a shallow grave by search dogs . . . nose broken, eye orbit shattered, three separate blows to the head with some heavy sharp-edged instrument, as-sumed to be a rock . . . skull cracked open."

Her skull was shattered; her face was broken. I had imagined what happened so often, but I never imagined this. I wonder what I have been imagining, whether any of it is true.

I am getting out of the car two days later when I start to cry. It is a funny thing: Nicholas and Max have a guest to dinner, a woman they admire very much, the president of the Black Women's

Association I think, and they are excited about it, and Nicholas makes honey-mustard chicken and rice. The woman seems admirable to me too, but I can't think of anything to say at dinner. Then Kim comes down in her white lace dress with the big sash and drop waist and asks me to drive her into the Square because she is going on the Booze Cruise, which is a cruise on Boston Harbor where they have dancing and drinks, and she is wearing high-heeled sandals and can't walk in them. I do, and it gets a little harder to talk, and then, just as I am backing the car into our driveway, it occurs to me I am about to start crying. I am not thinking about anything in particular, but I have the same sense of physical premonition that tells you you are about to sneeze or cough. I get out of the car, and start to walk toward the house, and wonder whether it will begin before I get inside. I don't want Nicholas and Max and their guest to see me crying for no reason. I decide it will and head back to the car, and just as I am putting my hands on the door, the crying begins. I have the presence though to lock the doors and roll up the windows before it gets too loud, and as soon as they are secured I start to scream. It is almost pleasurable, the screaming: it is so loud; I didn't know I could scream this loud. After a while I see a car pull into the other driveway, and I am worried that they will hear me and come over. Even though they don't and I watch them go into their house, the imagined intrusion spoils the nest of quiet of the car, and I realize I have to get to my room.

I open the car door a crack, and then cover my mouth with my hands so that not as much sound will come out, and then, in the way that you would run if it were raining, I dash from the car to the house. The kitchen is three rooms beyond the front stairs, but I'm not sure if they hear me as I go up, and before I am quite in my room I am screaming again. I slam the door and fumble for a picture from my photo album, peeling back the sticky page so that it tears slightly, and feeling pathetic I curl into a ball on the floor and hold it. Still, it's not enough, so I drag the covers off the bed and pull them over my head. I look at the picture again, from underneath the blankets, but it is damp now, promising wrinkles. I cry harder because my picture will be wrinkled now and now I'll never get a new one. After a while the crying takes on a momentum of its own, and I don't have to try any longer. I begin to think. For the first time I picture what happened—not metaphorically, not in light of the past, but as it was: Roberta, beaten, unconscious, cold, raped, dead, partially covered with twigs and forest matting, near a bush just off the side of the road along with some beer cans and trash, a hand sticking out, dirt in her face. (What if the dirt gets in her eyes? Did he close her eyes first?) The dogs find her, smelling something, bounding over and starting to sniff at it. The searcher comes over and sees it. (Did he pick her up so the dogs wouldn't poke? Or was he disgusted, and did he call the others and did everybody stare? He wouldn't be disgusted at seeing Roberta. Was he scared? Was Roberta scary to look at?) I hope Roberta wasn't scary. Her face: her beautiful face.

I try to scream louder, and then someone knocks at the door. I want to stop to tell them not to come in, but I can't. They sit on the floor and put their arms around me, and I think it's Nicholas but I'm not sure. My chest hurts and my throat hurts and I can't stop crying. It surprises me, not being able to, and I think to myself, interested: this is what they call hysterics. After a while whoever it is gets up and says they are going to call someone. I scream, "No." And then for some reason I sob: "Call Sam," and it surprises me, having stopped long enough to say it, but also that it is Sam I want. He is my eighteen-year-old brother and we're almost never not in a fight, and besides which we've never had a serious conversation. We kick each other on friendly days, and he steps on my feet under the dinner table, happily but hard. And the rest of the time we're mad and not speaking. Then the person goes downstairs, and I am glad to be alone in the darkness again, and keep crying, but more quietly.

After a while someone comes in again and it is Sam.

"You're all in a *heap*, Melanie," Sam says, opening the door and pretending to step on me, and then kneeling beside me and trying to pick me up, "a *big wet heap* with blankets over it." I know he is trying to be funny so I let him take some of the blankets off my head and put me on his lap and I try to stop crying again. I remember the first time it occurred to me that Sam was a good person. He had been living alone in the White Mountains all summer, working as the caretaker of a tent site, and he had come home one weekend early in the fall, and was telling us how this group of rowdy guys had come and thrown a stone at a chipmunk and broken its back, and he had had to kill it. "That's terrible, sweetheart," said my mother in a stupid way, and Sam said: "It ruined my week." I remember the almost physical sense of shock I had felt: *my little brother is a good person.*

I realize, after a while, that I can stop crying now, and that is somehow frightening too, so I cry a little longer, but the momentum has ebbed. And I ask Sam in a whisper: "What do you think Brad was thinking when he put up all those posters?"

There is a silence, and then Sam says in a small voice: "Maybe he forgot."

I turn around to look at him, and he says more definitely: "Maybe it was too scary to remember—just like it's too horrible for us to think about it. Maybe he thought he was doing some good, with the posters, and hoped he would find her. Maybe he hoped you would all find her, and she would still, somehow, in some way, be all right."

"God, I hope so too," I say, getting up suddenly. Sam doesn't correct the tense, and I wash my face, and he makes jokes about how puffy and ugly my face is now, "like a dragon," he says, "an ugly dragon." We go downstairs and we are just in time to watch the nine o'clock news show pictures of Brad's first hearing in court. It is crowded, his friends are there, crying, carrying yellow roses.

CHAPTER 5
Every Soul Standeth Single

Melanie, My Melanie,

    Thank you for brightening up my day with your letter. I showed it to Scott and he liked it too. Funny, how we all think alike on so many of these things.

    My schoolwork is becoming hopeless, but at the moment it doesn't matter (but only at the moment). This week most of what I've done is plough through MORE Nietzsche. Did Nietzsche have an editor? Oh well, I'm not unabsorbed. I've been having fun, really (!), in the city over the weekend. Last night I had workshift and washed dishes and sang whilst I worked. I did just fail a math test, but it turned out to

*be oke because I talked to the T.A. and she helped me understand my
mistakes. It's so surprisingly easy sometimes to feel "Oke, things aren't
so bad." My T.A. is great, she's a triathlon athlete who quilts; she
only does math for the fun of it.*

*I've got to stop torturing myself. GOT TO. It hurts too much Mellie,
you know?*

NO MORE TORTURE.

Oh, here's a funny little quote on the subject.

      Here Lie I, Martin Elginbrodde
      Have mercy on my soul, Lord God,
      As I would do, were I Lord God
      And You were Martin Elginbrodde.

*Well said, Martin Elginbrodde. Strong and admirable women
everywhere—coming out of the woodwork (What an image!). I met another, a Japanese woman who lived with a German guy for five years,
and saw he was changing, ignoring the good parts of himself, turning
up the bullshit. Counting on her like he'd count on an inheritance. So
she pulled out. It must have been painful, but she did it. I have no one
and nothing to leave, but I applaud her, and recognize the dilemma.
How nice it would be to be capable and strong. I'm not ENOUGH.*

*Here's another quote I like: "Women and men in the crowd meet
and mingle, Yet with itself every soul standeth single . . ."*

Right on.

*And me? Standing here, looking at what might be stars, but are
probably just streetlamps, and the clown in the field on the card which
I hope you like is laughing under blue and yellow heavens.*

In our lives, I wonder how much sorrow there will be.

Love to you!
Rosamunde

The Lees come back from California. They tell me there is going to
be a memorial service at two o'clock at Hancock Church early next
week, and it is being announced in the papers. I tell Kim about it.
Then Nicholas tells me that they called back a few hours later, and
they said to come at ten in the morning to the funeral home in
Lexington. I thought the service was in the afternoon, I say, but
Nicholas says: "No, that is the memorial service and this is the
funeral. The Lees have invited you to the funeral." I almost ask
what the difference is, but I don't.

The night before Kim asks me if I can drive her to the service.

"Well, no," I say, suddenly awkward, "I mean I'm going to be going out to Lexington a little earlier, so—so—do you think you could get your mother to pick you up?"

She stares at me a minute, and then shrieks accusingly: "You've been invited to the funeral."

I start to say no, and then I feel tired and shrug.

■ ■

Well, I tell myself, I'm already just as upset as I could be, everything I could feel I already feel, they cannot get any more feeling out of me. The funeral will be a formality. I am wrong, though, about this.

I call the funeral home in the morning to ask directions.

"There is a memorial service at two o'clock at Hancock Church today," the man on the phone says to me, his voice flat.

"But there's a funeral this morning, isn't there? For Roberta?" I ask, and then, remembering that everyone now used her pet name, "I mean, Bibi Lee?"

"The public service is this afternoon," he repeats, publicly.

"Oh," I say, "but I thought—"

"No," he says.

"But I thought," I say one more time, and he replies no again, and I can't think of anything more to say, so I hang up.

Nicholas comes over and asks what the problem is. I tell him, and he tells me I have to call them back.

"I can't," I say. "I'm too . . . shy," although that isn't exactly it. Nicholas hands me the phone.

"I've been invited by Francis and Teresa Lee to the funeral for their daughter Roberta Lee at ten o'clock this morning," I say as definitely as I can. "And I live in Cambridge, so could you please give me directions?"

And even though I'm pretty sure it is the same man who answers this time, he does so—formally, politely, calling me "miss."

■ ■

I get lost, though, on the way there. I wonder if I should stop and buy flowers, but I keep driving. Nicholas has left a Talking Heads tape in the car. *"Home is where I want to be,"* someone sings, *"But I guess I'm already there . . . Did I find you or you find me? . . ."*

I stop to ask a woman if she knows where the Lexington Funeral Parlor is. She explains, and I say okay, and as I am about to pull away she says: "Wait—are you sure you understand?" I look at her, surprised at the concern in her tone, and see her face is serious and concerned too. "I just wouldn't want you to get lost again," she repeats.

■ ■

When I walk into the room everybody is already there. On the table at the door is a book where people sign their names and a picture of Bibi in a white cotton dress holding a long-stemmed white carnation. I sign my name and go in. It is still and dark and people are seated in long pews. At the front is a large polished wooden box surrounded by gleaming flower arrangements, mainly dark red roses. All the people are Chinese adults, whom I don't know, and then I see Naomi. She smiles her big smile at me. She points out Kim's parents, who are there without Kim. People go up to the box, one at a time, and kneel before it for a few minutes. I want to go up too, but I'm worried I will do it wrong and start at the same time as somebody else. I wonder if there is a secret order to how people go up, and whether Naomi has figured it out, but she is sitting too far away to ask. A guy I don't recognize stays by the coffin a long time, his head in his hands, and I wonder who he is that he stays so long with Roberta. Then he walks back and sits down between Veronica and Olivia and I realize he must be Roberta's older brother. I wish I remembered his name. Mrs. Lee goes up next, and puts her arms around the box, and then puts her head down on it and stretches her hands wider, caressing the pale wood, and begins to claw at it. Mr. Lee gets up quickly and sort of pries her loose and then takes her back to her seat, and I think that it is the most horrible sight I have ever seen.

Finally I stand up, and just as I do I see that somebody else is also standing up, but I keep walking, and they sit down again. I kneel down, queer and frightened, and close my eyes tight for a moment, and then the moment is over and I go back.

The Lees get up and leave and people begin to follow. The attendant seems to be bringing people's cars to them in the parking lot, and they pull away neatly, one by one, linked to each other. I whisper to Naomi, "What's happening?" and she whispers back, "We are going to the cemetery."

■ ■

It begins to snow as we stand by the open hole at Mount Auburn Cemetery. I'm not wearing a coat because I didn't have a black one. I wish I had brought flowers so I would have something to hold. They lower the box into the hole and I stand quiet, not even trying to keep warm. Reverend Deer, who is the minister at my church, is giving the sermon. He says the blessing over it: "Into the ground, Lord, we commend the body. And we commend the spirit into your hands where it always was.

"Where it always was," he repeats, looking right at me. Because he is looking at me, it occurs to me to wonder whether this is true. I look down at my hands, in which I hold nothing, and then I look at the box. The sides are sealed tight. I wonder if I should do something before they cover it with dirt. I wish I could look inside and see that Roberta is all right in there. Unless I do something now, I think to myself, I will wish this forever.

Mrs. Lee starts forward, and Mr. Lee holds her back, tightly, his hands on her shoulders. They dump the first shovelful of dirt, and people start to walk away. I stand there, and Reverend Deer asks if I'm okay, and I'm too cold to think of anything to say.

■ ■

Naomi tells me afterward that before they covered the coffin she said to Roberta, "See you later, kid," just as she always would say it. I don't reply and then she asks me what I said, and I say, "Nothing."

■ ■

The memorial service takes place in the afternoon. Reverend Deer gives the sermon, and he says that, like Jesus on the cross, we must make a choice about meaning, and the choice is to believe that the world is God's, or not. If it is God's, then He is present in all events, in all our hours light and dark, and nothing happens outside the hold of His hands. In his death Jesus came to that moment of choice: either to believe what the crowd around him believed— that his life had ended, his God was a fiction, and he was dying senselessly for crimes he didn't commit—or he had to believe that there was meaning, and the meaning was God's, not his own, although he at that moment did not know what it was. He faced that choice then, on the cross, as we face it continually throughout our lives, on our most difficult days, on this day.

So we do not lose heart, he reads in a stern voice, and I imagine the sternness is particularly for me, *because we look not to things that are seen, but to things that are unseen; for the things that are seen are transient, but the things that are unseen are eternal.*

We choose to look not to things that are seen, he repeats, but to things that are unseen, and we choose—we choose, my friends, together this day at the funeral service of the murdered girl—we choose to believe in the unseen meaning present, always present.

I think about all the times I have been happy in this church, listening to Reverend Deer, and all the things he has said at other times. The church is decorated with flowers today, and not like at the funeral home—not bloody symbolic roses—but many-colored flowers, pretty flowers. I think about how the Lees asked Reverend Deer to give the eulogy and how he couldn't just say how lovely she was, or bright and gifted, because he didn't know her, but he still had to think of something else to say at the funeral of a girl who was murdered at twenty-one by a guy she used to date. It must have been difficult to think of what to say. And I think of how he did think of it, how he did find something to say to all of us.

My parents and my brother are at the service, and they are all dressed up. My mother is wearing a skirt of dark blue wool, and she looks pretty, and my father is wearing a suit and tie, although he usually is resolute about wearing jeans to everything, and even my brother is all combed, as he hates to be combed. He sits very straight and looks ahead, solemnly. I love him for being so solemn. And although I haven't really been talking to or seeing my family at all these days, I'm glad they are there.

A good sermon, whispers my father to me afterward, although—he adds good-naturedly, the familiar joke of his skepticism—he can't say that he quite sees that those are precisely the only two choices.

Dr. Shohet is there too, and I know that he has taken the day off from school, and he pats me gruffly, and Dean is there too and Gao and lots of people I haven't seen since high school. Robin has come all the way from Switzerland where she is spending the year, even though her family was supposed to visit her there over

Christmas and had already bought the tickets. And everyone I thought might be there is there, and no one was busy or couldn't make it or didn't notice that she was dead, and I realize for the first time that it is not private. Almost, I must have thought it had happened to me alone—Roberta's dying.

Adam has had to stay in New York, but his mother, Mrs. Mahoney, is there. I hadn't told her about the service, but she came on her own anyway, to think about Roberta and be sorry about it all. And she is sorry—she is giving it her best sorriness—and she didn't even know Roberta. A hard sermon to give, she says to me, a terribly hard sermon.

I am about to thank her for coming, when she says she hopes it is all right—she knows that funerals aren't for spectators, she hopes she isn't a spectator. I realize that she came even without knowing it was all right, so she must have really wanted to come, and I want again to thank her, but I am too grateful to think of what to say.

I introduce Dr. Shohet to a woman who goes to our church whom I have always liked. The woman walks away and begins to talk to a pretty girl standing nearby in a checked shirt. The girl is about our age, but I don't know her. Dr. Shohet asks if it is her daughter.

"No," I say, "she doesn't have a daughter."

"Really?" he says, looking at me quizzically. "I thought she did."

"No," I say again, and he keeps looking at me, and I don't know why, because I've never said it before—I am fond of the woman, but it isn't mine to tell or to speak about—but for some reason I tell him: "I think she had a baby girl who died or was born dead."

"Oh," he says, and then simply, with wonder: "How hard life is."

"Yes," I say, and we both stand there looking at each other, thinking about this.

Joyce, a Chinese girl from high school, is standing in the reception line. She asks me if I remember how Roberta and I gave her a birthday party, and how we talked about modesty in Chinese women, and how Roberta said she only knew the word for immodesty, but she'd never heard anyone say the word for modesty because when you're Chinese you are modest unless you are *immodest*. She is crying and laughing at the same time as she speaks, and I say I remember and she hugs me and it's good. And it's not strange—there's nothing, nothing strange in any of it. There's nothing bizarre or horrible or queer and no one looks at me funny or says anything insinuating or—or anything. There are white lilies and baby's breath, floating and ghostly, and it is proper and nothing besides proper. If I had died all these people would have come to my funeral too—not the same people exactly, but lots of people nevertheless, and Roberta would have been here. And it wouldn't be strange for the people because they would be in church, and it wouldn't be strange for Roberta because she would be with everybody else, and it wouldn't be strange for me because I would be dead.

Olivia, Roberta's older sister, comes up to me and tells me that she had found my copy of the *Duino Elegies*, and that anyone who gave Roberta the *Duino Elegies* must really be a friend, and she knew Roberta really loved me. I look at her, quiet I'm so happy. Naomi tells me afterward that Olivia told *everyone* Roberta loved them— she even said it to K, and Roberta didn't even *like* K. It surprises me, how disappointed I am to hear it.

Just as I am about to leave, I see Mr. Lee standing, small and overwhelmed, lost in the crowd. I feel sorry for him: I have never seen an adult look small and lost in a crowd. I look around and see that there are at least a hundred people there. "I never knew she had so many friends," he says to me with a little bewilderment. I say yes.

Kim is there, chatting with some people from high school, and I avoid her for a while, but finally I go up and ask her how she is, and she says she went and bought a basket of flowers and red and green apples for the Lees and left it at their doorstep. I'm about to tell her that that is really good of her because I don't know if I would have brought them anything if they hadn't invited me, and especially if they'd invited my parents without me, when she looks straight at me and says suddenly, her voice thick with awe: "It's too *bad*—they all loved each other so much."

I look at her, and think of all the things that go between those two statements: it's too bad she was so unhappy, it's too bad things happened as they happened, it's too bad because they needn't have, they really needn't have, because they loved her, they loved her so much. "It's too bad," I echo back, "it's too bad."

■ ■

I go over to Adam's mother's house that night, and she serves tea, and I read her some letters of Roberta's and she says they are perfectly beautiful. She says she will pray for Roberta, and for me too. I look at her to see if she really means it. I've never had someone pray for me.

CHAPTER 6
Matches

I'm frayed and forlorn and exhausted, in a permanent pervasive sort of way. SO WHEN CAN I QUIT? Supposed to be finding a job, and looking, but only sort of. I need the money, but I can't stand the thought of a job. Maybe people can tell that; no one's offering yet—or maybe they just don't like the way I look. The best of them was— curiously—a lesbian-run Italian ice cream shop. Haven't met any romance in so long I've forgotten how to scout it out. But they say it's around. So maybe it just passed me over and by. God, how do people get on top of things? Why is everything with me always so completely abortive? Pretty soon, we won't even remember that it's there. I mean really, things are just so out of hand. Maybe I better finish this later.

Well, IT'S LATER NOW and the dawn brought with it precisely nothing. Did I mention school is over? Saw a movie yesterday about punk called The Decline of Western Civilization: *stupid movie, and the title is bad too, you wouldn't have liked it either. That's one light anyway, in these gray days—to think of you and me disliking the movie together.*

We ought to make plans in the time that we have.

I wake up alone in my bed the morning after the funeral. It is cold and dark. I don't want to get out of bed, I don't want to get dressed, there is nothing I want to do. I start to cry because there is nothing I want to do. I look down and catch a glimpse of my stomach and feel such a hatred for my body that I can hardly move. I bury it in blankets so as not to see it any longer, and stay there, frozen, and after a time the feeling goes away.

In my old book of Hans Christian Andersen fairy tales, with its gray and red cover with the flowering vine embroidered in gold, is the story of the Little Match Girl.

It was terribly cold, it begins. Snow was falling and soon it would be quite dark: for it was the last day of the year—New Year's Eve. Along the street, in the same cold and dark, went a poor little girl in bare feet—well, yes it's true, she had slippers on when she left home, but what was the good of that? They were great big slippers which her mother used to wear, so you can imagine the size of them; and they both came off when the little girl scurried across the road just as two carts went whizzing by at a fearful rate. One slipper was not to be found, and a boy ran off with the other, saying it would do for a cradle one day when he had children of his own.

So the girl is beginning to freeze, and a boy is stealing her slippers in case they'd be handy in his own fairy-tale future when he has a little girl and might need a cradle. Lovely, I think: people are so helpful. A promising beginning.

So there was the little girl, walking along in her bare feet that were simply blue with cold. In an old apron she was carrying a whole lot of matches and she had one bunch of them in her hand. She hadn't sold anything all day, and no one had given her a single penny. Poor mite, she looked so downcast as she trudged along hungry and shivering. The snowflakes settled on her long flaxen hair, which hung in pretty curls over her shoulders, but you may be sure that she wasn't thinking about her looks. . . . You see, it was New Year's Eve; that's what she was thinking about.

Over in a little corner between two houses—one of them jutted out rather more into the street than the other—there she crouched and huddled with her legs tucked under her; but she only got colder and colder. She didn't dare go home, for she hadn't sold a match nor earned a single penny. Her father would beat her, and besides it was so cold at home. They had only the bare roof over their heads and the wind whispered through that although the worst cracks had been stopped up with rags and straw. Her hands were really quite numb with cold.

I pull the covers around me, feeling the rough of the wool, and sit up in bed and settle my chin on my knees. She couldn't go home until she had sold enough matches, but no one needed any matches since it was a holiday. There is a certain cruel little connection here: others' plenitude is her misfortune.

Ah, but a little match—that would be a comfort. If only she dared pull one out . . . ritch! . . . how it spurted and blazed! . . . The little girl fancied she was sitting in front of a big iron stove with shiny brass knobs and brass facings, with such a warm friendly fire burning . . . why, whatever was that? She was just stretching out her toes, so as to warm them too, when—out went the flame, and the stove vanished. There she sat with a little stub of burnt-out match in her hand.

Yes, I think, light and warmth, and the light is a vision and the warmth is the warmth within the vision, like the heat from the fireplace in the life she would like to have led.

Such a warm clear flame, like a little candle, as she put her hand round it—yes, and what a curious light it was!

The light of illusion, I think, the light of fantasy.

. . . It burned up so brightly, and where the gleam fell on the wall this became transparent like gauze. She could see right into the room, where the table was laid with a glittering white cloth and with delicate china; and there, steaming deliciously, was the roast goose stuffed with prunes and apples . . . She lighted another match. Now she was sitting under the loveliest Christmas tree; it was even bigger and prettier than the one she had seen through the glass door at the rich merchant's at Christmas. Hundreds of candles were burning on the green branches, and the gay-coloured prints, like the ones they hang in the shop-windows, looked down at her. The little girl reached up both her hands . . . then the match went out; all the Christmas candles rose higher and higher, until now she could see they were the shining stars. One of them rushed down the sky with a long fiery streak.

That's somebody dying, said the little girl, for her dead Grannie, who was the only one who had been kind to her, had told her that a falling star shows that a soul is going up to God.

How horrible, I think, that she catches the meaning—the falling star means someone is dying—but doesn't see that it's meant for her: it's her match that is falling to darkness. Only we see that meaning.

She struck yet another match on the wall. It gave a glow all around and there in the midst of it stood her old grandmother, looking so very bright and gentle and loving. . . . Oh, Grannie, cried the little girl, do take me with you! I know you'll disappear as soon as the match goes out—just as the warm stove did, and the lovely roast goose, and the wonderful great Christmas tree.

And she quickly struck the rest of the matches in the bunch, for she did so want to keep her Grannie there.

So I remembered it wrong, I realize. I had always thought that she didn't have enough: that she was sent out into the world with not enough matches. But not so; she used them all up by lighting them at once. She wanted a big flame. Had she been careful, holding one after another to her blackened fingers, she might have had enough to make it through the night.

And the matches flared up so gloriously that it became brighter than broad day-light.

It became brighter than daylight because illusions look brighter than reality. And the poorer you are—the less you have to pay with—the dearer is the vision and the more you are willing to pay for it. She spent all of her matches for this bright sight, these transcendent illusions.

Although, I remember, the writer was a Christian, and in Christianity the transcendent is not illusory. The snowy streets, the hunger and cold and loneliness—*those* were the fairy tale. What the matches lit was eternal reality. So say the Gospels. And so the story ends:

Never had Grannie looked so tall and beautiful. She took the little girl into her arms, and together they flew in joy and splendour, up, up to where there was no cold, no fear. They were with God.

Yet it's contrived, I think, closing the book. Contrived to suit the Christian sentiment. The old narrative has been given this

Christian meaning: the dead come back through the light of the candle of faith to lead her, by the hand, away from this world. Tarry not too long: God calls back soonest those he loves best.

To the others it was a little girl with a smile frozen on her lips, but the Christians know differently. *She was trying to get warm, people said. Nobody knew what lovely things she had seen and in what glory she had gone to the happiness of the New Year.* Death seems sad to the people on the streets, but the informed reader, the religious reader, knows better.

Forced, I think again: completely improbable. Yet, stories mean what you want them to mean: the writer was Christian, and this was the meaning he gave it. In the old stories when children die it is horrible: in his story the child is blessed. The first shall come last and the last first. It was his story, his to tell, and he told it this way. Why are you criticizing it?

■ ■

A pathetic ugly story of pain and death that has been told since the beginning of time about the world being cruel and children perishing—*the New Year dawned on the dead little body*—is twisted to carry a Christian meaning. New Year's Eve, a pagan holiday, has become a Christian one, thousands of years later. During pagan holidays they used to sacrifice men and children because they believed it brought them luck; in Christianity the sacrifice is sanctified for the sufferer—because it is suffering that is blessed. The story is still the same—loss, hope, loss—and she still freezes to death on the very same holiday. But the eve of Christianity dawns differently and the light of morning reinterprets it. The setting of the story is the last night between the old and the new year: the turning point between two interpretations. Yet the little girl is dead, and you know she is going to die even before you are done. Which way do you turn?

Of all sad stories, I think heavily, getting up from the bed, surely this is the saddest.

I write a poem about it later that morning, just to clarify verse by verse a few of the implications—the personal parallels—taking pains to be certain they scan properly. One thing I don't miss when I don't write poetry is scansion: the things I feel and think never do come out to the right number of syllables. The exercise does not make me feel better, as I had thought it would not, and I go downstairs. Sitting on the kitchen table is a large plant arrangement with a shiny red ribbon tied awkwardly around it.

"Someone sent you something, Kim," I say, looking at it.

"No," she says. "It's for you."

The plant has three large shoots and two small shoots and long strands of ivy hanging down the sides and little violets growing at the feet of the shoots. It is in an orange-brown clay pot, and it has a little white card attached to it. I open it up and it says, "Love, Bob." I read it again and it says the same thing, and it seems to me it is the nicest thing anyone has ever done for me.

I have the plant still. It sits on my desk; the violets have died, but the ivy is so long now it curls around the feet of the desk, and I always look at it while I write. I left it home one semester and although my parents claimed they took care of it, it got all thin and sickly, so now I always keep it with me.

■ ■

I find a piece of Adam's, reading through *The New Yorker*. It is unsigned, as "Notes and Comment" customarily is. He hadn't told me he was writing it, but I instantly know that it is his.

NOTES AND COMMENT

A young staff member writes:

I hadn't known her very well, but we went to high school together, and I liked her, and we shared friends. Six weeks ago—the Sunday before the Presidential election—a woman saw Roberta Lee, by then a junior at Berkeley, being dragged into a brown van by a bearded, beer-bellied man twice her size. Her body was found last Sunday morning. The effort to find her was run from a friend's fourth-floor apartment a block off the campus. Maps of Northern California lined the walls, with the areas where volunteers had posted leaflets outlined in red. The areas still to be covered were colored yellow, and though several million of the leaflets had gone out, patches of yellow remained at the end. Roberta's friends, and also a lot of strangers—such good people, all of them— sat on the apartment floor addressing envelopes to all the auto-body-repair shops in the Bay Area, or all the churches in Oakland, or all ten thousand postal routes in Northern

California and Nevada. An account in the San Francisco *Chronicle* noted that by the third week most of the weeping had ceased; the human mechanism weakens under the strain of endless, bottomless grief, and so people joked about the weather, or the classes they were missing, or the writer's cramp that comes after a couple of hundred envelopes. For a while, industriousness can keep dark thoughts away—thoughts about that damnable van. And the work itself was somehow necessarily divorced from the goal. People set out in the morning to put posters in every Quik Stop and on every telephone pole along Route 9 up in the mountains behind Santa Cruz—they didn't set out to "find Roberta." That way, at day's end they had accomplished something, even if it might never mean anything more than increased public awareness—even if the thug never drove his van through Boulder Creek or Felton or Ben Lomond.

Four weeks to the day after Roberta was abducted, a Harvard graduate living on the Upper West Side, Caroline Isenberg, was murdered during a robbery and attempted rape on the roof of her building. I didn't know her, except by sight—I had seen her act when I was at school. She was my age and had come to the big city for somewhat similar reasons (she to act, I to write), and she was close to people I do know and care about: a little of what they felt I could discern in their voices.

Early the next morning, Darren Styles, a messenger in the business department of *The New Yorker*, was shot twice in the head and killed, in the lobby of an apartment building in the Brooklyn housing project where he lived. Styles, who was twenty years old and had graduated from August Martin High School, in Queens, was going to school nights at De Vry Technical Institute. Last summer, he had testified against a thief who had robbed him of a gold chain, and police speculated that revenge may have been the motive for the killing. Or maybe not—maybe it was just that someone shot him. I knew him only to chat with in the elevator—no more than that—but I've been told he was an exemplary young man in every way.

Everyone who has read "The Brothers Karamazov" remembers the story of the Grand Inquisitor. Just a few pages before it, in the course of the same argument, comes a passage that sticks as solidly in my mind. Ivan, trying to prove the world beyond redemption, recounts a gruesome story to Alyosha: A noble, with "kennels of hundreds of hounds and nearly a hundred dog-boys—all mounted, and in uniform," notices one day that his favorite dog is lame.

He is told that a certain boy threw the stone that hurt, accidentally, the animal's paw. He orders the eight-year-old stripped, and in front of all the other serfs he sets his hounds upon him, and they tear the boy to pieces. Ivan and Alyosha are arguing theology, Ivan being unable to say, "Thou art just, O Lord." The case of the child, he says, presents "a question I can't answer."

And the events of the last few weeks present questions I can't answer—a position that chafes. The three crimes are not really similar except that they are all senseless, not explained even by sudden rage, say, or mercenary calculation. Ordinarily, my inclination is always to think of some program that will turn out healthy, well-adjusted people. Perhaps they need school lunches, or career counselling, or psychiatric evaluation, or more welfare. Right at the moment my gut is interested in vengeance, in locking people up and a lot worse. But both feelings are bogus. *Newsweek* recently ran an article on serial killers—men who murdered many people, one at a time. A drifter named Henry Lee Lucas confessed to about three hundred and sixty killings. "Killing someone is just like walking outdoors," he said. "If I wanted a victim, I'd just go get one." *Newsweek* called the rise in random murders an "epidemic," and it showed pictures of such men—most of them white, not looking especially poor, and, horribly, not looking especially evil. They weren't larger than life; they were smaller, if anything, but twisted. Welfare and food stamps and school lunches and psychiatric counsellors are good ideas for all sorts of reasons, but not because they will change people like these. And the thought that someone capable of killing a hundred people would calculate the odds of his receiving, say, a death sentence is a sick joke.

The deepest instinct is to gather close around you those you love, and live your life. But the world keeps intruding. I'm afraid that I'll begin to believe this world beyond redemption, not necessarily in a theological sense but in a human one. I don't want to hate the world. At one point in "The Brothers Karamazov," Alyosha comes across a gang of schoolboys stoning a pale, sickly classmate, and shields him with his body; with the same aggressive, individual, gratuitous, healing love, he turns a proud lad, Kolya, into a man. No other course of action suggests itself to me.

■ ■

I know that Adam has been thinking about all that has happened during this year. *"The deepest instinct is to gather close around you those you love, and live your life. But the world keeps intruding."* And then he remembers a story: Alyosha coming across a sickly child being stoned to death by a gang of schoolboys. I know why this story appeals to him so much. He likes to think of what Alyosha did because it was the right thing to do, the thing that worked, and which he himself would do. They don't usually go together, things that are right and things that are effective, but in that story they did, and the boys went away. "I don't want to hate the world," he writes, although there is much to hate within it—what happened to Roberta and Caroline Isenberg and the messenger who was shot in the head—and he uses this story to shield him from that hatred. Act in love, the story makes clear, in all situations, but particularly those ugly and cruel, and the situation will change. Alyosha held the sickly boy to his breast, and the tormentors dispersed. "No other course of action suggests itself to me," writes Adam.

It is a good piece, and written well, yet it makes me sad to read, as if it were written for me or about me—as if I were the wounded one he is holding so tightly to himself, by his own body kept from enemies. And too, it makes me sad that by the time the action he has chosen—writing—has come to be, it is already academic. Even the cast of characters has changed. The Man with the Van, like the boys with their stones, has already been exposed to be a fiction—a convenient one, perhaps—a story in which we could identify the perpetrators and thus defend ourselves. Adam must have written the piece several weeks ago and in the time it took to be published the Man with the Van evaporated, but the piece was outdated even before. Adam didn't find Roberta with all his brave beautiful action, and the aggressive individual gratuitous healing love he speaks about—the wonderful wonderful story he relies so heavily upon because there is nothing else to rely upon—has turned out, after all, not to be salvatory—not for everyone, not in all situations.

■ ■

I go to see Reverend Deer, and I carry my box of Roberta's letters. I read him some of them, and they sound unhappy and frightened. Especially frightened, they sound so frightened, I wonder why I didn't hear it before, and then I remember that I did.

Reverend Deer says that everything that happens can make you a better person or a worse person, depending on the meaning you construct around it. I ask him exactly what kind of positive meaning he has in mind, speaking carefully, trying not to sound too skeptical. She was unhappy and frightened and died young and violently by the hand of someone she trusted. She was beaten to death by the man she had slept with—naked, in trust, her body—and he buried her in a shallow grave by the side of the road.

I look at him, and I think he is about to answer, but he seems to change his mind, and he gets up and says: "I don't know." And then he kind of shrugs and adds: "Make something up. You're an imaginative girl. Probably you already have." I get up too and turn toward the door, and he says come back later, and I don't say anything, and he says come back and see me again later, and I say all right.

Dearest Melanie,

I got your wonderful card and poem. Do write again and often! They are perfectly expressive of some very common feelings. I've been busy and oddly enough am finding myself engaged (!?) well oke, getting caught up in my studies in a way that I haven't been in a long time. She says this as she frivolously blew off the day by going to the picture show in the afternoon! Last night I stayed up until odd hours working on a dissatisfactory paper and then I had to stay up all day feeling tired. Good God! As if I really had anything worthwhile to say. . . . Ugh I hate feeling sick. I will go to bed soon. I'm looking at Nietzsche's "The Advantage and Disadvantage of History for Life"—it's interesting as hell and very confusing. Like Alice in Wonderland. *No one but us chickens in here.*

I feel brave and tall and alone, indicative all of a prideful fall to come. Oh well. That's the stuff of tragedy or something like that. And tomorrow is St. Valentine's Day. You are my Valentine, hearts and lace girl that you are.

> *Neither footloose nor fancy free,*
> *but content for now,*
> *Love, Rosamunde*

I talk to Reverend Deer again. I'm half waiting throughout the conversation for him to say something about God—to ask me what happened to my faith, why it doesn't affect how I feel and think about what happened, which it doesn't seem to, and about which I'm wondering myself—but we talk of other things. And then, just as I am leaving, as I am buttoning my coat and finding my mittens, he adds: "And one of these days, you'll have to decide about God too."

It seems to me it's almost a line I've heard before, like a line the minister would say to a girl in a book about a girl getting over a death. I know there is a line the girl would say back, and then I remember what it is and try to say it flippantly, as she would: "Maybe He has to decide about me." My voice doesn't come out flippant, though, it comes out bitter, and when he replies, "He already has, Melanie. He already has," it's as if I were hearing the line for the first time and hadn't known what it would be—as if it weren't a line and I didn't know whether it was true and needed to know—wondering.

■ ■

Bob calls that night to find out how I am. I read him my poem about the Little Match Girl, and he says it's stupid. I ask why and he says, "Why do you think?" and then without waiting for my answer: "Because you made it up, that's why. You're choosing to see things Match Girl. Not everyone does, you know. I, for example," he begins dryly, and then says: "No, never mind, you already know what *I* think."

"It would be different," I say, "if—if it were different for me, I guess. If I had any—mmm—I don't know."

"And what is it you don't have?"

"I don't know. Matches, I guess."

"What exactly would constitute a match?" he snaps. "Number of friends left alive? Balance in your checking account? Whether your mother really loves you? Looks? SAT scores? Charitable acts done in 1985? Vague general sense of meaning or meaningless-ness? Save the Whales? United Jewish Appeal? Do you see how this list is deteriorating? I know you're always trying to tally things up to show it comes out negative and you're empty-handed—orphaned, whatever—and I don't want to be overly analytical because I know this is metaphor, but for God's sake *what are the units?*"

"You're such a bully," I say.

"Besides which," he says, "what about imagination?"

"What about imagination?" I say sullenly.

"A match of sorts, isn't it?" he demands. "The power to envision other characters in different stories—to choose your iden- tifications? Kind of a match. See," he finishes, and I can't figure out the ratio of mockery to affection, "I can make up metaphors too. Maybe I should be a poet."

■ ■

Later I am thinking about it, and thinking that, after all, the facts are still the facts—she did die, and she was unhappy, and it was her boyfriend who killed her, when Adam calls and says: "Guess what?"

"What?" I say, not anxious to hear any more news.

"Brad retracted his confession. He says he just said what the police told him was true, and he had wanted to know the truth so badly, he had been searching for so many weeks, he couldn't stand not knowing anymore. So when someone finally told him some- thing they said they were sure of, he wasn't in a position to disagree, he says. When he told them he didn't remember, they told him he forgot, so he figured if they said so then he must have because he was confused. I was, quote, confused, unquote, says Bradley Page. And now, he says, he's been tricked. They have tricked me, states Page, also quote. They entrapped and deceived me—they told me they had forensic evidence, they told me they had fingerprints on rocks, and a witness who saw me drive away, and that I flunked the polygraph test when it was indeterminate. Everything was undetermined, and they told me it was certain. They told me *lies*. It was all *fictional*. And they did make things up, of course, but they're allowed to make things up, and he isn't, as he should have known—if he did make them up, that is—if it isn't true. I guess that's what's going to be on the table from now on, so to speak: whether he made it up, how much he made up."

"*He made it up?*" I repeat. "*He was making it up?*"

"He says he made it up, sweetie," says Adam.

PART 6
Uninterpreting: Characters

■ ■

Man is an animal suspended in webs of significance he himself has spun.

—Clifford Geertz
Interpretation of Cultures

CHAPTER 1

Brad

Q. What generally did you learn of Mr. Page?

A. [Psychiatrist] Generally, I learned that Mr. Page came from a—what you would call a middle-class, fairly conventional background. He was brought up in a relatively sheltered area, acquired most of the conventional values of middle-class America.... He seemed to have rather idealized views about women ... He looked up to authority figures and did not appear to have much in the way of anger or animosity or mistrust toward them. In his own individual life, he tended to be rather idealistic. He tended to be compliant, concerned always with being seen as a good person....

Q. Do you see anything in his history, or have you learned anything indicative of any violent tendencies at all, or quick temper, or anything of that kind?

A. I have seen absolutely no indication of that. I notice in all the school records going back to the first grade, there is not one comment by any teacher that he has ever shown any aggressive behavior.

A. [Brad] We also at one time talked about my lack of anger. He asked if I had ever been in fights and if I ever got

mad at people and blew up at people, and I said no. And
he said: "Well, don't you think that's kind of strange?
What do you think would happen if you ever did get mad
at somebody? I said I thought I would be worried, but it's
never happened.

**Q. Now relations between a living person and a dead
person are referred to categorically as "necrophilia," correct?**
A. [Psychiatrist] Yes.
**Q. In this particular situation, how do you believe the
recital of certain facts relating to a necrophilia
type of relationship fit in generally to the fantasy
that he was spilling out?**
A. Now I know at first glance necrophiliac fantasies might
appear to be something quite bizarre and unusual, but
they are resident in almost everyone's unconsciousness.
      And certainly as a psychiatrist I have had people de-
scribe those fantasies ... and even more bizarre fantasies that come to them in dreams. And it is not anything
hard to understand when a person feels himself under
pressure to fantasize in a way that would satisfy his in-
terrogators this type of fantasy might come forth. It
would certainly fit in with his other romantic notions of
valuing certain bizarre thoughts and ideas ...

"So the fucking asshole is getting lots of press sympathy," I say to
Nicholas and Don, coming into the living room one day with an
armful of newspapers. "And all the students are saying the police
framed him in order to solve the case, which fits in with the
Berkeley Conspiracy of Authority theory so popular among the
young these days, and the reports are saying that he's going to get
off because she's Asian whereas he's young and pretty and white
and rich and the jury isn't going to want to send a young pretty
white rich person to jail. He's getting a hot-shot lawyer because his
family has connections and money, and she's getting some assigned D.A. because the victim has no say in these matters
because—" I say, and then stop, out of breath, trying to remember
why, and then I remember: "because they're dead.
      "And someone—I'm not kidding, I read this—someone had

the nerve to say he shouldn't be judged as harshly because it was a first offense.

"*A first offense,*" I repeat, and stop, unable to express the depths to which the concept of first offense does not apply to murder.

"And someone else actually said he won't be convicted because there wasn't any hard evidence. He fucking *confessed.* It's fucking incredible you can plead innocent if you already said you were guilty—like you can *change your mind* if you don't get your story straight in the first place. The whole under-pressure-from-the-police story is completely pathetic. I talked to the police plenty of times when I was under pressure, and I was never tempted to say *I* did it. And they were always trying to get information out of me, and implying I knew more than I was telling them.

"Which I didn't," I say, "*I didn't know anything more.*

"I didn't," I repeat anxiously, looking at them for confirmation. They don't say anything, and then I realize they are not disputing it.

"He—he—" I try again, and stop, confused at how to describe just how bad Brad is.

"Don't hate him too much, Melanie," Nicholas says solemnly.

"Why shouldn't I?" I say. "He's caused a lot of . . . *damage.*" *Damage* is such a feeble word. I grope for a stronger one. It doesn't come.

"He took Roberta's life," I say, "took it . . . *away.* And he took something from me that—which I needed. And which now I can't have—ever.

"Not ever. Not—" I say again, trying to think about this statement. It sounds dubious, as if I'm exaggerating, even though I know that I'm not—it is exactly true. I try to concentrate on how exactly true it is.

"He harmed me," I say, beginning to cry, "he harmed me."

Don and Nicholas exchange glances—solemn moral glances.

"What one man can do, every man can do," Nicholas recites gravely. "Isn't that what Christianity tells us? Every man is part of the whole. We are all capable of everything. I could never say I'm not capable of something someone else is capable of because there but for the grace of God, everything is possible, we live in a relative world and the only absolute is—"

"That there is no absolute," finishes Don for him satisfactorily.

"That's not true," I spit at them, worried. "Christianity says nothing of the kind."

"Goethe said: 'I have never read of a crime of which I myself am not capable,' " Nicholas says, switching sources to Romanticism. Don nods.

"What a stupid thing for him to say," I say. If anyone could have murdered Roberta, then I could have murdered Roberta, and naturally this isn't the case. I am not suspect—neither me nor anyone I love or like or even dated a couple of times. "It's not true," I say again, but more weakly. I stand there floundering, miserable for a few seconds, and then blessedly I think of something conclusive. "Adam Mahoney would never murder me," I say.

"Adam Mahoney is *never going to murder me*," I repeat. "Not under any circumstances! I'm *positive* of it."

They look at each other again. This time their glances clearly imply: the girl is getting hysterical. Say something, we ought to, calming. And then I realize that it doesn't really matter to them— they were simply making this little philosophical point, and it really does matter to me, and they are talking quietly and I am screaming. And I wonder why I even bother talking to people about my life, and I go upstairs to my room and cry.

■ ■

Veronica calls one day, about a month later. I ask her how she felt about Brad, whether she had guessed it was he. Of all the people Brad was unfair to, it seemed to me he was the most unfair to Veronica. He sat by her side for five weeks and watched her work fourteen hours a day, knowing all the while where Bibi was *and not telling her.* He watched her grow paler and thinner and her bones show through her sweater, and lose her job to do incalculable amounts of paperwork with three million flyers translated into seven different languages in case the Man with the Van had friends or informers who spoke only Vietnamese. Moreover, Veronica did most of his share of the work, as well as her own, when all along he could have spared her the whole. Unplug the phones, give Ken Lao back his apartment, go home, my friends, go home.

"Did you know?" I ask her. "What did you think when you found out?"

"No, I didn't know at the time. But as soon as I heard it," she says quietly, "I knew it was true."

Then she says that lots of students are defending him, and that

Meg in particular has defended him, and is willing to testify for him—to testify in court that Bradley Page is a nice person.

"She's going to fly in from Barcelona to testify on behalf of the defense when the trial starts," she says. I say, "Well," awkwardly, because I always liked Meg, and Veronica adds harshly, "And he committed necrophilia, too." I asked what necrophilia is, and she tells me, and I realize that I knew what it meant. For a minute I don't see how it relates, and then I do. But I guess she thinks I'm not imagining it sufficiently, because she says vehemently: *"Yes, in his confession he said he went back to the place and he saw her body stretched out dead, and knew she was dead because she wasn't moving, and he spread out the blanket he had in his car and put the body on it and caressed it and after a long time he thinks maybe he made love to it, and buried it.*

"He buried it well, he said in the confession, *because he wanted her to be happy."* Then she adds, "You didn't know all that."

"No," I say. "Nobody told me." She says, "It's true, you know," and I say, "Oh," and hang up.

■ ■

I try to throw up, but I can't. I am supposed to go to my exercise class that night, and I think I should go even though I feel sick and don't want to. I go to the spa, and stand in front of the mirror in my leotard, and the old nausea and hatred are upon me: I look at the reflection and it is *obscene.* It's too *big,* I think, almost crying, it's so hateful. My body, God I hate my body. *Flesh,* look at all this flesh. I look again and see: the same thing. *It wasn't up to me,* I protest, wanting to set the record straight, *I never decided to grow up. It wasn't my decision*—although there is no record and nothing to decide. I pinch it a little, and yes, it is perfectly real; not even around the edges is it beginning to fade. I stand there a few more minutes, staring. The class is starting, all the other women are going out, pink leotarded and black leotarded, not all of them thin, not all of them young, most of them not even pleasant looking. The warm-up music begins to play; they chat and smile. They live in their bodies and they like them. They are not homeless; they live in themselves. Not being thin or pretty enough is the feeblest of excuses for hating yourself, I think, and the urge to smash and be done grows stronger. The teacher is speaking in the background, saying, "All right, let us begin," and Madonna begins to sing, large and husky, calling, filling the room, and I want so much to begin as well but I stand just outside, in the next room.

And then, although I have not been thinking about it, I remember what Veronica told me—what was the word she used? And then: you know what it is, don't pretend you forgot or had never heard it before. I woke up in my body this morning, and it was all right then, and it's been all right for a while now—it's been all right since the morning after the funeral, in fact, when I was so sick I couldn't move. And then it went away. There must therefore be a simple connection between the news and the feeling, I think analytically. And therefore, although it feels so powerful and absolute and true—as if it weren't a feeling but a *truth*—it must, actually, be only a consequence of the news. It is a farfetched connection: three months later someone tells me the killer raped the corpse as well—Veronica says that Brad said that he had sex with the body, wrapped it in his blanket and made love to it—and I hate myself. Brad committed necrophilia, and I feel fat. Connections are so interesting, I think, so hidden and cunning, like strands of invisible heart-threads, threaded through everything. I stand there distracted and busy, puzzling, and waiting to figure out what it is—and forgetting, of course, to keep feeling while I am thinking. I am different this way from other people, not being able to think and feel at the same time.

The class ends, and nothing has been broken because I am still waiting, with that hopeful waiting-for-revelation expectancy, like the vague notion you have always that you do actually know everything necessary to know: all the connections, the story of what everything means to you, you could take your finger and trace each strand and come to the beginning—if you didn't get lost.

Your heart isn't going to tell right now, because it never does tell on demand, and it isn't even going to tell you when it is going to tell, but if you listen long enough and with the right interest, you will catch it at just the right moment and then it will tell. So I take off my leotard and fold it up carefully, putting on lipstick, and pursing my lips in the mirror, careful not to smudge, and like a vial containing some very interesting secret, I drive home in silence.

■ ■

I call Dr. Shohet, and I tell him what Veronica told me. He says carefully that he had heard that. "It is . . . strange," he says after a minute, and then stops. I can hear the concern in his voice, and hear too that he is not sure what to say about it. And I realize it doesn't matter what he says: I don't need him to try to think of a better light, a neglected interpretation by which it is less awful. It is awful, any way you describe it; the truth is, it is perfectly awful, and there is nobody I could call who could make it sound better. You call in order to feel better, and before he has said anything, I already feel better knowing he is wondering what he could say and can't think of anything.

■ ■

A few days later I call Adam. He picks up the phone immediately, his voice glad that it is me, and I get nervous, and am afraid to say anything.

"Is it all right," I ask, "if I tell you something . . . heavy?"

"Yes, love," he says, lowering his voice. I know he is listening to me completely, and I am amazed that he would give me this much attention, all of his attention—just upon asking, without prior notice, and without proving that what I am going to say will be significant. There is no one else in the world who gives me their complete attention upon such inchoate occasions. When I want my father's attention I say, "Dad, I need to talk to you," and when he's done with whatever he is doing, he finishes the chapter or turns off the game and says: "What?" This feeling of gratefulness to Adam comes over me, and replaces the need to tell, and I say, "Oh—nothing."

But he imagines I'm downplaying something important, and says urgently, "Tell me."

"Ahh," he groans, "darling—ehh." I can hear he is sick at the thought, and I don't want him to think about it more, so without thinking I say quickly: "It's all right. You'll make it up to me." As soon as I say it, I realize that it's true: if he were with me that night it would be made up for—he's that different from Brad. And even though he's not here, knowing that already makes up for most of it.

■ ■

Later I talk to Bob about it. He says he had heard, and makes a skeptical comment about a certain somebody's motivation for telling me in the first place. I say that if he knew he should have said something himself, he was keeping it from me, and he says he wasn't *keeping* it, he just hadn't bothered to pass it on.

"Bother?" I exclaim, getting mad. "How much *bother* would it have been? It's pretty important."

"No it isn't," he says, more skeptically.

"But it's so *revealing*. Why would someone want to have sex with someone who is dead? It's sex which doesn't include the other person—it is, in fact, the extremest version of that idea. At least in rape the victim is *thinking* they don't want you, if not actively struggling, so that even though the rapist is trying to take the woman's body, he isn't really *getting* it, other than the five minutes he has her pinned to the floor, because she isn't giving it. But in necrophilia you do have them, because they aren't an issue. It's the ultimate pornography: the woman not just objectified, treated as if she were an object, but really become an object—a thing, a body, a dead body. Like that blow-up doll that girl gave you for a joke on your twenty-first birthday, and everyone laughed at. What did you guys name her? Cheryl? It seems to say a lot about why he killed her in the first place—so he could *have* her—the dissolution of the other's will—"

"Oh, so what?" Bob interrupts me sharply. "*So what?* So you've figured it out? So some graduate student in English or linguistics can write a paper on the connection between sex and violence and jogging? The Sexual Politics of Forestry—sounds like a perfect *literary* sort of connection to me. Tie it in with the cave scene in *A Passage to India?*" His voice is thick with sarcasm and annoyance. "But for God's sake," he finishes, sounding really bored and disappointed, "it doesn't have to be you.

"I'm sorry, but I really think you're wasting your time."

"But," I say, "it's true."

"Oh, lots of things are true," he replies easily. "You always use that word as if it's so meaningful, but it's not. It's true that there really are men who rape and murder women for fun— several times a day—men who make a *habit* of it—but, so what? You don't see me all involved in thinking about them, wasting my time and heart trying to fathom their psyches, and figure out all the weird interesting little angles, like whether it means anything that it happened in a forest as opposed to a beach. I don't even care whether they're guilty, or are just jerks who imagine they're guilty. People are *paid* to do those things—psychiatrists and prosecutors and district attorneys and judges and policemen. There's no need for us to think about them—not for free, not in our spare time. *I spend my spare time thinking about my friends.*

"Are you being paid?" he demands suddenly.

"N—"

"Then what are you getting out of it?"

"N—"

"Why would you choose to think about things you get nothing out of?"

"I—"

"All right then—drop it. Point previously established. Never squander emotion. Didn't we talk about this before? Don't let Brad fuck with your mind.

"Besides which," he adds, an afterthought, thinking, I think, of a new angle, and I feel a certain weariness at having to hear it. I tell him something important and he throws out something glib and when it doesn't work he tries something else—slightly less glib but still several conversations away from what I want. And I wish we could just fast-forward, the way you fast-forward through a VCR movie to get to the good parts—that moment of passion or comfort or insight—when the characters finally stop screwing around and tell each other how they feel. And I wonder whether those moments with Bob seem so valuable because they're so long awaited—whether that is what gives them their beauty and their value—or whether they are just late.

"Besides what?" I ask.

"How do you even know it happened?" he says.

"What do you *mean?* Veronica told me. The paper said so!"

"Ohh," he says mockingly, "well, if it was *in writing,* I guess it must be true."

"What do you mean? Of course it's true—he said so in the confession. The papers are quoting the confession."

"Yeah, Brad's a *really* reliable source as to what happened. As I recall, he changed his mind about his statement the next day."

"But we know he was lying the next day."

"And how, might I ask, do you know that?"

"I thought— That's what everybody thinks. That's what you think! I mean—don't we—?"

"We don't know anything. There's no way to prove anything."

"You think he's *totally* making it up? Why would he make something up like that?"

"Who knows? There's no way to know he actually had inter-course with her," he says, flat and clinical. I have never heard him use such a clinical term before.

"He's totally making it up?" I persist, trying to figure out what exactly he is saying. Sometimes it seems that he's making fun of what I'm saying—"Oh, deep!" he'll tell me—and other times, when it really is deep, his sarcasm seems random, directed at whatever I say, as if he were trying to erode the concept of depth.

"He may have had *some* sexual feeling when he looked at her body," he replies, exasperated. "But so what? I have some sexual feeling when I look at a lot of people I would never touch. You have no idea what happened."

"But why would he lie?"

"Look, you choose to believe him, I choose not to. That's as far as it goes. No one's making you think anything. Just like you are choosing to be interested in it," he says evenly, "and I am choosing not to be."

I can't help thinking about it, though; I think about it incessantly and finally call Bob again a few days later. "Brad—" I begin for the hundredth time.

"Forget it," he says, cutting me off.

"How can I forget it?" I wail, but really confused, really not seeing that it is possible.

"Drop it. He's a sociopath. Don't worry about it."

"What's a sociopath?"

"Someone who is sick," he says.

"Oh. Is that all?" I ask, realizing even as I say it how insuffi-cient it is and wondering how much longer we're going to have to keep going through this song and dance. Of course it's not all—he knows it's not all—he must know that I know, yet he won't say anything meaningful until I've cornered him. The rape of my friend's dead body doesn't matter because Brad is a sociopath. He thinks he's indulging me and I think I'm indulging him.

"Uh-huh," he says, "that is definitely all."

I'm almost going to let him hang up though, but instead I say, "But Bob?"

"Yes?" he asks, nicer now. I suddenly know that the reason he has been so glib about it is that he was hoping that if he didn't give it serious attention, I would follow suit. I know, too, that at this exact moment he realizes that it hasn't worked. Our alignments are so seldom and identifiable; the next question I ask, I know for certain he will answer seriously.

"Are you sure it doesn't—matter?"

"The thing is, Mel, it's kind of a tree falling in the forest when there's no one there to hear it. You know? The only person who even knows whether it really happened is Brad, and in that way he's the only person to whom it really matters.

"Roberta wasn't"—he pauses, and says tentatively, as if afraid to put it hurtfully, and the thought that he doesn't want to say something hurtful somehow takes the hurt out of it—"with him," he says. "Roberta wasn't with him."

■ ■

"How are you?" asks Reverend Deer, as I am sitting in his office next to the glass door that opens into the garden with the fountain and the stone statue of the child with curly hair. It is a meditation garden because historically, I think, the Word of God was often received while people were waiting in gardens. It must be nice, I think, to have a job where a garden is a part of your working equipment. It must be nice, too, to have a name that matches your calling so well: Edward Deer, his name is actually the Reverend Deer. It's important, I think, thinking about my last name and how it doesn't match me. If I married Darryl Strawberry, however, and became Melanie Strawberry, then everything would match, and all of my children would be Strawberry children.

"Fine," I answer, and then feel the familiar twinge of disloyalty. (*Fine?* What do you mean you're fine? Roberta's not fine.) So I add hastily: "Except for Brad. He sort of—*festers* a little. But other than that—"

"That concerns me," he says gravely.

"Why?"

"Because you shouldn't let things fester. That is not good for you." His voice is very stern.

"But—he—"

"I do not want people to fester in your heart."

■ ■

In some of the articles Mrs. Page, Brad's mother, is interviewed. I decide to read them; I wonder what Mrs. Page has to say for herself.

4   The Boston Herald, Wednesday, December 12, 1984

MY SON COULDN'T BE THE MURDERER: MOM

By SHARON BERNSTEIN

OAKLAND, Calif.
Bradley Nelson Page was supposed to take his last college exam today and graduate with flying colors from one of the nation's most prestigious universities. Instead he will be arraigned for murder.

Page, 24, admitted he killed his girlfriend, Roberta "Bibi" Lee of Lexington, whose disappearance last month sparked a massive search throughout northern California.

Lee's badly decomposed body was found Sunday morning in an Oakland park.

One newspaper reported that Page, who friends describe as sensitive, even-tempered and artistic, admitted he struck Lee in the face, hid her body, then covered her body with leaves and twigs.

To Page's friends and parents, that scenario is impossible.

"This is just a tre-

mendous shock to the whole family," said Betsy Page, his mother. "Brad has been working with the police for the last five weeks. We just feel that there's some terrific mistake here.

"You could almost say to a fault that he was too pleasant," said Betsy Page.

She said her son and Lee, who had been dating since last February, were getting along very well.

"I took her to the ballet," she said. "I took her to see Cinderella with Baryshnikov."

Both Lee and the young Page were fond of classical music, and regularly attended the Oakland symphony, where Lee and Page's roommate, Jeff Dlott, were ushers.

"It's outrageous that they're thinking about Brad," said Dlott, 21.

Page's friends described the 6-foot-three-inch senior as handsome, with gray-green eyes and sandy hair. He writes poetry and makes handicrafts.

Dlott, who lives

with Page at a vegetarian housing coop, said his roommate was especially proud of a pair of drapes he sewed for Bibi.

"He decided he wanted to put these little lambs on the drapes," Dlott said. "So he experimented with little puff balls and he made these really intricate lambs with black legs.

"But he was kind of upset because the only puff balls that he could get to work were yellow, not white. He got little yellow lambs instead of little white ones."

Page was an organizer of "The Friends of Bibi Lee" and worked day and night to try to find his missing girlfriend, plastering San Francisco with posters. The blue and white walls of their room are adorned with photographs of Bibi Lee.

Dlott said Page doesn't use drugs, doesn't drink exept for an occasional glass of wine, and has never behaved irrationally.

Dlott said Page

studied philosophy, linguistics and poetry and enjoys cooking, poetry and crafts. He was on the lightweight crew team at Berkeley and was an avid bicyclist.

He recently finished near the top in a local triathalon where participants run, bike and swim the length of a marathon. According to Dlott, he was a "champion" ice-cream maker.

Chris Schardt, Page's next-door neighbor for 18 months, said, "He's a very, very gentle person. He's not at all hotheaded. The thought that Brad could have hurt anyone is kind of unthinkable."

Schardt said Page was too visibly upset by Lee's disappearance to seem a likely suspect.

"He was crying so hard and bawling so hard," Schardt said of the evening Page first realized Lee was gone.

"He just ran into his room and I could hear him through the walls. He didn't do that for my benefit. Incredible emotion like that you just can't fake."

ROBERTA 'BIBI' LEE. Found dead in California

The title of one of the articles is "MY SON COULDN'T BE THE MURDERER: MOM."

He couldn't have done it, she protests: I took them to the ballet. *I took them to the ballet. I took them to see* Cinderella *with Baryshnikov.* And in another article, in a section entitled "Community Standard," Mrs. Page is quoted as saying: "Around this community it was important to be good students, and parents exposed their children to art and music and intellectual things. We escaped the drug problems and those sorts of things."

I stop reading. I know exactly the sort of parent she is—just exactly. He couldn't have been unhappy, he couldn't have been troubled, he couldn't have murdered his girlfriend—she took them to the ballet. They escaped the drug problems and all that sort of thing—they all did, in fact, that was the kind of community they lived in. In their community, the consensus was that exposure to art and music and intellectual things enabled you to escape problems. She had succeeded, too: she had taken him and his girlfriend to see *Cinderella* with Baryshnikov, he was one exam away from graduating from Berkeley with flying colors, and no—her son couldn't be the murderer. "This is just a tremendous shock to the whole family . . . We just feel that there's some terrific mistake here."

It really does sum it up, I think to myself. A priceless quote. Sickening, of course, but sickening, too, to have to feel sorry for Brad on account of his family troubles.

■ ■

I speak to Meg on the phone one day. Meg knew Brad quite well; she had been Roberta's roommate the whole time Bibi and Brad were going out.

"No," she says surprisingly, "I know he didn't do it. There were too many good things in their relationship. Of course they had problems—I mean Bibi had problems with everyone—but it didn't mean we didn't love her very much. I think Brad is a very gentle person."

"You do?" I say.

"Yes," she says, "I really do."

I listen suspiciously to her tone for another minute, but it is completely sweet and sincere. I think of an article I read in which Brad's father said: "Brad was sweet, and I know that's something you're not supposed to call a boy. But I never remember raising a hand or saying a sharp word to him as a child. He was gifted in a lot of things, but he was most gifted in the way he gave his friendship.''

Gifted, I repeat to myself, a little shocked at the peculiar beautiful word. A word one uses rarely, about few people. She was gifted in many ways: the gifts she gave were so many, but most of all we were gifted to have had her for the time that we did: the fall of her hair, the small of her hands, the gloss of her voice: gifts of the dead, gifts which can't be opened until it's too late.

■ ■

Some policeman calls me, and then another policeman, and then a reporter, and they all want to know why he did it. It is strange, but it seems to me that I have never quite thought of that question before. "Perhaps she was pregnant?" an officer suggests. "No, no," I say. "Had he ever hit her before?" the police want to know. "Of course not," I say, wishing to explain that their questions are all on the wrong level. It isn't simple; it wasn't an ordinary thing like that—an action that fit into a pattern of actions. It happened only once, with no other expression, alone in the woods—buried hastily, and barely recalled. A deep thing. I know they would like me to tell them what it is, and I want to explain, but all their questions are so irrelevant that I keep saying, "No," and, getting confused, "I don't think so," and then, trying to be more definite, "No."

Finally someone asks: "But did he love her?"

"*Did he love her?*" I repeat incredulously. "I don't understand."

"You don't think he really loved her?"

"I have no fucking idea," I say, getting mad. "I don't understand on what level you are asking or what the meaning of the question is, or how, if it had any meaning before, it could possibly have meaning now, or how, *especially how,*" I say, really mad now, *"if it did, you could possibly expect me to know what it is.''*

"I'm sorry," he says, backing off, "I was just asking. I just figured you might know."

"I HAVE NO IDEA," I scream. "NONE."

■ ■

I wake up trembling in the morning. I know I have had another bad dream. Then I remember about Brad, how he must wake up trembling mornings, the fear and suspicion still upon him, and then he must realize that it is true—the worst of what he suspected about himself is true. There is no comfort in the daylight; even daylight is not a good omen for him because omens don't mean a thing anymore: *he did it.* Everyone knows—his parents, his friends, his elementary school teachers, his little sisters. His sisters will grow up knowing, and one day someone—a psychiatrist, a lover, a friend—will ask what's wrong with them: why they aren't like other girls. And they will be afraid to say—it is so ugly—their brother—their brother *murdered* someone. He will be a wound in the lives of everyone who knew him, and in his own life. A dark secret, *a revealed secret.* It's all over the papers; *it's true.* Murder. How do you wake up and feel better about that?

I am so glad, I think, opening my hands in the empty morning light—and wondering whether Bradley Page in fact has any sisters— that it isn't my trial that is coming up.

■ ■

"By the way," asks my friend Jerry one day almost a year later, "whatever happened to Brad?"

"Whatever Happened To Brad indeed," I say sarcastically. "That's a very good question—that ought to be the question of the year. That is, in fact, precisely what *I* want to know."

What happened to Brad, I explain, is nothing. The trial keeps being postponed because Brad's lawyer says he needs more time, and there are endless pretrials to debate what evidence is admissible and whether the confession was forced and that kind of bullshit and it doesn't matter because nothing is going to happen because people like him don't get convicted. There's this *New Yorker* cartoon which shows a jury foreman standing up to read a verdict, and the caption is: *"We find the accused not guilty, but not all that innocent either."* No one thinks it was anyone *else,* and we're not about to go back to looking for the Man with the Van—but they won't send him to jail. There's no evidence, they say—other than his own personal extended detailed confession, to be sure.

All the while I am explaining this as I always explain it, in my gay ironic tone, meaning isn't-life-a-drag-but-what-really-can-you-do?, when Jerry interrupts and says: "You want me to kill him?"

"Yes!" I shriek. "Jesus, why didn't you ask me *months* ago? That's *exactly* what I want!" I know I am shrieking, but I imagine it is all right because it is kind of funny—Jerry killing Brad. And it's funny too because as it happens Jerry does work for some vague intelligence organization in Washington doing something secretive and anti-Soviet I've never gotten straight.

"Okay, baby," he says quietly, and I realize that he did not see that it was a joke and I was just being funny. I get up, embarrassed, and he says, "It's okay."

"He is an asshole," I say.

"Of course he is," Jerry says soothingly.

"And you are going to kill him?" I ask, afraid he's going to change his mind.

"I am definitely going to kill him, sweetheart," he says. "Definitely."

■ ■

I think about going to the trial. I plan to go; I tell people I'm going to go; I think about calling for reservations and getting quarters to do laundry so I can pack to go, but I don't. I can't figure out quite why I would. There are several possibilities. I could be going for Roberta's sake, but it's hard to say whether she would care, being dead and all. No, just "being dead." I always add words like "and all" to make it seem as if there's something besides being dead, when there isn't. Reasons, other reasons to go to the trial. I could go for Adam's sake, but he doesn't want me to. He has, in fact, ordered me not to. I could go for myself, but I'd rather not. I could go for Bob's sake, but he thinks it's so ill-advised he won't even pick me up at the airport. He never sees anything important about being depressed, or doing depressing things. That leaves— whom? *Brad, that leaves Brad.* It's Brad's trial; I would be going for Brad. I would be giving Brad more emotions—hating Brad, being upset about Brad, being frightened of Brad, wondering who else is like Brad, etc. etc. ad infinitum, etc. Damn him to hell. Look at all these emotions I've already had; look at all this I've written. What have I gotten out of thinking and feeling so much about Brad? Adam can go, it is concluded finally, Adam will go.

"But you'll tell me everything that happens?" I ask anxiously, unable, as always, to really let anything go.

"Everything," he promises.

"No, I mean *everything*. You'll write down everything and you won't forget anything and you won't leave out anything and you'll ... you'll tell me everything, won't you?"

"I promise," he says. "I always tell you everything."

■ ■

The trial takes place in the spring of 1986, a year and a half after the murder. Adam does go and types up his notes for me and sends them along with a small pair of silver earrings and one gigantic gold earring, which is the biggest earring I have ever seen, and an olive sun hat and a calendar from Esprit and a very nice note. The note says that he is sorry I have to read the report; it is neither pleasant nor satisfying, but it is accurate. It also says he loves me and is proud of me, and although I know that there's nothing in particular he should be proud of me *for*, he says it twice in one short note, which is nice, and I read his report:

THE PROSECUTION

The prosecution spoke first, from about ten until about noon. Kenneth Burr, an assistant district attorney, handled the case. He is an odd fellow—very intense, always staring at the jury very hard, not laughing at other people's jokes. What follows is my attempt at a transcript of his remarks— not perfect but pretty accurate.

"This case flows around an incident that occurs on a Sunday probably very much like yesterday, when three young people decide to go jogging. The evidence will establish that Brad and Roberta were lovers, and had been for a little more than six to eight months. Robin Shaw was somewhat ac- quainted with both of them, her brother having been Brad's roommate at Lothlorien (I never did get this name right—at any rate, it's the co-op where Brad lived) the year before, when Roberta had also lived there. She didn't know Roberta that well, however, and didn't know that her relationship with Brad was anything more than casual. She didn't know that Brad had asked Roberta to live with him when he graduated in December. [All these 'facts' are the assertions of the lawyers.]

"Anyway, Brad had set up this run earlier in the week, asking other members of the house if they wanted to go but meeting no takers except Robin. They had agreed that

Roberta would meet them at eight-thirty. Brad was somewhat
acquainted with the area because he rode his bike, trained
for the triathlon, etc., in the hills. Brad and Robin went out
on the patio area and were stretching as they waited for
Roberta.

"Bibi was not in a very good mood. She was agitated,
irritated, and not very nice to be around. That was unlike
her, because she was a gregarious and outgoing person,
with a lot of friends. She was disturbed about a number of
things. One was her family. All the rest had gone to MIT,
and she was the first to leave the fold, and there was tension
about that. And, like many people who go straight from
high school to college, she didn't know exactly what she
wanted to do. She didn't feel she was putting that much into
her studies or getting that much out of them. And that
wasn't all that was bothering her. A rift had developed
between her and Brad. Not a major rift, perhaps, but a basic
jealousy. This was Sunday morning, and as we all know,
Saturday night is the time to go out with your boyfriend.
But they hadn't been out the night before. He went to a
party with his high school friends and didn't invite her.
Why? Perhaps he thought she wouldn't fit in, though the
evidence will show she always got along well enough with
nearly any group. Perhaps he was trying to put a little
distance between them? Perhaps. But, in fact, that night he
was picked up to be driven to the party by a high school
friend, a woman he had pined over for a number of years.
Bibi knew about her, and thought he had strong feelings for
her (this was Janet C? I don't know her last name). It wasn't
anything that serious, maybe, just transportation to a party.
But she was jealous. And Brad went dressed to kill [the
prosecution's exact words]. He was wearing a special bow
tie and pink socks that Bibi had given him. And he also
wore an Eiffel Tower earring that had been given him by
Janet, his high school friend. Bibi and he had had a tiff a
month or so before over the same issue. He was going to
Janet's birthday party. They had dinner in a restaurant that
night and Bibi walked out, stalked down the street. He got
up and followed her, but she made every effort to avoid
him, and eventually he left and ended up not going to the
party. Later they kissed and made up.

"That Sunday morning, when she got to the house shortly
before nine, she asked a couple of people where Brad and
Robin were. Upstairs in his room, they told her. She went

upstairs and they weren't there. She decided that they had gone running, and wrote a note that said, 'I guess you guys left—B.' She addressed the letter to Robin, not the defendant. Which was unusual, because she didn't know Robin that well. As she was leaving, she went out to the patio and found them. Her first words were, 'The least you could have done was wait ten minutes.' And they told her to calm down, they had waited. She went back into the house, and put a bag with her clothes [she was planning to go along on a trip to the Exploratorium in the afternoon] next to the couch in the living room. Then she came out, and the three of them walked/jogged four blocks down to Derby Street, where Brad's car was parked. There was a really strained environment, all emanating from Bibi. She was very upset, and she made her feelings known to the point where the others were uncomfortable. Perhaps you have been with two people having a marital spat [he is addressing the jury all during this presentation]. That was what this was like—uncomfortable, you didn't want to be there.

"At the car, Robin got into the front seat next to Brad. Bibi got in the front seat too, but next to the door. There was someone between her and her boyfriend. The atmosphere in the car was very strained, very little talking. They drove up Skyline to Skyline Gate, a total distance of about seven and a half miles. It took perhaps fifteen minutes. Now, the whole advantage of the drive is to take in the scenery. There are gorgeous views of the bay, of San Francisco. But because of the mood Bibi was in, no one had the opportunity to appreciate it. They piled out and started running. The defendant was familiar with the trail, had run the West Ridge before. Bibi and Robin had never been there. As they ran along, the strain was very evident. Bibi fell back a little bit—a few paces. They were going at a very casual pace—the defendant could easily have run faster, but the whole idea was to enjoy the trip. They got to the area by an archery range and read a trail map that showed the Roberts Park area, which they decided to run to. This area was more like a city park, with paved parking lots, a pool, etc. The whole trip took about twenty minutes. They came past a house, where a resident caretaker lives, and then ran through the trees, across the driveway, and into an area called Huckleberry, where they separated. The land here is not flat—it's rolling hills. Bibi went off in a southerly direction, according to Robin Shaw. A minute or so later the defendant stops to wait for the two girls. Robin Shaw soon catches up. Bibi doesn't. The two of them figure that she is taking a minute or so to get her head together, and decided to wait for her. They call her name out a couple of times—sometimes loudly, sometimes sort of jokingly. After fifteen minutes or so, they conclude she must have gone back to the car. It takes them about twenty minutes to run back, and they get there about ten a.m. She's not there. Robin Shaw suggests that Brad drive to Roberts Park—'I'll wait here,' she says. The defendant drives off. He later tells us that he drove to the parking lots, circled each of them, driving slowly, a couple of times calling out her name. At no time did he get out of his car. At no time did he climb up to look for her. At no time did he go to the people in the house to ask them. When he had no success he went back to Skyline Gate, where Robin was waiting. He said the total time he was gone was about fifteen minutes. Robin Shaw says it was fifteen or twenty minutes. They wait a little longer. It is clear to Robin Shaw that something is wrong. There is a change in Brad, a concern, an agitation.

"Brad wants to go back. Robin has questions: Can she run back? Does she have any money? The defendant says, 'We've inconvenienced you enough, Robin. Let's go.' Robin feels a little funny about leaving somebody that far from home. But the defendant says, 'I know her better than you do; she knows what she's doing.' The defendant says, 'She can take a bus. She can call someone. She can run home.' So they go back. When they reach the house, the first thing the defendant does is go have breakfast, a puff cereal of some sort. Then he goes up to his room, calls Bibi's house, speaks with Diana Freeman. 'Is she there?' 'No.' 'Tell her we're leaving for the Exploratorium at one p.m.' He doesn't tell her that we left her in the park, he doesn't say he's a little bit concerned. Nothing at all. He doesn't call anyone else. Instead he writes a paper. He thinks about going back up there to see if she's okay. But it's clear that people want to go to the Exploratorium. He says later that he had made a commitment to provide transportation. One of the girls who arranged the trip asks him, 'Is Bibi going?' And he says, 'No, she's not.' The group returns about six p.m. Brad is feeling really good. It had been a really moving experience, he says. He forgets all about Bibi. There was a really good dinner that night—enchiladas. He makes a call after dinner to Bibi's apartment. He tells Meg Luther he had left Bibi up there, and says, 'When she gets in, have her give me a call.' The defendant does nothing else. He doesn't call her family or friends or anything. About one a.m., a phone call comes from Meg Luther. She's panicked. She tells Brad to come over. She starts calling police agencies and hospitals. The police say they can't help because she isn't a missing person for twenty-four hours. The defendant stays in Bibi's room that night, and falls asleep.

"The next morning, the parks department puts on a massive search, with bloodhounds, the whole works. The defendant is asked to bring some article of her clothing. They explain to him how the dogs operate. They try to get a personality profile of Bibi. Dogs search the area and conclude that Bibi's not there. What they're looking for is not a dead body, but a live person, incapacitated.

"What next takes place is one of the most dramatic search efforts the area has ever seen. At first, it is primarily Meg Luther, Scott Lawson, and the defendant. Students who are friends are all coming together to help. This was back before people started putting pictures on milk cartons and such, so it was really dramatic. Within a week, two new people have entered the picture—Lena Grady and a man who works for the missing children group. They have some skills organizing this sort of thing. They set up a twenty-four-hour hotline. Newspaper reporters are all over the place. They play to the media, because that's how you find someone. They find nothing. Oh, there are a lot of tips. One in particular—a woman who says she saw Bibi five miles away, in Monterey, tussling with a heavyset man. From then on, the focus of the search is on the van man.

"This chain of events works very well in favor of the defendant. For there are two faces of Brad Page. The first face is the lover of Bibi Lee. This was the first real love. He is supposedly devastated. He is apparently caught up in the search. Then there's the other side, the other face—the killer of Bibi Lee who hides behind the mask of the devastated boyfriend. Who gets swept up in the search. He has to. If he doesn't, the finger of suspicion points to him [this last section delivered very emotionally].

"The body was found on December 9, when Lena Grady decides to have another dog-run through the park. This time it's not the Contra Costa rescue squad, but some German shepherd handlers she has worked with before. In a very short time the German shepherd finds her in some bushes seven hundred feet below the driveway, within this heavy, thick brush taller than six feet. There was a well-worn path, and they followed it in to the grave site of Bibi Lee.

"When the body is found, it is in the city of Oakland. Until this time, it has been under the jurisdiction of the Berkeley Police Department. But because of where the body was found, it is transferred to the Oakland police. Two sergeants are assigned to the case. The recovery of the body was an all-day effort—it took into the early-evening hours. And once that was done, the two sergeants assigned to the case— Lacer and Harris—decided to start their investigation by interviewing the last two people she had been with. They arrive at ten the next morning.

"The interviews with the defendant comprise five separate interviews, from 10:10 Monday morning until 2:18 Tuesday morning. The first interview, at 10:10, goes until 1:10 in the afternoon. At approximately 11:50, they tape-record what he has to say. Before he starts talking, they read him his Miranda rights. Between 10:10 and 1:10 the defendant tells them what I've said to this time. Sergeants Harris and Lacer have a good deal of trouble with what he is saying. As he describes the relationship they practically lived together. 'Well,' they say, 'you tell us this, but you're doing a few things here that don't sound right. You don't leave the love of your life in the hills and drive off. You don't go off to the Tactile Room of the Exploratorium when she's not back. You don't just drive around the parking lot a couple of times and never get out to look for her. There are concerns we have, things we feel uncomfortable about. Would you mind submitting to a polygraph?' The defendant agrees, and the test is administered by Sergeant Furry. In the preinterview, he asks him if he has read any accounts of her discovery, if he has any idea where the body was found. No. 'How did you sleep last night?' he asks. 'Pretty well—seven and a half hours.' He runs the test. The first sort of test is called 'peak of tension.' It asks, 'If you were the person who hurt her, you'd know what area she was injured—legs, head, chest, side, arms.' There was also a multiquestion format. On the third run-through, the defendant showed some emotion [he cried]—enough emotion that the test was discontinued. There were three things Sergeant Furry could conclude from the test: the defendant was being truthful, the defendant was being deceptive, or the results were inconclusive. Sergeant Furry concluded the defendant tested deceptive, primarily on the question 'Did you injure her?' Sergeant Furry told the defendant he had proved deceptive. He was taken back to an interview room—a small room with no windows, where all suspects, witnesses, etc., are interviewed.

"Half an hour later, Sergeants Harris and Lacer went in. 'You flunked the test,' they told him. The defendant has his head down on the table—he's wailing. 'But I loved her,' he said. 'I really loved her.' He wasn't crying—it was more a wailing type of moan. The sergeants say to him, 'You've got to pull yourself together. We've got some questions, some problems.' At that, he sits right up and snaps out, 'You don't think I did it, do you?' The interesting thing here is the lack of tears, the complete shift from apparent bereavement to apparent denial. 'We think you're lying,' they tell him. Within ten to twenty minutes he says, 'I remember kicking and hitting her, really whacking on her. I don't remember why.' 'Why?' they ask him. 'Well,' the defendant says, 'I must have blacked out.' They go over and over it. By six, he starts telling them a few things. By seven, when they start taping, he lays it all out.

"In the process of all this, the police had told him a few things—told him they have his fingerprints. And a witness who says he saw his car south of the driveway. These last two facts are not true. But they got a reaction.

"The story he gives when the tape is turned on is that he turned left and came down the road after driving around the parking lot twice. He sees Bibi on the forest side of the road, sees her walking on the shoulder. He pulls the car up beside her, gets out and runs up to her, tries to grab her and turn her around. On the one hand, he says she pulled away and he slapped her. On the other hand, he says, 'I tried to pull her to me, and I kissed her on the forehead. She said, "You don't care anymore." And that's when I backhanded her. She fell next to a tree. I think maybe I saw a trickle of blood from her nose.'

"His story for the afternoon is true—he went to the museum and all. And then he said, 'Right after dinner I went back up there and found her right where I'd left her. I knew she was dead because she hadn't moved. When I found her, I went to the car and in the back of the station wagon found a blanket. I took it back, lay down beside her, hugged her, kissed her, caressed her, and made love to her. Then I pulled her south to Skyline and I buried her. I buried her under some limbs of some trees.' 'What did you cover her with?' 'I covered her with some dirt and needles. I went back to the car, got a hubcap, and used that to move the soil.' [To the jury:] This is very important. You are going to see some very distasteful pictures. It is paramount that you study them very closely. It's not a grave in the sense you envision a grave. Not a hole, not six feet under. Basically, she's on the ground, and the humus and all is put on top of her. By the time her body is found, animals have gotten to her a little. But the coroner's office uncovered her very carefully, and you can see that it is not a grave. She is just nicely covered, just as the defendant described it.

"The defendant describes something else. And that is after his taped statement is done at 7:30. He's left alone while two people from my office are called in to talk to him. They arrive at the Oakland Police Department at 8:30, 8:40, they're briefed, and they go in a little after 9:00 that evening. In the hour and a half while he was waiting for that, the defendant realized what had happened. He realized that he had confessed. But he didn't want to be held responsible. When you listen to the confession, you can hear him trying to minimize the whole thing. He knew he had flunked the polygraph, thought there were fingerprints around, and figured the only thing to do was cut his losses—make it something less than it was, an accident. He just hit her once. But the coroner will tell you she had a depressed skull fracture, a piece of skull broken away and pushed into her brain. That requires a tremendous amount of force, likely a rock. Between 7:30 and 9:00 he is thinking about all these things—thinking, How can I get out of this? He starts seeing his life go down the toilet. How can I put the cat back in the bag? The answer he comes up with: I was so distraught, so psychologically fragile. I just wanted to help. And so I started my imagination going. [Prosecutor sounds very sarcastic as he says the above.] 'It was only logical to outline it the way I did,' he says. As if it were logical to make love to a dead body. We all know that. He tries to recant. 'No, I just made all that up. They convinced me. I'm so weak.'

"You listen to those tapes—not only to what is said, but how he says it. He tries to worm his way out of it. The interview with the men from my office takes about forty-five minutes. Then he's left alone as the cops do the paperwork. At 11:25 he knocks on the door. 'I want to straighten this out,' he says. At 11:50 they turn the tape recorder on. It goes until 2:18 as he gives them his spiel. 'I'm just devastated,' he says. He says one interesting thing: 'I heard she was bare from the waist up.' Well, her shirt had been pulled up above her chest. But no one had reported that yet—there was no way he could have known. The key evidence here is the tapes. You listen to them, and you hear a man who is trying to squirm his way out of responsibility for killing Bibi Lee.''

THE DEFENSE

This is the opening statement by the defense lawyer, William Gagen. It is a little less clear than the prosecution statement because he isn't laying out a story in as linear a fashion and because he is just more complex in his thoughts.

"You've heard a very professional, polished opening statement, and it contains a certain characterization of the evidence. I could have waited several weeks, until the prosecution closes its case, to present my opening statement, but I wanted to do it now because it is so important that you hear another side. The crucial day in this case is the day of December 10, but to understand the events of that day you have to have an understanding of who Brad Page was, and his interaction with Bibi Lee. Brad was twenty-three at the time, an average young man who had never been in trouble. He was thought by his friends to be gentle, kind and artistic. He liked nature and enjoyed literature. Perhaps because of his gentle nature he was very popular with young women. Roberta Lee was very bright, popular and attractive, and it was only natural they would be attracted to each other. At first they were friends, but by the fall of 1984, and perhaps earlier, they had a more serious kind of dating relationship. As with any young people, there were concerns and disagreements—just like young people anywhere.

"Lothlorien (I still can't get this name straight) was a coeducational living facility, where many of the young people shared certain philosophies, including vegetarianism. It was a most open place, men living with women, not necessarily in a sexual sense, but together. It says here that Bibi came in November of 1983. She and Brad began to interact early in 1984. That summer there was even a scare she might have been pregnant. She called him up to talk about it, but nothing happened—it was simply an overdue period. In the fall of 1984, their relationship resumed, though she moved into Fenwick. They spent some nights together, they socialized among the same people. Between Halloween and Thanksgiving, Bibi began to reflect some concern with what she was going to do with her life. She dropped out. They discussed if they would live together—there was no talk of marriage, just if they would live together, as kids do these days. Their relationship was very much up in the air on November 4. There had been incidents of jealousy, each saw people of the other sex, nothing was settled.

"One thing that is very important to understand here is the independence of Bibi Lee, because it relates to her thought processes and Mr. Page's. She was not dependent. She had hitchhiked to Mexico with a friend. She liked to take off when she was depressed, to distance herself. She took off on Brad some weeks before, the incident in the restaurant which the prosecutor described. There was a party for her at the house one night and she left. This pattern of leaving, of wanting to distance oneself, was not out of the ordinary for her.

"On the morning of November 4, Brad Page expected to meet with Robin Shaw and Bibi to take a run. Robin Shaw was a junior at that time. Her relationship with Brad Page was totally platonic; they didn't date. Bibi was, as we have heard, in a feisty mood that morning, from the events of the night before. Young people are very sensitive about these things. Bibi was upset because he'd worn a special bow tie and special socks she'd given him to a party the night before. Bibi snapped at him. Brad was perhaps sarcastic in return. It was a little tense, there was a bit of hostility in the air.

"They ran much as described by the prosecutor, and when they reached the Huckleberry area, Robin saw Bibi veer off to the south as if she were going toward Skyline. A little ahead, Brad and Robin stopped at Bay Vista for a while—a great view of the bay from there, they spent maybe three to five minutes. Then they trotted over to Diablo Vista, and waited there another three or four minutes. They called out her name several times, then decided she'd probably gone back to Skyline Gate and the car. They ran back. When she wasn't there, Robin stayed with the car; Brad drove back and drove around the parking lot several times and returned. It's a slow road with a lot of curves—it took fifteen or twenty minutes. When he got back, Robin was still there. Both felt a little uneasy, but Robin deferred to Brad, who said, 'This is like Bibi.' If he had struck her, as his statement indicates, it had to happen in that fifteen to twenty minutes. And, according to Robin, he didn't seem particularly upset or depressed, just like Brad.

"From one to five p.m. they were at the Exploratorium. Brad was the main cargo carrier because of his station wagon. He was happy that afternoon, enjoying himself. He has, according to his friends, a kind of playful quality. He's a playful guy. That morning, back in the park while they were waiting for Bibi, he'd fooled around, long-jumping over picnic tables. Anyway, at the museum he talked briefly with his roommate, Jeff, and showed some level of concern.

"The next few hours are critical. If his statement is to be taken at face value, he had to be gone for a significant time. The evidence will reflect he had dinner, and that he was at Lothlorien as late as 8:00 to 8:15. Between 8:00 and 9:30, he says, he was in and about his room; there is no evidence, as far as I know, of anyone seeing him. His roommate Jeff remembers that they went to bed at about 9:30. At about 10:00 p.m. Meg Luther calls and is told Brad is asleep. After midnight, Meg calls again and demands that he be woken up. This time he's very concerned. He goes over to her house and along with Meg places calls to hospitals and the like. The next morning Meg and Brad contacted authorities, and on November 5 a search effort begins.

"I want to interrupt my narrative here and explain that over the next few days, a number of sightings were reported. Four people had thought they had seen her between 10:00 a.m. and noon along Skyline. There was a woman going to church, a woman at the Woodminster Market, a woman at the Lincoln Woods shopping center. The last, most ominous sighting took place about noontime. This was Mrs. Marquand, who saw someone she identified as Bibi Lee being pulled into a van by a man. The police were able to find a similar van to photograph, and they did an artist's reconstruction of the man. These were put on literally thousands of flyers and circulated all over California. And the police, with the help of the TV stations, actually re-created what she'd seen and broadcast it.

"On November 5 there was a search of the park. Brad had been asked to bring some of Bibi's dirty laundry to the park, and he did, and then he waited in the administration building while the search progressed. There is one participant in this search that I would like to focus on in particular. This was a bloodhound, Duke—he had a 90 percent success rate finding bodies. By his breeding, he can smell blood for hundreds of yards. I am told the smell of it makes his nose almost literally burn. He once found a body that was under seventy-five feet of water. And he came within twenty-five or thirty yards of the burial site and, according to his handlers, ran over the exact location of the crime, if it happened as Mr. Page said in his statement it did. There is no evidentiary explanation for why he didn't find her. The Explorer Scouts also combed the area. These are not kids playing Boy Scout—these are eighteen-, nineteen-, twenty-year-olds. The leader remembers being in the area of the shrubs where the body was found. He cannot explain why he saw nothing.

"There then began a massive effort to find Bibi Lee. Brad Page, for the next five weeks, was intensely involved in the search effort. Nothing he did in that time indicated a desire to escape from the problem. He walked in the area with a reporter, pointing things out—they passed within seventy-five yards of the burial site. By Saturday, November 10, a woman named Lena Grady became the titular head of Friends of Bibi Lee. She had become almost obsessed—and I mean this in a positive way—with finding missing young women, and she organized the search effort. On November 12, the search headquarters was located at Treehaven—it was an almost military operation. On November 13, Brad returned to the park with the Berkeley police. On November 16, Brad and others brought in a psychologist to talk with people at his house because they were so grief-stricken. On November 17, a Saturday, they brought in a psychic. They were desperate enough that they were working with a psychic. Jeff had a guru that was helping him. On November 19, Brad wrote a poem called 'Suitable ending,' a summary of his feelings about her loss. He was artsy-craftsy to the point where he would sit down and compose a poem.

"Brad Page was in the cause of this search group all that time. Gradually he began to show signs of deterioration. He was suffering from strain. Friends remember hearing him crying from his room. He was drinking excessively, which he hadn't done before—these kids were always careful about what they put in their bodies. He began to dress in odd fashion. Bibi's favorite colors had been red and black, and he began to wear a black cape. And he and Veronica Lee painted two of their fingernails, one red and the other black. It was almost fanaticism by this point. One incident of note was December 4, when he was wailing bizarrely. His friends became so concerned that they called his mother, and she came in and he fell asleep in her arms. Her testimony, by the way, will have to come on videotape, because she died last year.

"The ninth and the tenth of December are the heart of this case. On December 9, a Sunday, her body was discovered. Brad spent part of the day with his mother in Lafayette. When he returned to Lothlorien, there was a note tacked up that a body had been found. He went to Treehaven, and while he was there, there was a phone call in his presence. He learned that she was buried somewhere close to where he had last seen her. His reaction was to break down. From the bathroom, where he went, there was a wailing sound. All the emotion seemed to be genuine.

"He slept at Lothlorien that night, and the next morning was asked to go to the Oakland Police Department, where two new officers, veteran homicide detectives, in effect began the case anew. What happened at the OPD is why we are here. The evidence rests on the statement Bradley Page made that day. At 10:00 a.m., a sixteen-hour period of interrogation was begun. Only three hours and forty minutes of the total interrogation were recorded, even though those rooms are set up to allow constant recording. [It will be an important question in the case as to why there are no tapes for the rest of those talks.]

"At 10:00 a.m., Sergeants Lacer and Harris introduced themselves. Brad was given his Miranda rights—the right to remain silent, etc.—and told it was merely a formality. At no time did he assert any right, or ask to call anyone except Lena Grady, whom he wanted to know where he was. All the interviews that follow were conducted in interrogation rooms—eight-by-five-foot rooms, about the size of a bathroom, intentionally barren. At the beginning, they tell him he's not a suspect. He talked. He talked about his relationship with Bibi. The officers seemed particularly interested in whether they'd had any sexual problems. He said there was some frustration about what type of birth control to use, but that generally they were good. We know this from the scanty notes the officers made. Why wasn't everything recorded? It's not critical at this point, but it will become critical later on. At the end of this first interview, the police suggested a lie detector test—not, they said, because they didn't believe him, but because they just wanted to have it as a record.

"Sergeant Furry is the man who gives the polygraph tests. He gives 200 or 250 a year. A vital question is whether this polygraph was given to actually determine truth or falsity, or as a technique of interrogation. It is not a pleasant process. The blood pressure cuff is put on the arm, and it stays pumped up for as long as the person can tolerate it. EKG-like devices are attached to the fingers to measure galvanic skin response. Straps are put across the chest to measure the breathing. Before being subjected to this test, Brad had never taken one.

"The integrity of the polygraph depends on the technique of the person giving it. Is he asking the correct questions? Does he have the subject in a proper state of mind? Is he taking his time? We will summon the chief polygraph expert in the nation—the very man who devised the scorecard Sergeant Furry used—and he will tell you that the test in this case was inaccurate, incomplete and improperly given.

"The first test they give is called 'peak of tension.' They ask, 'If she were injured, you'd know where. Was it chest, legs, arm, etc.?', and if your response rises at the correct one, it's a sign. Well, it's a stupid question—fatal injuries are very rarely to the legs, the arm, the side. That left head and chest, and in fact Brad reacted *more* strongly to chest than to head. Our expert, Clive Baxter, will testify that if he were grading Sergeant Furry, he would fail him. The next section of the test was called 'relevant questions.' They ask, 'Did you injure Bibi?' 'Do you know who injured her?' 'Do you suspect who injured her?' The test is scored from −4, which means deception, to +4, which means truth. They ran through this several times. On the third test, Mr. Page broke down and cried. Sergeant Furry stopped the test there. What he should have done was wait for him to calm down and done it some more—because the results had showed, according to Sergeant Furry, a mild tendency toward deception. According to Mr. Baxter, they showed a tendency toward truthfulness. At any rate, there was nothing conclusive. But the insidious outcome of the polygraph was that Sergeant Harris confronted Mr. Page and said, 'You failed. You flunked. And we have a witness, too, who saw you turn left on Skyline. And some fingerprints.'

"Now what happens is the critical time. For a three-hour period, Brad is subjected to continuous interrogation. From that whole period, there are three pages of notes. We know some of the things that were said: 'You failed the polygraph.' 'We have your prints.' 'We have a witness.' 'Do you believe in God?' they asked him. 'Then how can you lie?'

And they told him that people often black out, and that
there is a difference between an accident and a killing.

"And what Brad said was, 'No, I don't remember. But if
you tell me I was there, I *must* have blacked out.'

"Brad had very little street smarts. The officers dealt with
him now in an ingratiating way. And he began to conjure up
what he called a scenario. If I did it, it must have happened
this way. There were two cornerstones. One was a sexual
fantasy he had acknowledged earlier in the day. The second
was his statement that he could have slapped her or kicked
her. They knew that didn't fit with the physical evidence,
and they tried desperately to get a rock into his hands, but
couldn't. At the end of that three hours, they taped a twenty-
six-minute statement, which is the centerpiece of this case.
You will hear that tape, but I want to read you a few
excerpts. 'I *think* I backhanded her *or something.*' 'I *think* she
fell down on her side.' 'I *picture her* unconscious.' 'She
might have had a bloody nose.' 'I *assume* I drove back that
night.' 'I *think* I went back to the car.' 'I *think* I made love to
her.' 'I *envision* a slope, a little bit of a slope.' Now, in the
same twenty-six-minute tape, he says things like, 'Until yesterday I thought she was alive.' Does this track? This is
imagery, and nothing more. 'Did you ejaculate?' 'I *assume*
so.' Now, is that a truthful statement or is that imagery
created in these three hours?

"Now, the very expert OPD crime lab spent hours using
the physical evidence to try to corroborate his statement.
And not only were they involved, but also the FBI. A couple
of the physical items were incompatible. Could Bibi Lee possibly have been injured by being slapped, and then hitting her
head? Reasonable medical evidence suggests not. There were
three separate areas of injury to the skull, three distinctly
strong hard traumatic blows. Also there were nasal fractures.
'I might have backhanded her.' The next thing is the blanket.
Consent was given for a search of his car, and there are
photographs showing the trunk. [He displays one.] In the
well, they found a hubcap and a blanket. And these were
the subject of extraordinary efforts. There was no evidence
the blanket had even been unfolded, perhaps in this decade.
They found eight hairs on it, none of which matched Bibi
Lee's. There was no blood, and no semen. The hubcap had
no buildup of dirt in it. There was even a spiderweb in it.
And there was no indication it had been wiped clean.

"There was also a question about the burial scene—it was

not on a slope, as he had said. And there was no tree limb, as he had said. There are questions about its even being physically possible to bury her in the time he was possibly away from home. There was no evidence of cuts on his hands, and he doesn't have workman's hands. And if he was a manipulative killer, would he have returned to the scene in the dark of night, somehow found her body, somehow moved and buried it? The patrols in the area that night spotted nothing.

"And one thing I'd like to point out is that the place in which the body was buried has easy access from the road. It would have been very easy for someone to stop there, take out the body, and leave it there.

"Anyway, at some point that evening the D.A. arrives. 'I'm glad you're here. I want to talk to somebody. I'd like to go home.' I ask you, is that consistent with an intelligent man who thought he'd just confessed to a crime? He told them 'I feel guilty'—not about some act, but about going home and writing a paper. 'The first tape in the morning—that was everything I knew. All this other stuff, they just convinced me I was thinking: To think I could black out at a time like that and do horrible things like that—I didn't know I could.'

"Harris and Lacer come back in eventually, and they're displeased. 'If you lie, you're going to hell,' they say. That culminated with the final taped interview. Basically, it's an argument. They're confronting him, fighting him. And without the benefit of a lawyer, without the benefit of hours to think about it, he explains how it happened that he gave this false statement, this scenario.

"On December 10, he was a very scared man, an emotionally drained man. By education, he is a poet. He works on an intellectual level. Are things really as they seem? That kind of approach. And the two cops were good men, but tough, streetwise, and talking to him on a very different level. And that is how it happened.

I put down the report. It's too bad, I think, I'm so sympathetic to Brad's main argument—the argument that he imagined it. "By education, he is a poet. He works on an intellectual level. Are things really as they seem? That kind of approach." Are things really as they seem indeed? The cops told him they knew the facts, and so he made the emotions accordingly. Poetry begins with the real and ends in the imagined. They said he had done it, and they are real people—they are *policemen*—they know about these things. When people tell you something is true, it's true: you have to shape your feelings around the facts. We know this isn't the premise you were hoping for, but this is the premise we're giving you, so try to make yourself useful.

Imagine how it would have been if you had done it. It's important. There's no point in protesting. *You have to*—we just told you: we have fingerprints, we have a witness, *we know that you did it.* Let's work from there. Tell us how it happened. Come on: think. Don't you have any imagination?

But I thought I was at home writing my paper, Brad tries to protest one last time. But maybe I am wrong—maybe I . . . forgot. It gets so difficult to be sure of anything after a while. Especially if you think about it for a long time. I've been thinking so long now.

You don't have to be sure; we're sure. Just pretend for a little while—come on, play along. We really want you to; we need you to. Imagine, imagine, imagine what it is like. Your friend Roberta is lying on the ground. She is alone. *Alone.* Are you sure you weren't there with her? *You had nothing at all to do with it?* Alone and in the hands of a stranger. Wouldn't you rather he were you? You were with her only minutes before. Think. We'll turn on the tape recorder so you can think aloud. We just want to make sure we have everything down that you think. It's not such a large leap and it might be interesting. Crucial, possibly. Speak. Emote. Tell us a story.

All right: this is the story.

And then: wait! You misunderstood! I was just making it up. There is—a confusion of levels. I was speaking metaphorically. *I am a poet.*

■ ■

I call Adam. "I got your report," I say, "and I just wondered— umm—why you forgot to put in it that *one side was true, and the other side was lying.* I mean why, I wondered, didn't you put in that Brad's story—his story about his story—that his first story, the confession, wasn't a true confession—*that that story was a lie?*"

And then: "We do think that, don't we?

"Adam?"

He says, after a moment, he doesn't know.

"How can you say that?"

"I'm not keeping anything from you, child," he says in the old voice, the voice of perfect consolation. "I'm sorry—anything I knew I would tell you. I think he did it, but I don't know. Only Brad and God know for certain the whole story."

And maybe not even Brad anymore, I realize in sudden defeat.

Bradley Page at first arraignment

...in jogger's boyfriend arraigned

police say suspect, 24, is 'waffling'
dmission he killed Lexington native

Thomas Palmer
m Simon
al to the Globe

he boyfriend of Roberta [B...]
was formally charged with [...]
der yesterday morning, [...]
hours later, unshaver[...]
ting tired, he was arrai[...]
kland Municipal Co[...]
aded innocent.

Bradley N. Page, a 2[...]
nior at the University[...]
at Berkeley, was h[...]
ail pending a heari[...]
ay. No trial date w[...]
he two-hour court [...]
terday, attended by [...]
sons, but a preli[...]
was scheduled for [...]

Meanwhile, P[...]
on his initial [...]
that he str[...]
buried her b[...]
spokesman [...]
" District [...]

originally a case of a missing person.

Kennedy's office acknowledged
that his staff had called the Berkeley Police periodically to check
gress in the case. "The senator
the family and at their
abreast of the sit-
aide Brian

Lexington woman's body found in Calif.

By Thomas Palmer
Globe Staff

The body of a 1980 [...]

STUDENT, STATE SPLIT ON COED DEATH BLOW

By JOHN BIRTWELL

THE boyfriend of
oberta "Bibi" Lee
police he killed
Lexington wo-
tan by striking her
ith his hand, but a
reliminary autopsy
eveals she died
fter being hit with
a blunt instrument,"
california prosecu-
rs said yesterday.

Alameda County De-
ty District Attorney
rry Curtis said the
year-old coed
tely died after being
with a rock or a
ck.

Bradley Nelson
ge, 24, a senior at the
liversity of Califor-
-Berkeley, told in-
stigators he and Lee
d been jogging to-
ther on the morning
Nov. 4 when he sud-
nly struck her.

Curtis said the couple
d another friend had
en running together
en Lee left by her-
f.

The evidence is now
at Page came back
ne several hours
r and met Miss
," said Curtis.
e's decompo[...]
was found Sun[...]
ng in San [...]
ark, less than [...]
rom where [...]
ad said the [...]
arated.

pleaded in
to murd
at a brief he
kland Muni
officials sa
ll, sand
fendant w
eld witho
g a heari
ay, sa

Telephone (617) 426-3000

Dramatic confession ends hunt for

*** 25 Cents

Wednesday De[...]

BOYFRIEND HEL IN COED SLAYING

By JOHN BIRTWELL and ANDREA ESTES

THE BOYFRIEND of
slain Lexingto[...]

'Brainwashing' Hint In Bibi Lee Case

By Edward Iwata

Murder suspect Bradley
Page showed signs of being
brainwashed during a disputed
taped "confession" he made to
Oakland police, a psychiatrist
testified yesterday in Alameda
County Supe[...] Court.

The psyc[...]
Thompson of [...]
Page displaye[...]
ical symptom[...]
by military pr[...]
Betty Hearst[...]

have had severe amnesia and forgotten the killing, repeated questions to further confuse him and
convinced him he would feel better
if he confessed.

"In short, a confession
good for his soul, and without
lly damned

icipal Court f[...]

no win-
ize of a
he lan-
hadn't
lawyer
wationing
was

nd Sunday
Joaquin
200 feet
uple went

reached
her Oak-
it, called
Page 4

Friends remember Bibi Lee's 'spark'
'It was very beautiful to watch her dance...'

By LEIGH ANNE JONES
STAFF WRITER

Roberta Lee was a UC Berkeley linguistics student who disappeared on
Nov. 4. Her body was found Dec. 9,
five weeks after she was last seen. Her
description was inscribed into the
minds of the thousands of people around the Bay Area, the stat[...]
nation who [...]

when she couldn't find it. The day she
dropped out of school, she met up
with a friend on Telegraph, and told
the friend about her feelings. As the
two parted ways, Bibi took a few steps
and then turned back to quip, "Do you
think it's too late for me to start stu[...]
ing Russian?"

room and she used to come into my
room and turn on the radio and dance.
She would close her eyes and she had
such a comfortable way of movi[...]
that other people in [...]
stop th[...]

I reread the newspaper articles of the last two years carefully. I had forgotten how many there were, and how many different things they said and how many of the bits—the lines and tales— ring odd and familiar.

" 'Although it may seem like justice is being served, there is really no sense to me in all this, because, after all, Bibi's gone,' said Lloyd Nebres, who said he met Lee when she was a first-year student. 'What's taking place is painful to all—not only to Brad, but to her family and friends. It's pointless.'

"Nebres said he met Lee at one of his first classes at Cal, a seminar on Marx and Freud, and they instantly became friends . . . He remembers the candlelit vigils that were held for Lee in Sproul Plaza.

" 'I remember going out on my own, putting the posters up. I walked all the way down Telegraph Avenue in the rain to down-town Oakland, putting them on phone poles, stores.' "

" 'The night before [she was reported missing] we went to a punk Shakespeare production called "Otello." . . . She worked as an usher and could attend shows free.' "

" 'Alex Vorbeck . . . said she met Bibi when they both worked for a disabled woman. . . . The group . . . met on campus in front of the Martin Luther King Jr. Student Union before the search, where Page led a prayer directed to Lee.

" 'Brad led a prayer. He said something to Bibi about coming home, something like, "Our energy is coming out to you." It was real esoteric,' Vorbeck said. 'He said that we were all thinking about her and that she should come home.

" 'It gave me weird vibes when I found out he was arrested.' "

" 'We were postering, not really searching . . . we were going to bars and porno shops—places we thought the man identified would frequent. . . .' "

" 'It's outrageous that they're thinking about Brad,' said Jeff DeLott, 21.

"Page's friends describe the six-foot three-inch senior as handsome, with gray-green eyes and sandy hair. He writes poetry and makes handicrafts.

"DeLott, who lives with Page . . . said his roommate was especially proud of a pair of drapes he sewed for Bibi.

" 'He decided he wanted to put these little lambs on the drapes,' DeLott said. 'So he experimented with little puff balls and he made these really intricate lambs with black legs.

" 'But he was kind of upset because the only puff balls that he could get to work were yellow, not white. He got little yellow lambs instead of little white ones.'

"The . . . walls of their [DeLott and Page's] room are adorned with photographs of Bibi Lee.

"DeLott said Page studied philosophy, linguistics and poetry and enjoys cooking and crafts. He was on the lightweight crew team at Berkeley and was an avid bicyclist. . . . According to DeLott he was a 'champion ice cream maker.' "

" 'He was very artistic and liked art classes . . . where he painted and made stained glass windows and pottery,' Betsy Page said."

"Both Lee and young Page were fond of classical music, and regularly attended the Oakland symphony. . . ."

"As a prosecutor for many years, Burr said he has heard defense attorneys ask jurors to find their clients innocent because they had led deprived lives full of violence or had dropped out of school or had come from a broken home.

"But in this case, Burr said, the attorney is asking jurors not to convict Page because he grew up in a sheltered environment, went to the right schools, spent a year in France, traveled to Mexico and 'was not responsible for what he said.' "

" 'I thought I had stayed home and wrote my paper, but I didn't really know what I did that night,' Page said."

"Defense attorney William Gagen said his client's confession was 'ethereal B.S.' and discounted the prosecution's contention that Page is a child of privilege who can afford a high-priced defense."

" 'I wasn't getting very good sleep . . . I was having a hard time,' Page testified. 'I was crying, I was depressed.'

"At one point, Page said, he wore fingernail polish and put on eyeshadow "because 'I was kind of mad at the world for taking away my friend.'

"On another occasion . . . Page said he walked home 'and I started to cry . . . It got louder, and I was moaning . . . I was frightened.' "

" 'What do you do if you don't know what happened?' said Page . . . 'What's the cost of a life? We didn't know what was going on. . . . It was just left up to God for us to find out. . . . She was very dear to me.' "

"Midway through the search, Page said he and a group of friends enlisted the help of a psychic and a spiritual guru for leads on Lee's whereabouts."

"He wore a red flannel shirt of Lee's 'to be with her,' he said."

"In other testimony, Page referred to an incident that occurred when he was 18 years old. Page gave a sketchy account of meeting a man who asked him for $20 to wire money and ended up persuading Page to go to his bank account and give the man $1,000. Page said he never saw his money again."

" 'Didn't you find it somewhat revolting, the idea of making love to the dead body of the woman you had just killed?' asked Prosecutor Kenneth Burr.

" 'It was purely intellectual,' Page answered. . . .

" 'You didn't say, Wait a sec, guys; time's up; this doesn't work . . . ?' Burr asked incredulously.

"Page told him that he was confused and unable to assert himself."

"According to Dr. Thompson, Page had a strong sense of ethics, led a sheltered life and idealized women."

"He was fascinated by games, and he used to design board games."

" 'He was crying and bawling so hard,' Chris Schardt [Brad's next-door neighbor] said of the evening Page first realized Lee was gone.

" 'He just ran into his room and I could hear him through the walls. He didn't do that for my benefit. Incredible emotion like that you just can't fake.' "

Finally, there is a long interview with Brad in the *Tribune*, in the wake of the trial. Apparently, he has become engaged to a woman named Amy Hacker. She lived at Lothlorien and was a friend of Roberta's; they met during the search. She is pregnant; they are going to have a baby. There is a picture of them laughing, sitting side by side, Amy's hands resting on her belly. Amy has straight blond hair with bangs pushed out of her eyes, reminiscent of the little blond girl with bangs she must once have been.

"There's a lot in her personality and family life," Brad begins to say, "that I think would have been some elucidation, shed some light on what was . . ."

"She was a very obstinate person, very hard or easy to like, very opinionated. But I know it's not nice to say anything that could be construed as negative about someone who's been murdered," Amy chimes in.

What attracted you to Bibi? Brad is asked.

"That alone, that she—"

And Amy completes his sentence, "—never compromised herself for anyone."

"What Bibi does," Brad adds, "is if you say something she doesn't agree with, or that you aren't backing up what you say, she in mannerisms can offend somebody and put somebody on the defensive immediately, and make them substantiate what they're saying or go through their values, and she's willing to give and bend and learn from that, but that's what she's doing: Tell me how you know this so that I can know it, too.

"But," Brad adds, "she was also able to find beauty in a lot of ways—just in her little knickknacks, her plastic jewelry . . . it was just wonderful."

"Bibi's psychology was ignored at the trial," Amy tells the reporter.

I understand what they are saying. I know what psychology they are referring to, and why they are puzzled that it was not relevant. All the things you thought and knew about Bibi and what they meant and why she would disappear—the last paragraph of the last letter and all the rest—the tea house where we will meet, old ladies in an herb garden. The lawyers don't know; the D.A. doesn't care. It puzzled me too, how irrelevant meaning is. The case is about the criminal, it is not about Bibi. It is so difficult to always remember that.

He feels it is important, Brad says, that the jurors get to know him better.

"I think they would have to get to know me in order to make a decision on this case. . . . You would really have to know somebody to be able to say, Gee, yeah, he could say something he never did."

The article says that Brad attributes his confession to a spiritual philosophy among UC students that "nothing is certain, and anything is possible."

He is pleading innocent in the trial, Brad says, "because I could never plead guilty to something I didn't do."

Brad and Amy, the article concludes, plan to marry in the upcoming week. Amy says she believes that the jury will read the marriage as an ultimate expression of confidence in his innocence. "Yep," said Brad.

"I really do feel it's possible to completely know someone so they don't have secrets from you. And Brad also talks in his sleep," Hacker said with a laugh. "I mean, my God, if he were guilty he would talk about it."

If he were guilty, he would talk about it. It is possible to know someone completely, so that they have no secrets from you. Brad led a prayer. He said something to Bibi about coming home. Incredible emotion like that you just can't fake. The things that are real are things that we tell each other, and people tell what is in their hearts. The very kind of statement I myself used to make—have made, even here—but which in this story means something different. How do you read it here; here, what does it mean?

Because Roberta went running, I puzzle, Roberta got lost, and because she got lost there was a search organization, and because there was a search Brad met Amy. And because Roberta was found in Oakland, the Oakland police took charge of the operation, and they thought differently from the Berkeley police, and arrested the most obvious person, her boyfriend. And because they told Brad he had done it, he told them how, and because he was then guilty, he was suddenly alone and people hated him, and when he said he had been lying, didn't believe him. And because you had to feel one way or another, and because Amy knew him and must always have liked him, she decided to believe him. And then his mother died of cancer, and Amy became pregnant and he decided to marry her. And now they were going to have a baby. And so the story evolves, and suddenly instead of Roberta, you find there is a new person—*a person who never would have been born except out of the story.* The child will grow up a character in a story it will never be permitted even to read because the whole of the text is nowhere. The child will not understand: too many pages will have been turned already. I wonder how much of the story Brad and Amy will tell their baby.

And I understand—I even understand—why Amy married him. It is that powerful, this story: nobody—*nobody*—got out of it. We live, all of us, in the tangle of its narrative—telling it, imagining it, having opinions about it, believing Brad, not believing Brad, developing our own convictions about what happened. We want to: it is our story. Almost—if I didn't know better—almost, I would have married him myself just to stay within the story a little while longer.

■ ■

The jury, after three weeks of deliberation, was hung. There was, after all, apart from the confession, no evidence at all; it was his word against his word. How do you decide between two different stories when they are both told by the same person? He was acquitted of first- and second-degree murder, and a mistrial was declared on manslaughter. The vote, I am told, was eight to four in favor of conviction.

■ ■

I talk to Lena Grady once, a year later, to find out what is happening with the retrial. Naturally nothing is happening with the retrial, she tells me; maybe it will start next year, maybe later. It is expensive to retry cases, she wants me to know. She is working hard for Missing Children, she says; they have lots of missing

48 MELANIE THERNSTROM

children. *They have a seven-year-old girl whose mother sold her into prostitution.* Brad and Amy's child was born, she also tells me, and Brad is going to be a teacher, and he is living off Amy's money. *Amy,* she says significantly: *Amy had money. And he's fine,* she adds, nothing has happened to him, *he's going to Berkeley and he's fine.* Then she asks me if I remember meeting Amy at Treehaven and I say no. She says she was the busty blonde, and I say I still don't remember. I am about to hang up when she says maybe we should do some pretrial publicity, victim's family's aftermath and such, people forget about these things, it has ruined the Lees' life forever. Yes, I say, I know. And it has ruined your life too, she says. I don't say anything. "Because you were her *friend,*" she says, "because you *cared* about her."

"*And Melanie,*" she continues, after a minute, when I still don't reply, "you know there's no doubt he's guilty. If you could have heard the confession"—she lowers her voice—"the things he said about Roberta, the details he described in the burial, the way the body was laid out."

"The way her body was laid out. Oh, God," I say. "I don't care. I really really don't care." And I hang up.

CHAPTER 2

Bibi

*In a life remembered, there are possibilities for organiza-
tion and significance which could not have been available
to the person at the time. Moreover, in many cases, the future facts which contribute to our retrospective viewpoint will
be inescapable; we find it difficult to "unlearn" the fact that
this turned out to be a final parting, a vain hope, a fateful
meeting.*

—Richard Moran
"The Narrated Life"

*Oh, and I'm reconciled with Scott. Actually, he apologized, but I
told him I didn't care. He didn't have to apologize for telling the truth.
(Did I tell you about this? He wrote me a letter and said I was not cool.
Cool, he said, is to be hanging among the trees, crowded with pandas,
clutching like everyone else for a green branch.) It's curious, because above
all I would have liked so much to hold in my hands a few green sprigs.
I'm not describing this right but it made me sad.*

You write too.
Bibi

I take a train trip across the country two springs later and end up in
California, staying with Bob. I call Lena Grady when I am there,
and she asks me to come over to her house. She shows me

depositions from the trial. Stuck among the papers is a stunning photograph of Bibi; she tells me I can take it. The depositions aren't too bad; none of them say anything I haven't already heard. They consist of hundreds of pages of descriptions and little stories about Brad. I can't believe how well I'm getting to know him. Then the man Lena lives with—maybe her husband—comes home, and they say they want to take me someplace. So we get in their van, and drive for a while up a long road until we come to a wooded area. We drive deeper and deeper into the woods, and then we stop.

"Where are we?" I ask, worried.

"This is The Place," she says.

"What place?"

"The place Brad murdered Roberta. You can get out now."

I stare at her, unsure, and finally get out. There is nothing to see, of course—it is pretty and green and like any other part of the forest—but I get sick anyway. On the way back Lena starts to explain opposing hypotheses about the logistics of the killing— Brad, the Man with the Van, some potential other person, a theory that the body hadn't been there when it wasn't found by the first two dog searches because it had been moved and then returned. I get confused and stop listening, nauseated, the road bumpy.

Bob comes to pick me up when he gets out of classes that night. He and Lena talk for a long time, animatedly. For some reason, Lena especially likes Bob. It's curious because he is so skeptical about her. I sit on a chair in the corner and pull the afghans over me. I get colder and colder, and try to wrap them tighter around me.

"We had a very long day," Lena tells him. "Melanie was positively *green* at times. Of course, it is all *very terrible* and *upsetting* for her."

"Hmm," he says, glancing over at me, and standing up, "she looks a little green now. We're going home."

He stands up with such a swift, confident movement, and he looks so slim and fair, flipping his car keys, his white shirtsleeves rolled up, with his angled body and animated high-cheekboned face, that I imagine for a moment he looks like Brad. It is only a moment, though, before I think to myself I must be cold and tired indeed. I am always exaggerating resemblances, as in some overly structuralist reading of a story, which keeps insisting that it matters not who the characters actually are, but only what they signify as terms in the whole equation—X or Y: Brad is the X in Roberta's story, and Adam is certainly a Y. Bob must be an X too, then, since I already have a Y. Besides, he's a Californian, and his name starts with a B, and he has the same heart-shaped face and sunken cheeks, so the elements all line up. Tedious, I think, and not especially revealing really, trying to line up elements—as if life were some long algebra problem, formulated to be simultaneously complicated and reductionistic so that only those with the right education would be able to decode it. I must have read too much literary theory at an impressionable age. I think Roberta did too.

"Let's go, Melanie," he says, waiting for me.

"Yes," I say, "God, let's go."

■ ■

"Lena took you to Roberts Park today?" Bob says incredulously in the car on the way to his apartment when I tell him about it.

"Yes. Without telling me beforehand."

"You know she's taking advantage of you. Pure, unadulterated exploitation."

"But what's to be taken advantage of?" I ask, puzzled. "I don't have anything; what would I have to take advantage of?"

"Emotion," he replies, tangling his fingers in my hair, hard, hurting a little. "Emotion."

■ ■

I did, however, get the photograph from Lena. It is a blown-up shot of Roberta's face, looking at something. The thing about the picture is that you can't see what she's looking at; that's what makes it seem so important. She looks afraid too—her eyes are wide and soft as the eyes of an animal looking into a forest at things you can't see. She must have been looking at something when the shot was taken—probably the camera—but the gaze of the dead girl now falls on us, standing in the future, as she peers back through the lens, which is wide and near and dark-eyed as death as it winks shut around the moment and she wonders what will happen.

I take it out of the folder and I show it to Bob, and ask him if he thinks it's beautiful.

"Yes," he says, "it is beautiful."

"I'm going to hang it on my wall as soon as I get home," I say fiercely. He is silent.

"Don't you think that's a good idea?" I demand.

"If I had an old picture of me and Bibi, I would definitely put it on my dresser," he says. "Like a snapshot at the beach or something," he adds, amused at the idea.

"But I don't have any pictures at the beach. We never went to the beach," I say flatly.

"But honestly, Mel, you would only put up a picture like this if," he says, and pauses—lightly, ironically, but with a note of something else too—"if you had a friend who was murdered."

■ ■

Lena calls the next day and asks me to come over again. She has more things to show me, she says, maybe I should talk to the police commissioner, I can't leave without talking to the police commissioner.

"No," I say, "I have to leave tomorrow. I—I have to go."

"Can't you stay an extra day?" she asks. I think she is about to add *for Roberta's sake,* but either she wasn't, or she changes her mind.

"No," I say. "I really can't."

■ ■

"This is great," Bob says, when I hang up. "I know you're not going to admit it, but I bet this is the last time you'll do this. I think you're actually beginning to get bored with the whole thing. Do you realize Lena Grady almost convinced you to waste one more day of your life on it?"

"I know." And then, worried: "Wait—bored with what? Bored with . . . Roberta?"

"No, not bored with *Roberta,*" he replies, exasperated. "Bored with November 4th, 1984. Bored with the Place. Bored with the Story, and the Murder and the Search for the Murderer and the Trial and all the Murder Groupies. I hope you're bored with it—or getting there, anyway."

"But why—I mean—why do you care?"

"For the same reason that I suggest Chinese food early in the evening. So you'll be thinking about it and getting hungry by the time I want to eat. Because it's no fun eating alone, that's why."

"Oh, you mean—you want me—to be—"

"Happy," he says.

"Why?" I ask, still unsure.

"Because," he says, with the funny kind of irony that puts quotes around whatever you're saying: "I'm happy when you're happy." I'm about to ask if he means it when he adds, definitely ironic now: "Believe it or not." And I realize that the irony is only because he doesn't want to be caught saying directly what he always calls a mushy Christian kind of thing, and that in fact he does mean it. I mean I believe he means it, I think, feeling, as always at such times, the sudden slight sadness—consciousness of the seldomness of the moment, how precious it is, and how this one has come and will not come again for a long time. He is happy when I am happy, we feel this now, at the same moment: the rare happiness, the rare sudden belief.

■ ■

I bump into Don one day early the following fall in the Square. It is a wonderful fall day, school has just started again, and I am standing in the Square getting money from the money machine, and thinking it will soon be cold enough to unpack my woolen sweaters and skirts, when I see Don across the way. I try to remember if I've seen him since I left the house on Oak Street, a year ago almost, and decide that I haven't. I go back to the machine. After a minute, though, I see that he sees me, and is walking toward me.

"Hey," he yells, getting closer, "Melanie!"

"Hi, Don," I say, looking down.

"Hi, Melanie. How are you?" he asks, coming close. I can't imagine why he is so friendly.

"Good," I say, meaning: better—better than when I lived with you, better than when you knew me last. We chat for a few minutes: he tells me he's been living in France, and asks me about my plans, and I am happy to say yes, I do have some plans. I have managed to generate a couple of plans. There isn't much to say, though, because the unspoken question is sharp between us: you—why are you asking?

"I'm really sorry," he says suddenly, "about all that stuff last fall."

Funny, I think to myself, I don't recall your ever having been sorry before.

"Yeah," he says, looking right at me: "I'm really sorry about Roberta and stuff."

I look at him amazed. He looks back, straight, his eyes surprisingly blue. A year later he bumps into me on a street corner, and now he wants to tell me that he's sorry. He never did say anything at the time, of course, but I guess it's never too late. Curious: the way nothing is ever outdated.

"Oh," I say, "thank you. Umm—thank you. So—what did you say you were planning to do?"

"I'm going to graduate school in art history. All those pre-med courses I was taking last year—I kissed them good-bye. I'm going to be an art historian. Nicholas and Max are both in New York; Nick is studying music, and Max is trying to become a comedian, but he's also become an Orthodox Jew, which is a conflict, and I just spoke to Kim, and she's joining the Peace Corps."

"Kim is joining the Peace Corps?" I repeat incredulously. "My God—that's great, that's just great.

"I walked by Oak Street the other day," I tell him, "and there isn't a trace of us left. It looks like the house is being lived in now by a large Portuguese family. There are kids in the backyard playing on the jungle gym."

■ ■

I am talking to my father about Roberta, and at some point he corrects me, casually, "But it was an accident."

"An accident?" I say. "No, no, you don't see—you don't understand. She was *unhappy.*"

"But Mels," he says, "lots of people are unhappy when they are young. Most people, even. You grow out of it. I was unhappy."

"Nooo."

"I was."

"You, Daddy? You?"

"I know, I know," he laughs, "your big dumb father—the man with no interiority," he says using my favorite expression. "I was very unhappy at times.

"Okay," he adds, smiling, "maybe not tortured, like *Rilke* tortured, but definitely somewhat discontented."

■ ■

I'm talking to Sheila, a counselor at Harvard, about Roberta. Actually I'm talking about something else, but Roberta gets mentioned in passing and Sheila says suddenly, "You know, we've never talked about Roberta, and what she meant in your life, but I wanted to tell you I met her once."

"You did?" I ask, because I didn't know anyone at Harvard knew her.

"It was just for a minute in the summer. She was taking a writing course at the summer school, and she came into our office to look at other syllabuses. I caught a glimpse of her, and I remember her because she was so striking. She said she was from Berkeley and Lexington, and she was all tanned and athletic and—striking. She was wearing this cut-off T-shirt and shorts and she was so excited about her writing course that she wanted to find out what they were writing in other courses—and yes, that's how I remember her, just excited and hopeful."

"Hopeful!" I say, and realize for the first time that I think so too. Roberta was hopeful; she was, perhaps, the most hopeful person I have known. She hoped that life could be meaningful *all the time*—suffused with meaning, as light suffuses a dream in morning, when you are waking up. She was disappointed often, but not enough to stop hoping. I forgot about this when she died, in my disappointment. The first time Sheila saw her she thought she looked hopeful, coming in poised, tanned, and athletic, that summer afternoon. It is curious, having thought about Roberta so much, and having forgotten, after all, what she looked like.

■ ■

I am meeting my friend Edmund for coffee. The late-afternoon skies are dark and heavy on my skin as I walk over. Edmund isn't a very good friend, and certainly we've never had a serious conversation, but he is amusing and knows people I know and that sort of thing. And once, just once, I saw him across a room at a party, crowded and breathy with lipstick and cigarettes, and it flicked through my mind, with the sound of ice and the feel of bare shoulders, that he is someone I could be close to. His eyes were gray. Nothing has subsequently borne out that intuition, but I am patient that way: I can wait a long time, based on a momentary cocktail-party reflection, just as I can keep going to church and calling myself religious although years go by between even slight feelings of faith.

He is late getting there, and because I have had twenty minutes in which to think while waiting, I'm in a serious mood by the time he arrives. It is not a promising start for an amusing time, but the mood has settled in damply, and I can't shake it off. Also, we have agreed to meet at Café Algiers, and although I've been there millions of times without Roberta, today it is making me quiet. Because I am leaving him to do all the talking, he asks me what I did in my year off from college.

"Oh God," I say. "Nothing."

"And what, may I ask, constitutes nothing?" he asks with his clever elaborate way of formulating things—a British-mannered version of Bob.

"The first half of the year I stayed in Cambridge and worked as a security guard, to earn money and work on my poetry," I explain dutifully, leaving out the fact that my friend Roberta died then, "and in January I went to Canada and worked in a residential treatment center for delinquent teenagers—a godforsaken place. I had wanted to go to India with my old roommate Amy, who was also taking the year off, and we had applied to the University of Benares together, but my parents decided it was too dangerous—it was a third-world country—my mother once went to a third-world country and it was dangerous. So Amy went on this cozy American program, and sent back scented letters with lovely foreign stamps and pictures of elephants, and I stayed in Cambridge, because it was close to home and therefore safe and then went to the north and had a horrible experience. Tears froze on your cheeks, it was so cold; there wasn't anyone to talk to. Actually, it wasn't even the place that was so dreadful. It was me—I was dreadful, I was dreadfully unhappy. All I really did, all that year," I say, getting back to Roberta, "was be unhappy."

We talk about and around this for a while, and about Roberta, and then he says, surprisingly: "You know, Melanie, if I were in Europe or Tanzania or—anywhere—"

Absolute Elsewhere, I think to myself.

"And it turned out I wasn't coming back, I would want you and Claud and Ari and Tom and Amanda to murmur you were sorry occasionally, you liked having me around. But if every time you got together, all you said was how terrible it was, and how *depressed* you were about it, and referred to me as Our Friend Edmund Who Left Us And Is Never Coming Back—that would be kind of *nasty*. Of course it would hurt my feelings if you *completely* forgot me, but I think it would also be sad if you thought of me only that way.

"Besides which, she's not just Your Friend Who Got Murdered, is she? I mean, I'm sure she meant a lot more to you than just that."

"Oh," I say, "of course. *Of course.*"

He reaches across the table to give me his hand, and I get up and go outside. It has started to rain, I see. Rain falls hard on my face and I remember Roberta saying once (When was it? Was she walking in the rain or by a window, looking out? Was I with her? Was I with her?) only the handful of words, remembered words: "It's raining perfect now," she had said. "Perfect." Rain, I think, silvery rain, it is beginning to rain perfect, just as it did on Roberta's face: lifted, looking out, the rain falling silver all around.

■ ■

I am talking on the phone to DeWitt. I am talking about the glum state of things—the perpetual pervasive tedious themes. In Hopi time, time is not a grid but something in things—things grow later and later and further and further because distance and time are the same thing because they have no words to distinguish. Things that were long ago are far away, two days ago is two days away, November 4 is two years away and look how old I am. Even if I died now, I wouldn't die that young and I'd have to hurry to die young at all. DeWitt has almost talked me out of it for the night—the Hopis? he says, *the Indian tribe?*—but just when I am about to feel better I say, as I always say at these moments: "But what about Roberta?"

"Mainly what your friend Roberta was," he says decisively, "was unlucky." I like the way he says that: "mainly." I think about it a lot after we hang up. Of course there were some other factors involved. I have been thinking about these other factors for a long time now. I have not overlooked or repressed them—really, I can't be accused of convenient overlooking and sublimation and substitute formations—but even with all that was said, the general troubles and specific forebodings, and its having turned out to be Brad—even so, mainly what she was was unlucky. Mainly.

■ ■

I am working at my old security guard job. It has been a long night: a silent night. Just after midnight the phone rings.

"Hullo, dear heart," Adam says cheerfully. I have been silent for so many hours it is hard to form words to reply.

"What's wrong?" he asks, his voice changing. And then, swiftly, "Are you sad tonight?"

"No. It's just—why was Roberta's life—*meaningful?* I mean all that's left are letters and photographs, and she did write well and she was wonderfully pretty, and there were nice moments and nice descriptions, but I wonder what she would have said if she'd known that her whole life would come down to a couple of snapshots, like holding a white carnation in a white dress or whatever, and some letters her high school friend saved in a shoe box.

"And letters to some other people too," I add, thinking about it. "If they saved them."

"But—" Adam replies, and I know he is about to protest that while the things of this world rot and decay, the gifts of the spirit obviously endure.

"As for nontangibles," I go on, "they're not tangible." We talk for a while, and he tries various ideas, philosophic and such, but I talk him out of all of them. Then he tries religious ones, but for some reason they also carry no weight in the conversation.

"I don't know, sweetheart," he says finally, "but it feels as if it was meaningful, doesn't it? I mean it was meaningful to you.

"I know it was," he says, when I don't say anything.

"Was it?" I ask, still cold.

"Shit, Melanie, I'm no philosopher," he says, in his straight-blue-jeaned-reporter, I-am-a-good-guy-and-this-is-the-bottom-line fashion: "And I'm no good at this shit. You know you can talk tangles around me," he adds, and I smile. "I am looped in the loops of your hair, and lost in the labyrinth of your mind, but I'm still right. Okay?"

"Okay," I say, really smiling now at the familiar allusion, the old joke. The joke is that he is not clever but he is good-hearted and I am less good-hearted but have a fine mind. And although factually this is complete nonsense, and the reverse could as easily be said, or the inverse or some entirely different scheme for parceling out qualities, such as Adam is both and I am neither, this one must have had some persistent emotional resonance because it is our oldest, most affectionate and least tiresome joke. The joke is that he might be a Bear of Little Brain, but because of his good heart he knows Right from Wrong. And because I am clever I know this, as the clever always know the word of the good-hearted should be taken over the analytic every time. And sometimes just when I was about to win a disagreement or discussion, he would remind me—don't forget I'm right, he would say, because I'm a good guy—and I would instantly concede, arguments abandoned.

"Stick with me, kid," he would add then, at times, in a tone of satisfaction, meaning he is confident that I know I got a good thing when I got him and his good heart. And sometimes I would feel a pinch of envy and think that if we ever break up, as we must never break up—quick, say a spell, a talisman, even in the mind—if I ever have another relationship, though, I would remember, I am sure, that *I* want to be the good one. Let the other person monopolize the joys of the artistic temperament. Let *him* try to make up for it by looking sexy in black. It would be so lovely to be the one who is blessed.

I voiced this feeling to him once and he replied instantly, as if he were completely surprised and had never even heard the joke: "But you are good. You're the goodest person I know. I've told you that before. You—why you're my inspiration." I shook my head no, and the pinched feeling went away. And it was not until years later, years after we had been apart, that I realized that he did make me feel good. And smart and pretty and well read and other things as well, but the other things have been replaced and this has not. I have other friends, of course—I had other friends then, and I have made friends since then as well. I think of them, my own little list, late at night upon occasion, and they add up—accrue nicely, in their own way. And I know that all of my friends feel friendly toward me and interpret things in the best of lights and give me the benefit of the doubt most every time they can, but only Adam thought simply that I was good. Holy, blessed, sanctified, adored, made in the image of God: good. He believed it, and I believed his beliefs, and every once in a while I would put those two things together and be happy, in a different way than I am otherwise happy. No one else makes me feel this—not my parents, not my brother, not my grandmother, not anyone. Of all the irreplaceable things I lost when I lost Adam, this has turned out, curiously, to be the most irreplaceable; of all the things I miss about Adam, I think, perhaps, I miss this the most.

■ ■

I go over to Mrs. Lee's house one day for lunch. We talk about Roberta, of course, and she says people don't understand. People say their grandmother died or something, but they don't understand: their whole lives are different. I know, I say, there's no way that strangers can help underestimating it; it's not explicable, how big a thing it is. Then she says that if she had known this was going to happen, she never would have had Roberta. I don't reply, and after a while I go home. It is a good thing she didn't know because she never would have had Roberta. She could not have known; even if she had been told, she would not have understood all the things it would mean when it happened. It is not explicable, how big a thing it is. Their whole lives are different; their whole lives are different.

■ ■

I hang up the dark picture of Roberta that Lena had given me in my room—and, as I suppose it is supposed to, it depresses me. There is a big black button, too, which says REMEMBER BIBI LEE on it. I'm not sure why it was made, although I think Veronica gave it to me, to generate emotion for the trial or publicity for the search. I hang it up by the photograph, even though I don't really want to, because I can't figure out why it should depress me to be reminded to remember Roberta. It should be a *nice* thing, I tell myself, remembering your friends should.

But every time I walk by, what it says is: *This isn't a movie where you can walk out of the theater; this isn't a book you can put down before you find out what happened. It's true; it was. Remember.* I take them both down.

But, too, I hate to think of them lying in a drawer. Remember Roberta Lee. I worry about this for a few more days, and finally take a piece of material and, covering its face, hang the photograph up again, in a corner I can't see from my bed. I still worry, though, that I am cheating somehow, and wonder whether I am *covering things up*. I'm not neglecting it, I'm just trying to obtain a sense of closure, for the same reason you have a layer of flesh over your

heart—so it isn't all raw all the time. You don't need Roberta's face
raw all the time. It's misrepresentative.

   But she had a dark face, the old voice whispers. And I've had
this argument with myself so many times before, I can't believe I
have to go through it again. But I remind myself once more that
even Brad, even the character cut the smoothest, blue-eyed and
dangerous—a stranger, really, in the beginning and end—even
Brad didn't turn out precisely like *Brad.* You don't know what he
turned out to be. Maybe he confessed because he was trying to
pretend, just as you've been trying to pretend all this time, that he
knew what happened, what his role was, whom he played. And
yet he didn't, as you didn't, as none of the characters quite fit their
roles, and if the mythology hasn't unraveled completely it has
unraveled enough—enough not to be so enmeshed. The dark face
isn't eternal because you don't know what she would have looked
like when she got older. You always think that the things you
think must be true because why would someone want to think
dark things unless they are true, but it might be—it just might
be—that that kind of darkness has been easier for you than the
truth, the colorless truth that there is no way of knowing what she
would have looked like even a little later that same fall: there is
just no way of knowing.

■ ■

It is Wednesday afternoon, and Roberta, Naomi, Dean, Nora,
and I are in Dr. Shohet's office waiting for our independent
study in poetry to begin. For some reason on the table is a
dusty box of strawberries with little green stems. I stare at
them, surprised somehow. Roberta picks one up, and deliberately brings it to her lips. The strawberry is large and
red and her lips are a faint pale pink, and her eyes are dark
as always, her hair tousled and black, and there is something so odd about the tea-party strawberry and the Oriental girl, that I catch my breath. Dr. Shohet must have been
watching her too because he suddenly pokes Dean and says
in his gruff fashion: "Don't just stand there gaping, Mad-
den, look at Rosamunde. Take a picture, do something."
Everyone turns to look, and Roberta puts the strawberry
down and smiles her lovely secret smile and gets up and
the memory ends. It is curious, because no one had ever

called her Rosamunde before, yet no one thought to ask him why, and everyone immediately knew whom he was referring to. I try to remember if I am certain she put the strawberry down without tasting it, and I am. And as I remember, I remember too that the reason I remember the strawberry is because I remember the gesture. *Tess of the D'Urbervilles* had been made into a movie that year, and in the movie Tess's cousin puts a strawberry in her lips, and she eats it, and the eating foreshadows the rape, which foreshadows murder which foreshadows death and punishment. In this story, Roberta picks up the strawberry and holds it to her lips, and everyone turns to look. Someone says "remember," and what is meant is remember this moment, remember Roberta, and everyone turns to look, and as we look, because we are looking and trying, suddenly, to turn it into a symbol, because Dr. Shohet said to do something—*to make it symbolic*—Roberta puts the berry down, and the gesture becomes a symbol of all that is to come. The mythical imaginary excessive literary name with the life so really red and promising just upon her lips, but which turned out, in the end, to be untasted. And I want Dr. Shohet to know that I did do something—I am doing something—I am writing all this so that Rosamunde will be remembered forever. And I try not to wonder whether, if she had just been Roberta and no one had made up any names or noticed what she was eating and the theme of our study had not been symbolism, and this most of all—if we had never thought life and literature and film had anything to do with each other, and that our lives could therefore be written as such—whether the ending, which would no longer have to be an ending since only stories have to have endings, would have ended as it ended after all.

PART 7

Rewriting: The Little Match Girl

How She Tried to Tell the Story of Her Life So That It Would Be Just Like a Story

■ ■

The tendency of the fairy tale is always to externalize. No distinction is made between inner and outer worlds: all metaphor is displaced and transformed and treated as concrete reality.

—Max Luthi
The Fairy Tale as Art Form and Portrait of Man

CHAPTER 1

Bad Men and Scary Places

Which Tells How the Little Match Girl Came to Fall into Bad Hands

I don't trust men. I don't.

I am having a fight with my father as we are driving. This is a series of threats: he says he is going to make me get out of the car; I say fine. He says he'll never drive me anyplace again; I say I don't care. He says he is not going to pay for school and, determined not to feel threatened, I tell him to fuck off, and he roars: "I WILL LOCK YOU IN THE TRUNK OF THE CAR."

Even as he says it, he realizes how ridiculous it is. The last word is broken by laughter, and the fight ends. I hear this—that it has disintegrated into a joke before he has even finished saying it—but it has broken a second too late for me not to get upset.

"You *frightened* me," I sob violently, bursting into tears.

"It was a joke," he says, embarrassed now.

"It wasn't a joke! It wasn't a joke!"

"Of course it was. Do you think I would literally try to tie you up and lock you in the trunk? You wouldn't even fit. You're too big."

"That has nothing to do with it," I scream. "You know where you got that image from? You got it from a murder mystery. And you know what goes in the trunk? The body goes in the trunk— the dead body. It's when you've been murdered."

"I would never hurt you," he repeats. "You are so incredibly aggravating and impossible to deal with that I occasionally think I would like to kill you, in fact *I would like to strangle you with my bare hands this very minute*, but I would never do anything. I haven't laid a finger on you for years. When was the last time I hit you?

"In fact," he says, stopping to think about it, "I don't think I've ever hit you."

"Thinking counts," I shriek, and start to cry harder because this is so true. "And it doesn't help to say that it's a joke. What is a joke? A joke is something that has emotional reality without literal reality, and the discrepancy is supposed to make it 'funny.' Well, I take emotional reality pretty fucking seriously, besides which men really do rape and murder women and put them in trunks of cars and beat them and leave them in shallow graves. So that distinction— that line about which you think I should be so confident as to depend on it for my safety and well-being: the line between psychological and other realities—is a little *thin*."

"Well, I'm sorry, hon," he says, "but I think you are reading a lot into one remark, and taking the whole thing A LITTLE TOO SERIOUSLY."

Just to make sure he doesn't have the last word, I repeat that he did make me feel Unsafe, and he mutters that he is a simple man from Michigan and he can't imagine how he ended up in a family of such emotional women.

■ ■

My parents are supposed to pick me up and they are not there. I am standing at the subway station, sitting down and then standing up, looking for their car, and *they don't come*. There is a middle-aged man in a parked car, idly watching. I try to telephone them, but they aren't home, although their answering machine is on so it uses up my last coin. I get upset because I don't have any money, and there is no one else to call anyway. My parents aren't home, and I can't call Claudia because she doesn't have a car, and I can't call Lisa because she's with her parents in New Jersey, and I can't call Bob because he lives in California, and

I can't call Adam because—I can't call Adam, and that's it, that covers it. I'm standing at a pay phone in a subway station and there is no one in the world I can call who will come pick me up. I contemplate this for a while and then start to cry, really hard. The man gets out of his car and asks me if I need a ride, and I say no, and wipe my face.

"I do have parents," I say, laughing uneasily. "They are just a little late."

■ ■

"We are just a little late," says my mother, fifty minutes later.

"A little late," I moan. "I didn't have any money or anyone to call and strangers were coming up to me and—*and strangers are asking me if I need rides.*"

"Well, the truth is," says my mother, "I was kind of annoyed at you because last night—"

"Oh, don't even tell me," I cry, "I knew it. I knew it wasn't just an accident or that you forgot. I knew there was some special deep mean reason why you deliberately didn't pick me up."

"Well," she says mildly, "it was really your fault. I got tired of always being the one who makes all the arrangements, so I decided I'd wait and see if you called me to confirm when we were coming, and you had all last night to call and you didn't, so we didn't really have an arrangement—not an explicit one—for you to be picked up at all. But goodness, you don't have to look so *devastated*," she adds. "I mean we came anyway. Look, here we are. Arrived."

"You came," I say, "but you came late. *You came after I thought you weren't going to come.* It was awful. It was symbolic."

"It was not," says my mother, angry now. "I don't see anything one bit symbolic about it. Stop that, Melanie. I mean it—stop it this minute."

■ ■

Alexis, with whom I am going out that night, stops by my room to pick me up. While I am getting my things together, he looks around and, picking up an old picture of Roberta on my dresser, says: "Friend of yours?"

"Yes," I say, and keep looking for my things.

"What's her name?"

"Bibi."

"Where does she live?"

He whistles softly. "She must have a rough life," he says.

I turn around, startled. "What *exactly* do you mean by that?" I say sharply, although of course I know exactly what he means.

A little taken aback, he says, "I was kidding. I just meant she's very beautiful."

"And the connection is?" I ask, very slowly.

"Well—just—she would have an easier time with—things," he says, floundering.

"Like—what—things?" I ask, spacing my words apart.

"Well, men and—men. Jesus, stop it. You know what I mean, Melanie. What are you looking at me that way for?"

"You mean that because she is pretty men must find her attractive and therefore her life must have been easy because she must not have had a shortage of dates? Is that what you're getting at?"

"Well," he says, embarrassed. But somehow this makes me angrier, and I say: "*As it happened*, she had a rough life. She had an *extremely rough life*—and it was particularly rough precisely because some asshole thought she was beautiful—"

"Oh," he says, "oh. You mean . . . it's *that* friend. I didn't realize. I'm . . . sorry." And I realize that I'm sorry too. It's not his fault—none of it is his fault, and I wouldn't like it if he didn't think she was beautiful, because she was.

■ ■

"Oh, no," I explain to Adam, speaking in an exaggerated, childish way, which I know is exaggerated and childish, but which is nevertheless the way that I feel; "I'll never be able to go out with other people. It's too worrisome."

"Why?"

"Because I might fall among bad company. Harmful people."

"You won't. You have good judgment."

"I do not have good judgment," I say.

"You picked me," he replies, playful, friendly, a favorite tone of voice.

"No," I say, "for one thing, you picked me, and for another thing, it was an exception. You aren't really my type."

"What's your type?" he teases.

"*Bad,*" I wail. "Disastrous. Worse than disastrous. Someone just like me," I mourn, pretending. And with his unfailing judgment as to when the pretend strays into the real, ringing sudden and true, he checks me instantly. "Now, sweetheart," he says, and I think once again how safe he makes me feel, and how really different it will be to be without him.

■ ■

"It's fine," I tell Jim over pancakes at the International House of Pancakes at one in the morning. "It's fine. I'll be fine. I'm just never going to go out with anybody else, that's all. I'm not going to go putting myself in strangers' hands. It's not worth it; it's too risky."

"Well, to begin with," he says, "you don't have to *put yourself in anyone's hands.* I mean, that's kind of a funny image, isn't it? I go out with different people, and I don't put myself in anyone's hands, exactly. At least I never think of it that way."

"Oh," I say, "it's different for men."

■ ■

"But you don't understand," I say to Adam. "I'm not just going to miss you and be unhappy and stuff, the way people miss each other when they break up, the way you'll miss me. It's different for me because without you I will—"

"What?" he asks, sounding worried.

"*Perish.*"

"Why do you say that?" The surprise and innocence of his voice reassures me a little.

"Because, don't you remember, I asked you why I wasn't just like Roberta, and you said, 'You have me, and I'm not like Brad.' And that's why nothing bad was going to happen to me. And so now—"

"I never said that."

"You did. *You did.* I'm sure of it."

"I'm sure I didn't," he says. "Nothing is going to happen to you because of you, not because of me. Physical things can happen to anyone, and metaphysical things you will protect yourself from. I never thought that. I wouldn't—it isn't true.

"You know what I think, honeybunch?" he says, suddenly

cheerful. "Sweetness and Light?" he asks, and I smile, because he has not called me that in so long, and no one else ever will. No one else will ever even think it. "I think, darling," he finishes, "you imagined it."

■ ■

I'm explaining to Bob how Adam and I may break up, and not be together anymore, and how therefore everything will be over because he was the saint who rescued me from the darkness, and he was the person who took me off the streets, and he was the good man who said he'd take me home with him.

"Oh, Melanie," he replies wearily, "I've heard all that before. Isn't it time for some new metaphors? Maybe you don't need a saint to rescue you because there is no darkness to be rescued from. Maybe you imagined it; maybe the mistake lies in the meta-phor. I think, actually, the metaphor sucks and I think making things metaphorical is a mistaken idea."

■ ■

I answer an ad in the paper for a waitressing job. It turns out to be not close; it is a long subway ride to a bad part of the city, and when I get there it turns out the job is someplace entirely different, in an even worse part of the city. Hmm, I think, I've read about things like this. This is a front, and the job is in the part of the city where girls disappear. I should go home right now before I come to harm and my nice innocent-young-girl status is threat-ened. One of these days I'm going to get a letter in the mail telling me it's expired or been canceled—invalid, funds insufficient. I think about that letter a lot, how it will come with the complete itemized list of my sins attached for documentation, like a credit card bill with all the little names and dates and occasions—you'd forgotten how many there were or how they would add up. I can't figure out whether it's in order to speed up the process of expira-tion that I stay, or because I want to prove that niceness is not a thing like that and I'll be nice whatever I do, but I do stay. I nod and smile and get directions, and go over to the bar and tell myself: here you are, settle in. I put on some more makeup and a black dress, and name myself after one of my dolls, and although the manager tells me that isn't a sexy name and I should think of another, I say no, I like it.

One day, when I have worked there for about three days, I am at the bar serving this man drinks, and as he is drinking he is talking. He is talking to me and telling me things, real things about his life, and I am listening, but I guess he thinks I'm just waiting for him to leave so he will leave me my tip because all of a sudden he looks up, surprised, and I catch his surprise and laugh and say: "I was listening." And it's queer, but it suddenly occurs to me that this is like—like—what is it like? *Why, this is just like life.* There are people I like and people I don't like, and girls I'm friendly with and girls I'm not, and the owner is sweet, but weak and a little bewildered, as if he harbors illusions that he'd rather be a gardener and somehow just *fell* into being here, and his assistant is someone I would definitely not want to meet in a dark alley unless I had that short Italian man with the thick gold chain with me, who I'm pretty sure would look after me if I needed him to—you can tell, I think he comes from a family with a lot of sisters. And all this is just as you'd expect it to be. It's so curious: here I am, in this den of robbers, this house of thieves, *and I'm making friends.*

I'm so happy, I'm not sure what to do, so because I am in a bar I pour myself a drink, and things get a little blurry. And it might only be because of the blurriness, but the uncertainty I always feel about myself goes away for a minute, and it suddenly seems to me: I am nice. I like people; I listen to their troubles, and sympathize with them: no one will beat me up, no one will hurt me. I can get people to look after me in dangerous situations, dangerous people can be made less dangerous, and the situation is not always as dangerous as it seems. I pour myself another drink, and things get more blurry, and along with it the line softens some—the terrifying, demoralizing, imprisoning line that divides nice from not nice, safety from danger, and good men from other men. I go back to the table and sit down. The man keeps talking, and I tell him I am sorry for all the things that have happened to him, and I feel it, too: I am sorry, I really feel sorry, and stand up, dizzy, smiling.

I worked there, in total, for four and a half days. It was just long enough, it seemed to me, to have either permanently ruined my nice-young-girl status, or to have established that nice doesn't depend on not having walked through any particular forbidden doorways. I think about it sometimes, how it is something that I will always have done that most of my friends would not consider doing—a history of sorts, something to leave out of my résumé and those little accounts one narrates occasionally and at cocktail parties—of, for example, interesting jobs I have had. I know my parents consider it an *extremely dangerous thing to have done* and a sign I was *very troubled* at the time, which is perhaps the case, and all this may be a long excuse for that, but I'm pretty sure that whatever it was, it wasn't bad.

I want Roberta to know, too, that the fear that I will get lost one day and find myself on the dark side of the map and be murdered there is less clear now. The map can't be entirely accurate, I remind her sometimes, because I checked out a few places that definitely should have been on the other side, and the one thing they weren't—I actually am certain of this—is scary. I wonder, though, if I'll ever check out enough places to feel completely safe again, or whether complete safety, like complete happiness—*I was completely happy, suddenly I stood up and felt completely happy*—is a childish concept: one grownups learned long ago to live without.

CHAPTER 2

Doomed

What Will Become of Her?

"Well, I could be killed in some kind of accident," I say to Adam, trying to be more concrete. "Lots of people die in accidents."

"So could I," he replies, cheerfully.

"I could die of a drug overdose."

"You don't take drugs."

"I could get AIDS."

"Don't sleep with strangers, angel."

"I could starve to death. I could become very very poor, and then one day I would wake up and find I have starved to death."

"I would never let you starve to death. You know that."

"Even if we weren't together and you had married someone else?"

"Even if I hadn't seen you in twenty-five years. God, Melanie, don't you know that after all these years?"

I hear a certain sadness in his voice, and feel sad too, that I am still asking the same things after so much time, and say, "I'm sorry. It's just—I don't know." What is it? "It's just I could—I don't know. Commit suicide, I guess."

"But *why?* Why would you want to commit suicide?"

"I don't know. It's not that I *want* to," I say, confused, losing the thread of the thought. "It's just if it's *doomed.*"

It's difficult to explain to people like Adam that doomed isn't making lists of bad things that might happen so that you can cross them off as improbable because doomed is the thing you forgot to put on the list. The uninvited fairy; the appointment in Samarra. Doomed is the surprise ending—the person you didn't suspect in the murder mystery but who, in retrospect, is just right. Doomed is writing the book and trying to figure out the right kind of ending given the character you are, and doomed is knowing you can't cheat—the girl who must die must die. What can you do? I told you this was a sad story. Doomed is knowing this is a modern story and there is no deus ex machina anymore. Doomed is more than an event: doomed is, and I stop, unable to think of anything big enough to describe doomed. And then, remembering: oh yes, doomed, of course—doomed is—doomed is a way of thinking.

■ ■

"You don't think," I ask Bob, as casually as possible, "that there's anything especially wrong with me?"

"Anything especially wrong with you?" he repeats. "Excuse me?"

"Not a specific kind of wrong," I say, "a deep kind. Like something that marks me as, you know—*fundamentally different*—"

"Hmm," he says, suspiciously, "I recognize those italicized words, that breathless emphasis. I thought we were giving up that way of speaking."

And then: "Oh, you're talking about that LARGE PURPLE TRIANGLE in the middle of your forehead?"

"Yes, yes," I tell him tearily, passionately. "*Exactly* like that."

"Exactly?" he queries. And then: "No problem. Wear bangs."

■ ■

I am mad at my mother. We have had a relatively minor fight, but I have a terrible dream about it two days later. In the dream she is cutting me into little pieces and feeding me into the garbage disposal. She keeps turning it on for a few seconds because you're not supposed to feed big things into it because it can get jammed, but it's taking too long, and she's getting annoyed and frustrated and finally she turns it on full speed. My hair gets caught and clogs it up and then the blood gurgles upward and fills the sink and she gets madder and right about then my father walks in and tells her to calm down, it's okay, not to worry. But all of a sudden she is worried, she is sorry, she is very sorry—she was a little impetuous, she *lost* her temper. She says "lost," as if it got dropped or misplaced by accident—it could happen to anyone—it got lost, that's all, no use crying over single buttons and mismatched mittens. He repeats it's okay, hon, and the blood drains downward. I wake up so mad I don't speak for days.

Finally, she asks me what the problem is, and I say The Fight. She tells me she has never heard of anyone with such a long memory for grievances.

"What did I do to you?" she says. "I didn't do anything."

"You did, you did. *You wished me harm.*"

"What are you talking about? I get mad, I get frustrated, I get furious, I would like to dump you in the garbage pail—"

"The garbage pail?" I shriek.

"It was a figure of speech. A trope," she says, quoting. She once put her hands on her hips and told me and my friend Lisa that she never wanted to hear us use the words *trope* or *metaphor* or *mimesis* ever again; living with you girls, she said, is like being trapped in a high school English class forever.

"NO IT WASN'T," I tell her. "You could harm me."

"How?" she asks.

"Well," I say, after a minute, "I can't say exactly how it would happen, but when someone you love wishes you harm, it's like witchcraft—it has all sorts of funny ways of coming true. Ways you might not even relate to the wish—just odd little coincidences and things. You might even think they were just accidents if they weren't so very befitting—if they weren't wished beforehand, that is."

"What exactly are you talking about?"

"In the dream it came true," I say finally.

"The *dream?*" she repeats. "We're having this whole conversation because of a *dream?*

"Let me get this straight. You hold me responsible for the things that you dream?

"How would you feel if I started accusing you of things you did to me in dreams?"

"Oh," I say, considering, "maybe it is a little unfair."

"A little?" says my mother.

■ ■

Greta, a very good friend of Roberta's and mine from high school, and a poet, attempts suicide. That night, however, a friend of hers discovers that he has left a book in her room and decides to get it. When she doesn't respond to his knocking he assumes she isn't home and, knowing where a key is, he lets himself in, and finds her. She is crouched in front of a mirror watching the blood drip methodically from her wrists. Had he waited for her to return it, he would have waited forever. I am upset and surprised, but more upset than surprised.

"It has to make you wonder," I say, depressed, to Adam.

"Wonder what?" he asks.

"About us. About not being cut out for . . . things. You know, like not being suited for—well, for anything really. For life, I guess. Like Tonka in that story 'Tonka' by Robert Musil. The girl who didn't belong—'a snowflake on a summer's day,' he described her. You know the kind I mean," I say. *The doomed kind.*

"But this isn't a story," Adam says definitely. "And you aren't a kind. You are," he says, pausing to give that particular magical final note that makes whatever he says afterward sound as if it were the truth—as if it were really me and the question has been properly settled forever. "You are you," he finishes, pleased, as if he has just said something very clever: "You are you." And suddenly, momentarily, it seems to me that it is enough. The equation is sufficient and complete: I am I: it's all right, he likes me.

CHAPTER 3

Ugly

What Exactly Was Wrong with Her

> The direct opposite of the beautiful, the ugly, is in the fairy
> tale first and foremost the foil of the beautiful. The beautiful
> engenders its opposite just as good, poor and success call forth
> the opposite ideas of wicked, rich and failure. In this sense,
> one might say that the fairy tale is self-creating. . . . The
> polarities come into being according to the law of opposite word
> meanings.
>
> —Max Luthi
> *The Fairy Tale as Art Form and Portrait of Man*

I am wandering around the streets crying because I can't think of
a good place to cry. I don't want to cry in my room because I have
been crying there so much the room is beginning to be sad. I have
been in rooms I've spoiled before: it's as if the grief gets into the
wallpaper, and once that happens you can never get it off. Even
wallpaper with roses on it can be sad, or lilies; I realized that once
on a dark day.

I am passing a drugstore in Boston when I realize I want to go
in and buy something. I haven't been sure about anything for the
past few days, so I seize upon it as a good thing: a definite thing,
something I want.

I walk inside and go up to the counter, keeping my face averted so that the woman will not see I am crying.

"Can I help you?" she asks.

"Do you have any razor blades?"

She goes over to the wall. "What kind would you like?" she asks, gesturing toward them. "With a safety catch or without?"

I almost smile, in spite of myself.

"Without," I say, thinking what a good scene this would make. I almost want to explain it to her, I am so sorry she is missing all the symbolism.

I take out a damp dollar and hold it toward her.

"Wait," she says suddenly, in a cross southern voice: "what did you say you wanted this for?"

"Sewing," I say, looking down. I think my mother uses razor blades to slice the threads of the hem on a skirt when she is sewing. I hold out the dollar again to remind her that this is a commercial transaction—why should she question the actions of strangers?

She takes it, and hands over the blades. She is about fifty, with frosted blond hair and a magenta blouse. Just as I am turning to go, she asks again, sharp, quizzical, "Sewing? Did you say sewing?"

"Sewing," I say, opening the door and stepping out into the street. I hurry toward the bridge where the subway runs. I look backward once; she is standing in the doorway of the shop looking out after someone, who is, I deduce curiously, me. The train pulls up, and in sudden elation I step in. She does not know, naturally enough, she does not know what we know: that Adam is leaving me and I am supposed to be dead.

■ ■

The red light of my answering machine, I see, opening the door to my room, is on. This means that someone has called me—that is what the red light signifies. The green light signifies an absence of calls, and the red light signifies presence, but tonight it signifies something else as well, and I know what that will be. I listen to the message. It is Adam, and all he says on the tape is I love you, and although that is what he always says, this time I know what it signifies too, like the red light.

At first I try to do little things around my room—this would be an excellent time, for example, I think, to pay my telephone bill, and I actually begin to take out my checkbook, but I can't make the numbers add up, so after a while I just wait. I'm not sure how to just wait, though, and I remember how I read in the paper that the girl at Harvard who committed suicide did her laundry that afternoon. I used to think about that a lot: about why she would do her laundry first. I am prepared for the red light, I remind myself; I just bought something. Where are they? *I had them minutes ago.* I look around the room for them, but they are nowhere to be found. She was going to kill herself, but she lost the razor blades on the way home. Funny, I think: apropos.

The phone rings just as evening is coming on. It is, of course, Adam, and he says what I thought he would say; he says, Darling, I think we should be ending, but I love you and always will, and it is the word *ending*, not *always*, that I hear, and I echo back, ending, and replace the phone on the hook. It seems to me I have been listening for this word all my life, and a sense of ending gathers about me thicker than rain, but you can't just stand still and feel your heart dissolve. You must do something, and since there is nothing to do, you must do something ending. It is too sad otherwise, and too serious. You need a little action to break up the seriousness. I go into the bathroom and rifle through the cabinet looking for other razor blades. There are none. I find my roommate's razor, but for some reason there is no blade in it. I wonder why he would keep the blades elsewhere. All right then, I think, I will try a knife. I go down to the kitchen to find a knife, but none of them are sharp. I test them against my arm to see if they will cut but the skin doesn't even break. I go upstairs again, and look around my room, and finally find a compact mirror. I put it on the floor and step on it, and after a great deal of effort it breaks. It splinters crooked though, and when I hold it up I realize that it is made of plastic, not glass, but I don't have time to look for anything else because my heart is breaking. I run the edge along my wrists as hard as I can, and the thinnest lines of blood appear, beading, not even running.

I hesitate, feeling a slight tenderness for my wrists—my body, my own body—a reluctance, perhaps, to hurt it. I am ugly, I remind myself, and besides, Adam is leaving. God, what more are you waiting for? Adam is leaving me. Doom, doomed, the ending; the ending she had been waiting for all of her life. I pick up the broken mirror again, and slice harder. Finally, they begin to bleed a little, and I relax: the swift certain easy flow of blood, the easy easy pain. I watch the blood fall on the carpet until it has made a tiny pool, and then I feel better, and begin to bandage them. I go to the bathroom, and run them under cold water, watching, awed, at the way in which the water mixes with the blood and flows down the smooth white china basin into the drain at the center. It is so clean feeling, clear and clean as feeling itself, as the feeling of pain. And then I take my faded pink towel and hold it to my wrists, and they keep bleeding, but I press tighter, and the towel is so big and nice that the pain gets blotted up. I hold my arms cradled for a little while longer, just in case they still need it, and when I'm more than sure all the blood is gone, I put the towel away.

I look at the clock. It is almost half an hour later. I have an appointment in ten minutes. The feeling in my wrists dulls, and as it dulls I can tell my heart is still breaking, but not with the first pain, the unadulterated sense of ending. I missed feeling that: I was too busy looking for something sharp, and then thinking about the water and the towel and the knives that wouldn't cut, and the blade my roommate hid, and where the hell those razors went to. Adam said good-bye half an hour ago, I think to myself surprised, the ending has already begun. The beginning of the ending is already over, and I was busy doing something else. It's incredible how easy it is to distract yourself long enough to miss the most important moments of the most important events in your life. It was precisely, I think with satisfaction, the right thing to do.

■ ■

It is late when I get back to my room after the poetry reading. The reading was fine; I was good at the reading. There are shards of broken mirror and strands of wet Kleenex all over the rug. A bloody discarded towel is draped over a chair. The bed is unmade, the quilt half on the floor. My stuffed sheep, Sherman, lies face-down near the Kleenex.

"Well," I say to myself briskly, looking around, "well. Perhaps," I suggest, trying to generate more briskness, "perhaps this would be a good time to do a little writing."

■ ■

"Are you all right?" Adam calls the next morning. "What have you been doing? Did you sleep?" he asks anxiously, as if he really wants to know. It is early, maybe seven a.m.

"Well," I say, "I wrote a poem."

"You didn't sleep?" he asks again, sounding worried.

"Do you want to hear it? It's called 'Stanzas.' *Stanza* means 'room' or 'house' in Italian. Isn't that a lovely poemy coincidence? It was Petrarch's favorite coincidence," I say.

"Does it?" he asks, distracted.

There it is: the lighted windows, come over here
The lighted curtained windows
With the wide-hemmed white stitched curtains
Stitched by some white hand with a golden ring
Press your hand against the window
Rub in a circle to rub the glass clear
Otherwise you won't be able to see inside
To see this is the house

Of the house I want to live in.
There are my daughters, Daisy and Lucy,
Named the names we promised to name them.
Standing tall and almost to the kitchen stool
Yellow batter beaten bright, beat it harder
Until you can see the man I wanted to marry
Reading in an armchair, not looking up,
While winter whitens outside (not there, outside)

And it might be that the reason
That I cannot see myself
Is that I am in another room,
A room I haven't thought of yet
For the door is closed and no one knows
To open it
Writing, in the study, I must be writing

As I am, in fact, writing,
Crouched this winter nighttime, bent and peering
My face pressed close, too close, so close
To do anything but see clearly
Line by line
The milk from the batter separating out,
Stitches stitched too tight, gathering slightly,
An eyelash of cigarette ash scattering on the window glass.

"I don't like that poem," says Adam glumly. "I don't like it one bit. I think I'd better take the train up. You stay in your room and sleep in the meantime. And don't go anywhere, and don't do any more writing."

■ ■

He comes up from New York that night. I wear a long-sleeved black corduroy dress, which I imagine will cover my wrists, and forget about them. I am sitting on his lap crying a little, when all of a sudden he looks down and catches them and says: "Oh my God Melanie what have you done?" I mean to say it was an accident, I was trying to cut something, but his voice is so serious all of a sudden it seems there is nothing else I could have been cutting, and I can't find any words, and look down. He picks up my wrists and looks at them for a long moment. I want to say I'm sorry, but I don't have any breath, and then he brings them silently to his lips—my wrists, my ugly scarred skinless wrists—and kisses them. He kisses them gently, passionately, perfectly: the single kiss, the kiss of consolation which makes up for all that has happened and passed. And I think to myself, if I had known anyone would kiss me that way—if I had known I would ever be kissed that way again—if I had known, even, there was such a kiss, I would never have done it.

■ ■

"I can't go to the infirmary," I say.

"Why?" asks Adam.

"Because—what will people think."

"What do you mean, and who are people anyway?"

"You know—them. *People.* People will think I'm *neurotic.*"

"Well, I'm certainly not letting you go back to your room, sweetheart."

"Why not?"

"Because I'm not that dumb," he laughs. "The infirmary will just be a nice place for you to get some rest. I want you to think of it as a nice place to get a little rest."

■ ■

I am lying in the white infirmary bed, in a room with lovely
pale pink walls, and everyone is being nice to me. I am surprised at
how nice everyone is; the nurses are nice, people send flowers
and candy, Claudia calls three times a day, and Giles sends a box of
thin chocolate mints, even though I told my parents not to tell
anybody, and they said that they didn't, except Giles and Gabriella,
so I don't write him a thank-you note and my mother mentions a
year later how rude I had been and how I had hurt Giles. My
friend Sarah comes to visit, and brings dark pink nail polish and
Herbal Essence shampoo and *Cosmopolitan*. Something to wear and
something to smell and something to play with, she says. When I
had called to cancel our lunch date, saying I was sick, she had
asked promptly, "Mind or body?" and when I said, *"Mind,"* she
said she would come right over and bring me things. Everyone
keeps talking about when I get well and can go home, and I want
to point out that it is not like being sick: my heart is broken.
Broken. Rest has *nothing to do with it.* But it is such a pleasant
illusion, that the sickness of the soul is like the sickness of the body
and can be made well, and everyone is being so nice about trying
to maintain it, that I lie back in my white nightgown and don't say
anything. I listen carefully to see if they slip, but no one mentions a
single word about irreparable damage, and how ill-conceived,
doomed, and completely improbable the whole thing was from the
beginning anyway. And Adam sits by my bed and holds my hand
in both of his hands and tells me to rest.

"I'm glad you are resting," the nurse says, opening the door to
look in on me even though I'm not clearly resting: I'm thinking.
"Do you want me to make up your bed? Why don't I just make up
your bed here so that you can get some more rest. All you need, I
think, is a little rest. You look tired. Maybe it's been a tiring past
few—"

"Years," I finish for her sullenly. "It's been a tiring past few
years."

"It's not because I didn't grow up well, is it?" I ask Adam,
resuming the conversation. The long conversation.

"No, baby, you grew up just perfectly."

"I haven't been a disappointment to you, have I?"

"You know how proud I am of you."

"And it's not because I'm ugly." I have this sudden vision of someone asking me, shocked, what happened—as in, *What happened, Melanie?*—and my giving a long complicated explanation as to how we were so different and whatnot—I was so young, it wasn't meant to be, and the person suddenly interrupting and saying, "What you mean is: you're ugly?"

"You're not ugly," he says.

"Politics," I say flatly, to remind him. Adam once said thoughtfully that we had the curious effect of crystallizing each other's flaws, so that we seemed much more lacking in relation to one another than we ever did singly. He is not so unintrospective, he said, he just gets billed that way around me, and I, he added generously, am not so ignorant about politics or the workings of the world— the way clocks are put together, what the electoral college is. We're just different, that's all, so we exaggerate each other's differences. But actually plenty of people know less than I, he said—and stopping, trying to think of who, exactly: *"Some Eskimo somewhere."* And then: "Jesus, Melanie, *where have you been living that you know so little at the age that you are?"*

"And because I'm not sweet anymore, either," I add, connecting them somehow. I'm not political and I'm not sweet; I have nothing, therefore, to offer him. We used to have a whole series of trade-offs operating like: I don't know where Japan is, but I bake. You may be practical, but I write villanelles—and once, even, I wrote a pantoum. I ran out of ways to reimburse him so long ago, I think, with a sudden feeling of poverty. Pity it took him so long to realize: it is difficult to be caught this late in the day.

"Oh, child," he says.

"Or am too *emotional?* Or didn't come down to New York the weekend I said I would and you had made me red diet Jell-O? And brood and get depressed and make everything messy and am not really that much like your mother, or because—because—" I choke and start to cry because I've never asked anyone this.

"Is it because—" I try again, but I can't get the words out.

"What is it, darling?" he asks urgently, worried.

"Because—" I start again, but it's too frightening.

"What?" he says, sounding a little frightened himself. And then, "I'm positive it's not true, but you can ask me if you want to."

"Is it because—*you hate me? Because I have a demon inside me?"* I say, and then start to cry even harder because I'm so afraid of what he's going to say. There is a little silence, half a silence maybe, and then Adam—Adam who takes everything I say absolutely seriously and always has the perfect response—Adam actually laughs. I think I hear him laugh, and am so startled I stop crying instantly and listen, and realize yes, he actually laughed. And then the moment changes, and he makes an "ohh" sort of sound, in sympathy with the thought, and all of a sudden I'm not so positive about the demon. It seems as if it might be an idea that belonged to a moment passed, like a ghost story that slips from your hands and you look up to find the room is still fine, the wallpaper's roses bloom as well as they always did. But I can't let it go that easily because I never let things go that easily, and because it felt so true just a moment ago.

"But you are scared of me sometimes?" I ask.

"No," he says gently, and laughs again, kindly. "You're just not a very scary person, kiddo. I'm sorry."

"Never?" I ask, persisting. "How can that be true?"

"Melanie," he says, in the straightforward way he sometimes does, "the only time I've ever been scared of you was when I saw your wrists. But I'm not scared anymore because you're never going to do that again because you would break my heart."

"But you'd get over it?" I ask. "I mean eventually, wouldn't you? You'd get over it because people get over things eventually—because everyone gets over everything eventually because—because they have to."

"I would never get over it," he says flatly. "I'd like to say I'd be too mad at you to let it ruin my life, but no: they'd be feeding me with a spoon. I would never get over it," he repeats, heavily as a vow. And I think: I will always remember just the way he said this, and I put my hands on my wrists, ashamed and thankful.

"Anytime you want to ask me that, you can," he announces, as if some great problem had just been solved.

"Anytime?" I sniff.

"Anytime," he says, pleased. "You can call me up in the middle of the night in ten years and ask me.

"You can *wake me up* in the middle of the night," he offers generously. I am always waking him up with questions that could have waited until morning, and he is forever being big about it. "Even if you just happen to be idly wondering. I don't hate you; I never hated you. There's nothing wrong with you—nothing missing—you're not hateful or ugly or—or anything, and you don't have any demons.

"You don't have any demons," he repeats.

"Not even one, Pumpkin," he adds, smiling now.

And I think with sadness and relief how believable it sounds. The sadness, perhaps, is the sadness that everything is over, and the relief is the same thing, but felt differently. He hasn't, he never did, and now he never will. He'll never feel anything he doesn't already feel because everything is over now. We're clarifying our closing positions, getting ready to finish the old conversations. You can ask anything you want—all the questions you always wondered and worried about. It makes no difference now, but he never hated you. It has been settled at last, you see: you had imagined it, after all, that anyone ever hated you and wished you were dead.

■ ■

"I'm happy to be sympathetic anytime you want, Mel," snaps Claudia, interrupting, "but I'm not going to listen to you say stupid things. You can't talk as if you have no sense of self, because I know that you do. Adam is not breaking up with you because you are ugly or stupid or fatally flawed. The *two* of you are breaking up because there were problems in the relationship. He treated you like a child, for example. That kind of thing. Normal psychological problems," she says.

"He's not your sole source of self-esteem," she adds crossly. Claudia's father is a psychiatrist so she always uses psychology terms with a mixture of affirmation and irony—as if in quotes—her voice slightly sarcastic, her nose wrinkled.

"It's demoralizing just to listen to," she says. "Besides which there isn't even any such thing as ugly. Women are more attractive or less attractive; people have times when they look well and times when they look poorly; you look pale and wan at this particular moment, but only witches," she finishes definitively, "are ugly.

"If you want to dwell on the reasons, why don't you pick some real ones?"

"It's not that I need to be with him every second," I say. "It's that I can't be without him all the time. It's like being homesick: you don't want to live at home all the time, but suppose you were told you could never ever go home again—they had locked the doors and changed the locks. It makes my stomach hurt just thinking about it. It's like being sent off to camp *forever*."

"Except," Claudia says, "you aren't ten years old and he isn't your father."

■ ■

"I just wish," I say to Adam, thinking, "I just wish we had been married."

"Why?" he asks. He has brought me a calendar with quilts on it today, to show me how many days there are in the future. Doesn't it excite you, he asks, to look at all the days ahead that will be yours? It is a pretty calendar: each month has a picture of a different quilt above it with little squares of green and cream in lovely old Puritan colors and cloths, but I start to cry when I look at it because all the squares of days are blank.

"If we had been married once," I say, "then we would always have been married. We'd have history—a history that would never be undone. If you looked it up on a tombstone a thousand years from now, it would be inscribed that we were married. A history would be real and eternal and true."

"That's stupid, Melanie."

"Why?"

"I don't know why exactly," he says. "It's just wrong. It's like *literary*. It's melodramatic." He takes a piece of my lined notebook paper and prints out in his big clumsy hand: MELODRAMA. Then he draws a prohibition sign around it, with the line running right through the word. And in the corner he writes: *"By order, the Board of Health."*

"Okay," I say, looking at it, considering. I tape it next to my bed and look at it often. I have it still; it hangs over my desk, and I still look at it sometimes. No melodrama.

By order, the Board of Health

"No, no," I try to explain to DeWitt on the phone. "It's not that I'm upset or not adjusted yet. You don't understand. *I can't live without Adam.*"

"What do you mean *can't*? Figuratively? Physically?"

"I mean I can—" I say, "but no, there wouldn't be any point. I always had this idea—this fantasy—that one day I would grow up and become this happy beautiful person. It wouldn't even have to be anything excessive, just a nice normal very nice, very normal woman, like—like Adam's mother. Just like Adam's mother, in fact. You know the way when anyone refers to her they always say in a slightly softened tone of voice: 'Oh, Mrs. Mahoney—isn't she *the nicest woman?*' Like that."

DeWitt says he knows what I mean.

"Well, see now, when I get to be the nicest woman also, and happy and beautiful, there'll be no point to it because there'll be no one to notice. There'll be nobody watching. There will be nobody to be proud of me," I say plaintively. "There will be nobody to be happy for me when I'm happy."

"Well," says DeWitt, "Adam will still be proud of you, and so will I and your parents and Aunt Pat and lots of other people, but the main thing is you'll be watching you, and you'll be proud, and you'll be happy for you."

"No, that won't be enough. Not if there's no one else there."

DeWitt inquires again where exactly "there" is.

"The happy beautiful place," I explain vaguely, thinking of Roberta's last letter. "Where I am as I want to be. Where I would have been with Roberta, except Roberta is dead, and where I would have been with Adam, except Adam will be with someone else now. The place that makes it worth going through all this. Like a house in the country, a small gray house in the country set on its own pond and wood. *That* place."

"Laura Ashley dresses, braids, rosy children? *Little Women?* Yeah, yeah. I don't know—maybe you wouldn't have been happy in the happily-ever-after place. Maybe it wasn't your kind of place. Maybe it held some kind of danger for you."

"What kind of danger?"

"I don't know," he says, losing interest in the idea. "I couldn't say. But if it didn't and if it were the right place for you, you'd probably be there already."

"Besides which," he adds suddenly, as if he has just thought of it, "the only way of getting there isn't to have Adam take you into his home. He doesn't have a patent on happy beautiful places, now does he? Surely you can envision some alternatives. So why don't you bring that idea to somebody else? You invite him in. Think of that. A role reversal!"

"But there's no one like Adam," I say. "I'll never meet someone like Adam. Adam's *perfect.*"

"Ahh, Adam's not perfect," he says softly. "It's all done with mirrors."

"Really?" I ask, perking up. "Like why not?"

"I don't know," he says, "but he's not perfect." And then: "Take it from a former roommate. He's not perfect."

"Yeah," I say, still hopeful. "How?"

"Well," DeWitt says, thinking, "he isn't always neat."

"Adam," I say, "is neat—a deeply neat and organized person. He is always collecting my scattered possessions and making our bed when we are together. *I* am not neat."

"There's something—mmm--selfishly altruistic about him," DeWitt says. "Like if someone collapses on the street, Adam will always be the first one to push through the crowd to help him. And that's great," he says.

"It's pretty great," I agree.

"But it means no one else ever has a chance. Maybe I was hoping to be the hero occasionally. He sort of, you know, monopolizes all the virtue and generosity in the room and doesn't always bring out the best in his slower kinfolk."

"I don't think that counts as a fault," I say, depressed. "You should have been quicker. While the crowd was gathering their courage and resolving their ambivalence, the wounded one might die.

"I mean, look, he doesn't push his way through because he wants to show off or get there first, but because the rest of you are standing around like sheep trying to decide if you really want to help or if you're too lazy, while he's thinking solely about the man who's lying there—not about giving you a chance to practice being good."

"I know that," says DeWitt, "obviously. But are we trying to analyze Adam's motives here, or are we interested in the effect he has on other people? Fine, his motives are all pure, and we can chat about how lovely he is anytime you want, but I'm trying to talk about how you feel. And all I'm saying is I don't think he always brought out the best in you, and I don't think you felt that good when you were with him.

"For example," he says crossly, "remember when I was living with him, and I was always in such a black temper?"

I tell DeWitt I remember.

"Well, partly I was, and partly I was cast into the lonely shadow of his sunshine. He was always so damned good-natured and excessively generous about overlooking my mood, that I never had to snap out of it, or be conciliatory toward him. It's like that for you too," he says.

"No it's not."

"Well, I think it is. Look, he's abandoning our protagonist, and if he's such a good guy he must have good reasons—unselfish reasons—about how it is the right thing for both of you. So do you want to be helpful in figuring them out, or do you want to have a different conversation? It's perfectly clear to me that he doesn't bring out the best in flawed and tragic types. Not by a long shot," he says. "And that includes you. You're so sort of *ingenue* around him. You disintegrate into this round-eyed adoration and worship-fulness, which you don't get into around anyone else, and it's childish and aggravating. When I first got to know you in that class, I met you alone, and then later I saw you with your boyfriend and you were a baby. A good girl, a pretty petted child, but—it was such a disappointment. You want him because you think he has all these qualities that you imagine you're a little short on and hope to absorb by affiliation, and maybe he wanted you for the same reason, and maybe you're both right and it would be nice if you were a little more this and he were a little more that, but it's not a package deal: Thernstrom/Mahoney Enterprises: 'Together We Have It All.' In the old days people married for money, and now they marry for qualities. Let me guess: your mother once told you that you are high-strung and need to marry a stable man, and your father told you that you must find someone to balance your check-book. Not, of course, that they're trying to get you off their hands— they just want the best for you, and so they handpicked the very best, the candidate of choice. Aren't strategies demeaning? This is supposed to be a relationship, after all. I never saw what you had in common and I never understood why you weren't lonely with someone you were so different from. And I would have thought that you—especially you—would have realized it a long time before he did.

"Of course, you do have some things in common," he adds thoughtfully, "special unique things. I'm sure you'll miss each other in some ways forever. But you wouldn't have made it; you didn't have enough in common. Far fewer than would make a marriage, which is a day-to-day thing, which requires cooperation. You weren't partners, you were fans. You never had a partnership. You're messy and he's neat."

"You said—"

"Did I? You know, I always used to wonder why you weren't the perfect couple since I like you both so much. In a curious way, I always thought you were wasted on one another.

"On your journey through life," he finishes definitely, "dur-ing which I personally wish you so much real happiness and prosperity, Adam Mahoney is the last person who should be your tour guide. You guys aren't going the same way."

"We are too," I say, beginning to cry again, *"ultimately."*

"Oh, ultimately," says DeWitt. "Well, fine, meet him there."

"Besides," I say, remembering, "you didn't come up with any faults of his."

"What can I say?" he laughs. "I told you he's the perfect man. They don't make them like that anymore; they broke the mold. Words fail me; the light always falls just right when he's around. He's a great guy. But he isn't great for you, Mel, he wasn't even pretty good. And it's a good thing someone finally noticed besides me, eh?

"But I do understand how you're feeling now," he adds cheerfully. "You aren't going to live happily ever after with Adam. Well . . . welcome to the world."

And then laughing softly, invitingly: "It's not so bad out here. I mean it rains too much," he adds, liking the image, "but you'll see, you get used to it. You get to kind of like it. Look, my first three girlfriends are married. It was bad news at the time, of course—I might have jumped off a small bridge over some girl I didn't even *like*—losing people you love and being alone is definitely bad. But it's not *so* bad. Know what I mean?"

"Yes," I say, "I know the difference."

I have this sudden vision of journeying into the world, and waving good-bye to Adam at the doorstep of the house we never lived in. The important thing about this house is that we never lived there: that's what makes it so small and gray.

"Do I get to go back?" I sniff. "If I'm good?"

"No," says DeWitt. "You get to go forward."

I replace the phone on the hook, and get my towel and shampoo.

The nurse comes in to see if I need anything. She is a cheerful nurse, a nice cheerful nurse in a nice white dress.

"No," I say, "I'm fine. I'm going to wash my hair, so I can go home tomorrow with clean hair."

"What a good idea," she says brightly. "I think that's a very good thing for you to be doing right now."

■ ■

Just before I go to sleep, Lisa calls. She listens to me explain for a long time what is happening, and what the situation is, and why I'm in the hospital, and finally she says, "I know, I know. I've heard this all before. There's this whole elaborate totally imaginary configuration built around Adam and Roberta, et cetera, et cetera, but I wonder—I mean I'd really like to know—what you would think about them without all that? What would happen if he were just Adam? Your high school boyfriend? I mean, it's all so romanticized and mythologized and—and just *excessive*, Mel. Couldn't you think of him without all that for once?"

"No," I say. "I couldn't. But it's funny, because I wonder about that sometimes too. And it's funny too but, you know, you wouldn't kill yourself over a nice guy. Even a very very nice guy like Adam—the nicest I'll ever know or even read about, perhaps— exemplary even among fictional characters. One person would never be worth another's life. You would only kill yourself over a symbol."

■ ■

"So about us breaking up," I ask Adam first thing the next morning. I've stayed up all night writing. I have a whole new list of reasons that he might want to abandon me for. I am going home today; Adam is going home too. This is my last chance to find out *the truth*.

"Yes?" he asks.

"Was it because—" I begin.

"Oh, Melanie," he says, "how long are we going to have to keep doing this?"

"Until—until—it's just—you know—*the list.*"

"But baby, we've been through the list. There's nothing on the list," he says, opening his hands.

"I know," I say, and then, without thinking, "Weren't you happy with me?"

As soon as I say it, I see that it was what I had wanted to know all along. The one thing that was not on the list, the eternal list: was I—was I—oh God, it doesn't matter—only this one thing matters, sums up, cancels. Yet I have asked him this so many times before, there is a whole satisfactory history to the convention of asking this question, and he has always always said how very happy he has been with me. Ugly or not ugly, it matters not at all—dear Lord, weren't you happy with me?

"You weren't happy with me," he replies, suddenly flat. It is the first time I have ever heard him speak without affect, and I catch my breath and can't think of what to reply, it is so solemn. I stand there, stunned, in absolute defeat, waiting to think of what to say, and I can't think of anything and the defeat is that there is nothing to think of. He has said the one thing for which there is no reply. You can mourn and explain and contradict it for however many pages you like, but he will never change his mind. Our whole relationship had been one of language: no, no, I love you, I adore you, you're everything to me—*everything*—because I said so, just because I said so. And according to some long-standing arrangement, whichever of us brought up a doubt, the other would reconcile it, as all contradictions can be brought together if you believe in a larger order: no, no, no, it only seems that way, but really it's not, really we are perfect together. The shadows only reveal how real it really is, and the discrepancies, truth. And we would believe each other, and I always thought that was what love is: the willingness to believe infinitely in the idea that your love is infinite. She was not happy with him. The one sentence never spoken: the little phrase upon which the whole myth of our togetherness will unlock, the way a murder mystery unlocks when the missing clue finally surfaces and turns out to be so simple after all. It was the butler. I was not happy with him. And so I wait and another moment passes, and I'm almost ready to revert again to the old question, the question for which there had always been a safe and familiar answer—the question of whether he was happy with me—when he speaks.

"In the end," he says, "I needed someone who was happy with me. In the long run, not making you happy made me unhappy too."

I had almost forgotten this. We pretended to have other conversations, of course, we had hundreds of other conversations about what happened and why—we have them still sometimes—but really this was the last conversation. I always leave it out of narrations of our history. It was that final, really; I mean, there was that little to be said about it.

CHAPTER 4

Through the Golden Windows

How the Match Girl Was Alone at Christmastime

I spent the whole afternoon looking for a children's book I read
when I was little. An easy task it was not, considering I remember only
one line:
  "The children were coming through the snow and they looked
  up and saw the high lighted windows, the golden windows,
  which they realized were their own windows."
  Or something like that. Makes me think of Stevens: "In the house,
the windows are lighted, but not the rooms."
  The inner chambers of darkness . . .
  Oh, that reminds me: I will not be coming home at Christmastime.
When are you coming to visit me?

As it happens, one Christmas vacation I am alone. The fair version
of the story is that my family is going skiing for five days and they
are returning Christmas Eve anyway, and they did not *not* invite
me—I elected to stay at school and work. And to be especially fair I
should add that they were going to stay over Christmas, but because I didn't want to go they rearranged all their plans around

me. It was after rather a lot of negotiating, but they did. I said they should stay as long as they wanted to, and they said what did I want them to do, and I said I wanted them to do what they wanted to do, and they said I might feel lonely, and I said I didn't care. So finally my father said they would come back on Christmas Eve, and I asked if that was what they would have the best time doing, and he said they would have the *best time* skiing, but they would rather come home and be glum with me.

So they go and I stay, and they are together and I am alone, and it is Christmastime, and Adam has just bought a blue farmhouse in the country, and he is there with his family, who all like each other, and I am here, alone of course—did I mention that before?—alone. Also there is no heat in the dorm, and no food, and I have some money, but not enough. I try to take some food from home to bring to school, but I have a fight with my mother about it before they leave. She thinks she is being taken advantage of; I think she wants me to starve. She says I'm always trying to take their things. I say she never gives me the things I need. This leaves us not much to say to each other.

But why, I protest again, do things always have to be paid for in our household? Don't they want to give me anything; why is nothing *free?* She asks why I expect things to be free; what are they getting in return, and why should they always be taken from? I ask why everything has to be a good deal, a bargain, an exchange. What about unconditional love; I feel unloved. She asks what about unconditional love for them—she feels unloved too, she says, and I look at her and see mirrored the identical expression, and realize that she does, in precisely the same way as I do, and suddenly we have run out of things to say, the whole question of love and payment so complicated as to be almost hopeless. We look at each other again, lost.

It is concluded, some hours later, that I can take some tuna and the cheese and the English muffins but not the bread, because the bread is nice expensive bread, and definitely not the lettuce— no, it doesn't matter whether they are going to eat it before they go skiing, she wants it. "*Leave it*, Melanie," she repeats, starting to get mad again. Then she adds that if I don't have enough money for food, I can come with them, and I tell her what I think of that and we're in a fight again.

Hmm, I think to myself, this will definitely be prime Match Girl material. You ought to be careful this week not to get depressed. But the funny thing is, I'm not depressed. I'm in a good mood. I check a couple of times to make sure, but I do seem to be in a good mood. Never mind, I remind myself, wait until the food runs out.

I go to have dinner with Claudia and her boyfriend Chris the night before they leave for Claudia's house. My family is safe in Vail. Hanukkah is just beginning; it is the very first night, Claudia says, alluding to the candle on the restaurant table. Claudia and Chris are fun to be with and fun together, and I have a good time. Chris offers to walk me home afterward and on the way we stop at Store 24 to shop for my week. I wander around, unsure of what sort of food to buy, unsure even of what kind of food I like to eat. Everything looks like too much or too little; and nothing looks like it will last the eight days of vacation, and not longer or shorter, or end up spoiling or being sickening. And then I come across pancake batter. Pancakes, I think, God, I could actually buy pancake mix and make myself some pancakes. I read the directions: eggs, oil, water. I can't believe it is so purchasable. Two dollars and change. I go up to the counter, clutching the box. "But you need eggs and oil, too," Chris says, reading for himself.

"No," I say, suddenly vehement, "I can't afford it."

"But a bottle of oil is less than a dollar."

"No, I can't—I don't have the money," I say, somehow panicked.

"I'll lend it to you. I'll give it to you."

"No."

"You can't make pancakes without oil—they'll burn."

"I'm going to make them with water."

"Okay, Melanie," he says, humoring me.

As we are walking back to my dorm, we stumble across a bottle of oil lying on the sidewalk. Chris seizes upon it as if it were manna from heaven.

"Have you ever, ever seen a bottle of oil lying in the streets before? An unopened, unbroken perfect bottle of yellow Wesson oil?

"Isn't it incredible?" he repeats. "I mean beer is one thing—I once found a bottle of beer on the streets. I was just getting off work and needed a beer, and there it was—beer—but beer is the kind of thing people drop. But Wesson oil? Have you ever found Wesson oil before?" I say no, and yes, it is wonderfully coincidental, and no again, no.

■ ■

I make pancakes the next day. The first batch rises into perfect
golden circles from the hot oil of the frying pan. I turn the flame up
as high as it will go and watch them for several minutes, blackening. I write three chapters and six poems that week and one of the
poems is good and pleases me. And the funny thing is either they
forgot to turn off the heat in our buildings, or I was wrong that
they ever turn off the heat during vacations, because there is plenty
of heat—at least as much heat as usual, maybe more. Someone
offers to take me out to dinner the last night, but I say no, I want
to stay in my room. It makes me feel better, though, not having an
abundance of fine fruits and fresh things—no kiwis decorating my
windowsill—better, that is, not missing my family, and being able
to cook for myself, and getting so much work done, and not being
depressed about Roberta or feeling particularly homeless or unhappy or, honestly, actually that much like the Little Match Girl.

■ ■

"So what you're saying," Sheila, the counselor, says to me, "is
that in some ways this is really a very happy time for you."
        "I didn't say that," I say, getting worried.
        "Is there some reason it seems important not to have said it?"
        "I don't know," I say, more worried.
        "Is there something scary for you about being happy?"
        "I don't know." And then: "Maybe it sounds—*selfish*."
        "Who would you be hurting or leaving out by being selfish?"
        "I don't know."
        "Roberta? If you were happy, you wouldn't be like Roberta
anymore, would you?"
        "No," I say, really worried now. "I won't be like Roberta
anymore."
        "So it's as if you would be moving away from what you were
together?"
        "Yes."
        "And you have no idea what Roberta would have been like if
she had changed or moved away from it too?"
        "No, I have no idea."
        "That must be scary," she says.

■ ■

On Christmas Eve my family comes back from their vacation, and I go home and begin to brood. I can't decide whether I should go to the midnight service. I always used to go with Adam and his family on Christmas Eve. I went with them four Christmases in a row, and he would walk me home after the service, and give me presents when everyone had gone to bed, and then walk the five miles back to his house in the early dawn. He always had so many presents for me. My parents would be a little dismayed because he always had so many more presents for me than they did. The service starts at eleven. At ten-thirty, Bob calls from California. "You don't need to go to church," he tells me briskly when I say I don't know, and then, laughing, intimate: "It's kind of a one-on-one thing."

"What is?" I ask.

"J.C.," he replies softly.

CHAPTER 5

Matches and Matchlessness

*How the Little Match Girl Had to Sell Matches for Her Living,
and What Happened When Nobody Bought Them Anymore*

"Instead of feeling this vague existential sense of seeping away,"
my friend Lisa says at three-thirty in the morning in the middle of
a long conversation as I am sleeping over at her house, "you ought
to pinpoint specific incidents and expurgate them.

"Just pull them out," she finishes definitely, "like weeds in
your garden." Lisa is such a powerful person; she really does
pinpoint her problems and pull them out like weeds in her garden.
It makes me feel hopeful even to hear the definiteness with which
she uses the metaphor.

"For example," she says, "and I think this is the right kind of
example—suppose you don't have a subway token. Instead of
asking some man for sixty cents and knowing he's only giving it to
you because you're a girl, and feeling degraded and helpless in a
vague way and squandering a little bit of your dignity for pennies—
you do realize you throw away your self-esteem for other people's
small change—just don't. Walk. Really," she says, "that's the secret

to everything. Know that you can always do it alone. Everything feels different once you know that. Always be willing to walk."

"But—" I say, immediately forgetting that this is a hypothetical example, and imagining myself standing there, subway-tokenless, with that subway-tokenless feeling. "What if it's too cold, what if it's snowing, what if I never get home? *What if I can't get there all by myself?*"

"It's not that far," says Lisa. "It's never that far."

■ ■

I am looking for something, and I can't find it. I keep looking, though, long after it is clear it's not there, and getting upset. "For want of the shoe," my mother says, looking at me standing there cross and bothered.

"For want of the shoe, what?" I ask, not wanting to be distracted from thinking about Loss.

"For want of the nail the horseshoe was lost," she says. "Don't you know that saying? For want of this, this happened, and because of that, that happened, and at the end of it something really big happened, like the kingdom was lost, all because of the first thing. You've really never heard that?"

"Oh," I say. "That is exactly how I feel about everything."

"And what is it you're missing?"

"I don't know. But I bet it's something extremely small. Not even a thing, maybe just a feeling."

"Well," says my mother, "hope you find it quick."

■ ■

I go into Boston to see the modeling agency I have been to before. I haven't been there in a long time, though, and I'm not excited about it, but I need to earn money, and other people tell me modeling is exciting and a good way to earn money.

"Melanie Thernstrom!" says the woman at the desk, not too kindly. "We haven't seen you in months."

"Oh," I say, unsure, "I've been . . . busy."

"Too busy to take care of your skin, I can see," she says. I wonder if she is joking. "*Well,* if you want to model you're going to have to be a little more reliable. You're never going to get anywhere if you come in here once a year."

And then: "You do want to model, don't you?"

"Yesss," I say, less and less happy to be there.

"Well, you'd better get busy then, otherwise you'll be too old by the time we find work for you."

"Maybe I'm already too old," I say, wondering. Then she takes out a piece of white stationery and writes something down. "I'm giving you the name of Mr. Z. He is in charge of choosing models for a commercial—an *expensive* commercial. You go bring him your portfolio, and make sure he thinks you're pretty."

Make sure he thinks I'm pretty. "Wait," I say, "how do I do that?"

"Use your imagination," she says, and, unsure again of her tone, I get unhappier.

"What exactly do I have to do?" I ask.

"Nothing," she says, annoyed now. "You can wait out in the hall with all the other girls, and when your turn comes you go into his office and give him our card, and if he thinks you're prettier than the crowd in the hall you'll get the job. It's not complicated."

"Oh," I say, wondering if I should leave now.

"And come back and see us and tell us what happened."

"Yes."

"And Melanie—do something about your hair before you go. It looks like a mess. Didn't we tell you to cut your hair?"

"Mmm," I say, not sure how to reply because they did, perfectly plainly, tell me this months ago. I turn to go.

"She has quite a marketable face," she says to the other woman, and I turn around, startled as by the taunt of a boy in a schoolyard, and then it occurs to me this is a compliment, and I open the door and leave.

And it is not until I'm all the way out to the street and on the subway and saying to myself feebly, maybe I'll go to see Mr. Z tomorrow, I really can't see him today, and knowing I won't go, and feeling guilty and defeated about the fact that it isn't going to happen—even if I write it down in my calendar on my list of things to definitely do and promise to cross it off, it won't happen—when I suddenly realize *it doesn't have to.* I don't have to be too busy tomorrow because I don't have to go anywhere I don't want to. I'm not desperate, the snowfall isn't thickening, and I don't have to find someone before nightfall to buy any matches because I don't need any matches, because *I'm not selling anything.*

I'm not selling anything, I repeat, standing still to try to realize the magnitude of the statement. I don't have to convince Mr. Z I'm prettier than anybody else because I don't have to convince anyone of anything. *That's not my job in life.* There are other things to do, ways to be. Jesus, I wish I had realized this years ago.

A street man is leaning against the door of the subway, swaying, drunk. I go over and reach into my pockets and open my hands to him. "God bless you," he says, surprised. "God bless you too," I sing. *I'm not selling anything; I don't have to have anything to sell.* I wish I could tell Roberta about it: it is precisely the kind of thing she would have liked to realize too.

■ ■

I am picking up something in my dad's office. He is reading a manuscript when I come in, and my mother is sitting in a chair waiting for him to go home with her.

"Hi, Mels," he says, not looking up. "Listen, here's a quote you might like."

"Who's it by?"

"Emily Greene Balch. A student of mine is doing her dissertation on her. 'When I was very young, I decided to be beautiful, but then I discovered that God did not intend that I should be beautiful. So I decided that I would be intellectually brilliant. But alas, I soon discovered that God did not intend me to be brilliant. So I decided to be good.' "

"Oh!" I exclaim passionately. "Oh, that's so *good.* And was she good? Did she have the most meaningful life?"

"She was a reformer early in this century, reasonably important."

"Oh!" I say again, "I must copy it down! That's so nice; I like it so much. I must copy it immediately and remember it forever." I take my calendar out of my purse and begin to copy.

"Why do you want to write it down?" he asks. "It doesn't— I mean you aren't— You are—"

My mother begins to giggle, and he says, addressing her, I think, "But Melanie is beautiful."

I freeze. "And clever," he adds.

"But goodness there's no point in even trying for," my mother finishes, hysterically.

"Out of the question," he chimes in.

"No chance."

"Flunked that test."

"Once she decided she had those other things, she didn't bother with being good."

There are howls of laughter.

I am still bent over, holding the pen in midair. Then I realize that they are joking, that what this is is a joke, so I laugh, and finish writing, and turn to leave.

I have already started to move when I remember that things are supposed to be different now, and I'm supposed to be making a point of not feeling the same defeats. Unless you say something now, I tell myself, it is going to go on record that you have nothing. They're telling you that you seem to have things—beauty, cleverness—but in fact *things* are all you have, attributes merely, whereas the gifts of the spirit such as Goodness, like the things Emily Greene Balch wanted, were not parceled out at your christening, as when the fairy who was forgotten sent a spell instead. For of course once you have to sell things to make your living—to justify your existence—you know that whatever your matches are, they won't suffice. They will run out as soon as it gets cold and dark because things are frail that way. Cleverness is irrelevant and beauty boring. Only goodness endures because it isn't a match—it's a quality, a religion.

(Tell them you are religious.)

No, I couldn't do that.

(They have announced you have no soul. They're *laughing* about it. This is the moment for you to get tongue-tied?)

What could I say?

(Recite the Lord's Prayer backward. *Whatever*. Who cares? Make something up. Now. You *have* to speak up now.)

What if they're right?

(They'll definitely be right if you don't say something fast.)

I resist a tremendous urge to walk out. You know, I tell myself, if you walk out now you won't look where you're going when you cross the street on the way home because you will be hoping to be hit by a car to make the feeling of defeat go away. Of course, you'll feel differently in an hour or two anyway, but death wishes can be granted; you shouldn't count on their not being granted. People wish they could go away and never come back and then they do go away and never come back. You should not wish them in the first place: they are dangerous, like a bewitched child-

hood birthday cake where you blow out the candles and wish to
never grow older.

And, although it's almost too late because it is better to establish these things when you are still a child and can speak without
irony—it gets so difficult when you are older to speak without any
irony or qualification or self-doubt or hatred; irony especially robs
from everything the possibility of complete seriousness—nevertheless
I do my best, and I stand up stiff and awkward and announce to
them as bravely as I can: "I just want you to know—I am too a
good person."

CHAPTER 6

Safety

*Which Tells How the Little Match Girl Came to Feel at
Home in the World*

Dear Mel Again,

*The turkeys haven't shown their faces yet and it's getting later and
later and now we'll probably miss the bus. Shitface. So much for going
to Mexico with Ben and Manuel. And there are ants on my desk too.
Flying ones. How horrid!*

And now we are in Tijuana.
*We don't remember exactly how we got here but there were three
dusty buses, a trolley, a ride and a long walk over the border at 1:00
a.m. by foot. The stars were as big as flowers and it felt so late it was
early. Tijuana's a rathole in hell. This town's on the backside of
nowhere—seedy and rundown and sad. Everyone seems to be on their
way out—hucksters everywhere, loud and desperate. We're staying in
this lousy hotel for $8 a night, which is a rip-off, especially considering
the bedbugs in the bed. No one really lives here; everyone's trying to
get to the other side of the border and being hit up by someone who claims
they can help. But they can't. I don't remember having spoken to Ben
since before yesterday. I bought a pink clay Mexican cross, painted with
flowers and green birds. I've been wishing for a bath. A kitty is crying
outside my window. One feels this obligation to go places, you know?*

I am sitting in Café Algiers working on my thesis on a Sunday afternoon. I had been working in my dorm room, but it was depressing me. I tried the library, but I wasn't happy there either. I called my friend Claudia from a pay phone to see if I could come over, and she said I could, but I could tell she was busy packing. She is leaving tomorrow for warm faraway places, like Spain and Turkey and the magical island where her sister Luisa lives. I am worried about this—about her leaving me. I glance up from my table in the corner and notice that the graffiti on the wall says: "Home is where you feel safe."

I am startled; it is such an unlikely thought for graffiti. I scan the rest of the wall, but it contains only the usual collection of curses and random violent or sexual phrases. "Home is where you feel safe," I repeat out loud: safeness.

Okay, I say to myself with sudden resolution, I'm not going to leave here until I feel safe.

But, I immediately protest. It is an absurd idea—such a "literary" scenario—one day two years after the murder of one of the girls, the other girl walks into a café, reads something on the wall, decides safety is a state of mind and achieves it. But suddenly there is nothing I want to do less than sit in this café for another fifteen minutes: *I must go,* I think, I have work to do, I have my whole thesis to write, I can't just sit here doing nothing because of some psychological experiment.

Besides which, I remember, we're not even talking about anything.

Well, suppose this clichéd little gimmicky attempt to wrap things up neatly did have the power to be the concluding scene? The denouement? Suppose you pretended you felt safe right now, just to go along with this story being made up right now—to give it a nice ending. The end of the mythology of darkness.

I can't pretend that. Besides, there is no mythology of darkness.

You see, you are worried! Why can't you pretend?

And then the whole series of *buts,* the long-submerged, almost-lost-but-still-present list, surfaces.

But Roberta was murdered, I think. *But Adam has left me. But I have no future. I can't go back home, I have no home, I have no plans, and the things I plan won't turn out well. I know they won't turn out well because they've already not turned out well because—* And then, realizing for the first time the real danger: because there is no place I can be safe from these considerations. Not even this afternoon, not even for a couple of hours, am I safe from considering.

But safety is a feeling. No one knows what the future keeps. There are always bad possibilities. Maybe Claudia will be found facedown in an alley somewhere. *No one knows what time brings.* Yet right up until the minute it happened she would be safe, because she would have felt safe, and would have been leading her life as if she were safe. She would have had all these years of afternoons in which to feel safe and happy and homey, and nothing could take away all those years of afternoons. When people thought of her, they wouldn't just think about her at the end, they would think about how pleased to be in the world and how at home in it she was, how small and bright and fierce, and what a happy thing it was to be around her. Whereas for you the only safe thing would be for it to finally happen, because at least that would have the comfort of a real murder instead of just demons.

The waitress comes over and brings the check. I tell her I am waiting for someone. She asks if I want some more tea while I wait, and I say all right.

You could still be safe. It's not too late, even after all that has happened. Even this afternoon; even so you could still be safe.

It's just an idea.

It is always an idea. It is also an idea that you are unsafe.

I sit there, quiet, not even writing. The tea takes a while to come, and when it does come it is nice and steamy. I take the tea strainer out, and pour some cream into the teacup, and lift the pot in order to pour it. And as I begin to pour, it seems to me—and I could be wrong, I could be making it up, it could be just story thinking—but as I begin to pour, fragrant and tea colored, perfectly tea colored, I never knew safety would be tea colored, but just exactly tea colored—as I begin to pour, the safety feeling rises.

CHAPTER 7
The End of the Story

Which Tells What Happened to the Little Match Girl
at the End of the Story

*Incident repeats narration . . . Every anticipation cries out
for realization. Even when one knows long in advance that
something will come to pass—as can be assumed in the case of
the accustomed fairy tale listener or reader—one remains, so
long as the realization has not occurred, in a state of suspense
which is relieved only when what has been anticipated actually occurs, when the expected chord sounds.*

—Max Luthi
The Fairy Tale as Art Form and Portrait of Man

A letter arrives from Adam one day. It is May, six months after the
day I came home and found the red light of the answering machine
on. My name is typed on the outside; I recognize his typing. How
queer it is, I think, that even his typing is dear and familiar and
reminds me of him. His typewriter is old and manual and I know
exactly what it looks like, and why he hasn't bought a new one.
And although I love to rip open letters like wrapping paper, I know
somehow that I should wait until I get to a safe place to open it. I
am more careful, I suppose, than I used to be. I walk toward my
room.

"Dear Melanie," he writes. He is writing because he promised he would write and tell me as soon as he knew; and because he would never not tell me anything, because he keeps his promises, Adam does. I know this to be true, which is why I made him promise, I remember exactly the time and the way in which he promised: he is writing because he is thinking of getting married. Not soon, not definitely, but he said he would tell me as soon as he thought of it, so he is telling me. He is going to take a few deep breaths now, before he finishes writing this: perhaps I would like to also. But the hardest part, he says, is over now.

I put down the letter and take a breath. I look at the scrawl of roses sketched like an elegy into the wallpaper of the blue-green walls in the late-afternoon light. He is right: the hardest part is over. The waiting and the wondering and the uncertainty—but most of all the uncertainty, the years of uncertainty. (Will she marry him? Should she marry him? What will become of her if she doesn't marry him? How is this story going to end? *When is it going to end?*) I take another breath. It is over now; you can put the book away and go to bed. You must be tired; it has been such a long story. Even I was getting tired, and it's my story, but it's all right now because now we know. She didn't marry him; he didn't marry her, he married someone else. Roberta died, and Adam left; Roberta was found in a shallow grave, and Adam got married to somebody else. And Brad married too, another woman, and they have a little boy. Funny, for a long time I thought it was a girl: it would have made a better story; the irony is nicer, more obvious. I wonder what they named him. Oh, Melanie, it doesn't matter what they named him—it doesn't matter to you. It's their story. Ending. How easy it is; how quickly it happens. You could have guessed it would end this way, but you had to keep reading to find out for sure, to get the details. You can cry a little if you're sentimental that way: if you cry when sad stories turn out to be sad. I cry a little, and pick up the rest of the letter.

"I'm happy, of course, in some ways. . . . One question I had was whether to wait and tell you, but I was afraid it would poison things between us.

"And I have complete faith in you," he adds.

I am glad he has complete faith in me: whatever that means, and whatever it has to do with the situation at hand, but no, it couldn't wait any longer. Waiting is much harder than ending; if I had known that before, it might have ended earlier. And false endings are so much harder than real endings. I think about Roberta and feel certain she thinks so too.

"Knowing your turn of mind, it will be bound to occur to you one dark night whether you will ever be happy someday. The answer is yes. Or at least you have as good a shot as anyone; it is arrogant to think otherwise."

Arrogant to think otherwise. What a nice phrase; an Adam-like phrase. A nice way of thinking about things, Adam's way is. No wonder he is happy.

"I love you. Call me. It is difficult to make myself understood on paper. Do not worry about crying. I have been crying all morning. This will not be the last phone call or the last letter. God willing (and you willing) they will go on forever, and they will get easier and we will always know and love each other."

■ ■

Claudia and I are having our usual hypothetical discussion. I call her at her parents' house in Washington, where she has come back from the magical place for her older sister Luisa's wedding. She tells me that at the wedding all their relatives kept asking her, "So when is the next happy occasion?" and she would tell them when hell freezes over. The discussion begins with my saying, woe is me, I should have married Adam, and then she says, but you could have married Adam, you had years and years to make up your mind to marry Adam, and then I say, but I had this doubt and that doubt and the other doubt, but what would have happened if I had been a different person who had not had those doubts, a better person, for example, and maybe I would have gotten to be that better person after I married Adam, and then she says—and this is usually several hours into the conversation—she says a little more sharply that when I'm an entirely different person I can let her know, and we can figure out whom I should marry then. Then I add one more hypothetical, and the discussion gets a little more complex, in a widening web of could-be, and it eventually becomes clear that there is nothing one can say that is true, except that if the story had been different, the story would have been different, just as if Roberta had been ten minutes later to go running on the morning she was already late to go running, I might have gotten started a few years earlier working on being the happy person who might have been happy with Adam. And it is quite plausible, you see, because Roberta often *was* late to things or forgot about them entirely, but—(what is the but?) oh yes, Roberta wasn't late and Adam is engaged.

Before we have arrived at this wearisome conclusion, when this conclusion is, in fact, still quite far away, Claudia interrupts and says, "Oh, Mel, I know just the thing to do!"

I hear the word *do* and instantly perk up in hopes that she has thought of a real thing—a thing outside the train of imaginary speculations that lead to the same facts you began with.

"I'll send you some rescue remedy!" she says, with planning glee. "Luisa and I will make you up a special potion—a crisis potion—with secret special ingredients *made especially for your situation*, and we'll send it off right away."

Luisa lives a magical happy life on a little island near Spain where they make herb and flower potions called rescue remedies. Claudia gave me a bottle in the fall for general troubles and poor sleeping. It is made with flower essences and it comes in a dark smoky bottle, and you mix it with pure spring water and three drops of brandy and take it precisely as instructed and it works. Moreover, Claudia says, Luisa didn't always have a magical happy life: she used to be just like me—well, maybe not exactly like me—but not the way she's been since she went to this magical island and became happy. She used to live in Washington, D.C., and had an ordinary job and a boyfriend, and then she quit her job and broke up with her boyfriend and moved to the magical island and became *perfectly happy*. And not only that but she has just married this British writer who happened to live on that very island and who had written a book just before he met her called *Dance for a Diamond* in which the heroine was a small dark fiery girl called Lou, and then into his life arrived small dark Luisa, and it was a confirmed magical coincidence. It can happen to anyone, says Claudia.

"Will you send my potion off right away?" I sniff.

"I will Federal Express it," swears Claudia.

■ ■

"Ohhh," mourns my friend Lisa, "ohhhh—that's so bad. That's the worst.

"Ohhh, I didn't think that would happen," she repeats desolately, sounding so much like me and so little like her that I almost laugh. *"Married,"* she echoes, "oh, *noo."*

"Yes," I say, trying to sound desolate, but already feeling less desolate. I know that it is my sorrows she is lamenting because when she laments on her own, she doesn't sound that way at all. She doesn't usually lament, in fact; she analyzes accurately. At college, she studied economics. Although I'm happy she is feeling for me, I know the practical thing to do is to make use of her analysis while I have her.

"It is dreadful," I say. "Maybe we should go over all the ways that it is particularly dreadful to make sure we haven't missed anything. I mean I understand the basic horrifying concept, but I want to make sure we are lamenting all the different horrible aspects, with all their specific hideous personal implications."

"All right," says Lisa, thinking. "To begin with, you're going to have to watch him with somebody else."

"Like peering in the lighted windows of other people's lovely houses?" I ask. "Nah," I decide, remembering Christmas. "I mean, of course, but I've done it before. I can handle homelessness."

"But he might be happy with her."

"I want him to be happy."

"You do?"

"I think so," I say, puzzled. "I mean I don't want him to be *un*happy."

"You'll never be happy together though now," she says.

"Oh, I don't know," I say, thinking. "We might be much happier being friends."

"Well, okay," says Lisa. "What do you think the worst thing about it is?"

"Ummm—I'm not sure," I say, puzzled. And then, remembering, "That it might—I mean people might think—someone else might think that the implication is *I didn't really love him as much as I said I did.* It might imply I don't keep my vows—or worse, that *there was never anything behind them in the first place."*

"That's the worst thing about it?" Lisa repeats incredulously. "Who are you trying to prove it to anyway—whose story is it? It's up to you how much you think you loved him. Who is doubting you that you have to convince with a marriage license? I believe you; Adam believes you; you believe Adam. There seems to be a general abundance of good faith all around; what's the problem? That—if that's the worst thing about it—*that's ridiculous."*

And then: "Melanie?"

"Yeah?"

"What's her name?"

"I don't know," I say. "I didn't ask."

"Why not?"

"I don't know. Maybe I . . . forgot.

"So, mmm," I say, searching for an appropriate summary for the situation. The right summary can be such a useful thing, I think, thinking of what it might be. "Easy come, easy go?"

"Easy come, easy go," Lisa agrees approvingly.

■ ■

It suddenly seems to me that I have to get Adam a wedding present. I think and think about this, and the more I think, the clearer it becomes that it is an insoluble dilemma. If I don't get him anything, he will think I don't wish him happiness, and even if he knows better, his fiancée won't. And if I do—no, I can't. It is impossible.

"I'm not going to get you a wedding present," I tell Adam.

He laughs. "Guess what?"

"What?"

"That's okay, sweetheart."

"And I'm not going to wish you happiness, either."

"Not even a little happiness?" he says.

"Well," I say, considering, "maybe a small amount. A modicum. But nothing excessive. A car, some animals, maybe a couple of kids, but not much more. Nothing storybook—definitely nothing mythical. I wish you a small modicum of extremely average happiness."

"But you'll wish me a little more next year?"

"Maybe," I say, "but it's like one of those jobs where your salary can be raised to a certain point, but you reach that point and plateau. There is a very fixed limit on how much happiness I am ever going to wish you."

"What's the limit?"

"I don't know," I say. "I'll have to consult Claudia about it."

■ ■

"Out of the question," Claudia declares vehemently. "Presents? I mean, that's nice of you and all, Mel, but generosity is *completely* uncalled for! And I wouldn't bestow any matrimonial benedictions on them either! After all, he didn't consult you about marrying the slut! Presents," she repeats, "what a stupid idea."

I laugh, relieved at her dismissiveness. But then it occurs to me she might not understand, and even though I'm afraid it will spoil the moment, I have to tell her: "But you know, Claud, about . . . the woman. I don't really know anything about her, but I mean—oh dear, Claudia, she's probably *the nicest woman in the world.*

"I mean, after Aunt Pat and Adam's mother," I add, trying not to exaggerate. "Adam wouldn't marry anyone who wasn't nice. *Extremely* nice."

"I know," Claudia says simply, and then, "but goodness, I guess we can think of her any way we please! I mean I haven't met her, and you haven't met her, so no one's met her, and if you want to meet her years and years from now you can change your mind then. In the meantime, I don't think thinking of her as The Nicest or The Third Nicest Woman in the World is the slightest bit helpful."

"I could find out her name," I suggest dubiously.

"I wouldn't," says Claudia. "It'll make her sound a lot nicer. Why don't we work on thinking of a nice neutral term?

"Evelyn, for example," she says thoughtfully. "Or Jezebel.

"As for a wedding present," she adds, "if you must get him and Madame X something, it ought to be heavy, serviceable, expensive, dull, and nonreturnable. A food processor, for instance," she suggests helpfully. "Or a platter. And buy yourself a miniskirt while you're at it."

■ ■

"Adam," I say again, knowing I have asked him before, but needing to be certain, "if I don't send you a wedding present, your fiancée won't think I don't wish her well, will she? Or wish your marriage luck?"

"She won't think anything of the kind," Adam says reassuringly. "She doesn't think that way."

"Oh. But—Adam?"

"Yes?"

"You don't think it either?"

"No," he says simply and seriously. "I know you wish me happiness."

"Oh," I say, resting in the ease of his tone, the old contentment that used to lie so often between us. And then because I always need to ask one more question than I should, I say: "You're sure?"

"I'm positive," he tells me.

■ ■

I wake up, panicked, as from a bad dream. I don't remember what I'm dreaming about, but I know the panic. I try to think about it, and the panic becomes a question and the question is whatever the question is at the moment. *What if something has happened to Roberta? What if we don't get her back? What does homicide mean? Who did it, but who did it? What if Adam leaves me; what if*—and then I remember what this morning's question is, and I sit up very straight and say: *what if oh my God Adam marries—actually marries—somebody else?*

I sit still, breathing hard. And then I remember that he is going to. Roberta died, and Adam is going to marry somebody else, and there is nothing—*nothing*—for me to worry about anymore. Put away that story, and lie down, and try to think of something else. Like counting sheep. Try to picture some very boring sheep in a story where nothing happens, and count them for a while, until you remember there is nothing else you need to think about. I look around my room in the morning light and say once more that it happened, it all happened, long ago, and is finished. I look at my room to make sure it looks as it did before, and it does and I feel better and wonder if I will be able to sleep again.

■ ■

Aunt Pat is moving from her house. She isn't really my Aunt Pat; she is Adam's aunt, and her daughter Kathy, who died when she was fourteen and wrote a book of poetry called *Rainbow Dreams*, was Adam's childhood best friend. But everyone lets me call her Aunt Pat because I have so few relatives that I borrow them from Adam, who has a lot. Relatives always seem to me such a friendly idea. Aunt Pat has stayed all these years in the house where Kathy lived, but she is moving now, and she has found so many of Kathy's things, she tells me, as she has been sorting. There are letters and photographs and pictures Kathy crayoned and old medicine bottles still in the refrigerator with Kathy's name on them and even tapes of Kathy speaking and singing.

"Did you listen to them?" I ask.

"Oh yes," she says, "but I've heard them lots of times before."

"And it wasn't queer or strange or horrible or sad?" I ask in wonder. "It wasn't awful to hear her voice, to have it be that . . . familiar? Even though she has been dead so many years?"

"No," says Aunt Pat, "it wasn't queer or—or anything. In my mind, she's always kind of just in the next room, and I'm surprised and a little sad that the door never opens, but no—she's always there."

"In the next room," I repeat. "Do you really feel like that? All the time? How—wonderful."

■ ■

I half-wake early in the morning, disturbed, a sense of faint rustling. It is almost like the rustling Adam would make when he woke early in the mornings to go to work. Too tired to quite wake up, but too worried to go back to sleep, I would hear him, and think of him getting up alone, putting peanut butter on toast in the still apartment, gloomy with early light. Even in my sleep, though, I know that it is not quite the same rustling because I am alone here. No one is with me here. It must be the next room he is getting up in, I think, hurt with the impotence of worry. He is out of reach: he is in the next room. You can't help him. You don't need to help him: he is getting married. He is marrying, he is marrying, close your eyes. He has someone who will always wake up with him now and make things nice for him and fetch breakfast forever.

I almost feel jealous and wish I could be in the next room too, but the futility of the feeling is too obvious. It would be like wishing Roberta were alive when she was already dead, dead and buried. I pull the covers up, and even though I have lost both my friends, it suddenly seems to me I have done well with them. It's nothing I have done, actually; they went to their separate fates without me, and there was nothing at all I could do about it, but nevertheless they are in safe places, dead or with other people, and do not need me to worry about them. Really I have done quite well with both of them, I say again. Always kind of just in the next room. I close my eyes and go back to sleep.

PART 8

Misinterpreting: The True Story and Fictions of Memory

■ ■

Suppose truth were a woman—what then?
—Nietzsche
Beyond Good and Evil

CHAPTER 1

Payments

*There are places in the world you associate with loss
and, this being so, you should not go to them . . .
Darling, I say it
in earnest: we will never come here . . .*

—Michael Blumenthal
"Mt. Auburn Cemetery"

**"M," Bibi says, frowning with attention, leaning forward
slightly to look at me: "what are you doing here?"**

**"I am attending the trial," I say. "It's important. It's—
it's for you! The state is spending two million dollars and
it's all being done for you."**

**"Look, I already told you how I feel about all that shit.
So forget it, chica—okay? Just forget it. I mean I'm really
not interested. Tell them to donate it to a village in Af-
ghanistan or something. And send all those other spectators home too—who *are* all those other people?"**

The retrial—the mythical long-awaited fabricated and refabricated
trial—takes place in the spring of 1988, three and a half years after
the murder. I don't want to go, or rather, I don't know if I want to
go. I make plane reservations, and cancel and rereserve and recancel
them. On the whole, I think, I would rather not go, but I make a
lot of phone calls, and in one of them it emerges that my friend

DeWitt is going to California, or wants to go to California, or was thinking about it anyway, and when the night actually comes I find I have stepped onto the plane too. I have to go, and I'm pretty sure DeWitt decided that he had been thinking about taking this vacation anyway after he found out that I wouldn't go by myself, but I'm not in a position to question him. I don't pack, I don't arrange a place to stay, I don't go to the bank and get money, I just stare at the clock until quarter to two and then call a taxi, and my parents say it's not a good idea—it's not a good idea, Melanie, *it's just not a good idea*—and: *we mean it, Melanie, we do not want you to go*—but DeWitt is waiting and the tickets are nonrefundable and I step on the plane and then it's too late to change my mind. I am an hour late getting there, although the plane is later: as we are driving, the Greek taxi driver tells me to sit up front, and then puts his hand on my thigh. I move away and look out the window, too dispirited to think of what to say. And then the plane takes off and I sink down into the seat, depressed.

What are you doing here, Melanie? I repeat, overcome by an odd floating sensation of unreality, unlike even the old sense of being in a story. It's a parody, I think, a curious futile parody of the first search, three and a half years ago, when we didn't find her. And it is all so really far removed from Roberta: the retrial to discover the truth of the first trial which the first trial could not discover, the truth of the search in which we were searching to discover what happened, but didn't, and by the time you finish trying to sort out the sentence the word *truth* has lost all meaning. It's too many years later, and the "we" is not even the same we, although it is me, after a fashion or some version thereof, and we're vaguely trying to have the old conversation, and I'm too really tired even to pretend that it might lead somewhere, that we might learn anything more about what happened to Bibi on November 4th. She's been dead so long now, I think to myself, wonderingly. So long.

DeWitt is in a good mood; he tries various conversations, but I stare off into space. He has even brought cooking magazines for the occasion, and although they are usually a favorite thing of mine too, I refuse to take an interest and be better company. "Dammit, Melanie," he says finally, "snap out of it." I get up and go into the bathroom and look at myself in the mirror and put my hair in a ponytail and wonder if I'll look better when I get to California. "What did you do?" DeWitt asks, surprised, when I come out.

"You look better." And we order drinks and settle down with *Bon Appétit.* I don't want to go and become enmeshed in the story again, I think to myself; I don't want to go and find there is nothing to be enmeshed in. The story it took me so many years to get out of: the story I am so afraid to let go of: the story, the story.

As it happens, the courthouse where the trial is held is in downtown Oakland, in the Chinese and Vietnamese part of town. There are a large number of restaurants and grocers and fruit stands; this brings back not much memory—a teaspoon perhaps, or a little less. Department 41, when we finally find it, is a small room on the fifth floor of the courthouse, sparsely populated. On the left front side of the room in the courthouse sits the jury, and by an understood etiquette the Lees are sitting on one side and the Pages and friends of theirs are sitting on the other. I hesitate, walking in awkwardly the first day, unsure where to go, unwelcome some-how on either side. I want to sit on Roberta's side, I think, odd and stupid: I want to sit on Roberta's side. I resist a tremendous urge to walk out, and finally settle myself with the reporters. They are all alert note-taking young men, some of them handsome, one of them blond: they are unwelcome here also, I think.

Here we all are, I think, gathered in a most serious human enter-prise—the sorting of interpretation into truth. One is told all versions are equal: one interpretation as good as another and no meaning priv-ileged, since texts don't have meaning, they only have readers of meaning. But now, suddenly, no one is interested in readings: they want to know the truth, yes, no; he did it, he didn't do it. They have come to the end of the book and they want to know *who done it.* Guilty or not guilty; pregnant, not pregnant; alive, dead. Dead, she was dead. I am sitting in a courtroom, and this is ultimate reality.

Been reading I Never Promised You a Rose Garden *(a book about a mental institution). I copied out a passage for you I rather thought would appeal:*
> *The shop had a warm, normal look of work being done until one looked close and saw that it was only imitation. Patients were sewing or modeling clay, reading or making collages with paste and bits of fabric. Outcasts from the laws of the world seemed to be warming their hands before the illusion of satis-fying labor. They were vainly seeking its textures, papers and materials and raveling out old woolen scarves to extract reality from them . . .*
> *You know, Mels, it's kind of like that for us too . . .*

Ultimate reality, I think, trying to recall who promised it would be: ultimate reality has turned out to be not so interesting after all. As you enter, there is a sign saying "People vs. Page." It shocks me a little: I wonder what it is like to walk in and have your name opposed to People: to try to defend yourself in a case against you made by People. Next to his lawyer sits Brad; on the other side of the room is the assistant district attorney. He has an entire cart of notes by his side; I wonder momentarily what the notes are about. I wonder too what Roberta would say if she knew how many notes had been made on her—whether she would have lived differently. One would live more carefully, I suppose.

Amy, now Brad's wife, is sitting in the front row with the baby, who is large and blond, several years old by now. At her side is her father-in-law, looking thin and tense and pale. He frequently leans over to whisper something to her. Amy sniffles repeatedly, weeping at times with audible sobs; she is the only one in the courtroom who appears teary. The Lees are staring ahead, their faces like carved stone masks. Mr. Lee has resigned from MIT; I had heard he had been hospitalized repeatedly. Mrs. Lee too looks unusually unwell; her skin is sallow. I remember Veronica telling me her mother was taking antidepressants and other medications, and that she still visited the grave every day. Brad is wearing a suit; he is tall and gaunt and sober. His manner is appropriate: he takes the situation seriously, and yet is neither dramatic nor anxious, but attentive, dignified, and weary. He looks so much more grownup than I remember him; it is saddening to think this must be the occasion on which he wore his first suit. They were so close, I mourn suddenly, both of them, yet they never quite made it to adulthood. Brad was arrested two days before he was to take his last exam senior year, one credit away from graduation, and Bibi was buried when she tried to leave school. Bibi is buried, and Brad sits in his suit with his makeshift family and real baby, amidst the huge weight of relatives lined up on either side of the aisle, waiting for the proceedings to begin. A macabre version, I recall someone writing in a phrase I never liked, of the wedding that would never be. The wedding that no one would have imagined had she not died, had her death not made all possibilities—even those that were never in any way real or desirable or even possible—feel nevertheless like losses.

Idly, I wonder who the first witness will be and whether I will recognize him or her. Queer, I think, as if a play were over and the

audience didn't like it and demanded everyone emerge from behind the curtain to explain whom they thought they were playing
and why, but the main character had already left, and everyone
had to fill in for her. And queer, too, I think, looking toward the
jury with its sea of blank motley faces, that it has come to this: that
we have fallen into the hands of such an indifferent audience. I
hope they listen carefully.

"What started as a love story, and ended as a nightmare . . . ,"
begins Mr. Burr, the district attorney, the first day, opening his
speech before the hushed room.

Oh no, I think immediately, it didn't start as a love story and
end as true crime. Why do they borrow these formulas from
dime-store romances? You've got the genre all wrong—as if we
didn't have a genre of our own.

"What began," I say, trying to imagine how my version would
begin, "what began slightly ambiguously but nevertheless somewhat ominously, and ended extremely ominously and very ambiguously, as you might have guessed—indeed should have guessed,
and you know, you did kind of guess—

"What began as a nightmare," I begin again, thinking hard
about his formula, "and ended as reality . . . What began as imagination, and ended with Roberta dead . . . What began . . . wait—"
Jesus, Melanie, can't you speak any more clearly? Who is going
to buy your version?

Oh dear. What was it that began? And where does the word
love fit into my story? Oh dear, I think again, and try to listen to
the D.A.

■ ■

The first witness they bring in is the polygraph examiner. He is
fair of face and skin and creates an impression of guilelessness. The
polygraph, he begins to explain, the polygraph measures deceit. It
measures deceit through involuntary anxiety levels because *a man
can never lie to himself.*

But how is it measured? Brad's lawyer inquires: What shows
up is anxiety. How do you know that it is anxiety connected with
guilt? Maybe it is just anxiety. You asked my client whether he
murdered Roberta Lee, but my client felt responsible for her death.
He wasn't responsible, of course, but he felt it. He felt guilty

because he went home to write a paper the morning that she died. What he needs is a psychiatrist, not a jail sentence.

But a person can never lie to himself, the man repeats.

A polygraph measures feelings; who or what can ever judge whether a feeling is true? queries the defense attorney. They ask a number of questions along the lines of: a) Is today Tuesday? b) Is black the opposite of white? and c) Did you murder Roberta Lee? And then they see which you react to most strongly.

Because you can't lie to yourself, the man explains again, with more conviction: *if he felt guilty, he was guilty.* If he said he did it, he did it. He looks at the D.A. for reassurance. Brad patiently takes notes, his eyes a calm and lovely blue, his countenance gentle.

But men lie to themselves all the time, I think: they even lie to themselves about whether they are lying to themselves. *Everyone knows that,* I think, disgusted—everyone.

Coming out at lunchtime the first day, I bump into Brad. I had wondered what it would be like to see him again, and am surprised to find the first thing that I think is: What about my photographs? You promised you would send me those photographs. The last time you and I were together we walked to the photo shop to get copies of Bibi made for the search, and I was leaving to go back to Boston the next day, and you said: Don't worry, I'll send you copies when they come out. And for the past three years it's been on my mind that you promised you would not forget to send me photographs, and how you never did, and how now you have pictures of her that I'll never have. And do you keep them; do you cherish them? Do you still have them in your photo album and do you look at them now?

Things. Other things I could say to Bradley: Hello. How have you been? This must be a difficult situation. Did you—umm—did you murder my friend? Did you murder Roberta?

"Hi, Melanie," he says. Then we both walk toward the elevator, where Mr. and Mrs. Lee are standing. Brad glances at them, and then takes the stairs, and I stand, uncertain, waiting for everyone else to leave.

I talk to Mr. Page, standing in the hall, once. "How do you like San Francisco?" he asks, awkwardly. "Do you have friends here? Do you have a place to stay?"

"I like it okay," I say nervously. "I have a place to stay and some friends here. Five anyway," I add, thinking hard, and pausing to puzzle over whether my fifth friend counts. I always begin to calculate when I am anxious. I'm funny that way: about things that are calculable—budgets, for example, which are good things to calculate, or whether Darryl Strawberry is having, all things considered, a disappointing season—I'm oblivious; whereas for things about which speculation is both impossible and dangerous—love, for instance, language or meaning—I am forever generating false likenesses between things unequal and unknown.

"I wonder where the Lees stay," Mr. Page asks me timidly.

"I don't know," I say, likewise timid. "Do you get on with your lives—in between times?" I ask hesitantly, suspect myself in the same way—as in: *You*, why do you want to know? Why are you asking? Why would Mr. Page want to tell his motivations, and why are you always trying to elicit false confidences?

"No," he says, as if he is thinking of how to explain, and then changing his mind. "No," he says again. I think of Mr. and Mrs. Lee, sitting straight-backed and silent in the back row of the courtroom, punctual, daily. Mr. Lee, unable to work anymore, sitting on the bench, stroking Mrs. Lee's hand and taking notes three and a half years later. Three and a half years later they are *taking notes on the trial.* Why are they taking notes, I wonder suddenly—what will they do with all of their notes?

Haven't you all done enough already, I think. Can't you all just go home and call it a day? I think the parents should all go home together; I think the parents should walk out now.

But of course I don't say it because I already know the answer: if home were still intact, they would be there.

■ ■

Mr. Burr, the prosecutor, I discover after a while, has the meanest voice imaginable. He has a whole collection of menacing, guilt-producing expressions: his favorite is asking, rhetorically I suppose, *and this is the woman you loved?* This comes up often, but particularly in the phrase: why did you leave *the woman you loved* in the park after twenty minutes? Just how many minutes a day did you spend exercising when *the woman you loved* was nowhere to be found? Could you explain to me one more time why you didn't worry when you came back from your little outing at the Exploratorium and *the woman you loved* was not home yet? It took you, umm—how long did you say?—to start having sex with Amy Hacker after *the woman you loved* had disappeared forever and not returned?

I keep picturing Mr. Burr as a boy trying to decide what he will do when he grows up, and I can hear someone saying: "Why don't you be a D.A., Kenneth? You have *the meanest voice imaginable.*" It is an effective voice, of course, as mean voices go, and he is stunningly articulate and intelligent. He wears dark blue Italian suits and is handsome in an aggressive sort of way. I keep trying to feel grateful that he is taking such an interest in us, but the gratefulness gets queer and choked and I never end up quite feeling it. Mr. Peretti, the defense attorney, on the other hand, is soft-spoken and gentlemanly, dressed in gray and white, with a quiet let-us-be-reasonable-about-this manner. Let us be reasonable, my friends: why would this nice, nice-looking, nicely brought up, nice young man want to have killed this, ah, Roberta here? Really, reasonably. That kind of thing. It is difficult not to feel sympathetic with Brad, because he trips over precisely the questions I would. For example, Mr. Burr acidly points out that Brad had testified in the last trial that he didn't know what "booking" meant when he was arrested. Does he still maintain that? Mr. Burr says he would be interested in knowing.

Yes, replies Brad, tremulously—remembering, perhaps, that day.

Have you ever seen *Miami Vice?* Mr. Burr shoots out. The judge smiles.

Yeah, says Brad.

Checkmate, says Mr. Burr, precluding protest. And yet the protest is the real protest, the true objection: because it doesn't mean the same thing when Don Johnson says it to the bad guys as when Sergeant Harris said it to me. *That was television.*

Most of my time in the courtroom, though, I spend watching the stenographer type; I brood on how she could possibly get down every word of every sentence. Everyone speaks quickly: it is infinitely mysterious that she is able to type it all.

Who is it, I wonder, attempting to pay attention: who is going to benefit from this trial?

Justice will be achieved. Justice. Hmm. Of all concepts, I think, justice is surely the least interesting. The blindfolded lady holding two scales. I begin to draw a picture of a blind lady on my notebook. I try to remember if justice has wings as well as being blind. It seems to me she does have wings. Justice, I think, stirs no emotion whatsoever, even though usually I am fond of personified abstractions. I try to recall the quotation to the effect that there are no courts of justice, but only courts of law. Curious, I think, for a man to be tried in a court of law but not justice. Who is the beneficiary of justice?

The Lees? The Lees. The Pages? Justice will not help the Pages. Lena Grady? The Friends of Bibi Lee? Me? DeWitt? Society? Protection of Society? I try to dwell on Protection of Society for a few moments. It is difficult. Society and its protection is another concept that moves me, I think, not at all.

Roberta? Oh yes, Roberta, I remember: this is all being done for Roberta. But Roberta, Lord knows, Roberta of all of us, open-handed, palms spread flat, sums scattered and calculations betrayed, it matters not at all to Roberta. None of our words weigh or are worth weighing, signify or have signifiers, because Roberta alone has nothing more to lose or to gain.

■ ■

The rest of the time I spend imagining what would happen if Roberta walked in.

Through the little square door at the back where the jury files through in the mornings and evenings, Roberta walks in. She is wearing a short black dress, cut so that the hemline falls unevenly, and she is impatient. Hmm, I remind myself, it is three and a half years later. I try to picture Roberta three years older. She would be twenty-four; several years out of college. Unimaginable. Roberta— well, Roberta looking just as she did last, Roberta who happens not to have changed at all—Roberta walks in. She sees Brad first: she goes over and kisses him (She kisses him? She kisses *Bradley Page?* Oh no, he wasn't Bradley Page then.). Okay, skipping the kiss, she sees—Amy? What are you going to do with Amy? All right, so Roberta doesn't see Brad, then; she doesn't see Brad or Amy or their baby; she goes right over to her parents, Jesus, her parents, and everything is put together again. I try to imagine the Lees with everything put right—the unbound bound, the broken restored, the wounded not wounded. And Roberta, Roberta then comes over to me, and she wants to know what am I doing at the trial, why am I not in school, whom am I sitting with, where is Adam, how come I look so odd? You don't look good, M: why don't you look good? I want to answer, but the answers all involve death, and change, and time passed for us but not for her. I begin to try to explain (Oh God, didn't you know, Adam and I—oh, Bibi, things are different now). But by the time I finish explaining to her how things got to be as they are, things in the dream become identical to things outside the dream, and everything becomes as it is: one room, where we are. And Roberta loses interest, and the whole of the dream is so completely qualified anyway that it is no longer a dream and I give up and start listening to the testimony again.

There used to be a sign on my parents' refrigerator saying: "Speak Chinese." Ha. And then someone took it down. Ha, Ha. You are never going to learn to speak Chinese. They say Eskimos have twelve different words for snow. Someday someone will say Roberta had twelve different words for depression. Yes she did, twelve: they were just all the same.

Oscar looks bored too.

■ ■

"Keep an open mind until this case is submitted for judgment," the judge repeats to the jury every time we break, framing the testimony with silence: "Do not discuss the facts of the case with anyone, and allow no one to discuss them with you." An injunction intended not for us but for the jury, of course, but that nevertheless rings more and more false every time it is repeated. What is there, after all, in the case besides discussion? Conversations about conversations about conversations. The first trial was a long conversation interpreting a conversation between Brad and the policemen one afternoon three years ago: this trial is a longer conversation concerning the inconclusiveness of the first one. There is nothing to say other than comments on what has already been said. What else can you do? I ask the reporter next to me if he wants to have lunch.

The reporter next to me, it turns out, works for the local Berkeley student paper, the *Daily Californian,* and his name is Michael M. He is big and broad-shouldered, with wavy dark golden hair, and bright blue eyes and big tortoiseshell glasses that fall slightly forward on his nose. One of his ears is pierced with a small silver earring. He had been in the Navy for two years, I later found out. He flashes a large white-toothed smile with dimples, and sticks his tongue slightly through his teeth when he laughs. He looks like the thoroughly nice person that I discover he is: he is from an Irish-Catholic family in a small town in upstate New York, and he has five older sisters and no brothers, and each of his sisters is named after one of the girls in *Little Women,* except Ann. He is exactly the kind of person, I think, that I ought to spend time with while I am in California.

He, DeWitt, and I sit on the scanty Oakland park lawn, on the damp downtown grass, and eat Chinese dumplings. I wonder what Michael thinks about the trial and he wonders what I think. I hate dim sum, I decide, although the consensus is it's great. The sea gulls hover progressively closer: I feed them globs of sticky rice and swampy vegetables.

"Does Brad still have friends?" I ask Michael.

"Apparently. A friend of mine was supposed to go camping with him and Robin over Thanksgiving, but she got sick. So I guess he and Robin Shaw are still friends."

Robin Shaw wants to go *camping* with him? "I guess she doesn't think he did it," I say, making a ball of some more of my rice and seeing how close I can make the sea gulls come.

"I guess not," Michael says. I reach to take his rice too, and he laughs and offers it to me.

"There's a great line in a movie this reminds me of," DeWitt says, leaning forward, "where the main character is accused of murder. And he protests vehemently: 'Well, I loved her and all, but not enough to murder her!' " DeWitt is a movie critic, and generally has a store of good quotations on hand.

"Not enough to murder her," I repeat. "Yeah, that's good. I don't think it has anything to do with Bradley, but it is really very good."

"If he did do it," DeWitt asks, leaning forward, still thinking about that line, *"what do you think in their relationship would have caused him to do it?"*

Michael and I look at each other askance: the question is so naive. It is difficult to explain why it is so naive, but it is. No one who knew Bibi and Brad asks that anymore; no one who knew them has asked it for a long time.

■ ■

"Well, kiddos," says Bob, as he and I and DeWitt are on our way to dinner, "did you hear any new stories in court today?" I watch admiringly as Bob switches lanes, glancing in the mirror, twisting his wrists. He is an awfully good driver. When I was younger I used to think that kind of thing wasn't important, but I have changed my mind. What I mean is, he doesn't make mistakes. In the poem about John for Chrissake look out where yr going because John was expounding on the darkness that surrounds us instead of looking at the road, Bob would not be John. This is a virtue.

"No," I say sullenly. "Did you?"

"Hmm," he says, "let me think. Oh, a friend of mine said he and Amy were with a bunch of people, and at one point Amy said, 'So, I wonder if he did do it.' "

"She did?" I gasp. And then, "Bob," I say, as he begins to laugh his familiar laugh, "is that really true?"

■ ■

Lena Grady comes to testify. Bradley wasn't working very hard on the search, she testifies: he took lots of nights off. *She stayed in the center on Thanksgiving Day, and she didn't even know Bibi. He was her boyfriend, and he did less than she, Lena Grady, had done. In the Friends of Bibi Lee, he was hardly even a friend. He—he—she—she—*

I don't hear her testimony: Michael repeats it to me on the telephone. "You were at the search, weren't you?" he asks quizzically. "Was it true?"

"No," I say angrily, "I mean of course it is true, but . . ." and I stop. It is, actually, precisely true: he did much less than Lena Grady did. Everyone did. She was the one who organized the second search of the park when they had given up searching the park, who called the volunteers with the dogs and said we—not the police, but we—are looking for people to do another search of the park because we think it should be done one more time. Bibi has been dead three and a half years, and Lena's still keeping tabs on who did what which afternoon. Lena is still racking up points and donations; Lena has not lost track of the score for the search that went nowhere. It makes me so mad, thinking about it, I can hardly explain.

■ ■

"Well, the thing is," DeWitt says to Bob and me over beers, *"if he hadn't done it, he wouldn't have confessed."*

Bob is graduating from the University of California at San Francisco this spring: he is moments from being a doctor. He has been nominated for some award with a metaphorical name, a Golden Cane award, in which they actually give the winner a real golden cane to carry around, to designate that he is exemplary at what he does. We are all waiting to hear. I know, it seems to me, with every bone, that there could not possibly, ever anywhere, be a finer doctor than Bob. Fine: that perfected combination of insight and accuracy, kindness and pragmatism. People often possess one quality or the other, but not both. Bob has decided to be a radiologist, and develop technology for photographing the mind. And although I had wanted him to deliver babies, I know exactly why this appeals to him.

"But why would anyone confess to anything they didn't do?" DeWitt persists, looking at the two of us as if he is really waiting for an answer. DeWitt was not involved in the search; this is the first time he is thinking hard about these events, so he is still thinking new things and coming up with questions that feel new and true and important to him.

"It's impossible," he says thoughtfully, "to imagine confessing to something you didn't do."

"Impossible for you," I say. "But we don't send people to jail for lack of your imagination. Besides which," I say, "I can imagine it perfectly. They told him they had evidence. If someone—someone in authority—told you they had *evidence* about you and it was *a fact that they knew you were lying*—well—what could you say?"

"You would say you didn't do it."

"But they had *evidence.*"

"Melanie and I have this conversation all the time," Bob says, laughing. "Of course not—neither would I. But Melanie would. Melanie would confess. So I guess it's a good thing," he finishes gaily, "that they didn't arrest Melanie, because it would probably take us a lot of years to bail her out."

"You probably wouldn't try," I sniff, appeased nevertheless. They would probably be unsuccessful, but they would both of them, I decide, looking around and feeling suddenly liked, definitely try.

"And by next week," he adds to DeWitt, "she'll have figured out who the plaintiff is." The immediate response—*I do too know*—rises on my tongue, but I check it, realizing, dismayed, that Bob is watching me, all ready to say: "Yeah? Who?" That familiar foreboding of innocence and ignorance—insufficient information about my environment, like a disease prefiguring extinction—comes over me. Like: how is it I got to be so old without having come by the requisite knowledge of the world? How come I was absent that day in school? And then: *What day?* How do other people know who the plaintiff is? I glance at DeWitt: he looks as if he knows.

It always seems to me that I would have been perfectly competent—unusually competent even—if only I had been born before the Industrial Revolution. The world is round. No matter how far you walk you will never fall off the end of the earth. *It's a myth.* If you wish to keep a fish fresh, you must soak it in milk. I might even have invented something. Who knows? I used to have

this fantasy that one day I would find myself transported into some
earlier age—through the looking glass, or behind C. S. Lewis's
closet—and would thus personally have the chance to enlighten
humanity, centuries ahead of schedule, and bear certain great
news. All men are created equal, bloodletting doesn't let out the
disease, and energy equals mass times c squared. And it would be
right about then that I would realize that *I can't remember what c
stands for*. No, worse than simply slipped my mind: I had never,
in point of fact, known what c referred to, let alone the difference
between a wave and a particle, because my section leader in
quantum mechanics was nice to me because I was a girl, and gave
me a B+ all the same. And so on it would go—from interval
estimation to the objective correlative, algorithms to autosugges-
tion, antinomianism, apraxia, apriorism, avant-garde, contempo-
rary, modern and postmodern—it would turn out that although I
did just fine on my SATs, after all, and can always make conversation at cocktail parties and with my parents' friends, upon any real
inspection my understanding of all the founding concepts of modern civilization—or even of the precise definition of modernity
itself—dissolves. What, for example, is the *surplus* in surplus value?
Surplus of what and who gets it? Or the zero in the zero-sum
game? Is the intentional fallacy entirely fallacious? And the interpretation of *Tess of the D'Urbervilles*—the one about her getting hung
because she disobeyed her parents—that interpretation has got to
be wrong no matter how many exchange students from the People's Republic tell you their teachers told them to read it that way.
If a deconstructionist had a chance to have a chat with Mallarmé,
do you think he'd tell the poet, sorry, I'm busy, I have my own
theories as to what *ptyx* signifies? Is modern architecture actually
uglier than all previous architectures, or does it just look that
way—all the little diamond windows and gargoyles with dragon
feet having been replaced by allusions to geometry. Why doesn't
falsifiability work in the reverse, and how do you feel about living
in a world where the only things you can be certain of are the
things that are *not* true? Did Dr. Skinner really raise his daughter in
a box, and are daughters always just as mean to their daughters as
their mothers were to them? In that case, why not keep pets
instead? The Nazis, I read, were not in favor of cruelty to animals.
Do commodities traders care a fig about corn and hogs—or really
even about the price of corn and hogs, since whether it goes up or
down they can still take advantage of price fluctuation? How much

money do you have to spend on therapy before quitting isn't *resistance?* A piece of bubble gum will stay in your stomach for seven years, but if you swallow a watermelon seed it will never grow a watermelon. Before I go to graduate school I'd like to get straight the difference between synecdoche and metonymy, and which is the king to the crown, as opposed to the sail to the ship, or sex and the sword, meaning women and war. Regression to the mean, however, has also always been one of my favorite ideas. It's metaphorical, I think, somehow. If the Germans had invented the Bomb first, would not the world be a dreadful place? The law of comparative advantage is not really to everyone's advantage. How come no one I know knows how to break-dance? What is break dancing exactly, and how does it differ from slam dancing? What kind of vocabulary do people have who know all the words in crossword puzzles? If you drop a mirror, you will have bad luck for seven years; if your brother drops your mirror when he is helping you move, do you get the bad luck or does he? In other words, is luck a variable or a constant? Does absence make the heart grow fonder, or is out of sight necessarily out of mind? Does it depend on your face or their soul? How long do you have to wait before you call him back? Did you deliberately abandon me, or did it just happen that way? If Maud Gonne had married Yeats, would his poetry have been as good; does this hold true for Petrarch; and did you know that he only saw Laura a couple times in his entire life? And what of Sir John Suckling? Is a sequel to *Gone With the Wind* an immoral idea, was Hitler a vegetarian, and are the *Newsweek* statistics on marriage accurate, especially the part about forty-year-old women being more likely to be shot by terrorists than to find husbands? That is a mean statistic. If you had three wishes, would you wish there were no insects? How come grownups never have favorite colors? If people don't have enough money, why don't they print more? Where do butterflies go when it rains? What is the least number of these questions you can answer and still consider yourself educated, or can you proceed through the whole of life perpetually *vague?* I look at Bob crossways. Are these questions the same questions; are these questions important questions? If you listed all your questions, would the list add up, organize, conclude? Would you come to some final formulation: would you know at last what you need to know? Would you recall all the bits of nursery rhymes you thought you had forgotten forever? Did you do it, Bradley; did you do it?

"You have until Friday," Bob tells me in his friendliest manner. "That gives you three days to figure it out: look it up in the dictionary—that's *p* for *plaintiff*—write Ann Landers, or ask Adam or your father.

"And there's no need to look so wide-eyed," he adds. "Extensions are negotiable. Get psyched," he tells me encouragingly. "You're covering a trial. Pretend it's a made-for-TV movie. If you don't do your homework they're going to pick someone dumb to play you. Like a *blond* dumb person.

"C'mon, Mel, you're starring in it," he coaxes. And then, "No, actually I'm starring in it. But get busy, M's. I'm happy for you. It's going to be fun."

"You can't have fun at a murder trial," I state primly. "It's disrespectful to the dead."

"Yeah, you're right," he says. "I take it all back. Concentrate as hard as you can on being as miserable as possible all of the time. *Suffer*. That definitely ought to help matters. O depth and symbolism; maybe we should skip dinner after all."

"Like Oxfam night in college?" I ask. At Oxfam night in college everyone was asked to skip dinner, and the price of the meal would be donated to starving people. And everyone with a conscience always did it, and then went out for dinner. What Bob always wanted to know was whether, instead of skipping dinner, we could donate the price of the restaurant meal he was about to save by not ordering in Chinese food at midnight when we got hungry. *Which*, he would point out, would far exceed the three and a half dollars they calculated our meals at. And when I told him it was the principle not the actual amounts that mattered—the whole point was that it was an exercise in principle and you had to be hungry or it didn't count—he raised his eyebrows and said: "Oh, really? And I had thought the point was the starving people." I could never make up my mind whether or not this was cheating.

"Mmhmm," he says. "Just like that."

■ ■

"What," I ask Michael one day in court, for some reason really wanting to know, "what will become of Brad? I mean what does he do?"

"He was working in a day-care center, but the parents found out who he was and had him fired. He says he wants to get a teaching certificate, but you need an FBI clearance in order to enroll."

"I can't imagine who would ever hire him," I say vindictively, half horrified, half sorry.

"Of course if he did it he should be punished and all," says Michael, in a way that is somehow picking up on the last note, "but," he finishes quietly, "he seems like kind of a nice guy."

"A nice guy," I repeat, a little shocked: we know what we know, but he seems rather nice. She was a temperamental girl, moody, volatile, but she met a nice guy; important, for high-strung women to find nice men and stay with them.

■ ■

I am standing at the bathroom sink mirror jabbing my hairpins back into my braid, when Amy walks in. I am in that state of giggly elation that comes at the end of a long and absurdly pointless day. Analysis of bone specimens; a traffic analysis expert making impossible calculations about the speed the Man with the Van might have driven by with his Van. Or perhaps it was the amount of time the women who thought they saw him would have had to see him, if they had seen him. I forget. Jolly improbable, at any rate, as Michael said. And there was the professor of persuasion, too, who came to testify, as if only an expert psychologist would be astute enough to have unearthed the news: *"The confession cannot be taken at face value."* He was *persuaded.*

The professor had brought with him this documentary piece of evidence that shows that people can be persuaded of anything; he drew lines on the board, he told stories about airline pilots who learn to trust the barometer over their own senses that say: you are now upside down. He mentioned Milgram. Stanley Milgram, in his book *Obedience to Authority,* describes a certain famous ghastly experiment: he had volunteers administer what they thought were genuine electric shocks, at progressively higher levels, to other volunteers whenever they gave the wrong answer to a question of some kind. Most of the volunteers—ordinary Americans—would administer dangerously high levels of electric shocks to their subjects, who were screaming and begging them not to. The experiment concludes that most people will do what they are told to do, as the professor tells the courtroom Bradley Page has done.

The professor's own personal specific, however, which he pulled out as if it were a kind of glorious trump, seemed to be a study of three people in a room, with three lines of unequal length on the board.

Apparently one volunteer could be persuaded to change his mind about which line was longest, despite the obvious fact that he could see one was much much longer and drawn on the board, if the two other people, who were secretly paid just to confuse him, told him he was wrong. The short line, they would tell him, was really quite long. He had underestimated, they would say persuasively, the length of that short line. Nine out of ten people, the study concluded, are persuadable.

In a volunteer study about lines, interrupted Mr. Burr.

A relevant study, the professor told him politely.

Where the volunteers were not criminals and the examiners not police trained in methods to extract truth from pathological liars who have a grave personal stake in continuing to lie about their past, said Mr. Burr. There is no stake in the lines, Mr. Burr says, there is no reward, and more important, there is no penalty. Mr. Burr would like to know if the professor has done any studies of this nature. No? Mr. Burr is not surprised; he had imagined not. Not to be overly literal, but he does think there are some differences between the lines and the murder of this young woman, which could possibly prove significant.

Amy, standing next to me in the bathroom at the other sink, runs a comb through her short fluffy blond hair and reapplies pink lipstick. She is a passionately pretty girl; she purses her lips: she is defending her family. Outside, Michael is leaning against a wall waiting for me, and lounging next to him is Brad, waiting for Amy. We walk out at exactly the same time and smile at the men. Someone says something; someone else laughs. Just at that moment the Lees walk by, their glance taking the four of us in wordlessly. Michael and I freeze, implicated.

"You know," DeWitt tells me angrily as we are on our way to court, "even if he gets a sentence, it is going to be a light sentence. It's manslaughter. *Manslaughter.* That's like when you run over a child with a car by accident. Like five fucking years. Subtracting parole."

"I know," I say, wondering why it doesn't seem to matter at all. "But—does it matter? His life still isn't worth living. It's still all *spoiled.* I mean he's still—damned. Is there a penance for murder?" How could even God pardon him: the work of the murderer's hands cannot be undone. It's the stone so big He can't move it; anything can be repented, but she'll never be here again.

A group of reporters gathers outside the courthouse each day when court adjourns.

"The thing is," Michael says, as we are standing with them one day, chatting, "it's not like you're being asked to choose between two viable scenarios, one likely and one unlikely. Between the dogs and the hubcap and everything testing clean and no trail of blood on the one hand, and the Man with the Van having driven her back to the place she was last seen by Bradley Page, although those women saw her someplace else, on the other, the options are really not that good." Michael throws up his hands with a balancing gesture.

"Yes," I say, thinking how nice it is to be outdoors and in California, "absurd. They are both absurd. But the Man with the Van is an absurdity too.

"Between two improbables, I'd rather it be Brad. It would be better that way." And it would be better: it is much better if the killer was someone she knew and didn't know was going to kill her, than that she was tied up in a truck by a beer-bellied moon-faced stranger she knew would harm her, but had to wait to find out how much.

"Anyway, I mean this is a trial. They are going to decide. If they don't vote for a conviction, then we'll never know, but if they vote that he is guilty beyond a reasonable doubt, that means we're positive."

"But they're just twelve people," shrugs Michael. "Twelve other people might have voted differently. In point of fact," he says, "in this case, they did. Eight to four, was it? Four to eight?

"But I don't think I'd vote for the Man with the Van," he adds, seeing my disturbed face.

"I don't know," says Marc Sandalow, one of the reporters, squinting into the lovely late afternoon light. "It doesn't sound one little bit more implausible than that Brad murdered her, picked up Robin fifteen minutes later, went to the Exploratorium for the afternoon with five of their friends, came back and had sex with the corpse. And then went over to her room at midnight to make phone calls to hospitals, and slept quietly in her bed. Why did he sleep in her bed? He lived a mile and a half down the road; why would he sleep in her bed that night?"

■ ■

"It's good," my friend Lana tells me on the phone, as we discuss the current situation. "It's important," she says definitely, passionately. "The trial is important. It's payment."

Payment, I think, what an attractive idea. A satisfying concept, I think: precisely what we have been in need of here. A metaphor to explain what we are doing here and why. I have been feeling in need of just such a metaphor of late. A good metaphor, I think, thinking too hard—a good metaphor, that is, if you don't realize that there is no one to pay to, and nothing to pay with.

"Yes," she says, "a metaphorical payment." A metaphorical payment in lieu of real coinage or hands into which to deliver it. A payment of time and absence—the absence of all the things that time would otherwise have been full of, the life that would have happened: the time Brad would have spent with his child as it grew, the person the child would have grown into being had his father not been in jail. A sacrifice made for no one, a gift made of unknowns, nothing handed to nothing, from the empty-handed unto empty hands. A better metaphor than one might have thought, perhaps, after all.

L is for LEO who swallowed some tacks

L IS FOR LEO WHO SWALLOWED SOME TACKS.
(But surely not—M IS FOR MAUD WHO WAS SWEPT OUT TO SEA)
Dear Melanie,

Tacks, classes. *Back from Mexico and back in school and I still don't quite believe it.*

Believe it, babe.

I'm taking Linguistics, Economics, Anthropology, a folklore class and Feminist Theory. Oh child, you'll never make it. You're lost. Who, me? (This paragraph ends in confusion.)

Concerning Ben in Mexico: don't be concerned. We missed some connection and never reconnected, he turned around twice and I was gone. Chalk up another one . . . So now I'm back in the rut—classes, rain, sleeping in sections, getting sick again or thinking about it or remembering the last time. Behind, as usual, and I'm an usher three concerts in the next few days. I don't make any pocket money, but I do get to see free shows and let my friends and pals owe me one. One of them is Elvis Costello, your favorite (isn't he?) Al-lis-son—if you'd known it was The King, you'd never have let him down. Our tastes don't always agree

but I concede

Costello is twee

With that and Bowie and somebody else I can't remember I should have no trouble getting farther behind. A muffled cry from the deep shit: help!

Too bad about Leo, eh?

Rosamunde

The person on the stand the next day is one of the two policemen who interviewed Brad. Brad glances at him; they both tense. I wonder what it is like for them to realize that this entire case consists of a conversation they had one afternoon three years ago. I keep waiting for one of them to say, oh, c'mon. No one remembers what was said. *It was years ago.*

Could you tell the court, Mr. Peretti begins, why you were questioning Mr. Page?

Because I was convinced there was some deception there, the homicide detective replies. Look, he tells me he remembers everything: *he remembered he had puffed wheat for breakfast,* he remembers the paper he wrote when he got home from the park, and he doesn't remember whether what he told us about murdering Bibi Lee was true.

This makes, I think, a modicum of sense.

We were determined not to start taping until his memory returned, the detective continues. It just didn't make sense leaving a young girl like that up in the woods. He looks at the D.A., and the D.A., as if by some prearranged signal, puts his finger on the button of the tape recorder. He presses it, and it begins to play. Brad looks shaken; this is the first sign of emotion he has shown. The courtroom stills. So we are going to hear the confession after all; the policeman and Brad and the district attorney and the judge and everyone in the room and Michael and I are going to hear the confession.

"You have the right to remain silent . . ." the officer begins, his voice in the recording so formulaic it sounds like "once upon a time." The opening, I think; this is the opening to the story. This is the recitation of the rights you must give up in order to tell the story and find out what happens in a land far, far away. We know already, of course, but Brad was telling it for the first time then, with wonder in his voice. For some reason, an aphorism I heard in a beginning writing class comes to mind: "No surprise in the writer," says Robert Frost, "no surprise in the reader." *In a good story the writer himself doesn't know what he is going to say before he begins to write.*

I understand, Brad says, his voice almost a whisper, what these rights mean.

The first thing I remember is going off on her—hitting, kicking her—but I don't remember why. The voice of the afternoon three years ago through the veil of the recording is trancelike.

I was driving along when I saw her by the side of the road . . . I tried to kiss her on the top of the head, but she turned from my caress.

What did you do then?

I think I might have backhanded her.

What did you do then?

I don't remember. I think she might've had a bloody nose.

Where was she?

She was lying by the foot of the tree.

Was she dead?

She wasn't moving. But I loved her, I really loved her. I loved her. And then: *You don't think I did it, do you?*

After what you just told us, I hope you are damned to hell. Did you tell anyone this? What you knew about the whereabouts of Ms. Lee?

No, because I didn't know until today.

Because you thought, given the condition you had left her in, she might have been able to leave the woods?

I thought until today that she was alive. Brad's low puzzled voice fills the courtroom. *I didn't know,* he stammers. I immediately feel sympathetic—the old protest, the familiar protest: *I didn't know, I didn't know.* I have protested this very protest myself. I didn't know. And I didn't, either.

I thought maybe there was some way she was still alive because you had to think—he says, and stops, confused—*in order to hope, to search. A person had to hope.*

Yes, you had to hope in order to search. I remember that too—the search and the dilemma about hope.

Well, says the officer, breaking off their conversation briskly, the tape obviously running out, *I have a picture of an attractive Chinese-American girl here. Is this Ms. Lee?*

Yes, says Brad, tentatively.

And is this the girl you have been referring to in our conversation? the officer asks.

Brad hesitates, and his hesitation feels long. Is this the girl in the story? Is the girl in your story the girl in the photograph; is the girl in the photograph Roberta? Are you sure? How can you be sure? Are they identical?

Yes, says Brad, *I think that it is.*

■ ■

The last witness called to the stand is Bradley Page. Both Mr. Burr and Mr. Peretti question him extensively: the same questions, asked differently. Brad describes Bibi as having gone off in a snit. "As time progressed, it became more and more clear that Bibi was in a snit and left without us," Brad says. "It was a little awkward leaving," he says, but she had been prone to emotional outbursts in the past. After returning to his cooperative, he testifies, he ate breakfast and finished a term paper. "If it had been anybody but Bibi, I wouldn't have left the hills," he adds. "That day it made sense—and I feel so badly about it, but that's what I did," he says. He describes the circumstances surrounding his confession: "I had so much guilt throughout the search, and I still do, and trying to figure out what happened is so important to me," he says; his voice quivers. The papers represent his speech as being much more emotional than at the first trial. Apparently his nervous fidgeting and ashen face had been interpreted as a sign of guilt. "I feel I am now much more capable of expressing myself than I was at the first trial," the paper quotes him telling reporters.

So, he's a more practiced witness, says Michael.

A reporter who, curiously enough, had gone to high school with him and who had written a long article defending him, called "The Strange Confession of Bradley Page," tells me that she went to visit him in jail. He was doing origami, she says, and writing a book about the male and female principles in the world—a sort of yin-yang thing, she says. She felt so queer going to visit him there, she tells me, he looked so out of place. He was using his time there well, though, she adds, sounding dubious somehow.

Brad's testimony goes on for three days: over and over the details are hashed out: Brad's history, other women he knew, his and Bibi's sex life. He was a virgin, he says; Bibi was the one with experience. She had slept with someone in China when she was fourteen years old.

Michael and I sit in the back row. I draw in my notebook. Mr. Burr has a penchant for ending his sentences in prepositions, I note. The witness splits his infinitives; modifiers are misplaced. *Concretize* and *prioritize* are not verbs; *flyering* cannot be used in lieu of *to put up flyers*, as in: to put up flyers with Bradley Page, advertising the unknown whereabouts of Roberta Lee, when all along he knew exactly where she was but thought he should put up flyers anyway as some kind of sick penance or joke or simply self-deception. I am sitting at the trial, I think, and she is dead, and people are trying to figure out what happened and why, and I am correcting their grammar. She has been dead three years; she will be dead even more by the time people who never knew her but are paid by the state to be interested in the situation are finished constructing their explanation. There were tensions in their relationship of a sexual nature; sexual tension, the policeman surmised. He raped the corpse. What kind of birth control did he say they were using? I am sitting in a courtroom in Department 41 and I have nothing to do but correct other people's grammar.

Melanie, can you stand to listen to even one more typical story from the land of Bibi? First I was in Modern Greek and decided I didn't want to be in it. So I got the forms signed and did the kowtow and got out, switched to Modern History. But "Modern History"? What kind of course is that? Sounds like "Modern Life." So there I was, antsy and bored with an undercurrent of frustration, sleeping through lectures, when I saw so clearly that I just DID NOT WANT TO TAKE THIS COURSE. More kowtowing, more forms. Serious avowals of seriousness. And where does the girl go? Back to Modern Greek. Oh brother.

Mr. Burr questions Brad finally about the pregnancy scare. Brad replies that she was tested and was fine and Mr. Burr goes on to the next item on the agenda. I am surprised: usually he interrogates in minutest detail. I stop him in the hall at the next break. You missed an odd little angle, I tell him afterward in the hall: that test—that pregnancy test—it came back positive. It was only later it turned out to be a false positive.

I had heard that, Mr. Burr said, but I decided to leave it out. It isn't worth the publicity. Abortion, et cetera. Headlines. I felt it would be exploited by the tabloids. I didn't know if the Lees knew about it, and I didn't think they needed to know.

They know, I say. Or they should know. She was their daughter, for God's sake, and there wasn't even any abortion. And maybe they don't want to hear it said aloud in public, I think, trying to scrutinize his face, and wondering why he's worrying about it now considering the things he says all the time. Like the way he refers to the Lees' daughter with impersonal pronouns: "it," meaning the body, Roberta.

It may be so-called women's lib, Mr. Burr says, but if a man is having sex, he's scoring, and if a woman is, she's promiscuous. That is precisely the kind of thing people pay twenty-five cents to read about, and I don't want to feed it to them.

Roberta wasn't promiscuous, I say, shocked.

Mr. Peretti asks Brad about injuries, and then, almost incidentally, at the close of the third day of Brad's questioning, two months into the trial, he mildly inquires: "And did you kill Roberta Lee?"

"Now that you mention it," whispers Michael.

"NO," screams Brad, his scream filling the courtroom. "I DIDN'T—OH GOD, I DIDN'T, I DIDN'T."

"I am innocent," he moans, wailing, the thin, high-pitched, horrible sound filling the courtroom: *"I am innocent."*

"Kind of buried the lead there, didn't they?" Michael remarks to me pleasantly.

*   *   *

Walking out of the courthouse that afternoon, I stop and buy an oversized tangerine at a wooden street stand from an old Oriental woman, and then a dark lace dress and some perfume black as poison at a used-clothing store. Roberta, Roberta, Roberta. Roberta, I think, conjuring quarter memories, Roberta in San Francisco less than a handful of years ago, she too must have done precisely this kind of thing.

CHAPTER 2

Ways of Seeing: Fictions and Lies

Fiction—lies, damn lies, all.

—Mark Twain

Distance concerns the relation of the narration to its own materials. . . . One important aspect . . . is the difference between narration—the act and process of telling a story—and narrative—what it is you actually recount. When I tell a story about myself, as in autobiography, the ''I'' who does the telling seems in one sense identical with the ''I'' whom I describe, and in another sense different from it. We shall see later how this paradox has interesting implications beyond literature itself. . . .

It was impossible any longer to see reality simply as something ''out there,'' a fixed order of things which language merely reflected. Reality was not reflected by language, but produced by it: it was a particular way of carving up the world which was deeply dependent on the sign-systems we had at our command, or more precisely which had us at theirs . . . Meanings are not so stable and determinate . . . and the reason they are not is because . . . they are products of language, which always has something slippery about it.

—Terry Eagleton
Literary Theory

One free day in a crowd of free spring days in an interlude so that closing arguments can be prepared, I walk down the street to the white building where the transcripts of the first trial are kept. I want to read how Brad told the tale when he first told it, although everyone keeps saying what a better job he is doing now. A bright-haired girl comes and asks if she can help me. "Oh, the Bibi Lee case," she shrugs when I tell her what I want: "Of course you can read it.

"Which one would you like?" she asks, beginning to pull volumes down from the shelves as if they were Books of Hours or ancient Chinese dictionaries. All of them, I tell her, and settle at the table, my hands flat on their dusty covers, hesitant, as if I were holding a corked bottle that looks empty but might nevertheless contain a genie. I wonder which volume is the first volume and where to start reading, and whether to start reading the long story, the long legal manufactured story. I wonder how it will read: how it will compare to the version I know. Everything is so long ago, I think, as I have thought before, yet here in this unlikeliest of places, on shelves dusted by strangers, our story is kept. I curl up in the chair, pulling my red corduroy jumper down over my knees and taking some linty gumdrops out of my pockets; I open the first blue-bound volume and begin to read.

The judge opens the trial:
"As jurors," it is written, "you must not be influenced by pity for a defendant or by prejudice against him. You must not be biased against the defendant because he has been arrested for a crime or because he has been brought to trial. None of these circumstances is evidence of his guilt, and you must not infer or assume from any or all of them that he is more likely to be guilty than innocent. . . ."

Wait, he tells us, to choose an interpretation. Begin the story as if it were the beginning—even though it is not.

"If, on the other hand, one interpretation of such evidence appears to you reasonable and the other interpretation unreasonable, it would be your duty to accept the reasonable interpretation and to reject the unreasonable."

But I *know* how to interpret; I've read this all before. There is nothing more for me to learn, my heart breaks, *nothing*. This story doesn't go anywhere. At the end of six volumes, the jury was hung.

I continue to skim the dull pages half-heartedly, though, until I recognize bits of their lives coming back to me. Surprised and pleased, I take out my notebook and my green-ink pen, and begin to copy down randomly scattered bits that appeal.

"Before Christmas break she wrote him a letter saying quote Bradley Page, who are you? unquote."

Did she find out, I wonder, did she find out?
The lake. The idea of the lake.

"My thirty-second assessment of Brad was: pretty face, shallow. . . . I'm not impressed." [Veronica]

"He had gone out the night before wearing a pink Eiffel Tower earring."

Q. Did she have friends in the Bay Area?
A. She was friends with a man who collected mannequins.

Q. At any time, Brad, did you and Bibi discuss the possibility of marriage?
A. No.

Of course they didn't discuss it. . . . They talked, at best, about living together. We don't make commitments.
Question irrelevant, I write in the margin.

Q. As of the first part of November 1984, did you know what the future held for you and Bibi? By that I mean what your plans were.

Plans? I write. *Plans like adults make plans for adulthood to ensure that it happens? Like planning to go to law or medical school or work for a computer company? God, no, Bibi never had any plans. Trips, fantasies, escapes to exotic imaginary places—these were things she thought of. None of us ever had any plans.*

A. She had invited me to go to Brazil during Christmas break if I had the money. And also we had planned to go to the desert for two weeks during Easter. But other than that, no.

Q. Did you know where she was going to end up after the Brazil trip?

A. No.

Q. Did you know where you were going to be?

A. No.

And as it turned out, she was right. There was no need for other plans—even Brazil and the desert were too far away.

I wonder, the old restless futile wondering, if things would have unfolded otherwise had she made plans.

Q. And if I understand correctly, this is, as you had described her before, this was a woman that you truly were in love with, is that correct?

A. Correct.

Q. And the fact that you did not know or have any plans or your plans were somewhat vague at this point in time . . . this was the woman that you loved, correct?

A. Correct.

The psychiatrist for the defense is questioned:

Q. And I should tell you that several witnesses have testified to Brad's comments about the trauma he suffered in France. Are you familiar with that incident?

Oh, the French incident. The host mother of the family he was living with in France was attracted to him—he thought—and this became what he described as a formative damaging experience. He says that that was the time he first realized he was capable of functioning on two different levels—one of which he didn't know about. On the one hand, he felt that something dreadful was occurring in the house, something secret and illicit—the woman who was supposed to be his mother in his host family wanted to take advantage of him—and on the other hand, she never did, and everyone in the family seemed to be proceeding as normal. He constantly compares this to Bibi's disappearance—although what the analogy is, we don't know. And when Bibi called, in that telephone conversation of long ago, to tell him she was pregnant, he told her he had had a similar experience in France. He called it "psychological rape."

A. I had a little trouble understanding exactly what happened because from my point of view . . . very little . . . happened.

But Brad was quite upset over the fact that while he was living in the home, this lady appeared to get closer and closer to him. He had a great deal of difficulty understanding if that's the way the French are, or if she was really trying to make a pass at him.

When he had the feeling she was trying to make a pass at him, it horrified him and he tried to keep that feeling in abeyance.

Q. Now, doctor, why did this particular incident cause Brad . . . to describe a great deal of trauma from this?

And I ask this particularly because we are in the 1980s. We have a twenty-one-, twenty-two-year-old nice-looking young man. Why was this not brushed off as perhaps an experimental encounter in a foreign country, something like that?

A. I think that is a very interesting question because in all of my contacts with Brad we have never been able to get, at least in a way that he can understand, to the bottom of this.

Because there was no bottom to get to. Nothing happened. Like Roberta's pregnancy—like waiting for her the times she didn't show up—like all the unhappiness for which there was no reason, and no analysis could explain, and no explanation was sufficient. Like Bradley's confession?

And finally, the question:

Q. After seeing Mr. Page, did you come to any conclusion as to whether or not he suffered from any mental illness or defect?

A. No, I didn't feel Brad had suffered from any mental illness or defect.

Q. And there is no question in your mind he did not suffer from any type of so-called diminished capacity or any other mental problem that would make him unable to deal with his emotions?

A. None whatsoever. . . .

Q. How would you categorize the maturity level of Bradley Page? By that I mean his way of just dealing with worldly problems.

A. I would think that if you want me to put it on that dimension, I would categorize Bradley as being quite immature. He had the sophistication about the world of someone five years younger than his chronological age. He was still basically a teenager in his outlook on life. . . .

Q. When you say basically a teenager in his outlook on life, what are you referring to?

A. I think he had little awareness of evil in the world . . . He tended to be rather trusting, naive . . . He tended to see things in a very optimistic—I would say at times overly optimistic fashion. So he had never been really—and if you will pardon my use of the street term—I don't see that Bradley had ever really been kicked in the ass during his lifetime.

Q. Had he been in situations in his life where there was the kind of confrontation that occurred in the police interview room?

A. Never.

Q. To your knowledge, and based on your history, had Bradley ever been in a position where he was accused of doing something wrong?

A. No, he was never in a position where he was directly accused of doing something wrong. . . . I think Bradley was brought up in a home where very conventional ideals were portrayed. The values of his home were all very positive, very moral, very ethical, very concerned about the rights of others and so forth. . . .

I noted in our meeting . . . Bradley came in with a thin gold ring. He was wearing a T-shirt and blue jeans, purple scarf, a pink hat. The shirt was pink and blue. He had pink socks on. He had a diamond-shaped earring in his left ear. I found myself wondering if I was totally out of touch with young people on that occasion . . .

I wonder what the psychiatrist would have said about Roberta— black-lace black-leather black-onyx silver-ringed black-jeaned Roberta. I wonder what he would say about me.

Q. What does that say about him?

A. I think this is the way Brad has of being an individual. Of sort of expressing himself or projecting himself in a nonaggressive fashion.

Pathetic, the importance of costume.

Q. In addition to the various personality traits that you have mentioned about Bradley Page, I want to ask you about your observation on another one, and that is a tendency to be a bit scattered, to be, as I believe one witness has described him, ungrounded. Have you found this in Mr. Page in your clinical evaluations?

A. Yes. I found that to be so. From the time of the very first interview I noted . . . that at times he was vague, at times he seemed not really to realize the seriousness of his situation. At times, he tended to deal with life in abstractions when he needed something very concrete. And I attributed this to his overall immaturity. I didn't feel it was anything that pointed to mental illness, but it was just part of his not really being able to enter into the mainstream of life and understand what things were really about.

Scattered, I note, *ungrounded. At times, vague.*
—Ditto for me and Bibi and everyone else we knew, I write in the margin of my notebook.

Q. When you say he tends to deal with life through "abstractions," what do you mean by that?

A. You might ask him a specific question: "Well, Bradley, what do you think the effect of this particular situation would be on you?" And he will say something like, "Life is growth." I say, "That is fine, what does that mean with reference to this situation?"

Mistakes of metaphor—the substitution of the abstract for the concrete.
Reality becomes language; perspective is everything. Not mental illness, maybe, but a fatal flaw all the same. Bibi is dead; life is growth.

I think the depth of these feelings is suggested by several episodes described by others and he described at least one of these episodes to me of involuntarily wailing or screaming or doing some vocalization in the nighttime . . . He himself had the feeling that he was beginning to become catatonic . . . frozen.

Q. Now you have mentioned the reports . . . of the police officers of wailing?

A. Yes.

Q. Was there ever an episode in your office . . . ?

A. . . . I believe it was the July of 1985 . . . As I was again discussing with Brad some of the aspects of his quote confession unquote . . . I had been confronting him more with my concern about how anyone could possibly believe when he is in a police station what he says might not be a source of later distress to him. Brad became, I think, very concerned.

And out of the blue he let out a rather loud wail that continued for many seconds and was really shattering. I had worked in that office and my preceding office close to thirteen years, and I don't think I've ever heard anyone, including some very very disturbed people, make such a loud, unearthly sound.

And my secretary heard it very clearly, and she herself was concerned, she told me later, as to what was going on. Brad continued this sound, I think, for—it was probably a few seconds, five seconds. At one point he held his head in his hands. There were a few tears that showed in his eyes at the time, but certainly there was no copious tears. And he pulled himself together . . . and proceeded with the interview as though not much had happened . . . And this was after Brad had consistently shown such a control of his feelings in sessions.

. . . I think Brad tried to control himself to the point that some of these emotions just reached a point that he couldn't control them anymore, and they came out in this rather dramatic fashion.

The emotions just reached a point where he couldn't control them. But I loved her, I really loved her.

Q. Now my question is, having seen Brad repeatedly during the period of time that his mother was dying and died, how did he react to that outwardly?

A. Very little show of emotion.

Q. Did you consider this to be unusual?

A. Well . . . I thought his reactions were somewhat different than most of the reactions of young people to their mother's dying.

Q. Why in your opinion did he react this way?

A. I discussed with Brad his apparent lack of feeling about something that was very critical. He came out with a number of

abstractions . . . indicating that this is something that he had
to resign himself to.

So it was an attempt on his part to see all the events
that occurred in his life, tragic or otherwise, as part of an overall
plan to which he simply had to adjust himself. . . . He indicated
that he has always had a hard time talking about his feelings,
relationships. On that occasion he seemed to feel it maybe had
to do with the fact that he did a lot of things with his left hand.

Excuse me?

Q. Did you understand what that was all about?
A. . . . I think he was referring to some of his problems called
     dyslexia, spatial disorientation, confusion about certain types of
     intimate relationships, et cetera.

Diana Freeman, one of Bibi's roommates, is questioned. She had
received a call from Brad shortly after he returned from the park
that Sunday morning, in which he simply asked if Bibi was home.
When Diana said no, he had her take a message that he had called.
Q. When the defendant spoke with you at about eleven
   o'clock, eleven-fifteen in the morning, that Sunday morn-
   ing, he said nothing about his and Bibi's separating that
   day, did he?
A. No.
Q. He didn't make mention of the fact that he had left her
   in the hills at Roberts Park, did he?
A. No.

I know I had just left her ten miles away ten minutes before without
a ride home, but I just wanted to see if maybe there was a way she
was somehow home. And maybe it wasn't totally logical, but I was, you
know . . . concerned. I felt guilty.

Bradley Page is questioned:
Q. Did Bibi talk during the run or was she quiet, or how
   was she?
A. No, she didn't say anything the whole time. . . .
Q. So, Brad, it seems, the sergeant is asking you how Bibi
   was acting at that point. And your answer is this [he
   reads from the transcript of the police interrogation]:

"The only way I can answer," you start to say, described apparently from that John Berger book, "is that sometimes you love somebody so much that when you first see them you are overcome, and the only thing that kind of relieves it is to make love to them. Or, in this case, you know, she saw me and just needed me that much, whether it was physically or emotionally. And until that happens, it's agonizing." ...

What?

... Two questions, I will ask the first one first: Who is John Berger, and what are you referring to?
A. I was referring— He wrote the book *Ways of Seeing,* and Bibi had given that book to me.
Q. And what is that book about?
A. About different ways of seeing things, different perspectives, how different people look at a picture and see different things.

Ah, perspective!

Q. I don't understand what you are talking about with reference to the John Berger book and seeing Bibi and loving somebody....

We don't understand.

Q. Did you discuss with him why he wanted you to take a lie detector?
A. That he just wanted—that this would be helpful to confirm what we said, that he did not know me and if I would take a lie detector test ...

I was hesitant, and he said, "Well, it helps ... to go on with the search. We can get this behind us and we can go on and look for Bibi's killer."
Q. And did you believe that?
A. Yes.
Q. Did you object in any way to taking the polygraph?
A. No.

I feel sorry for Brad, with his eagerness to please, to the point of taking a polygraph that would condemn him.

He is asked about his interrogation:

Q. What were you doing during that period of time?
A. Probably halfway through I started crying.
Q. Why?
A. I don't know. Just—feeling badly over the loss of Bibi.

The loss of Bibi. The recurrent phrase: loss, losing. How she was lost; how we lost her.

Q. How did you feel toward the officers after you did stop crying?
A. I was grateful.
Q. Why?
A. To get me to stop crying—I was really frightened during those cries—they said, "You have lots of things to look forward to, and you have got to get it together." And they just comforted me a lot. Your future, they said, is still bright.
Q. Now, how would you characterize their demeanor during this part of the interview that began at three forty-five?
A. They were concerned for me. . . .

How grateful he is for their crumbs of attention! How eager to think that they like him and want to help him! How stupid he is.

A. Just before I completely stopped crying, and got myself together, they said, "We still have some questions to ask." And as soon as I stopped crying they said, "Why did you do it?"
   I sat down, and they said, "You are lying." And I looked up at them and closed my eyes.

I think about that one moment of defeat, when if he had sat up and asked to telephone his attorney—if he had said, nice talking to you, gentlemen, but the party's over, I've tried to be helpful but now I have to be going—his whole life would be different. But instead he closed his eyes.

Q. And, as you closed your eyes and tried to remember what happened, did the officers continue to talk to you?

A. I closed my eyes. They said, "That's good. Close your eyes. Sit back, relax and remember what happened." They said to remember seeing Bibi.

Q. And as you thought about seeing Bibi, did anything come into your mind?

A. After about ten minutes of having my eyes closed, I had an image of making love. . . . They said, "You must have done it. You might have blacked out hitting or lashing out at her, but you have to remember everything before."

Q. What subjects were discussed between you and Harris?

A. Bibi and my relationship, the duration of it. And also Sergeant Harris mentioned the time that he had had a trauma in his life and how he had gotten over it. He said that . . . it's important to get things off your chest, and you know, it was obviously hard on me and it's best to get rid of, divulge, everything and let things go so you can feel better about it.

Q. And then did he specifically relate to you an incident in his life?

A. Yes.

Q. And do you remember what that was?

A. He shot a man on duty.

Q. And did he tell you what effect that had on him?

A. Yeah, he said it was really hard on his family and him. After a while he sought counseling and he was over it now, and he is fine.

Confess, own up, and you too can seek counseling and end up with a fine family, like Sergeant Harris.

Q. Tell us how you described Bibi for the policemen.

A. Just that she was very bright and that she was probably more academically inclined and was looking for somebody who was more like that than I am.

Q. Did you tell Sergeant Harris that there were any resentments or bitterness or agitation because of this?

A. No. That was his suggestion.

Suggestions. The power of suggestion. Inventing motives.

Q. What did he ask you specifically regarding your sexual relations with Bibi?

A. We talked about birth control. He said, "What did you use?" I said, "I withdrew." Sergeant Harris said something about, "Well, didn't that insult your manhood that she would get all the pleasure and you didn't?" And I thought that was weird.

But you didn't want to interrupt?

Q. Did you tell him it was weird?
A. Believe it or not, I still trusted Sergeant Harris.
Q. But later you explained [he reads from the transcript of the interrogation]: "I was so under stress and pain from a lot of ideas that you had given me about sexual-frustration stuff. I know they came from me, but I never tied them into any possible motive until then. And until then it was such a shock, and such—I mean I have learned so much about myself in five minutes."

Amazing, I note, *the personal transformations that can occur in five minutes.*

Q. While Sergeant Harris and you were talking about some very personal and private subjects during that half hour, what was your thought as to why they were being brought up?

Why did you think they were asking, Bradley Page?

A. That obviously I had just gone through a trauma, and that sharing some of the things, understanding our relationship better, would have helped me in coping with getting over the loss of Bibi.

They were therapy-oriented law officials.

Q. What was your reaction? And by that I mean what were you thinking about Sergeant Harris and his relationship with you?
A. Well, I thought he was being very comforting and helpful. And at one point I thought he was going to take me home to dinner with his family.
Q. And why was that?

A. He had just been so nice.

Q. Did he say anything about that?

A. No, but he had mentioned his family earlier and talked about how they can now sit around the table and eat and things were well after his trouble. . . .

Sergeant Harris always invites all the murder suspects home for dinner after he finishes interrogating them. He's that kind of guy.

Brad explains how the confession evolved:

Q. And did the police ask you if you had seen Bibi again?

A. I said I don't remember ever seeing Bibi again, and they said I must have remembered seeing her, and they went through that list again, and I said no, I don't remember seeing her. And they said, "What about what you told us earlier?" I said, "Those are images." And they said, "What happens if they are real?" and I said, "I'd be scared."

I would be scared too.

Q. When you said these images, if they are real you'd be scared, what did you mean at the time?

A. Well, these were things I had made up earlier—they were not actual recollections from somewhere—that I didn't know where they came from, if I'd actually done it.

Q. Now, at this point, Brad, what was your state of mind as to whether or not what the police had related to you was true or not?

A. I couldn't remember any of it, but if they were so persistent and adamant that they had this other evidence, and if I was up there, if they had people that saw me up there, and I couldn't remember, then maybe I was capable of doing it.

. . . We went back and started from the scene of hitting and kicking her and added details to that.

Don't worry—let's just get a basic narrative out so you'll have something to work with. You can go back and add the details later.

Q. When you say "we went back and added details," whom are you referring to?

A. Harris and Lacer. I closed my eyes and they went back to,

"Let's start with the hitting and kicking." They said, "How did you hit her?" I said, "I don't know." They said, "Did you use your arm?" I said, "Yeah. Maybe I backhanded her."

And they said, "Well, what happened next?" And I said, "Well, she fell down." And they said, "You know, she hit her head on the rock." And they said, "Didn't she land on a tree?" And they said, "Well, is there any blood?" And I said, "No, it was not bloody. It was kind of a bloody nose."

Q. Going back, reconstructing, why could you picture a bloody nose?

A. Well, if you backhanded someone they would probably have a bloody nose.

Q. Did you ever backhand someone?

A. No.

Q. Had you ever struck Bibi before?

A. No.

Q. Did you ever strike Bibi?

A. No . . .

Q. Brad, at that point were you thinking that, yeah, you had done it, or did you not know, or what was your state of belief at that point?

A. I thought I hadn't done it but that somehow it might have been a possible way that I did. . . .

Paradox is an inextricable part of the fallen world. It was like—you know—ambiguous.

Q. The things you told the officers, were these things you recall actually occurring, or were they something different from that?

A. They were images that I had at that time for the very first time.

Q. Let me stop you at this point. While you and the officers were talking about the details of how something could have happened, why were you doing this?

A. If there was a possibility that I might have done it, I was trying to find out, and help them find out, what had happened.

Q. How would it help them by telling them these things were images?

A. Well, they said that there was a possibility that they were real, that they had already had me up there doing things I couldn't remember, so that somehow we had to make up a story that I could have done it.

Q. What in your own mind was the benefit to you of making up these stories?
A. That if I had done it, I needed to know.

And the logic is so simple and stupid and completely improbable it appeals—as the stories of children appeal. He couldn't possibly expect anyone to believe him, as when a child tells you he did do his geography homework, but it was eaten by a dinosaur. You want to believe him just because no one else would. If he had done it, he needed to know.

Q. What happened then?
A. We had gone through the scenario, and I had gone—gotten driven up and said we'd gone up to the— Bibi—hit Bibi. Decided that I must have made love to her. And I said, well, this took more than fifteen, twenty minutes, I know I hadn't done this unless I came back later. . . .

By which you mean the reason you decided that you went back to bury the body that night was because, when they told you to picture Bibi, the first image you had was of having sex, and you figured that would have taken more than fifteen minutes, so there wouldn't have been time while Robin was waiting, so you must have gone back later that night? Is that how you're saying the scenario was invented? By default?

. . . Somewhere around then there was a, like, change in attitude by the policemen. Like, well, we have got to take notes and get the story written down.

Oral transmission is becoming inadequate.

Q. Who mentioned that?
A. Harris, because we didn't have the chronology yet. We worked backwards, and we wanted to go through forwards this time.
Q. When you say you had worked backwards, what did you mean by that?
A. We started off with an image of hitting and kicking her and we worked backwards to hitting her, and I decided I must have seen her.

But at any point you could have said: this isn't true, I don't like your images, you're putting words in my mouth.

Q. [The D.A. reads from the transcript of the police interrogation]: "Okay, it wasn't us that brought up the blanket. . . . You took the blanket as something to cover her body with. And you told us you got it from the car. Now, let's go back and now you've got the blanket. Now where are you going with the blanket?

"Answer: I went and covered her."

[And then, addressing Brad]: They told you it wasn't they that brought up the suggestion of the blanket, right?

A. That the blanket existed. But that it was put in the scenario later on.

Q. And that was something you put in, correct?

A. How this came about precisely I can't remember, but it was something—

Q. Throughout the whole tape, as you listen to the tape, they are asking you: why are you giving us this answer, correct?

A. But they also—they are asking that on two different levels, like . . . in this scenario, how would this fit in? Or, why did you put it in knowing that it was a scenario?

In other words, does the narrative function primarily ontologically or mimetically? What is lost in the distance between the signifier and the signified?

Difficult questions, of course—even with your background—no wonder you were confused. But then again, confusion was probably their intention. A cunning plan.

Q. You were asked in some detail about your rights. Did you have any reservation about waiving your rights other than what was expressed on the tape?

A. No.

Q. Did you see any problem with waiving your rights?

A. No.

Q. Did you see any need for a lawyer?

A. No.

Q. In fact, Brad, at any point in the entire day, did you ever ask for a lawyer?

A. No.

Dumbo.

Q. At the end of the tape with the district attorney and the district attorney's investigators, the last statement from them, I believe, was, "We don't have any more questions." And the next response was from you: "I would like to go home." At the time that you finished the interview with the district attorney, what was your expectation as to whether you would or would not be going home that evening?
A. I was uncertain, but after talking to the D.A. I thought I would go home.

Can I go home now? Can I go home?

Q. Why?
A. I had already helped him all I could and I felt they would understand what had gone on, they would let me go.

Since we were all just there to help one another, you remember.

Q. How did Sergeant Harris view your recantation of your "confession" to the D.A.?
A. Harris was very upset and said, "So you told the D.A. that everything you told us before was a lie?" And I said no. And so we argued about lies and fiction, images and truth for about twenty minutes . . .
Q. And when you say you lied about—pardon me, that you talked about lying and fiction and truth and these different subjects, what again, with an overview, was the nature of the discussion?
A. That I said that I was sitting there trying to remember that these were—they were fiction, and he said, "They were lies then." And I said, "Well, no, they are not lies."

And so Bradley and the policeman sat in the room for the next quarter of an hour and discussed the difference between fiction and lies—you know, willing suspension of disbelief and the like. How handy Bradley's studies in linguistics must have come in! What luck he was taking jazz dance and creative writing!

So we had to argue about what was a lie and what was a fiction. And he said, "Anything that isn't true is a lie, son," and "So we will use this definition that even fiction is a lie."

Q. What, as you were arguing with Sergeants Harris and Lacer, what in your mind was the distinction between a lie and fiction as it related to the previous statements?
A. That something that was hypothetical was fiction, and they said no, those were lies.

Score 1 for the Men in Blue.

. . . They obviously didn't understand. I was trying to explain to them what had gone on. They asked me questions about my motivations for things . . . why I had left, what had actually happened on November 4th, or motivation of this scenario.
. . . They had me convinced there was a possibility I might have done it, and that's why I had to . . . figure out if there was a way.
Q. Did you explain that to them?
A. Yes.

They obviously didn't understand.

Q. Did you specifically talk to the officers at this point in the interview process about the things that you knew concerning Bibi's death before you began to talk to them?
A. Yes. But they were jumping around. They'd ask me one question about what I actually knew, and they'd also ask me, well, what had I known before, before I had done it. So they'd sit there and we'd be talking about one thing and they would confuse me about where we were at. See, we were talking on one level and all of a sudden they would ask another question as if they were on a completely different level.

Oh, muddling levels!

Q. When you say you were talking about levels, could you be specific?
A. Like motivation about why would I say something would hap-

pen in the scenario. If I were in the scenario, what would I have—why would I have said it? And outside information that I had, because I wouldn't know that the dogs—that the dogs couldn't find her. . . .

Q. So something like the dogs not finding her, what did this assist you to do in creating the hypothetical?
A. Well, assuming she must have been buried.

You told the policemen that you had buried her because she must have been buried because why, otherwise, would the dogs not have found her?
Yeah, I get it.

Like we wanted to know why I had parked the car where the officers had said it was parked, and so I just tried to make up something. So we never came up with a reason for parking the car any one place. So at the end, we said I just parked it someplace random.

No kidding.

Q. What is linguistics?
A. I am not precise. The study of languages.
Q. What is it about, the study of languages? What have you been studying for three or four years?

What have you been studying for the past three or four years?

A. It—there is a common thread between different languages if that is a basic structure of language that all other languages have a basic structure that's common to all.

A unified-field theory of linguistics, of sorts.
Sounds like he isn't quite ready for his orals.

Q. And at that point did you have any problem with continuing to talk to the officers?
A. No.
Q. At that point did you again voluntarily give up your rights?
A. Yes.

Q. Did you feel you needed the assistance of counsel?
A. No.
Q. At this point did you make any requests for phone calls?
A. No.
Q. During the entire day that you were at the police department and on into the next morning now ... did you ask any of the officers to call anyone on your behalf?
A. I made a phone call to Jeff to have him cancel my psychiatrist appointment.

How responsible. Wonder what Jeff told the secretary.

Q. But as you are listening to the first taped confessional statement ... the policemen are saying: "Well, look, we want to go through and have you explain to us, how did you have this information to give us, and why did you give it to us? Like, how did you know all those details to make up for your fantasy murder scenario?"
A. Right.
Q. And in there, there's not anything along the lines that you are saying: "Wait a second, you gave me that piece of information," correct? "Don't put this on me—you fed me those lines."
A. Because they were there. Why should I have to tell them?

It was a group effort! A committee confession!

At the time I did not realize that's what this would all be used for.

I always have these kinds of conversations.

Harris said I would be booked for the murder of Roberta Lee. And I said, "What does that mean?" and I said, "Does that mean I can go home?" And he said, "That's up to the D.A. to decide."
Q. When he told you you were going to be booked for the murder of Roberta Lee, did you know what that meant?
A. No.
Q. Did you know what booking meant?
A. No.

Q. Did you ask him?
A. No.
Q. Did he explain?
A. No.

You must have been somewhere else, my friend.

A psychiatrist testified for the defense:

A. Brad can't and never has been able to completely understand what his mental state was at that point that would have caused him to have naively—his own words—accepted these suggestions or to have gone on to express thoughts which came from his imagination. . . .

It was after many rehearsals, he states, that the recording was made. . . .

Q. What was there about that interrogation process, the conduct of the officers in interrogating Page, which would have had the effect of causing him to invent this scenario of what might have happened?

A. I think that at the time Brad was initially questioned by the officers, he saw himself as someone who was there to help. When the situation, to his awareness, became one in which he was the suspect, to him this was a tremendous shock and he suffered a certain degree of psychological disorientation. I think anyone can understand, if he goes down with the idea that he is going to help law enforcement do something, and he ends up becoming the suspect, this is a very disorienting and upsetting experience.

This type of experience, in addition to . . . occurring in a setting where you are totally controlled, you move from the free world into a setting where now officers have complete control over every aspect of your life . . . suddenly you are in a totally controlled situation, and this tends to accentuate the very deepest dependency strivings of individuals that we all have as part of our early development. And it produces regression. By the term "regression" we mean that certain features in the way you feel and the way you think become more close to those feelings you had as a child. So you'd tend to become more suggestible to ideas that are placed before you by people who are in authority over you . . . and to believe more of what you are told.

Q. Let me stop you. This disorientation that you refer to, and the regression, is that a condition that is common to humans, generally?

A. Yes. This is very common to humans in general, and it has been described over and over in the literature as "coercive persuasion."

And yet was he really coerced? Tortured? Threatened—starved— locked up—defenses shattered, perspective warped?
   No. Not at all—not, at least, in reality.

I think that Bradley had never had any contact with the police before. He never had any reason to see police as anything but on his side. He's never been in an adversary relationship with them either, personally. He didn't grow up on the wrong side of the tracks where there is always a certain degree of suspiciousness toward the police. He identified them fully as agents of his type of society. In addition to which he began to have severe doubts about his own ability to rely on his thinking when certain bits of quote evidence end quote were introduced by the police. This furthered disorientation on his part. . . .

There are elements in the police interrogation which unintentionally approximate those seen in so-called brainwashing or other forms of interrogation. Specifically, what I saw happen to Brad in the interrogation has a great deal of similarity to processes in those undergoing other forms of coercive interrogation, including identification with the inquisitor. He identified with the large policeman as though he were a paternal figure. . . . Bradley felt they then made the continuing statements to him that people sometimes, under the shock of such an experience, black out, develop amnesia, and it would be important for him to try to recall everything that went into clarifying the issues and making himself feel better. He felt the emphasis that, were he to confess, any pain he might be feeling and which he might not be able to attribute to any specific cause might be thus relieved. . . . In other words, confession was good for his soul, and without confession he was literally damned in the hereafter, if not in this world. . . .

His disorientation was certainly not to the degree that is frequently seen in the more extreme forms of brainwashing, but we must remember that Brad is a much more suggestible, less sophisticated, immature person who has never had any preparation for this type of encounter nor any training for it.

Q. Now was Brad's response consistent with his tendency generally to abstract as opposed to deal with things as they are?

Bibi's tendency, Bradley's tendency, my tendency. The tendency.

A. It is consistent with a very creative imagination, and it is not at all unusual for people to imagine things of this sort.

CHAPTER 3

The Warmth of Her Smile

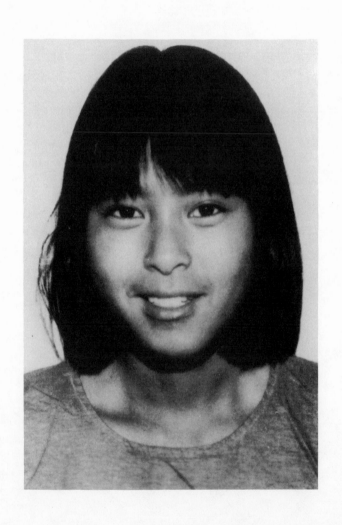

Yesterday I was sitting out on the front steps drying my hair, and a woman stopped and said, "I see you all over the place, and I really get a strong sense of style from you. I just wanted to tell you that I really like it." That certainly made this girl's day. If only she knew what I was really like . . . I guess that's the nice thing about strangers.

And then closing arguments began. It is curious, Mr. Burr addresses the jury conversationally, that this is the eighth of April. It's curious because I first started speaking to you on the eighth of February, and I told you then that the evidence was going to show you some things that it has shown. I also told you then that you were going to have to be very careful of a process happening that now has happened, and that is getting to be familiar with Bradley Page. He comes to court every day: we see him in the halls and in the elevators, we see his wife and his father, and everybody, Mr. Burr says, gesturing with a sarcastic sweep, *everybody* has seen his baby. And there's a natural process, a sort of human sympathy that gets generated which renders it increasingly difficult to keep in mind that this man murdered someone. We aren't tempted into the same affection for Bibi Lee because we don't know her. We'll never know what it is about her that made forty people rush to form the Friends of Bibi Lee and volunteer their time when they heard she was missing.

He pauses here for a minute, as if trying to think of what it was, and then, as if it has just occurred to him: "We never saw the warmth of her smile." That that single image is the one thing he is able to summon up about Roberta, who was so describable, confirms it: he never had seen her smile. How could he think of anything else? He didn't know her. She didn't, actually, smile very often, so it was almost the wrong image to have chosen, but not quite. You would have had to know her well to know that her smile was warm, but it was: her rare beautiful seldom warm smile. The warmth of her smile. A good epitaph, I think, deciding.

"You know how hard he must have worked to generate that phrase," Michael, sitting beside me, whispers tolerantly.

Brad had gone out the night before with Janet C, Mr. Burr continues. Now, Jan is just an old high school friend—he says he's been in love with her for years, to be sure, but nothing was ever going to develop from it, he says. They were just getting together with some old high school buddies of theirs, and he doesn't consider it a date. But Bibi does. And he thinks this is unreasonable of her. She is silent and hostile and unreasonable the whole car ride; she embarrasses him in front of Robin, and then when they finally do start to run, she takes off on him. Disappears, makes a nuisance of herself. They have to stop the run to go back and look for her. *No Bibi.* What the hell does she think she's doing? So the defendant finally leaves Robin at the parking lot, and drives along the road. What he tells us is that *he didn't turn on Skyline Boulevard:* when he came to it, he says, he turned around and circled back to the parking area.

Now, that's funny: why wouldn't he turn onto Skyline? It's the obvious place to go. And the answer is equally obvious: he did. He drives down it and finds Bibi standing by the side of the road. The police had told him they had two pieces of evidence when they were trying to elicit a confession—they said they had fingerprints and a witness who had seen his car on Skyline Boulevard. Do you know why these ploys were so effective in scaring our defendant? Because they were true. He turns onto Skyline and sees Bibi, and calls to her. She continues to walk. Not only has she left him, but when he has gone out of his way to find her, she *ignores* him. He runs over to her and kisses her on the top of the head. She struggles out of his arms. Rejection. He is being controlled—as she has always controlled him. All of a sudden he loses it. Snaps. It's that fast. He backhands her; she falls to the ground, and he kneels down and smashes her head into a rock—a tree root, something— three times. It happens so fast it almost doesn't happen. And then she's dead. His life disintegrates before his eyes. And so he begins the long process of trying to cover up.

Mr. Burr pauses, resting perhaps. And we too rest, as if in preparation for the process ahead: the long narrative of concealment and disclosure.

The defendant receives two big initial breaks, the strength of which he is still trying to get by on. He tells the Berkeley police he didn't see her again, and when they search the park the next day, they don't find her body. This is so unlikely that it must have appeared to Brad like an act of God, and to the policemen it served as a confirmation of his story. Meg and others make a big fuss, and an organization begins to be formed. Now, Brad was in a very tricky situation here—in fact, one of the most tricky situations in the world. Participating in Roberta's search while knowing all the while where Roberta is, is an unprecedented act of deception and hypocrisy. He can't look too hard because he knows where to look.

She's dead. On the other hand, if he doesn't search then the finger of suspicion points at him. And so, what we see is his attempt at compromise. He has to stay involved, but he can't bring himself to be really involved like the ones who are truly devastated, like Scott Lawson or Meg. He is asked to talk to the police frequently, and he talks to them so frequently, in fact, that a certain convention is established. And that is the convention that he is innocent.

How easily everything follows, I think, once you have established a narrative convention.

And then the defendant receives the second big break. A woman thinks she remembers seeing an Asian girl being forced into a truck by a moon-faced man. Then a second woman remembers a variation on the same thing, and suddenly there is a credible suspect. The search for the Man with the Van begins, and the defendant begins to relax. Imagine the relief he must have felt that the object of the search was now securely someone else—an imaginary someone, about whom he knew nothing more than anyone else. With what a clear conscience he could now put up those posters.

But then one day the game's up. Only thing is, it's been going on so long he can't believe it's over. He's called in for questioning. Since the body is found in Oakland, it's the Oakland police who question him, and they don't buy his story. By this time, however, he's so confident, he even volunteers to take a polygraph test. And surprise—he flunks. The defendant tells us that the reason he confessed is that he wanted to help the police find Bibi's killer—if he had done it, he wanted to know; but that's not what the tape tells us. The tape shows a man trying first to avoid, and then to minimize responsibility.

You see, what happens now, folks, is that he panics. Right after they tell him what the polygraph shows and the other evidence they invent—the fingerprints and witness—he thinks to himself: *all is lost; they know.* But then they tell him that in fact all is not lost—if he confessed, it would be an accidental killing, whereas otherwise it could be seen as a cold-blooded murder. Accidents can happen to anyone, they tell him—why, Sergeant Harris himself was involved in a fatal shooting. And so, according to the well-known law of self-preservation, he decides to make a clean breast. He confesses. Cat's out of the bag. But soon after, he decides it was premature, and he wants to change his mind. An accidental killing may be better than a cold-blooded killing, but no killing is

best of all. Gentlemen, he says when the D.A. arrives, I'm glad
you've come because I think there's been a misunderstanding and I
want to go home. He's got himself in a box, and he's trying to claw
his way out. Only thing is, it's a bit late. Because the things he says
in the confession are true.

I don't know who Lynn Eberts or Karen Marquardt saw, but it
wasn't Bibi. Lynn Eberts saw her being picked up at ten o'clock;
Karen Marquardt saw her being picked up on Montclair at noon.
What was she doing on Montclair right near the park two and a
half hours later? It took her two and a half hours to get to
Montclair? Let's suppose Lynn Eberts was telling the truth, but
Karen Marquardt was mistaken. So the Man with the Van picked
her up on Monterey Boulevard, and drove her back to the park to
bury her? Right back there to the place where she was last seen by
the defendant? Only thing is: *how did he know where it was?* He was
supposed to have picked her up miles away, remember? Why
would he return her to bury her body right where Bradley Page
coincidentally last reported seeing her? Speculation is so interesting; it can go on forever.

Brad tells us that when he goes back to the woods that night,
he moves the body. In the confession he describes himself as
having dragged it. Why doesn't he say he picked her up and
carried her in his arms in the classic romantic Rhett Butler gesture?
Because in reality a corpse is stiff and heavy and unwieldy and
would be dragged. An alive Bibi would have been cradled in her
lover's arms—but that's the difference between fiction and reality.
He doesn't imagine it that way because it wasn't imaginary.

The police ask him where the body was, and he gives an exact
location of where he first struck her down. Then he says that he
moved the body toward Skyline that night, a quarter of a mile
south of Roberts Park Driveway. And lo and behold, the body is
discovered a quarter of a mile south of the driveway to Roberts
Park. Why?

In the third tape—the retraction tape—the police asked him,
in his so-called imaginary scenario, if he was making it all up, why
for Chrissake did he see himself moving the body toward Skyline?
And you know what he says? *Not:* you guys fed me that information, don't you remember? *Not:* that was part of the committee
fantasy, as he's trying to tell us now. What he says is: I don't
know. *"Those are images I have in my mind, and if they're true, I'll be
scared to death."*

So you see, even his recantation confirms the truth. At one point during the third tape—the tape where he's trying to worm out of it—he says: the cops say bushes, and I imagine bushes. *But bushes are nowhere on the confession tape.* They existed in real life, not in the confession. He slips. She was found under a bush, but the cops didn't tell him that. You see, it's difficult not to make any mistakes—not to borrow one detail too many from reality to be able to put them all back where you found them and not be caught.

I remember Claudia once telling me, I think to myself, that there was a Faulkner novel where Faulkner had made a mistake—he said at one point that a house was stone, and then later in the story he said it was wood. And it's important because the house burns down. But it's all right, Claudia said, we forgive him because imagining an entire world is a big job. Brad said bushes. He slipped the other way—not making his fiction too far from reality, but too close. And he's still trying to protest, *this story is purely fictitious; any resemblance to persons living or dead is purely coincidental*—except that he forgot and used bushes, instead of palm trees. For some reason, I remember just the way Claudia used the word *forgive*.

And then there's the question, Mr. Burr continues, of his whereabouts that Sunday night. When we asked him where he was, he said maybe he was in his room studying, but he couldn't exactly remember. He told us to ask Jeff, his rommmate; he said maybe Jeff'll know. Well, we asked Jeff, and Jeff didn't know. All he remembered for certain was that by ten o'clock Brad was back in their room. Jeff DeLott was his best friend; Jeff was devastated by his arrest. You can bet that Jeff tried as hard as he could to recall seeing Brad, yet he couldn't come up with anything. Brad must have asked everyone in Lothlorien, and in spite of the fact that there were dozens of people in the house that night, no one had a single memory of Brad in the large chunk of time between dinner and bed, the time in which—he tells us in the confession—he was burying the body. No one, that is, except his pregnant wife two years later at the trial, who remembered then that she happened to be walking beneath his lighted window outside Lothlorien right around the time no one else knows where he was and he himself can't quite pinpoint it and she saw him at his desk, studying.

Now folks, this is the day that he personally lost his girlfriend. He took her to the woods and he *lost* her. Now don't you think every detail of the day is going to be indelibly etched in his memory? Every other detail seems to be. He remembers what time he went to sleep, he remembers the phone rang twice before Jeff picked it up at midnight when Meg called to say Bibi hadn't come home, he remembers he had enchiladas for dinner, but he doesn't remember what he was doing all evening long? He could lie, of course, and say he does remember, but he needs to check his story with Jeff. So, hoping to bluff us, he tells us talk to Jeff. Perhaps he hopes his best friend will lie for him. At any rate, he's covered himself by not risking contradiction.

But perhaps the most convincing thing about this confession is not the crucial details, like him saying he backhanded her, and our confirming that her nose was broken, but the extra, unnecessary ones. *I went up to her and kissed her on the top of the head.* Why does he kiss her on the top of the head? Why not the cheek, or the lips? *I went back to the car to get the blanket, and saw that it was parked on the left side—the east side of Skyline Road.* Why? Why would you imagine having your car parked on the wrong side of the street going in the wrong direction, unless that's what you did?

I knew she was dressed from the waist down, he says on the tape. Why the waist down? Why not completely dressed or completely undressed? How would he know her shirt was found pulled over her chest? "Extra details" is the only answer the defendant gives. Why?

One of the things the defense is going to tell you is that there is no physical evidence. Well, no kidding; the murderer had five weeks to get rid of any physical evidence. For example, the blanket— not the moldy one we have in the lab, but the tarp that Robin Shaw remembers seeing in the back of the car—*where is it?* What became of the blanket?

We have the physical evidence of her body, and the way it was found. There were no bruises or marks or signs of a struggle; she was not kept in captivity, her wrists were not bound, her shirt was not torn. There were only the three decisive blows to the head from the single struggle. The struggle with Bradley Page. Listen to those tapes. The evidence is all there. You can hear the quaver in his voice. That alone should make up your minds.

"Unfortunately," says Mr. Burr, with a sweeping gesture toward the Pages—the most generous of all his gestures, as if to say, I take the Pages into account in my version, you can believe what I believe and not have forgotten about them—"unfortunately for his family, he is guilty."

The Page family at the second trial.

CHAPTER 4

We Don't Know

I don't think you should make Adam a tapestry. A tapestry will take too long. Just buy him a nice eelskin wallet, made of unlucky eels. A tapestry would be excessive. I saw a book with an eelskin cover today— a special and specially expensive small printing ($300), in which the spine of the eel was made to match the spine of the book. Sick little bit of metonymy there, eh?

I wouldn't give it to any of my boyfriends, had I $300—had I a boyfriend. I know, I know: what happened to Brad you want to know?

What Happened To Brad? Oh, what happened?

There is a significant question, Mr. Peretti says in his gentle fashion, as to whether Roberta Lee was in that park. There are two things that would lead one to this conclusion. There is, first of all, the search of the park on November fifth, and secondly the sightings of Roberta Lee after they left, which show that Robin and Brad were not the last ones to see her alive. These sightings were not of an Asian female in a shopping mart or in a car stopping for gas—they were sightings of a *jogger. An Asian jogger wearing black and white striped running shorts.* Moreover, one of the women saw not only a jogger, but a struggle—a young woman being forced into a van by the side of the road. How often does that occur? And this sighting was deemed to be sufficiently credible by the police that they concentrated all their subsequent efforts on finding the Man with the Van. The first sighting was corroborated by Duke, one of the search dogs, who determined that her scent stopped at a point in the road, so we can assume she must have gotten into a car. These sightings were believed at the time, and there is no reason now not to believe them, except for the fact that they don't happen to fit with the state's case against Bradley Page. These were women who were trying to be helpful, who were doing their civic duty, as all of us should, and then all of a sudden they receive a call saying thanks for everything, but we don't need you anymore. Why don't they need them now? They are unreliable now because the prosecutor wants them to be unreliable.

The search of the park on November fifth was very extensive. These were professionally trained German shepherds, one of whom was specifically reported as having gone within ten feet of where Bibi's body was later found, partially exposed. One of the searchers tells you that his dog did react to that bush, and that he went in with a flashlight and didn't see anything. He shined a flashlight in the place where the body of Roberta Lee was partially covered and he didn't see anything—not the burial mound, not the exposed flesh—*nothing*.

Moreover, you have heard the pathologist testify that the kind of head injury on Ms. Lee would have produced a fair amount of blood, yet *nowhere*—not on the rocks, not in the grave site—*nowhere was there any blood.* In the so-called confession, Bradley says that he dragged the body. That should have left a tremendous trail of blood for the dogs to find. And the dogs, who howl at the sight of flesh or the smell of blood, were silent.

A lot of the testimony of the prosecution rests on so-called accusations of what Bradley Page did or didn't do about the search. Well, what I want to say about this is: hindsight. All of a sudden everybody remembers something Brad didn't do: all these people who never had a complaint at the time. And yet as you listen to the testimony, what you discover is that each one accidentally reveals some new little contribution Brad had made. And yes, maybe he didn't do as much as Lena Grady, but that woman was a saint. Still, I don't think he should be indicted because he chose to go swimming every day. People handle stress in different ways: Brad felt he could do best by keeping himself in shape, by keeping grounded.

"Lena Grady," Michael whispers to me, "was a saint."

I once read a story in the newspaper, Mr. Peretti continues, about a Japanese man who was walking on a beach with his two children, when a tidal wave came and washed the two children away. I probably remember that story because I have two children myself. There was nothing the man could do, but think how terrible he must have felt. Well, that's what it was like for Bradley Page. He went running and he lost her, and all of a sudden the finger of suspicion pointed at him.

"Run that by me again," says Michael. "Japanese what?"

Out of his shock, his profound disorientation, emerges his confession. Read it carefully, and it's obviously fictional. For example, in the so-called necrophilia, the most abused and publicized part of this case, what Brad says is: I spread out a blanket, and I lay next to her and caressed her and cried, and after a fairly long time, I think I made love to her. That's not necrophilia. He's talking about making love to an alive Bibi—not pulling the legs apart, with the rigor mortis already setting in. I don't mean to be indelicate, but come on, folks. That's fantasy; that's the difference between fantasy and reality.

"The difference between fantasy and reality," repeats Michael. "Didn't Mr. Burr use that phrase?"

Amy and Robin testified that he appeared normal and unaffected at the trip to the Exploratorium. Robin saw him fifteen minutes later, and she saw nothing; Amy and the others who went with him to the Exploratorium *noticed nothing wrong*. Now, this is not a cold-blooded killer, this is not a practiced murderer; were he to have done such a horrible and appalling thing for the first time in his life, he would hardly have had such a pleasant afternoon afterward. Remember, this is someone about whom it has been universally testified, from his kindergarten teachers onward, that he was sweet and gentle and had never to anyone's knowledge hit anyone before. How do you think he would feel had he suddenly done such a thing? He probably would at least have made some excuse for backing out of the trip.

He slept in her bedroom that night. Would you sleep in the bedroom of the woman you had just murdered? He chose to sleep there, even though his own room was a four-minute bike ride away.

At several times during his speech, you heard Mr. Burr refer sarcastically to how Mr. Peretti was going to explain such and such. For example, I'd like to see Mr. Peretti explain what Bibi was doing on Montclair two hours later, he said. Well, my answer is: I don't have to. That's Mr. Burr's job. I'd like to say I had this case all wrapped up for you, but I don't. I can't solve it for you; I can't fill in all the details. Maybe the man had picked her up in the park, and she was trying to get out of the car on Montclair. Maybe he was bringing her back because that's where she told him to go. Maybe she hitchhiked, maybe a lot of things. Who knows? I don't know what she was doing there. But neither do you. We can speculate, of course, but speculations get us further and further away from the realm of reality because speculation is endless. How shall we stop once we begin to speculate?

But of course you *have* to speculate if you are going to convict Mr. Page, because this entire case is speculation. There is not one shred of physical evidence. The hubcap with which he supposedly buried the body tested clean, and the blanket he supposedly wrapped her in tested clean, and the polygraph showed no conclusive results. Not deceptive, as Mr. Burr keeps referring to it, but inconclusive.

Remember, it is not enough to think Brad is guilty. It's like a carnival bell—it has to ring the bell. You can have as many climbing doubts as you want and they don't matter: they have to reach the high bell of moral certainty. And what I propose to you is that there is not just some doubt, there is significant doubt. It doesn't ring the bell.

It is your moral obligation not to convict someone if there is any other conceivable way to understand the configuration of events. I think in this case we all have to admit: there are many.

CHAPTER 5

The Blue Screen

"It's like making a movie," Page told the officers. "It's not actual memory. . . . ."

It is almost three. The trial is supposed to close today: that gives Mr. Burr an hour to say whatever he is going to say. I imagine for a moment that he will find something, some final disclosure that will alter all the other disclosures. I look around at the jury: their blank faces appear slightly less blank; the courtroom is slightly restless. You wonder what they are thinking—if they are thinking anything—and wonder too, even if this were all fictional, a trial scene, and you were writing the lines for the D.A., what you could think of for him to say that would be powerful enough to close the story—to tie up all the stray threads of a narrative too long—an image, an idea, an epitaph. I notice a video machine in the corner.

"It was there before," Michael says.

"No, it wasn't," I say, "I remember." We both turn to stare at the silent black face with its sleeping single eye. Mr. Burr, as if the idea has just occurred to him, goes over and turns it on. The room stills. An image appears on screen and at the same time, mysteriously, the familiar voice begins to speak out of a tape recorder: Brad, telling of the burial. They are playing the confession tape a last time, a voiceover now to the images on screen. "Those are images I have in my mind, and if they're true I'll be scared to death."

The first thing you think is how blue it is. The entire image is suffused in light blue light. It might be that it was taken in early morning, or late late dusk, or was meant to look as if it were, or perhaps, simply, you were sitting too far away from the screen, and the distance somehow makes it look blue. Or likeliest of all you remember it as blue because there is something blue or blue-colored about memory and remembering death, and particularly remembering things lost and inaccessible, as what is lost in and illuminated by this blue light is utterly lost. I want, I need, I believe, I think. You imagine, at first, that you see only branches, and then you realize that they give way to something in the center, and entangled submerged in black earth and branches you see white limbs—a knee, part of a thigh, half a face, long dark hair. But perhaps they are all only branches and parts of trees in which you see human shapes. A vine grows from what you think was her stomach although it may be a tree stump. You imagine she could still shake it free, this earthsleeping girl—brush the brambles from her black hair and dust the dirt from her shoulders—but already she is so laden with black ground, it is difficult to distinguish which is which. It worries you, that you can't distinguish; you strain forward in your seat, trying to tell them one from the other—limb from branch, dark shape from dark shape and blue mist. Five weeks' sleep and look how wedded already she is to the earth; think how she would look now that years and years have passed, the transfiguring blueness, distance changing hue. Blue is such a lonely color. The loneliness as morning or dusk or distance or light is lonely: the loneliness that the image is so far away and was taken so long ago, and the loneliness that it doesn't really exist anymore—it is an image on a blue screen, which will be turned off and blank before you have finished thinking about it.

Mr. Burr reaches over and turns it off.

Michael, sitting next to you, has his eyes closed. So he did not want to look at it, the lost girl alone in the blue blue room. You tell him it is over, and hear, dumbly, Mr. Burr saying: "It's not a pretty picture, but it wasn't a pretty thing.

"He is guilty."

And in the same dumbness you realize that the trial is over, and you walk out with Michael into the sunlight, and Michael asks why you are so quiet, and whether it was those pictures, and you shake your head, no.

It doesn't matter what she looked like; she was dead.

The hole in her skull was so big you could put a child's hand in it, with all the fingers spread wide. Or an adult man's fist, smashed through as hard as he can, or a rock with jagged edges, or a vine with many flowers that could grow out and have its roots protected in the curving white basin.

It doesn't matter what she looked like; she was dead.

The skull was so thin; you had never realized before how thin a skull is. Eggshell thin; shattering thin, shattering and shatterable. Imagine, it held all those thoughts and could be shattered so simply.

It doesn't matter what she looked like; she was dead.

The vine was growing from her stomach. The D.A. said the roots had already taken hold; it was that deep by the time they found her, it was that deep. There was a vine growing out of her stomach when they found her.

They must have pulled it out by now.

Her knee was intact; but the animals had gotten to her thighs; her thighs were eaten away.

The first thing they saw was a hand, sticking out of the shallow grave, along with the trash and brambles.

It doesn't matter what she looked like; she was dead. Repeat this before you sleep, a little litany, a chant, and you won't dream about it ever.

But the grave was robbed. The body was unidentifiable, even the sex. They brought in a video camera and the D.A. or someone like the D.A. told them to move it closer so they could get a good shot of the decay and show it in court. We knew she was dead, but they wanted to make sure we knew what she looked like.

It doesn't matter what she looked like; she was dead. She was sleeping in the earth; she was held in the blue light, she was dead, she was dead. The machine is turned off, the image dissolved.

CHAPTER 6

A Malignant and Abandoned Heart

My friends aren't writing me so I'm reduced to visualizing them. Perhaps I'm unimaginative. When I see them, they look just like me— but somewhere else. Oh well, what are friends for if they don't stand in for you in places you've never been?

On April 20, 1988, the jury hands down the verdict. Manslaughter was the only charge available to them since the first jury had exonerated him of first- and second-degree murder. Apparently murder requires both intent to kill and malice: first-degree manslaughter also involves the same intent to kill or cause grave bodily harm but without the presence of malice. The difference is considered crucial: the sentence for murder is twenty-five years to life; the penalty for manslaughter is punishable under California law by a sentence of two, four, or six years.

I go over to my friend Robin's apartment one night to look up the difference in her huge lawbooks. She has just completed her second year at Berkeley's law school. I had thought she should go on in Spanish literature—that she was selling out to go to law school—but I was wrong. She is happy in law; she likes it, and she is such a small blond person and her happiness so quiet, that one feels happy with her. What, I ask Robin, is malice?

" 'Malice,' " she reads aloud, " 'is the presence of a malignant and abandoned heart.' " First-degree murder depends on malice aforethought—that is, planned malice, although the law adds thoughtfully that "to prove the killing was deliberate and premeditated, it shall not be necessary to prove the defendant maturely and meaningfully reflected upon the gravity of his or her act." I wonder if it was ever the case that a defendant had. "The use of the premeditation-deliberation formula as a basis for identifying murderers deserving of the greatest punishment" has recently been called into question, the textbook notes, as "prior reflection may reveal the uncertainties of a tortured conscience rather than exceptional depravity," whereas "the suddenness of the killing may simply reveal callousness so complete and depravity so extreme that no hesitation is required." Second-degree murder is without planning, caused by malicious passion.

Manslaughter, on the other hand, is defined as "the unlawful killing of a human being *without malice.*" It falls into two categories—voluntary and involuntary or first and second degree. First-degree voluntary manslaughter stems from unmalicious passion; second-degree involuntary manslaughter is a result of accident. "What," I ask Robin again, "is the difference between malicious intent-to-kill passion and unmalicious intent-to-kill passion?"

" 'Murder,' " she says, leaning over her lawbook, " 'must be committed under circumstances in which ordinary men would not be liable to have their reason clouded or obscured by passion: and the act must be prompted by . . . a wicked, depraved or malignant mind—a mind which . . . is cruel, wanton or malignant, reckless of human life, or regardless of social duty.

" 'Manslaughter, on the other hand,' " she reads, " 'is when the acts of killing, though intentional, be committed under the influence of passion or in the heat of blood, produced by an adequate or reasonable provocation, and before a reasonable time has elapsed for the blood to cool and reason to resume its habitual control, and is the result of a temporary excitement . . . rather than of any wickedness of heart or cruelty or recklessness of disposition: then the law, out of indulgence to the frailty of human nature, or rather in recognition of the laws upon which human nature is constituted, very properly regards the offense as of a less heinous character than murder, and gives it the designation of manslaughter.' "

I wonder what "adequate or reasonable provocation" the jury thought Roberta provided that made Bradley, as it would have made any ordinary man "of fair or average mind or disposition," be so suddenly overcome by passion that he would beat her to death. The law goes on to say that "in determining whether the provocation is sufficient or reasonable, ordinary human nature ... should be taken as standard," unless, the law adds, "the person whose guilt is in question be shown to have some peculiar weakness of mind or infirmity of temper, not arising from wickedness of heart or cruelty of disposition."

So, perhaps the choice of manslaughter rather than murder was made not due to reasonable provocation, but because they felt Bradley's passion arose from some peculiar weakness or infirmity of temper. I am glad the law is so confident of the distinction between weakness and wickedness. The sentence for manslaughter is usually less than a quarter of that for murder.

■ ■

The court secretary calls Michael on Wednesday morning, because he is a reporter and is on her phone list of courtesy calls, to tell him that the verdict will be handed down that day. We take a taxi over; the taxi driver tells us he has been following the case in the papers and Page is clearly guilty. In the papers that day a black teenager has been sentenced to fifteen years for selling cocaine. Brad is sitting in the hall when we get there, reading *The Hobbit*. No one has told him that the jury has reached its verdict; he is sitting in the hall as he has been every day they were out deliberating. It has been a week thus far; last time, he waited three. We tell him what we were told and he goes to a pay phone and calls Amy. And then the court is called to order and the jury files in and the TV cameras crouch forward and everyone hushes and the foreman hands the slip of paper to the bailiff and the bailiff hands it to the judge who looks at it and hands it back and the bailiff walks over to her desk and reads: "We find the defendant guilty ..."

Brad begins to scream, his countenance crumbling, covering his face with his hands. "No, no," he screams, "oh God, no," as the wailing sound, unearthly, thin and blue, fills the room. I remember they had discussed during the trial the fact that Brad wails instead of sobs, and whether that constituted genuine emotion. The bailiff asks the jury one by one if this was their decision. It is difficult to hear them reply through the sound of moaning. Mr. Peretti, looking sorry, puts his arm around Brad's shoulders. The

TV cameramen move in, waiting for him to look up so that they can get a good shot of his face. Amy, sitting next to Mr. Page in the front row, begins to sob hysterically, and Brad gets up and puts his arms around her. She buries her face in his chest and he leads her, her shoulders still shaking, out of the room. "It's like watching a wounded animal dissected," a reporter says, his hands on his stomach. And the phrase stays with me for several minutes and I realize with nausea that one would not dissect the wounded, only the dead. Mr. Burr tells the larger circle of cameras around him that he is very pleased; the Lees, he says, feel they can finally put their daughter to rest. Someone asks him if he feels sorry for Page. Not after having watched, these past three years, the horrendous suffering of the Lees. "Horrendous," he repeats, "the snuffing out of the life of their youngest daughter." There was "not a fact, not a single fact," Jack Page tells reporters. "It was a trial by innuendo and sneers and upturned lips," he says. Mr. Peretti tells a group of reporters that a mistake has been made.

"It happens," he says flatly. He no longer has a professional obligation to defend Brad; if anything, it seems unprofessional to question the unanimous decision of the jury. I ask Michael if he thinks that means Mr. Peretti actually believes in Brad's innocence.

"I mean he's not being paid to say it anymore," I say anxiously.

"I know," says Michael, "and they did convict him without any evidence, but—" he says, opening his hands and shrugging.

"Yeah," I say, looking at him again, feeling the lump of doubt in my palm, small and grainy, like the grain of a mustard seed, the smallest of seeds, immaterial almost. But it's merely the doubt, perhaps, that you always carry with you, that things might be different than you think they are, and that whatever you think they are now, if you thought a little longer you would think of something else—neither the Man with the Van nor Brad, but some third possibility—and had you waited some more you would know what it is. The doubt is the doubt that they knew nothing more than they knew the last time he was tried, and last time they decided that they didn't know enough. But Michael buys me breakfast afterward, and I order a Bloody Mary, and by the time breakfast is over I've forgotten about it, and I think of how, as the jury filed out, Mr. Page had leaned forward and hissed: "It is an evil thing which has been done."

Bradley Page at verdict.

The sentencing takes place early in June. A range of sentences is possible; the D.A. says that the Lees request the maximum. They are not vindictive people, he says, but they want the maximum punishment. He reads passages from letters each member of the family has written him, stating this. Veronica describes how her life has been destroyed: she quit work, dropped out of graduate school at M.I.T., was abandoned by her boyfriend of seven years. She also talks about how close she and Brad were during the search: she held his hand when they received word that the body had been found in the park. "While waiting for the identification of the body, I was holding the hands that killed her," she writes. Mr. Lee writes that at the very least Page should spend three and a half years in jail—the amount of time he and his family have endured the agony of uncertainty waiting for the trial to conclude. He also writes about Mrs. Lee. He once saw a dog hit by a car, he says, and he remembers how it looked, humped with pain, limping in a circle, unable to cry out. He has frequently recalled the image, he says, in seeing his wife's suffering. Mrs. Lee's letter is not read.

But the district attorney's office has also received letters on behalf of Bradley Page—sixty letters, I read later—from his friends and family and relations, expressing shock. Mr. Page writes that the time he feels the saddest is when he sees Brad with his son. As a father himself, he knows the judge will understand these feelings. Brad himself has also written a letter. He says that he did not kill Bibi, but that he "takes full responsibility for the action" of leaving her in the park. "Those actions were immature, and lacked aware- ness . . . ," he says. "I am pained and truly repentant for my . . . indiscretion and poor judgment that led to Bibi Lee's death. I fear for my sanity, safety—mostly from myself at present—and from unknown punishment from individuals and institutions yet to come." Mr. Peretti writes: "Either he killed her or he didn't. . . . If he didn't, his position is perfectly appropriate. If he did, he is not consciously aware of it. He genuinely believes he is innocent."

Mr. Peretti asks the judge that Brad not be sent to jail at all, but do community service instead. He is capable of being a produc- tive member of society, he says; he has proven that through his exemplary behavior in the past three years. He clearly poses no threat; "Don't destroy Page's life by sending him to state prison," he says. Besides, he has a wife and baby; he has other lives to think about now. Mr. Burr says the idea that anyone's life would be destroyed by going to prison is ridiculous. "He did more than take the life of a young girl," Mr. Burr says. "He destroyed a family." As if the family were the most important thing, I think.

The judge sentences him to six years because, he says, he has seen no sign of remorse in the defendant.

Under the community service program, however, he will be eligible for parole in two years. He will file an appeal, of course, and the sentence will not begin unless the appeal is denied, and it will take at least a year to determine that. Amy cries again as he is handcuffed and led away, although Brad is quiet.

"You have condemned," says Mr. Page, "the best and gentlest soul in the courtroom."

Examiner / Kim Komenich

Bradley Page reacts as he is convicted of voluntary manslaughter in slaying of Roberta 'Bibi' Lee

Page convicted of killing Bibi Lee

'Oh, my God — I didn't do it,' he sobs to jury after hearing its finding

By Don Martinez
OF THE EXAMINER STAFF

OAKLAND — Bradley Page, sobbing hysterically upon his conviction of voluntary manslaughter, proclaimed to jurors as they filed out of a tense courtroom Wednesday that he hadn't killed Roberta "Bibi" Lee in November 1984.

The lanky defendant crumpled on the shoulder of defense attorney Gene Peretti and moaned, "Oh, my God — I didn't do it," as court clerk Jennifer Hodges read the guilty verdict following 5½ days of deliberation.

It was the dramatic end to Page's second two-month trial, which centered on the bludgeoning death of the popular, 21-year-old UC-Berkeley student.

Her decomposed body was found buried in a shallow grave in thick shrubs five weeks after she vanished while jogging with Page in the Redwood Regional Park area of the Oakland hills.

The 27-year-old defendant had been acquitted of first- and second-degree murder in the first trial, but the jury had deadlocked on manslaughter, which the second jury unanimously agreed upon.

The jurors said they were unable to find evidence beneficial to Page, according to prosecutor Kenneth Burr, who huddled with the panel after the verdict was returned.

Jurors said several factors pointed to Page's guilt, including:

● His conduct in leaving Lee, his girlfriend at the time, in the remote park area after they separated when she jogged down a different trail.

● His reportedly dwindling participation in the five-week, statewide search for Lee organized by her campus friends.

Witnesses who organized the huge search for Lee testified that Page's participation had decreased as the weeks progressed.

● Page's confession to Oakland

— See PAGE, back page

TWO FATHERS IN 'BIBI' LEE SLAYING SHARE SORROW, GRIEF OF TRAGEDY

The Associated Press

Father's Day is likely to be painful for both Francis Lee and Jack Page, as one recalls his daughter who was beaten to death by her boyfriend and the other contemplates life for his son, who was convicted of the crime.

Lee's daughter, Roberta "Bibi" Lee, was beaten to death in November 1984 after jogging in Redwood Regional Park in Oakland with Bradley Page. In 1986, Page was acquitted of first-degree and second-degree murder. He recently was convicted of voluntary manslaughter and sentenced to six years in prison. He is free pending appeal.

The fathers of Page and Lee said they harbor no ill will toward one another, and said each has suffered intensely because of the tragedy.

Lee, formerly a computer science professor at the Massachusetts Institute of Technology, said his previously good health has declined and he has resigned from MIT.

He said he has been hospitalized five times since his 21-year-old daughter's death and stepped down from MIT "after realizing that I would never be able to teach and do research at my previous level of performance."

His wife, Teresa, "cannot conduct her life without the use of anti-depressant medication," Lee said. He and his family, who sat through every day of each of Page's two trials, have gone through individual and group counseling.

"We are just trying to put our lives back together," Lee said.

He said he also feels bad for Jack Page.

"I sympathize with him," he told the *San Francisco Examiner* in a telephone interview from his Lexington, Mass. home. "It was his son who did this terrible, terrible thing . . . I don't think his son told him everything."

But Page, a journalism instructor at Merritt College in Oakland, insists his 27-year-old son didn't kill "Bibi" Lee.

"I still think my son is innocent. I think this is a miscarriage of justice," he said, criticizing the media coverage of his son's trials.

"The people covering the story know, at one level or another, that by this time they have given their readers a pretty firm notion of the defendant's guilt . . . What's more, they are probably pretty well convinced themselves."

Since the slaying, Bradley Page's mother died of cancer. He has married and is the father of a 2-year-old son.

"My own feelings of sadness seem to grow deepest when I see Brad with his son, Ky," Jack Page wrote to Alameda County Superior Court Judge Martin Pulich, who tried the case.

"As a father yourself," he said. "I know you can readily understand the hurt this tragic affair has engendered—for the Lees and for us."

Bradley Page was one of the thousands of volunteers and law enforcement officials who participated in the search for Lee, who initially was reported missing by Page when she failed to return home after the jogging exercise. Almost 50,000 fliers with Lee's photograph were distributed nationwide before the body was found five weeks later.

PART 9

A New Story: Memory

■ ■

*"A man who dies at the age of thirty-five," remarked
Moritz Heimann once, "is at every point of his life a man
who died at the age of thirty-five." Nothing is more dubious
than this sentence—for the sole reason that the tense is wrong.
A man who dies at thirty-five will appear to remembrance
at every point in his life as a man who dies at the age of
thirty-five. In other words, the statement that makes no sense
for real life becomes indisputable for remembered life.*

—Walter Benjamin
The Storyteller

CHAPTER 1

The Story

> . . . *But narratives and lives (like descriptions and their objects) are different sorts of things: my life is not in English, a good life often makes a bad story, my death is gratuitous.*

> —Richard Moran
> *"The Narrated Life"*

Here's a Chinese saying that comes to mind: "Have mercy on me, O Beneficent One. I was angered for I had no shoes; then I met a man who had no feet."

Cheerful, eh? Cheerful and cheering. Somehow the thought that things could be worse never carried much weight with me.

Are you disappointed in me? I hope not. Your letter didn't sound as if you were. I HOPE NOT. I've been mulling things over, going round and round. And feeling like there's not much I can do now that we're bi-coastal again, except worry and be chagrined and ask you. I did try to call you from the airport, but your mother obviously didn't tell you.

Speaking of "bi," I'm still enmired in the Problem of the Two Boyfriends (sounds like a Chinese proverb). And today I'm wearing a button I found which says: "Dare To Be Androgynous." Something to mull over. . . .

Your letter made me feel good, it did.

"Wait a minute," interrupts Claudia, "you can tell me about your life anytime you want, and I'm perfectly happy to listen, but I don't see what it has to do with Roberta, or why it always has to have something to do with Roberta."

"Everything has to do with her, it has to, it does. Because we were so similar, you see—our stories were *the same.*"

"I don't think you are particularly similar," Claudia says, "and, as it happened, I don't think your lives have turned out similarly, either."

"Claudia!"

"Look, my best friend and I used to dress alike in fourth grade too, so we could pretend we were identical. When you get older you discover that there are other ways of being close to people."

"There are?"

"Oh God, Melanie," she says, "you know that."

■ ■

"So what's the story?" asks my friend Lisa. "I don't understand. How do you feel about it now that's different? Like with Roberta— was she doomed or wasn't she? Sometimes you talk about her as if she was doomed, and sometimes that's the *old* way of thinking."

"I don't think she was doomed," I say. "I think she died. Doomed is what characters are; I don't think of her as a character anymore. I think things just conspired to make her *look* like a character.

"She did die of course," I say, "and she did feel as if she was going to and saw herself as a person who would—doomed, dreading, depressed—so it was as if the plot and the character meshed, and meshing seems like a storylike thing. She was depressed and then she died, and these two things became coupled, and the more you think about it the deeper the linkage becomes, and you forget that actually they coincided only carelessly, and easily might not have. She was depressed, of course, but in a way she didn't mind it that way. It made the statement she wanted to make about certain things in her life at that time—like family and school—and when the situation changed, as it would have, she would have changed her statement. Remember how Roberta once asked Brad how he felt about her, and he said she looked sexy in black? Well, it's like that—she did look sexy in black. She was scared sometimes, and depressed, and it was depressing at times, but it was also funny and seductive and ironic, and suited somehow to adolescence. It's a classic adolescent persona. It would eventually have ceased to serve and been replaced. Claudia once told me how she had gone on holiday at the seashore when she was little, and she hadn't been playing with all the other ten-year-olds, so this friend of the family finally took her aside and asked her what the matter was. Claudia told her she didn't know, she felt sad or tired or something. The friend nodded and told her that she had *angst* and some very important people like Goethe had had it. And small Claudia asked, 'Really?' and instantly brightened.

"Even November fourth could so easily have been different. She was unhappy, she went running, she died. What is the connection between these things? What do they *mean?* She was picked up by a man with a van: *she put herself into the hands of dangerous strangers.* She was murdered by her boyfriend: *the dangerous stranger is someone she knew.* You think and think and pretty soon you have discovered all these secret connections and hidden meanings. She was depressed and then she got involved in this bad relationship, because she was likely to be involved with that kind of person, and he murdered her because that was the kind of person he was, and it was all beautiful and inevitable. And Roberta becomes Rosamunde, the Dead Girl, and I am the Little Match Girl and Brad is the Bad Boyfriend and Adam is the Saint, and Bob is —mmm—the Chorus maybe. But it's all fictionalized. I remember Claudia saying to me once, frustrated, when I had just finished convincingly explaining the cast of characters: 'Look, Mel, I don't care what you say, I just know it has to have something to do with your world view because I'm a perfectly perceptive person too and *I* don't know any saints or doomed people—and neither does anyone else.'

"I wasn't exactly wrong," I say. "Roberta wasn't not doomed, and Bradley certainly isn't good, and Adam is not *un*saintly, but it's also true that these things are true because they were true for me. I forgot that: how much I read in all the time, when actually she kind of liked being depressed as well as was depressed, and I was unhappy and happy with Adam, and all I thought about Brad when I met him was that he was pretty, and that I don't know what happened between them, and never will.

"And I wanted to forget, too, how it really was because I thought that fictionalizing was the way to make things more meaningful. I didn't know that the meaning of meaning can be that meaning is uncertain, or that the real story could be that we don't know what the story is, and that that is sufficient. Maybe it was an accident; maybe it had to be; maybe however it worked out, it would have worked out badly, and however she died, she would have died young—and maybe that's all nonsense. There's no way to know—and there's no need to know.

"It's better murky," I say. "It's—mmm—a modern fiction."

"But still a fiction?"

"No, not a fiction," I say. "It's so hard not to keep talking about it that way. I don't mean to, though. There's a story I think of sometimes which is about just exactly that. It's from *I Never Promised You a Rose Garden*, about a young woman called Deborah, who is struggling to recover from a mental illness. The story is a story that her psychiatrist tells Deborah's mother, to help her, I suppose. Her psychiatrist is German, and was practicing in Germany during the Nazi regime. One of her patients was a Jew who had been sent to a mental institution because he would practice the most terrible tortures on himself, exactly like Nazi tortures. When the psychiatrist worked with him, she discovered that he did it, of course, precisely because he was afraid that this would be done to him.

"At that point in the book Deborah's mother asks anxiously, Well, then what happened? The psychiatrist tells her that he got well eventually, and was let out of the hospital. And she asks: *But then what happened?* And the psychiatrist replies: Oh, he died in Dachau.

"That is exactly the way I feel about the whole thing. I wasn't wrong about the things I used to think—the truth isn't different in the sense that *it wasn't something else.* She was found in a shallow grave and Adam did marry someone else and I did lose my two favorite people, and no one would say that this is any less serious than I thought it was—but I feel it differently now. It's like the difference between fictional horror and real horror—between the man inflicting the tortures on himself in imitation of real tortures, and the real tortures. I used to spend all my time being afraid of imaginary things so I wouldn't have to be afraid of the real ones, which happened. Just like I used to spend all my time thinking about the meaning of what happened so I wouldn't have to think about how bad it really was.

"It's easier to think about fiction and the construction of fictions and anything likewise elaborate than the feeling that lies beneath. All the simple things, which you would think someone would naturally feel right away, I never got a chance to feel. I only felt the exaggerated versions—the story themes. I said all these things, but I never got to say the plain ones, like my friend Roberta was an especially wonderful person and had the loveliest glossiest hair."

"Unhuhn," says Lisa. "I get really tired of you talking about everything in terms of reading and writing."

"I used to have this idea I would think about all the time: that there was a book somewhere where the story of my life was written down. I mean I have the story of the past in my diaries, but this would have the whole story, so I could read ahead and see all the new chapter titles *and find out everything that was going to happen.* The only catch was that I never got a copy, so I had to spend all my time imagining what would be in it were I to read it and know what to do, and I kept worrying I would guess the wrong thing and fuck up the narrative. I came up with all sorts of motifs that would be in it and little illustrating parables—stolen mainly from fairy tales. So anyway, I finally decided there is no book. There is no book, and it's not a story."

"So how do you feel about it now?" Lisa asks. "I mean I've noticed that so much of what you talk about seems to be Adam said but then you talked to Bob and he said, and you read this poem and had this thought, and do I think it's the right thought, and I always feel like telling you: you know it's your story and you can feel about it any way you want. So, anyway, Mel, how d'you feel now?"

"I don't know," I say, getting worried, as I always do when people ask me that: "I couldn't say."

CHAPTER 2

Opening a Window and Lighting a Candle

"I will not forget. See, I have carved you in the palm of my hand."

—Isaiah 49:16

Me too.
Roses,
Roberta

It is cold out tonight: for an early-summer day it seems unusually cold. I look out the window of my bedroom; even through the pane I can see the cold plainly. I press my fingers against it; they become cold, and I press harder. I stand there for several minutes, trying to figure out how cold it is. Finally, I walk past my parents' bedroom in my white nightgown and go downstairs and open the front door. It is dark out; I can't see anything in the darkness, but I can feel the cold on my bare shoulders. There is a nice moon above; it floats through the trees and doesn't glint on anything because there is nothing to glint on. If there were gravestones and this were a graveyard, it would glint there so that you could read the inscriptions on the stones. Roberta is outside tonight. She isn't cold though, of course, she isn't cold.

It's not even that I miss her that much, I explain to nobody in particular, I just don't want her to be cold. I go up to my room and stare at the window a long time, trying to decide whether it would help to open it. I read somewhere that when a Gypsy dies, the Gypsies open a window and light a candle. I could open a window right now, of course, but I don't think it would help. I'm not sure, but I don't think so.

■ ■

"I don't understand," says the therapist. "What about windows?"

"Well, the Gypsies," I explain, because I always explain things in terms of other things, "the Gypsies, when someone dies, open a window to let the spirit out and then light a candle to tempt it to return and to keep the memory bright. They want the spirit to feel remembered, but still free to come and go. That way the dead person doesn't feel shut out or shut in and something is lost and something remains. So—it's like that. I don't want her to feel shut out.

"It's like," I say, trying to think of what it is like, "it's like in *Wuthering Heights*. You know how the ghost of Catherine comes back and she's trying to get in but the stranger is sleeping in her room, and he won't let her in. She keeps clawing at the window, and finally he takes her wrists and runs them along the jagged edge of the broken window until they bleed and she goes away. And it's *the meanest thing*—" I say, getting upset. "He won't let Catherine in because he's afraid of her, and she has to stay outside on the cold miserable damp moor—

"Have you read *Wuthering Heights?*" I ask, suddenly distracted.

"Now, Melanie," she asks in her don't-switch-the-subject-to-books tone: "I want to hear how you feel about it."

"Oh—I don't know. Like that, I think. I feel just like that. I don't want Roberta to be shut out in the rain and dark, as if she were a ghost no one would let inside because it was too dark and dead and . . . lonely."

"Let me get this straight," she says finally, "since our hour is almost over. You don't want her to be—lonely? Is that it?" she asks quizzically.

"Do you think the dead are lonely?"

"What could you do to make her not lonely?" she asks.

"I don't know," I say, beginning to cry at the place where I always begin to cry. "I have no idea."

■ ■

I am sitting in a dark crowded movie theater with Tom and
Edmund and Ari watching *Robocop*. It is set in the future, and it is
about a policeman who is made into a robot and blows away lots
of criminals. First he has to die, though; that is how he gets turned
into a robot. I know he is going to die at the beginning of the
movie, so I sit there, pulling my black miniskirt down and hugging
my knees, waiting for it to happen. I look over at Edmund; his face
is tensed; he must be waiting too. They get Robocop in an abandoned building, and there are three of them, and one of them
knocks his gun out of his hand and they have him on the ground
and the mean one steps on his chest and the music hurts, loud as a
heartbeat, and I get up to leave.

"Hey," Ari says, catching my skirt. "What's wrong? Don't go,
Mel. Here—I'll trade places with Edmund and hold your hand and
nurse you through it."

"Cops don't like me," the mean-faced criminal is drooling.
"So I don't like cops," he explains logically, blowing Robocop's
arm off.

"It's a cartoon," whispers Tom, leaning across. "Meaningless,
gratuitous, unadulterated violence."

"Does it hurt?" one of them asks as he presses the trigger again
amidst laughter.

"I'm going to fucking blow you away," the criminal says to
Robocop. Robocop, who is not yet a robot but only a smallish,
blue-eyed young man named Murphy, whimpers, no. His face is
very white. The music thickens.

I sit down. The criminals are speaking accurately; in less than
five minutes Robocop is going to die. Nothing is going to happen
between now and then to stop them. I know; this is the plot: *Ari
told me before we came, and he read a review of it.* Robocop is going to
be murdered, I say to myself. Look look: this is what it is like to be
murdered. The music becomes too loud to breathe. I look at
Robocop's face and he looks frightened too, but I remember that
when you are murdered there is no music, so you have to discount
all the fear that comes from the music and the mood of the music.
The criminal puts his finger on the trigger and bullets spill out and
into Robocop's face, and the man keeps holding the gun and firing,
moving all the way down Robocop's body, and it goes on for what
must be I think several minutes, and then it is over and Robocop

lies still and sleeping and bloody on the floor. I close my eyes in absolute relief, thinking.

So I was wrong all this time about how scary it is. It seems scary: it seems more and more scary and more and more as if something is going to happen, and then you realize that it is going to happen and it is not less but also not one note more scary than that. They are stepping on your chest and threatening you and help is too far away, and there is only one thing they're stepping on your chest about because there is only one thing they can take. Your life. Difficult to imagine, neither larger nor smaller. She died. Her heart stopped. No more, not more. The criminals hustle out of the building and leave him to the stillness, and the music saddens, and I relax in its tears and catch a glimpse of Tom's face and see that he looks sad and relieved too. The sadness lasts all the way through the movie, through the long complicated revenge that Robocop, the metal robot reconstructed from the shattered body, eventually enacts on them—to try to dissuade himself, I suppose, from the knowledge that there is no revenge because he died. They took it away; they can't give it back. Even if he makes them sorry—even if he does the same thing to them and makes them as sorry as they can be—even anything you can think of—even so, he will not live again. We get up and walk out to the car.

"Your buddy DeWitt said that it was about humanity flickering through the mask of technological society, as embodied in Detroit," Ari pipes up in the still night air. "A deconstructionist allusion," he continues more confidently, "you know, a copy of a copy of a copy, I can't remember of what but it's made by some famous Dutch movie director as an in-joke, I think—"

"On postmodernism," I say, because that is what people always say. "And futility."

"Yeah," says Tom, fishing for DeWitt's review in the paper. "Listen to this, guys. When DeWitt saw *Robocop* he 'got off on how it made people crazy, on how they screamed and laughed and pounded their chairs . . . But apart from its satire, *Robocop* belongs to the vilest strain of the modern action genre. I don't know whether to laugh or to cry about how much I loved every brutal perverse demagogic minute of it. The corruption is painless.'

" 'The corruption is painless,' " repeats Tom, "that's a great phrase."

"It's not true," I say. "It's not true."

And then: "Hey, Melsky, I'm sorry. I didn't know it was going to be that kind of movie." Ari always calls me Melsky as if I were Polish.

"You did too, but—oh, it's all right. I mean it was lousy—it was definitely a lousy cheap miserable movie—but it's okay. I didn't mind watching it."

And it is not until long after I'm back in my room, and Tom has played for us on his guitar and I have said sing lullabies and he has sung lullabies, working our names into them—*good night, my friends, Melanie and Edmund, good night, good night*—and I have settled Edmund on the couch where he is staying and closed the door to my bedroom and brushed my hair and gotten into my nightgown, that I start to cry. I gasp, trying to find breath, I am crying so hard. "I'm just so sorry it happened, Roberta," I sob. "I'm so fucking sorry."

Looking up, I realize that was the first time I ever said that. I knew it would be a simple thing when I finally got to feel something.

■ ■

I am just getting ready to go out for the evening in the dream when Roberta knocks on the door to my room. I am almost finished dressing; I am poised before my mauve leather jewelry box, its white satin insides displaying different pieces of jewelry, and wondering which I should put on. I am wearing a plain black dress, which is a nice dress with the right jewelry and a plain dress otherwise. She enters before I have had a chance to tell her to come in, and stands behind me. She is also wearing a black dress, although I know that her black dress means that she is dead, whereas my black dress means that I have a date. She is not wearing any jewelry, though, and it occurs to me that soon she is going to go back to the graveyard and be buried and dead. Her dress will rot and her hair will turn to dust, and she will be a skeleton. And then when people dig her up all they will see is bones. They won't know that she is not just any skeleton—she is special, loved, my friend; no one will know that this skeleton is my beautiful friend Roberta. They are all the same, the dead; I would have to give her something different if I wanted her to be different— something of mine. It would have to be so beautiful and lasting that if they didn't find her body for a thousand

years it would still be there, shining. I would have to give her my necklace.

I can't give her that, I say. Why, my grandmother gave it to me. It wouldn't be right to give away something of my grandmother's. I have to keep it in her memory.

I look at Roberta. Her face is impassive, heavy, sculptured. She does not say anything.

Give it to Roberta. Give it away.

I fondle another necklace, pointing out that it is also gold, although I know that it is solid metal and diamondless, and not set with stones gleaming and clear.

"Do you like this one?" I ask her miserably.

"I don't care," she says, exasperated. "I have to go."

I look at the other necklace. I want to give it to her and be done with it, but I can't; I hate to think of people digging her up and seeing that she is someone to whom people gave their second-best things. It might make them think that she is not loved best and above all.

I look at Roberta again. She is impatient, bored. She has to go, she reminds me, she has to go.

I pick up the other one but it also makes me sad. It will be buried underground, lightless. A waste, not even a jewel, just a stone in dirt lost among the dead. What if it is never dug up and found again? Why would you give your best jewel to one who is dead? She doesn't care; she is going to leave in a minute no matter which you choose. She is dead dead and nothing you do matters any longer.

Go on. Risk it then. Even if it means nothing, at least you will have tried. Even if she doesn't care and no one ever knows, it is better to have given it. You'll get nothing from keeping it—it will be worthless as soon as she leaves. You'll never wear it again, you'll be ugly, your date bad.

I have to go, says Roberta. She opens the door, and undecided—time, as always, ended before I have come to conclusion—feeling in either hand the weight of a necklace, I awaken.

■ ■

Claudia and I are walking back from dinner. For no particular reason things are heavy that day, and I keep fighting tears. Finally Claudia asks what's wrong, and I say: "Nothing new."

"Look, I just know you're going to be happy someday," she
says fiercely. "I'm just sorry you have to go through all this now. I
wish I could go through it instead for a little while, and you could
take a break.

"Like napping," she adds hopefully. And then: "Why don't
we try it? I'll be unhappy about Roberta and Adam and all that
stuff, and you can have the night off and be me. If you need
something to do, you can wonder why they haven't handed my
thesis back, write my Aunt Rebecca, or mend my carpet."

Claudia has this ancient Persian carpet that unravels itself day
by day, and that she is forever stitching at because she can't
decide to buy a new one because she's not sure whether it's
important to have a nice carpet or whether that is bourgeois. We
had a bet about happiness once where the winner would receive
her heart's desire, although it would take at least ten years to see
who was right, and Claudia was worried she wouldn't have anything to want, and then she thought about it and decided she
would want a new carpet. She has devoted her entire college
career, she says sometimes, to mending this one.

"You can't eat anything, though," she tells me, contemplating
the terms of the deal, "because I might want to be going on a diet
soon.

"And between us," she adds confidentially, "I think writing
Aunt Rebecca will be the most fun."

"If I gave you my troubles you would take good care of
them?" I ask suspiciously. "And give them proper attention?" She
is one of my few friends who can maintain a fiction long enough to
have a whole conversation in it.

"And you would definitely return them?" I say. The funny
thing is, even as I'm pretending to be suspicious, I realize, I actually
am a little suspicious—worried somehow that if I gave them to her,
if I stopped being unhappy about my losses for an evening, I might
not get them back again and then they would be *lost* losses. And I,
who always think of loss as inflicted upon me, realize that of
course it isn't. Or maybe it was at first, but by now it is something
that I want, choose, and wouldn't give away even for the night.
White bones, cheekbones, sad things, forgotten things—things, remembered things.

"But you know," she adds, "it isn't even like it's just pretend.
They really are shared things. I think of your troubles when I'm
alone anyway."

"You do?" I ask.

"All the time. I mean obviously Roberta died long before I met you, but I think about her too. I used to imagine meeting her— how we'd have lunch the first time, and we'd both be a little hostile, and it would be a little awkward, but as soon as it was over we'd decide we liked each other, and each tell you separately. If you died now, when I thought of you I would definitely think of her too."

"You would?"

"Of course I would," she repeats, in both her real and story voice.

■ ■

Claudia and I are having tea and talking about our futures. In the middle of the conversation it occurs to me, though, that we can't keep talking as if we were the same and there were no differences between us, because there is a difference. She is still infinitely hopeful; the definitive events of her life are yet to come. She wrinkles her nose thoughtfully and reminds me of our bet. (The bet for which Claudia might collect the carpet is about whether I'm going to be happy in ten years. I say I have to be happily married for her to win, and she says I might be a lesbian by then, or a monk, so the bet only refers to whether I think I'm happy at the time. I say I need a ring and a small gray house and three daughters named after flowers—Lily, Rosie, and Poppy or Fleur, or she loses. She says my ideas about happiness are pretty incredibly fucking conventional, not to mention somewhat unrealistic, and I say yes, and she says that's another thing that might change, and I say never.) It's a lopsided bet, of course, but we can't bet about whether Claudia is going to be happy because she's already happy.

"But anything can still happen," she says, not quite understanding. "You can be depressed about now, but there's no need to be depressed about later."

"But the old things can't unhappen," I say.

"To begin with, Mel," she says emphatically, "I absolutely refuse to let you mention Adam, your mother, and Roberta in the same breath. They have nothing whatsoever to do with each other. Lots of people have family problems, Roberta was unlucky, and you broke up with one of your boyfriends. Not everyone does marry their first love; people outgrow each other, or they outgrow the kind of love they have together. You can't expect that the things you have as a young girl, you'll have as an adult. Things *change*—that's what growing up is about.''

"But these were promises—''

"So you promised them then and now you make new promises,'' she says. "Renegotiate. Right now everything is lumped together in your mind under the general category of loss and pain and despair and stuff, but as time goes by you'll separate things out and rearrange them. You'll see. You'll always miss Roberta, and you'll always miss Adam, and you may always have some sadness about your family, but it will feel different because you'll imagine them differently. And once it is packaged differently, it won't feel so burdensome.''

"But it will always be the same amount of loss,'' I say, "so it will always be as heavy. The way the murder of a whole person is always the loss of the whole person.''

"But you'll be bigger, so it will feel smaller.''

"Hmm,'' I say, standing up.

"No, wait, I don't want you to go home sad,'' she says, standing up and taking my arm. "Let's—I know—'' with sudden inspiration, "let's go get our picture taken at the photo booth at Urban Outfitters.''

We walk over and the picture booth is broken and closed and there is a sign on it saying: *"No, we don't know where else in the Square they have one,"* in coy fashionable style. I look at it for a few minutes and think that they never used to have signs that were quite this aggressive. I must already be somewhat bigger, I realize, because it doesn't feel nearly as heavy as it used to, and it's not even that I think about them less. It's a funny idea, people getting bigger, and I can't imagine how it has happened—I don't recall having had any strong brave revelatory enlightening or even positive experiences in the past couple of years. So I keep walking, but yes, I must be at least a little larger because it does—I think it does—yes, I am almost sure—it does definitely feel lighter tonight. Claudia and I go to the drugstore, and we try to buy a camera ourselves, and the man keeps telling us that they just got in some good cameras, but it finally becomes clear that this is not true so she buys me some heart-shaped candies with writing on them and I buy her *Cosmopolitan*. I shake the hearts out of the box and hold them in my palm, small and intricately shaped, like jewels, like griefs, like candle drippings from a memory candle you lighted once in a foreign church and thought how pretty they were—so pretty, almost you would have liked to keep one. Almost, I think, fingering the hearts slowly, walking home—almost, except you can't.

■ ■

Cleaning my room one day, I find an old letter from Adam. It is quite out of date, not as out of date as Roberta's letters, but almost, I think, two years old. I reread it.

Dearest,

I'm beginning to get the hang of this computer, but I still like to use the old typewriter sometimes—it would feel disloyal to cast it aside just because some screen winked at me. And anyway, I like it. So today is my 25th birthday, and when I think about it, it is hard to imagine 25 happier years—though I expect and hope that the next 25 will be happier still, and the 25 following that to be even more fun, and as for the 25 after that I'm sure we'll enjoy them.

I went to a birthday party last night for Ed Koren, who is one of the cartoonists, and a great guy. It was a surprise party arranged by his wife, and he actually looked surprised and very happy when we all shouted. There must have been a hundred people there, all in good cheer. It was his 50th, and he didn't seem in the least decrepit. I hope you don't worry about getting old; you will be wonderful and beautiful and kind at every stage.

Tonight we are going out—about twenty of us from the office—to watch Halley's comet from a beach on Long Island. I doubt we'll see much, but I bet we have a good time nonetheless.

At four o'clock in the morning when the D train reaches the end of its run in Coney Island, about 20 men get off and cross the platform into the inbound train. This is where they live. And there are probably a hundred trains running at any given point in the night, so you do the math. . . . It isn't always a happy world, but we shall be happy in it—not by ignoring the sad, but by doing what we can and loving each other. I am the luckiest fellow on earth, mainly because of you.

Adam

I read it a couple times. "It isn't always a happy world, but we shall be happy in it—not by ignoring the sad . . ."

So even Adam, I realize, even whole happy garden-happy Adam, takes sadness into account. You don't have to ignore anything in order to be happy: we shall do what we can. And I, who am so used to thinking of happiness as a small and superficial thing—privileged but parochial—am surprised. He wrote this letter at a very happy time, when we were perfectly happy together—and he still thought of sadness. He wasn't writing about personal sadness, of course, because Adam isn't sad that way, but he still thought of other people's sadnesses. This is where they live: you do the math. He had no idea of the sad things that would happen to me between then and now, and that I would read the letter one day when I was sad and that the things he wrote would seem helpful and true. And too he did not know—he could not know—that he would be one of the sad things, and the sadness would be the sadness that I lost him as well, so that the letter is not really true anymore, or not literally true, just as I am not going to see Roberta again soon as she said sometimes at the end of her letters. It is the sadness that the letter could never be written again because everything it refers to is lost, and the sadness that it is only lost things you read in this way because it is sadness that makes the letter what it is: it is sadness that allows you to read it the way that you do.

■ ■

"But the thing about Kathy," I ask Aunt Pat once again, although we've talked about this before, but I particularly want to know today, "is that you always knew she was going to die, didn't you?"

"Yes," says Aunt Pat, "since she was two."

"And you were never tempted to—give up on her?" I can't believe I've asked, it sounds so cold, but I want to make sure that I know exactly.

"No, sweetie," she replies innocently, unhesitatingly—struggling, I think, to think how to explain. "I used to have this dream—well, not even a dream, but just an image—of Kathy and me swimming across a lake. And at some point it became clear that it was too far to go and we weren't going to make it, and I decided I'd rather stay with her."

"And drown," I say, thinking she was right. It was too far to go; Kathy had a fatal disease. She was born that way. Aunt Pat spent fourteen years with her, and Kathy was this and that and everything to her, and Kathy died. It seems to me it had to have been at least partially a decision: Aunt Pat had a career, but she chose to make Kathy the most important thing. She chose to live this way: she could have chosen the opposite. She could have had other children, or taken up Chinese cooking or become more serious about silk screening—whatever. In one way or another she could have decided she wanted to be attached only to the living— to the people on the shore.

I look at her again, trying to figure out why she doesn't look more bedraggled, like one of the drowned.

"And you aren't—mmm—sorry about it?" I ask carefully, meaning: *you aren't sorry now that you have nothing but sadness left, and other people's children are in college?*

"When Kathy was dying," says Aunt Pat, "I told her how lucky—how incredibly privileged—I felt to be her mother: that it was the best thing that ever happened to me. And it was true.

"Sometimes I'll be with other mothers and I'll think, how come they get to keep their children, and I didn't get to keep mine, but then I'll think about Kathy, and I'll realize I probably got more out of her than some mothers get out of ten children. So no—I don't feel unlucky or regretful, or—no," she says again, to everything I wonder and worry about and waste my time worrying about so often: "I never wonder if it was worthwhile."

■ ■

There is an Indian tale in which a woman takes her dying baby to a guru to ask him to make it well. Bring me, he says, a mustard seed from a house that has never known any sadness, and that will heal it. So the woman sets out and knocks at the door of the first fine house that she comes to.

Oh no, say the people there, you have surely come to the wrong house now. We have no such mustard seed here. And they start to tell her about all the terrible things that have happened to them: their daughter was to marry a man who left her; the man was in love with her younger sister. The younger sister didn't love him, but married him anyway, and the older one drowned in the pond by their house. They had no children; their household was unblessed. And it has stayed unblessed; unblessedness lasts for three generations. *You don't understand,* they say, telling their tales of woe, *poverty isn't the only kind of sadness.* So the woman goes to the next house. However, they too have their own terrible stories: it turns out, in fact, that each house has *its own terrible stories.*

The Gosches' son Johnny was delivering papers on his paper route one September morning in 1982. His father always accompanied him on his route because it was still dark out, but Johnny didn't want him to because he was already twelve, the oldest of all the paperboys. So one day he took their dog Gretchen and left the house early and by the time his parents had awakened he was gone. His father went to look for him, but all the other boys could tell him was that they had seen Johnny being followed by two men. Johnny had said he didn't like the men, he was taking his papers and going home, but the men followed him around the corner and someone had heard a car door slam. I read the story in a magazine: Mrs. Gosch still keeps a light burning on the porch, she says, and Johnny's room is as it was. She sits there sometimes. There is a picture of her, with dark curly hair and face averted slightly, standing by the empty newspaper cart, the only thing that was ever found. It rained the second night, a cold rain; she kept thinking of him, she says, in the rain, wondering if they were still looking for him. The Gosches have followed thousands of leads; they've spent all their money; at night they read child pornography magazines looking for a picture of him. A detective heard about a child auction once where they were selling boys to foreign buyers, and they hired someone to buy him back, but Johnny wasn't on the block that night. People call sometimes and laugh at them: describe the horrible things that could have happened to Johnny, tell them he's dead. The police traced the calls and many were from people in their neighborhood—some children, some adults. Once, after he had been missing six years, they received a letter signed, "Your son, Johnny Gosch." The letter was typed, but Mrs. Gosch said that of all their children, only he would sign it that way. They used to tease him about it: you don't have to tell us your name, they would say, we know who you are.

My roommate Daisy's father died when she was ten. Her mother had left him; he was an alcoholic who lived on a farm in Minnesota. He wandered outside during a blizzard one March, drunken, and froze to death, and they found him a few weeks later, when the snows melted. Daisy told me she remembers her mother telling her, and it meant nothing at all at the time to her: she might as well have been told her father had won the Nobel Prize, she said. But of course it meant things later. It was like being handed a dossier diagnosing all the personality deficiencies and symptoms she would suffer as a result, she said: she doesn't trust men, she's lonely, she smokes, doesn't eat. She used to drink, too, but she has stopped now.

The husband of Caroline Isenberg's sister, Emily, was shot and killed when he was working as a security guard, with a plastic gun at his waist, substituting for someone who had called in sick. And then a few years later Caroline was murdered. The Isenbergs divorced and then her mother died and Emily was estranged from her father, who had not wanted her to marry so young. The Mitchells' child was killed in an accident at an amusement park on a carousel; our neighbors' little girl was retarded and they gave her up for adoption. Her father had wanted to keep her. Anne's mother was stabbed to death in the middle of the day in a park near a busy street by three men who were never caught. Cecil fell out of a tree and by the time he got to the hospital his arm had gangrene and they had to cut it off. Robin's father wanted a boy. Giles's brother and his best friend died in a car accident on a holiday in France. The truck driver who hit them claimed it was their fault; there were no witnesses. My teacher became engaged late in life, and went on a trip to Mexico with her fiancé where he came down with a sudden virus and died; she never met anyone else. And there was another woman I met once whose first husband had gone to Mexico and had picked up a rare blood disease from a dirty needle when he went to a Mexican doctor; he died three years after they married. They had been childhood sweethearts.

Jason's mother married a man she didn't love because she was an immigrant, fleeing in bad circumstances, and needed someone to take care of her; Jason's father abused him. When he grew up, he asked his mother once whether she had ever loved his father, and she told him, Jesus no—she had never even liked him. He repeated that to me, amused: she had never even liked him. A woman told a friend at a party that she had had three children in case two of them died, and then two of them died. Two of Adam's cousins died also, one in a rock-climbing accident and the other another way. All the animals on my mother's family farm died: the horse fell down and broke its leg, the ducks froze on the pond, the pig Bess ate the poison that was meant for the rats, the goat got its head stuck in the milk pail and smothered, and the sheep Alice drowned and the other sheep was so lonely they had to kill it and eat mutton all winter long. My mother's childhood was unhappy.

At the sentencing of one of the men who shot her husband, the man turned around and looked at Emily Isenberg and apologized: I'm sorry, he said, your husband did not need to die. She wrote him a note and gave it to the bailiff to give to him: he was the first person connected with the murder, she said, in all those years who had ever apologized for what happened. He called her collect from the prison and they talked for an hour. When he is up for parole she will be there, she says, supporting his release. She is engaged again now; I read about it. I knew some people would think I was being taken advantage of, she says, but you have to do the right thing for you, I spent all those years being angry, and this is the right thing for me. I cried when I read it: I remember wondering whether I used to cry about stories I read in newspapers, but I can't remember. In Dave's living room hangs an embroidered picture. Stitched in colored thread it says, *"With every good-bye you learn / you learn to say good-bye / you learn."* He is a happy person— complacent, I had thought: I wonder why he keeps it there. The woman in the Indian tale returned to the guru empty-handed, and the baby died.

I think about the story of the mustard seed often. I think, too, how funny it is that I've thought about it so much and it still makes me sad: sad that the baby died, sad that the woman couldn't find such a seed, and sad too that I am now one of the people who wouldn't have had it to give to her. If she knocked on my door, I would send her away. I try to remember a time before this was the case, but I can't: it is so long ago it seems almost imaginary— mythical, storylike—not nearly as real, really, as the story just told.

■ ■

In midsummer, just after the second trial is completed, Mrs. Lee dies. It is early autumn before I learn the news. She was not old, as Mrs. Page was not old when she died just before Bradley was first tried, but Mrs. Lee had been unwell for a long time. I remembered how she had missed one day during the trial; Mr. Lee said she was ill. They had been together each day in the courtroom, holding hands. It is at a pay telephone that I am told that she has died; it is raining; the person wonders I did not know already. As he is explaining, and I am explaining that I had not heard, that no one told me, I remember how Mrs. Lee and I had planned to work on her English together. In China she had studied Chinese literature at the university and planned to teach, but then they had come to America. She had worked in a flower shop for a short time, but she had never learned to speak the language fluently, or to read well. I was not to tell her husband that I helped her, that was important. We had planned, too, to go to Roberta's grave and plant violets. The grave is only a few miles from home and, standing at the funeral in the freezing snow with nothing to hold because I had not brought flowers, I had promised myself I would return often with pansies and snapdragons and pink and yellow tulips, but I never wanted to. I imagined, I think, that I was saving the trip for another time, like feelings to feel when you are older and feel differently. I remember too going over to the Lees' house just before the funeral, and seeing how unnaturally clean and strange with roses it was, huge darkened arrangements covering every surface, each with a white card of grief. Mrs. Lee had plucked out a stem and given it to me—one of their flowers, sent to them by someone else in sympathy. I remember saving the petals and drying them in a book. I made them a tart of strawberries just after the funeral and left it on their doorstep, and when Veronica came to bring back the tin, it was filled with small triangle-cut honey pastries, brushed with nuts. It was a Chinese custom, she told me; her mother never returned a dish empty. I remember too, a few weeks later, I had been leaving their house and she had looked around, and I had kissed her quickly, not wanting her to give me something, and she had seen a bag of oranges lying on the counter. She had taken out an orange and placed it in my palm, and I had put it in my pocket awkwardly and gone outside. As I walked home, leaving bits of the thick rind like a trail to find your way back through the white world, I wondered if oranges were rare in other parts of the world. And looking around at the streets and bent branches, gifted with snow, I remembered it was Christmastime and tasted the bright fruit. Once, in high school, Roberta had been staying late at her computer job and she hated it so much she had gotten scared. She had called her mother, I remember her telling me, and her mother had come and sat with her until it was time to go home. *"I can hear my mother's voice,"* Roberta said to me once. *" 'Oh child,' " she says, " 'oh child,' " but it's no use, it's just no use.*

I had thought all memories would be returned to me eventually. It is not so; there are too many. Nearly all are torn, but handed from the living to the living are things we have said, gestures, the breaking of a fruit in a certain season, a petal from someone else's bouquet, thoughts about language, the things that you wrote, gifts to give before you die.

so mels

humdeedum mel

i got to get going here
as noemi says

"i love you more than i miss you."

happy all hallows eve
"art is a house that tries to be haunted"

—*e. dickinson*

jack o'lanterns

李美化

keep a candle

It is a cold night, tonight. Summer nights are often cold; one forgets that. I look out through the glass of my bedroom window, and press my hands against the pane. She isn't cold of course, she isn't cold.

CHAPTER 3
Memory

Dearest Melanie,

SO it's raining tonight, I'm staring out the window watching the rain open a window into evening, and what I want to say is: I'm sorry. I know it's been rather up and down with us this summer; but it'll be oke. Thank your parents for picking me up, too, that night at Arlington Heights: had they not, I'd probably be there still. Besides, I still have your bicycle, and you've my key, so we are all twined! We shouldn't worry so, about losses and losing. It's tangled, but our lives are twisted thick as hangers on a tree. Let's keep each other's things for a little while longer. That way you can come over anytime you like and pick them up.

Here is a quote for you from Winnie the Pooh.

"Let's go and see everybody," said Pooh. "Because when you've been walking in the wind for miles, and you suddenly go into somebody's house and he says: 'Hallo Pooh, you're just in time for a little smackerel of something,' and you are, then it's what I call a Friendly Day."

Piglet thought they ought to have a Reason for going to see everybody . . .

"We'll go because it's Thursday," he said, "and we'll go to wish everybody a Very Happy Thursday."

So Happy Thursday from me too, and one more small quote too, also chosen especially for you, this one from Thomas à Kempis, who was a good saint.

> *And I offer also for all those whom I have in any way grieved, vexed, oppressed, and scandalized, by word or deed . . . that thou mayest equally forgive us all our sins and our offenses against each other.*

What is she trying to get at in this roundabout way? I'm saying: I'm still yours, I hope you are still mine, things don't get lost, perhaps, as easily as we had thought they did. Will we?

> *With time*
> *and patience*
> *and compassion*
> *we will find one another.*

> > *Roberta*
> > *Bibi*
> > *Rosamunde*
> > *Mei-hua*
> > *B.B.*

> > > > *August, 1984*

I am sleeping over at my friend Lisa's apartment in New York. We have had a good evening: we ordered in Chinese food and watched reruns of soap operas Lisa has taped and then settle on the couch for a long talk. I haven't seen her in a while, so it is a serious talk, and she is telling me about her life and I am thinking a lot, trying to explain how I feel about things. We talk about things that have happened—about Adam and my mother and my family and Brad and plans, and I narrate them in the way I feel like narrating them tonight, and every once in a while she asks a question—a big question about why it happened as it happened and whether it had to happen thus—and I say I don't know, and she says you must know, it's your life, and I hesitate and then make something up, and after a while I begin to wonder if anything I'm saying is true. She asks another question, and then another, and it suddenly occurs to me that if she asks one more question I will have nothing to say. I brush away the thought, though, and keep talking. It recurs: I've done all this talking, and I've had all these realizations, only I can't remember what they are this minute, and the things I do remember don't mean anything tonight. I had so much to tell, and now it's been told, I've forgotten exactly what I said, and the story slips away. I stop, confused, tired, I tell Lisa I am tired.

It is late when we finally get to bed, and I did think I was tired, but I guess I'm not. I lie there, listening to Lisa's breathing, and all of a sudden the old questions, all the terrible hypotheticals with their desperate imperative to know, are upon me and they must be answered, they must be answered tonight.

Am I happy, am I sad, is my life meaningful, why aren't I sleeping? Was Roberta's life meaningful, would I have been happy married to Adam, what if I had died instead of Roberta, how would she be thinking about me right now? Were we alike; would we want the same things for each other? What if it hadn't rained the second night when it rained in the park and the rain washed away the scent and we didn't find her for weeks and the weeks washed away the evidence? How does she feel about having been murdered? Did Brad not love her, did Brad love her and kill her, did Brad not love her but she was killed by someone else? Who are they and why did they do it? Did I really love her or do I only remember it that way? Do my parents really love me or do they just like to tell their friends that they do? Does Adam really love me, does anyone really love me, am I good, am I happy, am I worth loving, do I love anyone, what does Bob think, is my life meaningful, is my life meaningful at all? Are these questions the same; are these questions the right questions?

I sit up and see that the horrible little green glow of the clock says it is after four in the morning. It is past four o'clock and years and years have gone by and you wake up in the middle of the night and you don't know any better than you ever did. *I don't know,* I wail, helpless as a child quizzed on the multiplication tables: *I don't know, I don't know.*

But the questions, I remember, as I have remembered before, have been answered. I decided I didn't need to answer them because—I remind myself, annoyed, as it is annoying when you spend your whole life realizing the same little insights you already realized before—*I don't need to answer them because I have my own feelings about them.* Meaning is uncertain: I opened a window and lighted a candle and discovered feeling, and feeling is important and meaningful, an offering, like a jewel. I might not know who did it or what happened to her, but I know I am mad at whoever it was. I might not know what Roberta was really like, but it doesn't matter because I really loved her and I'm really sorry that she died.

Feelings, other feelings. First you have the story and then you have your interpretations of the story, and then you have the feelings out of which you interpret. Feelings endure. Begin at the beginning: think of Roberta. I try to think of some little thing that she did or said, but I can't, and then I try to picture what she looked like, but I can't do that either, so I try to picture a picture of what she looked like, or even how I used to feel looking at those pictures—I used to feel, I used to feel so much—but I look at the green light of the clock and feel nothing. There is the story and there is the memory of the story, and then you wake up one empty night and you don't have anything. I remember the story of the anthropologist who was trying to find out about the Indian's religion.

"What is the world made of?" the anthropologist asks.

Tell us, tell us what the world is made of. We need to know what you believe. We need to know what other people think the world is made of.

"The world isn't made," the Indian explains patiently. "It rests."

"But what does it rest on?"

"It rests, sahib, on the back of an elephant."

"But what does the elephant rest on?" the anthropologist asks again, with Western persistence.

"It rests on the back of a turtle."

"And what does the turtle rest on?" The story gets a little tedious, although you have to keep listening because you want to know. You can't help it; you need to know what the world is made of and you won't be able to put down the story until you know.

"It rests on another turtle."

"But what does that turtle rest on?"

"Ah, sahib," says the Indian, sighing. "After that it's turtles all the way down."

Turtles all the way down. The story is probably apocryphal. I must go to sleep. Down to what?

No more questions. The Indian had the last line.

Beneath the turtles there is nothing, and no one can tell you anything about it. The sick green light of the clock says five. It is five o'clock and you are awake. Lisa is sleeping, everyone is sleeping, there is no one you can telephone and ask, everyone in the world is sleeping besides you.

I get up and go into the bathroom and lock the door. The medicine cabinet is filled with pills. There is a razor on the edge of the bathtub; Lisa must use it to shave her legs. Emptiness and desolation, boredom and loss. Loss, irreversible loss. Loss of story, loss of memory, loss of feelings about memory. Everything you do, you do to avoid waking up in the green desolation and realizing that you lose everything, and already have. I stand in the bathroom and hold in my hands absolutely nothing. *Nothing, nothing.* You would reach for a razor blade just to have something.

I kneel down on the bathroom floor and press my hands against the walls. There might be a deeper meaning—it might be that this moment, which seems so empty, lies within some larger structure of narrative, but I don't know what it is. I press my hands against the walls and they don't give at all. If there is meaning to meaning, I'm not going to figure out what it is. There are turtles upon turtles; we gave up asking before the Indian explained if there was anything beneath turtles, and how we would know to recognize it.

But in your religion they tell it differently. In your religion you know what is there because you have faith. Faith gives shape to what is there. *Our knowledge is imperfect and our prophecy is imperfect; but when the perfect comes, the imperfect shall pass away. For now we see as through a glass, darkly, but then shall we see face to face. Now I know in part; then shall I understand fully, even as I have been fully understood.*

I look over at the cabinets. Now you see through the glass, then you shall know. *Then you will see face to face. Then.* How do you get to then? I think I am going to get up, but instead I keep kneeling on the clean cold tiles and close my eyes.

Dear God, I say, I return the story. I return the story and the meaning of the story and the need to make meaning of the story. Our knowledge is imperfect and our prophecy is imperfect and I can't do it anymore and I never could and I return it all so I have nothing left.

When you open your eyes you shall have nothing left. You will be alone in the bathroom, with the razor blades and the pills.

Dear God, that time belongs to you. I return it. I can't see face to face. I can't see past the darkness. I thought I could, but it was too hard. Take it back. Please take the story back.

The story will be taken back, and then your life will have no story. If you rest even for a moment from reading and writing you will see by the green light of the clock that nothing is there. If you get up and go to sleep just like nothing happened, then it will be just like—

It will be just like—what? What is it that you're so afraid of?

It will be just like nothing ever did happen. It will be just like Roberta is dead.

But Roberta is dead. I don't even remember what she looks like.

And then, clear as a vision—it must be only a memory, but it appears so clearly I imagine it is a vision—I see her face. The real thing, not a photograph: her face.

So I have been wrong after all about this: it is this many years now, and I still know what she looks like. It hasn't ebbed or blurred or faded or done any of those things they tell you pain and dead friends and memories of youth all do eventually. I realize, too, that I must have known what she looked like all along, only I was thinking too hard to see. There is a place where everything is intact, and you can put your hands on it, not often but sometimes. You push and you push and you think there is nothing there, but it opens up and you realize you remember perfectly what she looks like. You remember everything, everything is there, nothing has been lost, only you were too busy trying to find it to realize that it was always there. Not a word, her face. You can pick up the story anytime you want to feel, and you can put the story down anytime you get tired because before and after and there all along there was something besides the story; there was her face. Dear God, her face.

We commend the body into the ground and the spirit into Thy hands, Lord, where it always was. The plot belonged to many things, but the meaning, which was what I was so worried about, the meaning was with God all along. *In His hands.* I didn't have to write hundreds of pages to remember; I never forgot. *"I'm still yours, I hope you are still mine."* She *told* me I hadn't lost her. How could I not have remembered that she answered the anxiety of that last question—*will we?* before she even voiced it? *"Things don't get lost, perhaps, as easily as we had thought they did."* All that was left was for me to answer that she hadn't lost me either. I could have said that years ago. *Love never ends. As for prophecies, they will pass away; as for tongues, they will cease; as for knowledge, it will pass away. . . . So faith, hope and love abide, these three; but the greatest of these is love.*

The greatest of these is love—that is the rest of the passage, I remember, the same passage about the dark veil of glass. I had forgotten that. *Love never ends* was how the passage began.

I get up and I go back into the bedroom and watch Lisa sleeping for a moment. Her hair falls across her face, red in the early light, her pale skin translucent. Then I get into my bed and settle the blankets around me, and for what feels like the first time in years, I close my eyes and fall to sleep, a real sleep, weighted and dreamless, a sleep for forgetting, a sleep not to be remembered.

It is August, and Roberta is leaving. I know she is going to leave in a few minutes, because someone is coming to pick her up, and then they arrive. The car pulls up and she turns to go. "Good-bye," she says, getting in.

Calling after her, anxious, the slight anxiety, "I'll see you soon—I'll see you at Christmastime."

She turns and looks at me through the glass, smiling, silent. The car pulls away. She did not reply, and the car pulled away. She did not think I would be able to hear her, perhaps; there was not time. There was not time. Your friend has to be leaving now; it is time for your friend to be leaving. Say good-bye to your friend now, Melanie—come now, come on, it's time to go now—say good-bye, Melanie, say good-bye.

"Good-bye, Roberta," I say. "Good-bye."

POSTSCRIPT

■ ■

During the time in which I knew her, Roberta wrote me many extraordinary letters. Even in high school, when she lived down the street, she would often write me when she had something important to say, and during college, surrounded by others, I had the peculiar feeling that my correspondence with Bibi was among the most real and immediate things in my life. I wanted very much to be able to reproduce these letters within the book. They were originally a seed text—Bibi's own voice, speaking through the veil of memory. The copyright law upholds the curious distinction that the physical property of the letter belongs to the recipient, but the copyright belongs to the author—or the author's estate. And the copyright law concerning unpublished letters grew increasingly stringent during the time in which the book was being prepared for publication. Thus rights to the letters Roberta wrote me now belong to her family, who have denied permission to reproduce or quote from any part of them. The letters in the book as it has been published are imaginary: I hope that they remain true to her spirit in some measure. But no one can write for another because no one's spirit is like another's. The loss is, as it was, irreparable.